What is VAK?

YOU CAN APPROACH the topic of learning styles with a simple and powerful system—one that focuses on just three ways of perceiving through your senses:

- Seeing, or *visual learning*
- Hearing, or *auditory learning*
- Movement, or *kinesthetic learning*

To recall this system, remember the letters VAK, which stand for **v**isual, **a**uditory, and **k**inesthetic. The theory is that each of us prefers to learn through one of these sense channels. To reflect on your VAK preferences, answer the following questions. Circle the answer that best describes how you would respond. This is not a formal inventory—just a way to prompt some self-discovery.

When you have problems spelling a word, you prefer to

1. Look it up in the dictionary.
2. Say the word out loud several times before you write it down.
3. Write out the word with several different spellings and then choose one.

You enjoy courses the most when you get to

1. View slides, videos, and readings with plenty of charts, tables, and illustrations.
2. Ask questions, engage in small-group discussions, and listen to guest speakers.
3. Take field trips, participate in lab sessions, or apply the course content while working as a volunteer or intern.

When giving someone directions on how to drive to a destination, you prefer to

1. Pull out a piece of paper and sketch a map.
2. Give verbal instructions.
3. Say, "I'm driving to a place near there, so just follow me."

When planning an extended vacation to a new destination, you prefer to

1. Read colorful, illustrated brochures or articles about that place.
2. Talk directly to someone who's been there.
3. Spend time at that destination on a work-related trip before vacationing there.

You've made a commitment to learn to play the guitar. The first thing you do is

1. Go to a library or music store and find an instruction book with plenty of diagrams and chord charts.

2. Listen closely to some recorded guitar solos and see whether you can sing along with them.
3. Buy a guitar, pluck the strings, and ask someone to show you a few chords.

You've saved up enough money to lease a car. When choosing from among several new models, the most important factor in your decision is

1. The car's appearance.
2. The information you get by talking to people who own the cars you're considering.
3. The overall impression you get by taking each car on a test drive.

You've just bought a new computer system. When setting up the system, the first thing you do is

1. Skim through the printed instructions that come with the equipment.
2. Call up someone with a similar system and ask her for directions.
3. Assemble the components as best as you can, see if everything works, and consult the instructions only as a last resort.

You get a scholarship to study abroad next semester in a Spanish-speaking country. To learn as much Spanish as you can before you depart, you

1. Buy a video-based language course on DVD.
2. Download audio podcasts that guarantee basic fluency in just 30 days.
3. Sign up for a short immersion course in which you speak only Spanish.

Name _____ Date _____

Now take a few minutes to reflect on the meaning of your responses. The number of each answer corresponds to a learning style preference.

1 = visual   2 = auditory   3 = kinesthetic

	Visual	Auditory	Kinesthetic
My totals			

My dominant Learning Style(s): _____

_____

Do you see a pattern in your own answers? A pattern indicates that you prefer learning through one sense channel over the others. Or you might find that your preferences are fairly balanced.

Whether you have a defined preference or not, you can increase your options for success by learning through *all* your sense channels. For example, you can enhance visual learning by leaving room in your class notes to add your own charts, diagrams, tables, and other visuals later. You can also key your handwritten notes into a computer file and use software that allows you to add colorful fonts and illustrations.

To enhance auditory learning, reinforce your memory of key ideas by talking about them. When studying, stop often to summarize key points and add examples in your own words. After doing this several times, dictate your summaries into a voice recorder and transfer the files to an iPod or similar device. Listen to these files while walking to class or standing in line at the store.

For kinesthetic learning, you've got plenty of options as well. Look for ways to translate course content into three-dimensional models that you can build. While studying grammar, for example, create a model of a sentence using different colors of clay to represent different parts of speech. Whenever possible, supplement lectures with real-world audio and video input and experiences, field trips to Spanish-speaking neighborhoods, and other opportunities for hands-on activity. Also recite key concepts from your courses while you walk or exercise.

These are just a few examples. In your path to mastery of learning styles, you can create many more of your own.

VOLUME 2

CUADROS

INTRODUCTORY SPANISH

Sheri Spaine Long
University of Alabama at Birmingham

María Carreira
California State University at Long Beach

Sylvia Madrigal Velasco

Kristin Swanson

HEINLE
CENGAGE Learning

Australia • Brazil • Japan • Korea • Mexico • Singapore • Spain • United Kingdom • United States

HEINLE
CENGAGE Learning™

Cuadros
Sheri Spaine Long, María Carreira, Sylvia Madrigal Velasco, & Kristin Swanson

Vice President, Editorial Director: PJ Boardman

Publisher: Beth Kramer

Senior Acquisitions Editor: Heather Bradley Cole

Senior Development Editor: Kim Beuttler

Assistant Editor: Sara Dyer

Editorial Assistant: Claire Kaplan

Senior Media Editor: Morgen Murphy

Senior Marketing Manager: Ben Rivera

Marketing Coordinator: Claire Fleming

Marketing Communications Manager: Glenn McGibbon

Senior Content Project Manager: Aileen Mason

Senior Art Director: Linda Jurras

Senior Manufacturing Planner: Betsy Donaghey

Rights Acquisition Specialist: Mandy Grozsko

Production Service: PreMediaGlobal

Text Designers: Carol Maglitta, Susan Gilday

Cover Designer: Harold Burch

Cover Image: © GEORGE STEINMETZ/ National Geographic Stock

Compositor: PreMediaGlobal

For product information and technology assistance, contact us at **Cengage Learning Customer & Sales Support, 1-800-354-9706**
For permission to use material from this text or product, submit all requests online at **www.cengage.com/permissions**
Further permissions questions can be emailed to **permissionrequest@cengage.com**

Library of Congress Control Number: 2011937474

Student Edition:

ISBN-13: 978-1-111-34115-2

ISBN-10: 1-111-34115-X

Heinle
20 Channel Center Street
Boston, MA 02210
USA

Cengage Learning is a leading provider of customized learning solutions with office locations around the globe, including Singapore, the United Kingdom, Australia, Mexico, Brazil and Japan. Locate your local office at **international.cengage.com/region**

Cengage Learning products are represented in Canada by Nelson Education, Ltd.

For your course and learning solutions, visit **www.cengage.com**

Purchase any of our products at your local college store or at our preferred online store **www.cengagebrain.com**

Instructors: Please visit **login.cengage.com** and log in to access instructor-specific resources.

Printed in Canada
1 2 3 4 5 6 7 15 14 13 12 11

To the Student

¡Bienvenidos! Welcome to the *Cuadros* introductory Spanish program. Spanish is one of the most useful languages you can learn; it is spoken by nearly 500 million people across the globe, including over 50 million Hispanics in the United States alone—one out of every six Americans. It is the most spoken language in the world after Mandarin Chinese and English. As you undertake your study of the Spanish language with *Cuadros*, keep in mind the following:

- We strive to present the Spanish-speaking world in all its diversity, with particular attention to indigenous and African-Hispanic populations, as well as European and Latin American immigrant populations.

- We guide you to make cross-cultural comparisons between the cultures you learn about and your own. Too often, the emphasis has been on the differences among cultures, when what may be surprising is the number of things we have in common with Spanish speakers around the world.

- We encourage you to look at your own community and to meet and interact with the Spanish speakers you encounter in both local and global communities. Spanish is all around you—just keep your eyes and ears open for it!

- *Cuadros* is designed to enrich your language-learning experience—while you are learning another language, you are also gathering information *about* the people who speak it and the countries where it is spoken. At first, you may think that you are unable to read or understand much Spanish, but in *Cuadros*, the focus is on getting the main ideas, and the tasks expected of you are limited to what you have already learned or what you can safely deduce from context. You will be surprised to see that you can comprehend more than you think you can!

- *Cuadros* features a variety of resources to help you achieve your language-learning goals more easily. Media icons at relevant points throughout the print book tell you exactly which component to use for additional practice or support. Or, work right from the eBook for direct access to all of the program's resources, including audio recordings of key vocabulary and grammar terms, instant activity feedback, and online chat and commenting functionality.

- Learning a language is easier if you relax and have fun. Keeping this in mind, we've included humorous and contemporary content with the goal of making language learning enjoyable and interesting.

We hope you enjoy your introduction to the Spanish language and its many peoples and cultures. Learning a language sets you on a course of life-long learning. It is one of the most valuable and exciting things you can do to prepare yourself to be a global citizen of the twenty-first century.

—The Authors

Student Components

Student Text

Your **Student Text** contains all the information and activities you need for in-class use. Volumes 1 and 2 each contain a preliminary chapter followed by five regular chapters that contain vocabulary presentations and activities, grammar presentations and activities, video-related practice, cultural information, reading selections, and writing practice. There are also valuable reference sections at the back of each book, including Spanish-English and English-Spanish glossaries and verb charts. In addition, Volume 2 contains an appendix that reviews all of the grammar presented in Volume 1.

Student Activities Manual (SAM): Workbook / Lab Manual / Video Manual

The **Student Activities Manual (SAM)** includes out-of-class practice of the material presented in the Student Text. Volumes 1 and 2 of the SAM are each divided into a Workbook **(Cuaderno de práctica)**, which focuses on written vocabulary and grammar practice, reading, and writing; a Lab Manual **(Manual de laboratorio)**, which focuses on pronunciation and listening comprehension; and a Video Manual **(Manual de video),** which offers extra practice of the storyline and **Voces del mundo hispano** segments.

iLrn Heinle Learning Center

An all-in-one online learning environment, including an audio- and video-enhanced interactive eBook, assignable textbook activities, companion videos, assignable voice-recorded activities, an online workbook and lab manual with audio, interactive enrichment activities, a chapter- and volume-level diagnostic study tool for better exam preparation, and now, media sharing and commenting capability through Share It! The iLrn: Heinle Learning Center is offered separately for Volumes 1 and 2.

Premium Website

You will find a wealth of resources and practice on the *Cuadros* **Premium Website,** accessible for Volumes 1 and 2 at **www.cengagebrain.com.** The **Premium Website** assets should be used as you work through each chapter and as you review for quizzes and exams.

To get access, visit CengageBrain.com

- It provides access to the text audio program, Web activities and links, Google Earth™ coordinates, and an iTunes™ playlist.
- The premium password-protected resources include the SAM audio program, the video program, grammar and pronunciation podcasts, grammar tutorial videos, auto-graded quizzes, and more!
- The web quizzes focus on vocabulary and grammar and provide automatic feedback, which helps you understand errors and pinpoints areas for review.
- The web activities offer the opportunity to explore authentic Spanish-language websites. Cultural web links relate to the **Voces de la comunidad, ¡Fíjate!,** and **¿Quieres saber más?** activities as well as **Tú en el mundo hispano,** which covers volunteer, study abroad, and internship opportunities throughout the Hispanic world and **Ritmos del mundo hispano,** a section that explores traditional and contemporary Hispanic music through music and video links.

Acknowledgments

Reviewers and Contributors

We would like to acknowledge the helpful suggestions and useful ideas of our reviewers, whose commentary was invaluable to us in shaping *Cuadros*.

Many thanks go to the following professors, each of whom offered valuable suggestions through their participation in live and virtual focus groups:

ACTFL: Introductory Spanish Focus Group
Aleta Anderson, *Grand Rapids Community College*
Yolanda González, *Valencia Community College*
Monica Montalvo, *University of Central Florida*
Renee Wooten, *Vernon College*

Pasadena Focus Group
Esther Castro, *San Diego State University*
Mercedes Limón, *Chaffey College*
Ofelia McQueen, *Los Angeles City College*
Markus Muller, *California State University, Long Beach*
Rosalinda Nericcio, *San Diego State University*
Yelgy Parada, *Los Angeles City College*
Victoria Tirado, *Chaffey College*

Philadelphia Focus Group
Norma Corrales-Martin, *Temple University*
Judith R. Downing, *Rutgers University – Camden*
April Jacobs, *Temple University*
Maríadelaluz Matus-Mendoza, *Drexel University*
Patricia Moore-Martinez, *Temple University*
Eva Recio-Gonzalez, *University of Pennsylvania*
Kimberly Ann Vega, *Temple University*

Development Reviews
Karen Berg, *College of Charleston*
Genevieve Breedon, *Darton College*
Matt Carpenter, *Yuba College, Clear Lake Campus*
John Catlett, *Cabrini College*
Daria Cohen, *Rider University*
Carmen García, *Valencia Community College*
Martha García, *University of Central Florida*
Diego Emilio Gómez
Yolanda González, *Valencia Community College*
Laurie Huffman, *Los Medanos College / Florida State College*
Isabel Killough, *Norfolk State University*
Lori Lammert, *Chattanooga State Community College*

Jill Loney, *Urbana University*
Richard McCallister, *Delaware State University*
Meghan Mehlos, *University of Wisconsin – Eau Claire*
Deanna Mihaly, *Eastern Michigan University*
Dianne Moneypenny
Lisa Nalbone, *University of Central Florida*
Janet Norden, *Baylor University*
Catherine Ortíz, *University of Texas at Arlington*
Sieglinde Poelzler-Kamatali, *Ohio Northern University*
Rosalea Postma-Carttar, *University of Kansas*
Laura Ruiz-Scott, *Scottsdale Community College*
Lester Edgardo Sandres Rapalo, *Valencia Community College*
Erika Sutherland, *Muhlenberg College*
David Tate, *Brevard Community College*
Wendy Westmoreland, *Cleveland Community College*
Sandra Wise, *University of Texas at Arlington*

Testing Program Consultants
Bárbara Ávila-Shah, *University at Buffalo, The State University of New York*
Patrick Brady, *Tidewater Community College*
Marta Nunn, *Virginia Commonwealth University*
Helga Winkler, *Ventura County Community College District – Moorpark College*

We would like to extend our gratitude to the Graduate Teaching Assistant and Adjunct Faculty Focus Group, which discussed the tools needed to ensure a successful transition to a new edition and successful use over the course of the semester.

Graduate Teaching Assistant / Adjunct Faculty Focus Group
Alison Atkins, *Boston University*
Alison Carberry, *Boston University*
Alejandra Cornejo, *Boston University*
Daniela Dorfman, *Boston University*
Megan Gibbons, *Boston University*
Rebeca Hey-Colón, *Harvard University*
Magdalena Malinowska, *Boston University*
Glenda Quiñónez, *Harvard University*

Finally, special thanks go to the following professors and writers, who have written the outstanding supplements to accompany this program:

Meghan Allen, *Babson College – Volume-level diagnostics and Web assets*

Flavia Belpoliti, *University of Houston – Bridge chapter teaching suggestions*

María Colina – *Lesson plans*

Juan De Urda, *SUNY Fredonia – Web quizzes*

Karen Haller Beer – *Testing program*

Maribel Lárraga, *Our Lady of the Lake University – Testing program and audio script*

Sarah Link – *PowerPoint presentations*

Jeff Longwell, *New Mexico State University – Volume-level oral assessments*

Nina Patrizio-Quiñones, *Our Lady of the Lake University – Testing program and audioscript*

Joshua Pope, *University of Wisconsin – Madison – Information gap activities*

Nidia Schuhmacher, *Brown University – Web searches*

Sierra Turner, *University of Alabama – Activity worksheets*

A hearty thanks to our fine VAK system, Learning Style worksheet writers: **Carlos Abaunza, Rebeca Hey-Colón** from **Harvard University** and **Magdalena Malinowska** from **Boston University**. Through creativity, hard work, and proactive communication, these writers took full ownership of the project from its incipient stages to create a comprehensive set of intuitive and valuable tools for visual, auditory, and kinesthetic learners.

We would also like to thank the World Languages Group at Heinle Cengage Learning for their ongoing support of this project and for guiding us along the long and sometimes difficult path to its completion! Many thanks especially to Beth Kramer and Heather Bradley for their professional guidance and outstanding support. We would also like to thank Kim Beuttler, our development editor, for her enthusiastic support and dedication to the project, her unflagging energy and enthusiasm, and her unerring eye for detail, Sara Dyer for her creative and focused work on the supplements that support *Cuadros*, and Morgen Murphy for her dedication to the quality of the media package. Thanks also to Aileen Mason, our production editor, for her meticulous care, and for her cheerful and good-humored tenacity in keeping the production side of things moving efficiently, and to Katy Gabel for her excellent project management work. We would like to extend our appreciation to Lindsey Richardson, Marketing Director, and Ben Rivera, Senior Marketing Manager, for their outstanding creative vision and hard work on campus, and to Glenn McGibbon, Senior Marketing Communications Manager, for his phenomenal work on marketing and promotional materials. We would like to acknowledge our copyeditor Janet Gokay, our proofreaders Pilar Acevedo and Jonathan Jucker, our art director, Linda Jurras, for her inspired design work, our illustrators JHS Illustration Studio and Fian Arroyo, Hilary Hudgens for his creative design contributions, and the many other design, art, and production staff and freelancers who contributed to the creation of this program.

¡Mil gracias a todos!

To my inspirational students, who helped shape *Cuadros*, and to *mi querida familia*, John, Morgan, and John, who have accompanied me on my life's magical journey as a Hispanist. *Gracias por el apoyo infinito.*
—S. S. L.

I am particularly appreciative of the help and encouragement of my husband, Bartlett Mel, my father, Domingo Carreira, and my colleagues Ana Roca, Najib Redouane, and Irene Marchegiani Jones.
—M. C.

I would like to thank my parents, Dulce and Óscar Madrigal, for bequeathing to me their language, their culture, their heritage, their passion for life, and their *orgullo* in *México, lindo y querido.*
—S. M. V.

A special thanks to Mac Prichard and to Shirley and Bill Swanson for their constant support and encouragement, both personal and professional.
—K. S.

Scope and Sequence

- the textbook
- numbers 0–100
- objects in the classroom
- classroom commands

Reference Materials

Mi identidad

Tu identidad se forma de una variedad de elementos: tu sexo, tu edad, tu nacionalidad, tus relaciones familiares, tus gustos, tus estudios, tus actividades, tu personalidad y tus características físicas. Hasta la tecnología que usas a diario puede influir en cómo te percibes a ti mismo y cómo te presentas al mundo.

¿Cómo te identificas principalmente? ¿Como hombre o mujer, joven, estudiante, ciudadano *(citizen)*, hijo, deportista, músico o amigo? ¿Por tu personalidad virtual?

In this chapter, you will review

Communication

- **identity:** personal information, greetings, introductions, phone calls
- **likes and dislikes:** interests, activities, personal and physical descriptions
- **studies:** classes, schedules, time and dates
- **technology:** hardware, software, Internet, electronics, emotions
- **family:** family members, professions, daily routines, personal care items

Grammar

- **hay** with nouns
- nouns, articles, and adjectives
- the present indicative tense of regular, irregular, stem-changing and irregular-**yo** verbs
- **gustar** and verbs like **gustar**
- interrogative words
- simple possessive adjectives
- **ser** vs. **estar**
- adverbs
- reflexive verbs
- the present progressive

Culture

- un podcast de una estudiante méxicoamericana

iofoto.com/Big

A repasar

Activity 1 practices **hay** with nouns, using **Volume 1 Preliminary Chapter** vocabulary.

1 **¿Qué hay?** Con un(a) compañero(a), túrnense para decir si las siguientes cosas están en el salón de clase. **¡OJO!** No deben usar el artículo con los sustantivos plurales, ni tampoco en las oraciones negativas con **hay**.

MODELO Tú: *Hay un diccionario en el salón de clase.*
Compañero(a): *No hay notas en el salón de clase.*

Cosas: una calculadora, una computadora, un diccionario, un escritorio, un lápiz, unos libros, una mesa, unas mochilas, unas notas, una pizarra, unas sillas, unas ventanas

Activity 2 practices nouns, articles, and adjectives with the verb **ser**, using vocabulary from **Volume 1, Chapters 1, 2, and 3**.

2 **¿Cómo son?** Con un(a) compañero(a), túrnense para describir las siguientes cosas y personas, usando adjetivos de la lista.

MODELO *Los libros de la serie* The Hunger Games *son interesantes.*

Cosas: la canción (título), la clase de..., el libro (título), la película (título), el programa de televisión (título), ¿...?
Personas: el actor (nombre), la actriz (nombre), tu mejor amigo(a), el presidente de Estados Unidos, el profesor de..., la profesora de..., ¿...?
Adjetivos: aburrido, antipático, cómico, divertido, estúpido, extrovertido, fantástico, inteligente, introvertido, mentiroso, simpático, serio, tonto, ¿...?

Activity 3 practices the present indicative of regular **-ar, -er, -ir** verbs and the verb **ir**, using vocabulary from **Volume 1, Chapters 2** and **3**.

3 **¿Qué hace?** Trabajen en grupos de tres o cuatro personas para crear una historia larga usando verbos de la lista u otros verbos. La primera persona empieza con una oración corta. Después, la segunda persona repite la oración original y añade otra parte, usando un verbo nuevo. Sigan así hasta que la historia llegue a ser *(becomes)* tan larga que nadie pueda recordarla. Después empiecen otra historia con un sujeto nuevo.

MODELO Tú: *El estudiante perezoso va a la biblioteca.*
Compañero(a) 1: *El estudiante perezoso va a la biblioteca, pero no estudia.*
Compañero(a) 2: *El estudiante perezoso va a la biblioteca, pero no estudia. En vez de eso (Instead), habla con sus amigos...*

Verbos: abrir, asistir a, bailar, caminar, cantar, cocinar, comer, compartir, conversar, correr, escribir, estudiar, hablar, ir, leer, mirar, patinar, trabajar, vivir, ¿...?

Designpics/Glow Images

4 **¡Compárense!** Con un(a) compañero(a), túrnense para contestar las siguientes preguntas. Después, hagan una lista que resuma (*summarizes*) sus respuestas.

Activity 4 practices **tener**, **tener que**, and **tener años**, using vocabulary from **Volume 1, Chapters 1** and **3**.

MODELO   Tú: *Tengo dos libros en la mochila y también tengo...*
Heather: *Tengo tres libros en la mochila y también tengo...*
(Resumen): *En las mochilas tenemos libros y también tenemos...*

1. ¿Cuáles son dos cosas que tienes en la mochila o en la bolsa (*purse*)?
2. ¿Qué clases tienes este semestre o trimestre? ¿Qué clases tienes hoy?
3. ¿Cuántos años tienes? ¿Cuántos años tiene tu madre o tu padre?
4. ¿Qué tienes que hacer hoy? ¿Qué tienes que hacer esta semana? ¿Y este fin de semana?

5 **Preferencias** Con un(a) compañero(a), túrnense para decir si le gustan o no las cosas y actividades indicadas. Después, escribe un resumen de lo que les gustan y lo que no les gustan.

Activity 5 practices **gustar** and verbs like **gustar**, using vocabulary from **Volume 1, Chapters 2, 3,** and **4**.

MODELO   (Resumen): *A mí me gustan... pero a Abe no le gustan...*
A nosotros nos gusta...

1.
2.
3.
4.
5.
6.
7.
8.
9. ¿...?

6 **Preguntas, preguntas** Trabajen en grupos de cuatro. Cada persona debe escribir los nombres de tres clases que tiene este semestre o trimestre. Las otras personas del grupo tratan de adivinar cuáles son las clases, usando palabras interrogativas para hacer preguntas. Después, túrnense para adivinar las clases de las otras personas.

Activity 6 practices interrogative words, using **Volume 1 Preliminary Chapter** and **Chapter 3** vocabulary.

MODELO   Compañero(a) 1: *¿Quién es el profesor?*
Compañero(a) 2: *¿A qué hora está?*
Compañero(a) 3: *¿Qué día de la semana tienes esta clase?*

Palabras interrogativas: ¿a qué hora?, ¿cómo?, ¿cuándo?, ¿cuál?, ¿cuántos(as)?, ¿dónde?, ¿por qué?, ¿qué?, ¿quién?

7 **Presentaciones** Trabajen en grupos de cuatro personas, dividiéndose en dos parejas. Cada pareja debe turnarse para hacerle las siguientes preguntas a su compañero(a) y anotar las respuestas. (Pueden contestarlas según sus datos personales o inventar otros.) Después, en su grupo original de cuatro, túrnense para presentar a la persona que entrevistaron al grupo completo. Sigan el modelo.

Activity 7 practices the simple possessive adjectives, using vocabulary from Volume 1, Chapters 2 and 3.

MODELO Entrevista: —*¿De dónde es tu familia?*
—*Mi familia es de...*
Presentación: *Quiero presentarles a Cassidy Caitlin O'Brien.*
Su familia es de...

1. ¿Cuál es tu nombre completo?
2. ¿De dónde es tu familia?
3. ¿Cuántos años tienes?
4. ¿Cuál es tu clase favorita?
5. ¿Cuál es tu clase menos favorita?
6. ¿Cuáles son tus libros favoritos?
7. ¿Cuáles son tus películas favoritas?
8. ¿Cuáles son tus canciones *(songs)* favoritas?

8 **¿Ser o estar?** Con un(a) compañero(a), túrnense para escribir ocho oraciones completas, usando palabras de las tres columnas. Cuando sea posible, añadan detalles a sus oraciones para hacerlas más interesantes. Sigan el modelo.

Activity 8 practices the verbs ser and estar, using vocabulary from Volume 1, Chapter 4.

MODELO *Yo estoy cansada después de mi clase de computación porque es muy difícil.*

A	B	C
yo	estar	cansado(a)
tú	ser	de...
él		en el centro de computación
ella		mi profesor(a) de...
nosotros		nervioso(a)
ellos		un(a) estudiante...
¿...?		¿...?

9 **Generalmente...** Con un(a) compañero(a), usen los siguientes adjetivos para crear adverbios. Luego, túrnense para usar los adverbios para decir cómo hacen las actividades indicadas.

Activity 9 practices adverbs, using vocabulary from Volume 1, Chapter 4.

Adjetivos: correcto, difícil, eficiente, fácil, (no) frecuente, lento, rápido, seguro
Actividades: cambiar tu contraseña, correr, escribir mensajes de texto, hablar, jugar videojuegos, instalar nuevas aplicaciones, sacar fotos, ¿...?

10 **Para mí...** Trabajen en un grupo de tres o cuatro personas. Cada persona debe indicar sus hábitos y preferencias en la siguiente tabla. Después, túrnense para resumir los resultados, según el modelo.

Activity 10 practices stem-changing verbs in the present indicative, using vocabulary from **Volume 1, Chapter 4**.

MODELO   *Yo prefiero dormir ocho horas por noche, pero Emma y Keegan prefieren dormir seis horas. Todos nosotros comenzamos a estudiar a las...*

1. ¿Cuántas horas prefieres dormir por noche?	4. ¿Quieres comprar una nueva computadora o tableta este año?
2. ¿A qué hora comienzas a estudiar?	5. ¿Puedes programar una computadora?
3. ¿Cuántas horas juegas videojuegos al día?	6. ¿Pierdes tus cosas frecuentemente?

11 **Preguntas personales** Con un(a) compañero(a), túrnense para contestar las siguientes preguntas.

Activity 11 practices irregular-**yo** verbs in the present indicative, using vocabulary from **Volume 1, Chapter 5**.

1. ¿Conoces a una persona famosa?
2. ¿Sabes hablar francés?
3. ¿Sales todas las noches de la semana?
4. ¿Dices mentiras *(lies)* de vez en cuando?
5. ¿Haces la tarea todos los días?
6. ¿Cuántas horas de televisión ves al día?

12 **Mi rutina** Con un(a) compañero(a), túrnense para decir cuándo haces cada una de las actividades indicadas. Después, escriban un resumen que compare sus hábitos.

Activity 12 practices reflexive verbs, using vocabulary from **Volume 1, Chapter 5**.

MODELO   Tú: *Mi hermana y yo nos peleamos cuando tenemos que compartir la computadora.*
    (Resumen): Nate y su hermana se pelean cuando... Sophie y su madre se pelean cuando...

Actividades: acostarse, divertirse, enfermarse, levantarse, pelearse, preocuparse, quejarse, reírse

13 **¿Qué están haciendo?** Haz una lista de cinco familiares que conoces bien. Después, trabaja con un(a) compañero(a) y túrnense para comentar lo que crees que cada uno(a) está haciendo en este momento.

Activity 13 practices the present progressive tense, using vocabulary from **Volume 1, Chapter 5**.

MODELO   *Mi primo Ian está trabajando en la computadora.*

A escuchar

ESTRATEGIA

Listening for the main idea

When you are listening to Spanish, it can sometimes be hard to know what to focus on. There are often words you don't understand. Also, the difference between seeing words on the printed page and hearing them spoken can be huge. A good way to organize your listening task is to focus on getting the main idea of the segment. Don't try to understand every single word, but instead try to get the overall meaning, tone, and feeling of the speaker. Later, with the help of textbook activities and as many listenings as you need, some of the other details will emerge.

1 Trabaja con un(a) compañero(a) para contestar las siguientes preguntas.

1. ¿Qué es un podcast? ¿Qué clase de persona graba y publica podcasts? ¿Para quién son los podcasts? ¿Cuál es el motivo para publicar un podcast?

2. Piensen en los temas de las actividades en la sección **A repasar.** ¿Cuáles de esos temas les parecen *(seem)* ideales para grabar en un podcast?

3. El nombre del podcast es "El día a día de una estudiante cansada". ¿De qué creen que se va a tratar *(is going to be about)*?

4. Lean la información biográfica de la autora del podcast.

Nombre: Olivia Reyes
Edad: veinte años
Nacionalidad: méxicoamericana
Profesión: estudiante en University of Texas at Austin
Familia: los padres (Óscar y Yolanda), dos hermanos (Gabriel y Agustín), una hermana (Teresa)
Pasatiempos: tocar la guitarra, mirar televisión y películas por *streaming*, salir con amigos, jugar juegos interactivos

Jenkedco/Shutterstock

2 Para prepararte a escuchar el podcast de Olivia, haz una correspondencia entre las frases a la izquierda y sus equivalentes en inglés a la derecha.

1. me identifico
2. no me malinterpreten
3. la mayoría
4. me acuerdo
5. qué sé yo
6. me quedo dormida
7. adivinar
8. de nuevo
9. facetas
10. alguien dígame

a. *I remember*
b. *again*
c. *I identify myself*
d. *I fall asleep*
e. *someone tell me*
f. *don't misinterpret me*
g. *facets*
h. *the majority*
i. *what do I know*
j. *to guess*

>> Escuchar

🔊 **3** Ahora escucha el podcast "El día a día de una estudiante cansada" en la
Track 17 que Olivia describe un día en su vida universitaria.

>> Después de escuchar

4 Contesta las siguientes preguntas sobre el podcast de Olivia para
identificar la idea principal y comentar algunos de los detalles. Escucha el
podcast otra vez si necesitas buscar algunas de las respuestas.

1. ¿Cuál es la idea principal del podcast?
   a. Es importante tener muchos pasatiempos.
   b. La vida de estudiante es difícil.
   c. A Olivia no le gustan los estudios.
2. ¿Dónde vive Olivia?
3. ¿Cuál es la identidad que ocupa la mayoría de las veinticuatro horas de su
   día?
4. ¿Cuándo son sus únicos momentos de libertad (*freedom*)?
5. ¿Qué hace después de su última clase?
6. ¿Qué hace ella con sus padres y hermanos durante los fines de semana?
7. ¿Cuáles son tres cosas que ella hace con sus amigos durante los fines de
   semana?
8. ¿Cuándo recuerda Olivia que ella es mucho más que una estudiante?

5 Con un(a) compañero(a) de clase, comparen sus rutinas semanales con
las de Olivia. Contesten las siguientes preguntas y después hagan un resumen
de sus respuestas. Al final, júntense con otra pareja para compartir y comparar
sus resúmenes.

1. ¿Cuáles son las diferentes partes que forman su identidad personal en
   su totalidad?
2. ¿Cómo son sus rutinas de lunes a viernes?
3. ¿Cómo son sus rutinas los fines de semana?
4. En general, ¿cómo son sus vidas? ¿ocupadas? ¿fáciles? ¿difíciles?
   ¿aburridas? ¿divertidas? ¿...?
5. Completen las siguientes oraciones:
   ▪ En mi opinión, lo bueno de ser estudiante es...
   ▪ En mi opinión, lo malo de ser estudiante es...

A escribir

ESTRATEGIA

Using a bilingual dictionary

You've already learned a variety of writing strategies in your introductory study of Spanish. As you write, always focus on a mix of strategies to help you approach a specific task. Given the nature of this task, this is one strategy that will help you prepare your information before you write.

Since no textbook can provide all the words you need when you write, you will want to use bilingual dictionaries and online sources to supplement the words you already know. Follow these steps to get the best Spanish equivalent for the word you need.

- Look up the word you want to translate, along with several other words that are close to it. (For example, *weird, odd, strange*.) Compare to see which Spanish words come up as the best translation for each. If the same Spanish word comes up several times, it is likely a good translation.
- Choose one of the Spanish equivalents that came up more than once and look it up to see what its English translation is. Is it your original word or one of its synonyms? If so, it is probably the word you want. If not, focus on another option until you find one that matches.

1 Mira la información biográfica de Olivia en la página P2-8. Después, crea una tarjeta como la de abajo que incluya tus datos personales.

Nombre:
Edad:
Nacionalidad:
Profesión:
Familia:
Pasatiempos:

2 Vas a escribir un guión *(script)* para un podcast. Como ya sabes, los podcasts tienen un enfoque específico y comparten algunas de las opiniones o ideas del (de la) autor(a). Por ejemplo, el podcast de Olivia se enfoca en "El día a día de una estudiante cansada". Con un(a) compañero(a), hagan una lista de por lo menos cinco ideas para un podcast. Pueden tratar los temas de las actividades en la sección **A repasar**, la **Actividad 5** de la sección **A escuchar** u otros, según sus preferencias.

3 Ahora, selecciona una de tus ideas para elaborar en tu podcast. Antes de escribir, crea una lista de palabras relacionadas al tema. Usa un diccionario bilingüe para buscar palabras desconocidas *(unknown)*. Después, piensa en algunos detalles *(details)* relacionados al tema que quieres incluir en tu podcast.

4 Escucha otra vez el podcast de Olivia. ¿Cómo está organizado? ¿Cuál es su tono? Puedes usar su podcast como modelo. También repasa la siguiente lista de sugerencias para los podcasts antes de escribir.

- ¿Quién y cómo eres? Debes presentarte al principio del podcast, igual como lo hace Olivia. Usa los datos de la **Actividad 1** (y, si quieres, otra información pertinente).
- Debes incluir ideas y opiniones interesantes y tratar de presentarlas de una manera divertida.
- Usa un estilo informal y familiar y recuerda que las oraciones cortas *(short)* son más fáciles de entender que las oraciones más largas.
- No presentes demasiada información – escoge un tema muy específico y limita el número de detalles que incluyes.

>> Composición

5 Ahora, escribe el borrador de tu podcast. Incluye la información de las **Actividades 1** y **3** y usa el podcast de Olivia como un modelo. Trata de escribir un podcast interesante y personal que va a divertir a tu audiencia.

mascough/iStockphoto

>> Después de escribir

6 Mira tu borrador otra vez. Usa la siguiente lista para revisarlo.

- ¿Tiene tu podcast un enfoque específico y detalles interesantes?
- ¿Hay concordancia *(agreement)* entre los artículos, sustantivos y adjetivos?
- ¿Usas las formas correctas de todos los verbos?
- ¿Usas bien los adverbios y los verbos como **gustar**?
- ¿Hay errores de puntuación o de ortografía?

¿Adónde vas?

COMUNIDADES LOCALES

Cada barrio o comunidad tiene su propia personalidad que lo define y que también influye a la vida diaria de sus residentes.

¿Crees que los vecinos *(neighbors)*, los barrios y los centros comerciales de nuestras comunidades locales todavía tienen importancia? ¿Por qué sí o por qué no?

Communication

By the end of this chapter you will be able to

- talk about places in town and the university
- talk about means of transportation and food shopping
- talk about locations and give directions
- make polite requests and commands
- agree and disagree
- refer to locations of objects

Jeremy Woodhouse/Getty Images

Un viaje por México

México es el segundo más grande de los países donde se habla español y tiene la población más grande de hispanohablantes. Su nombre oficial es Estados Unidos Mexicanos.

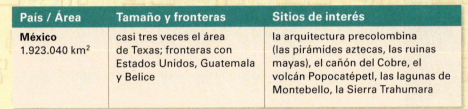

País / Área	Tamaño y fronteras	Sitios de interés
México 1.923.040 km²	casi tres veces el área de Texas; fronteras con Estados Unidos, Guatemala y Belice	la arquitectura precolombina (las pirámides aztecas, las ruinas mayas), el cañón del Cobre, el volcán Popocatépetl, las lagunas de Montebello, la Sierra Trahumara

¿Qué sabes? Di si las siguientes oraciones son ciertas **(C)** o falsas **(F)**.

1. México es mucho más grande que Texas.
2. Hay ruinas de por lo menos dos civilizaciones en México.
3. México es un país sin *(without)* mucha diversidad geográfica.
4. México tiene la segunda población de hispanohablantes más grande del mundo.

Lo que sé y lo que quiero aprender Completa la tabla del **Apéndice A**. Escribe algunos datos que **ya sabes** sobre México en la columna **Lo que sé**. Después, añade algunos temas que **quieres aprender** a la columna **Lo que quiero aprender**. Guarda la tabla para usar otra vez en la sección **¡Explora y exprésate!** en la página 221.

Cultures

By the end of this chapter you will have explored

- ancient civilizations and indigenous populations of Mexico
- the Spanish conquest and the Mexican Revolution
- linguistic diversity in the Spanish-speaking world
- **el tianguis**, a special kind of open-air market
- Mexico City teens and where they go for fun

¡Imagínate!

SERGIO: Oye, ¿adónde vas con tanta prisa?

JAVIER: Primero tengo que ir al gimnasio, y después al **centro estudiantil**.

SERGIO: Pero, ¿por qué la prisa, hombre?

JAVIER: Después del centro estudiantil, tengo que ir al **banco** a sacar dinero y después al **súper** para comprar la comida para la cena.

>> **En la universidad**

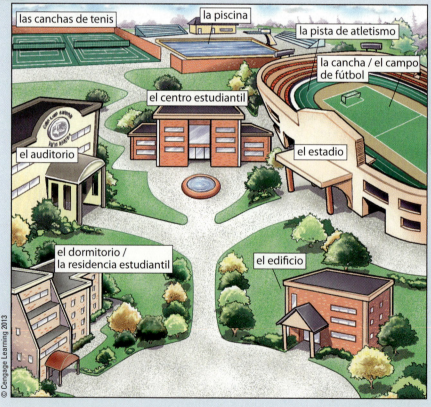

las canchas de tenis

la piscina

la pista de atletismo

la cancha / el campo de fútbol

el centro estudiantil

el auditorio

el estadio

el dormitorio / la residencia estudiantil

el edificio

>> En la ciudad o en el pueblo

el aeropuerto *airport*
el almacén *department store*
el apartamento *apartment*
el banco *bank*
el barrio *neighborhood*
el cajero automático *automated teller machine (ATM)*
la casa *house*
el centro comercial *mall*
el cine *cinema*
el cuarto *the room*
la estación de trenes / autobuses *train/bus station*
el estacionamiento *parking lot*
la farmacia *pharmacy*
el hospital *hospital*
la iglesia *church*
la joyería *jewelry store*
el mercado... *market*
  ...al aire libre *open air-market; farmer's market*

el museo *museum*
la oficina *office*
la oficina de correos *post office*
la papelería *stationery store*
el parque *park*
la pizzería *pizzeria*
la plaza *plaza*
el restaurante *restaurant*
el supermercado *supermarket*
el teatro *theater*
la tienda... *store*
  ...de equipo deportivo *sporting goods store*
  ...de juegos electrónicos *electronic games store*
  ...de ropa *clothing store*
el (la) vecino(a) *neighbor*

ACTIVIDADES

1 **¿Dónde está Javier?** Javier necesita varias cosas. ¿Dónde está él? Escoge de los lugares en la tercera columna.

1.

2.

3.

4.

5.

6.

a. la joyería

b. el cajero automático

c. el supermercado

d. la farmacia

e. la oficina de correos

f. la tienda de ropa

The names of many places in the city are cognates. With a partner, take turns reading each other as many of the cognates as you can while the other guesses the English translation.

Other places of worship besides **la iglesia** are: **la mezquita** *(mosque),* **la sinagoga, el templo.**

2 **En la ciudad** Indica adónde debe ir cada persona, según lo que quiere hacer o comprar. ¡No te preocupes si no entiendes todas las palabras!

1. —Es hora de comer. Tengo muchas ganas de comerme una pizza enorme.
2. —Tengo que estudiar las pinturas de Picasso para mi clase de arte.
3. —No puedo hacer las compras todavía. Primero necesito ir a sacar dinero.
4. —El doctor dice que necesito esta medicina para controlar mi alergia.
5. —No quiero cocinar en casa. Quiero salir a comer.
6. —Necesito comprar muchas cosas y después de las compras, podemos ir al cine.
7. —Voy a visitar a Mariana y para llegar a su casa, tengo que tomar el autobús.

3 **¿Adónde van?** Habla con varios compañeros. ¿Adónde van después de clase? ¿Qué van a hacer en ese sitio? También diles adónde vas tú y por qué vas allí.

MODELO Tú: *¿Adónde vas después de clase?*
Compañero(a): *Voy al dormitorio.*
Tú: *¿Qué vas a hacer allí?*
Compañero(a): *Estoy cansado(a). Voy a descansar.*

Opciones: cenar, cocinar, correr, dormir, estudiar, hacer la tarea, jugar (al) tenis / fútbol, levantar pesas, mirar televisión, nadar, trabajar

In some varieties of Spanish, to indicate playing a sport, **jugar** is used with the preposition **a: jugar al tenis, jugar al fútbol**. Usage of **a** with **jugar** varies from region to region.

¡Fíjate! La diversidad lingüística en el mundo de habla hispana

Todas las lenguas exhiben variaciones geográficas. El español de México no es exactamente igual al español de Puerto Rico ni al español de España. Estas variantes regionales de una lengua se llaman *dialectos*.

En general, el léxico o vocabulario es lo que más varía de una zona dialectal a otra en el mundo hispano. Por ejemplo, algunas de las palabras referentes a los medios de transporte exhiben variación dialectal: **carro, máquina, auto, automóvil** y **coche** se usan en diferentes zonas del mundo hispano. De la misma manera, **autobús, bus, guagua, colectivo, camión, ómnibus** y **micro** son diferentes maneras de referirse a *bus*.

La fonología o pronunciación del español también varía de una zona dialectal a otra. Por ejemplo, en algunos lugares del mundo hispano, la letra **s** se puede pronunciar con aspiración, como el sonido inicial de la palabra *hand*. En los dialectos que aspiran, la palabra **español** se pronuncia frecuentemente como [ehpañol].

Es importante recordar que las diferencias entre los dialectos del español son relativamente pocas. Por esta razón, dos hablantes del español de zonas dialectales muy distantes generalmente pueden comunicarse con facilidad.

Práctica ¿Puedes dar unos ejemplos de variación léxica dentro de EEUU o entre los países de habla inglesa del mundo?

Vocabulario útil 2

SERGIO: ¿Vas **en bicicleta**?

JAVIER: No, voy **a pie**. Mi bici se desinfló. Bueno, adiós —¡me tengo que ir!

© Cengage Learning 2013

>> Medios de transporte

a pie *on foot, walking* | **en metro** *on the subway*
en autobús *by bus* | **en tren** *by train*
en bicicleta *on bicycle* | **en / por avión** *by plane*
en carro / coche / automóvil *by car*

ACTIVIDADES

4 Para llegar… Quieres llegar de un sitio a otro. ¿Cuál es la forma más lógica para llegar?

1. ¿Estoy en el dormitorio y quiero ir a la biblioteca. Voy…
   a. en avión.   b. a pie.   c. en tren.

2. Estoy en Los Ángeles y quiero ir a Nueva York. Voy…
   a. en bicicleta.   b. a pie.   c. en avión.

3. Estoy en casa y quiero ir al parque qué está a dos millas de mi casa. Quiero hacer ejercicio. Voy…
   a. en bicicleta.   b. en tren.   c. en autobús.

4. Estoy en la Calle 16 y quiero llegar a la Calle 112. Voy…
   a. en metro.   b. en avión.   c. a pie.

5. Estoy en la universidad y quiero visitar a mis padres. Tengo muchas cosas que llevar y quiero hacer muchas paradas *(make many stops)*. Voy…
   a. en bicicleta.   b. a pie.   c. en carro.

> In Mexico, **carro** is more commonly used than **coche**, and **camión** is more common for *bus* than **autobús**.

5 ¿Vas a pie? Tu compañero(a) tiene que ir a varios sitios. Pregúntale cómo piensa llegar a esos sitios. Inventa destinos lógicos para cada forma de transporte.

MODELO Tú: *¿Cómo piensas ir a la fiesta de Carmen?*
        Compañero(a): *Voy a ir en autobús.*

1.   2.   3.   4.   5.   6.

© Cengage Learning 2013

DULCE: Pero, mujer, ¿adónde vas con tanta prisa?

CHELA: Quiero ir al gimnasio antes de **hacer las compras** en el supermercado.

DULCE: Pero si no es tarde, son sólo las tres.

CHELA: Ya sé, pero si me da tiempo, quiero ir a la **carnicería** para comprar unos **bistecs.**

In Spanish-speaking countries, the ending -**ía** indicates a store that specializes in a certain product. It is clear what the store specializes in because the name of the store contains the product. Notice the names of stores that end in -**ía** in **Vocabulario útil 1**. Notice that the **í** always carries an accent. Can you name any other specialty stores that end this way?

>> **Hacer las compras…**
En la carnicería

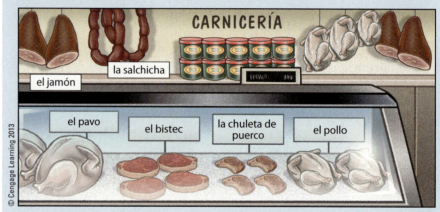

>> **En el supermercado**
La comida

ACTIVIDADES

6 En el barrio Hoy en día, las tiendas especializadas como la carnicería y la panadería no son tan comunes como en el pasado. En las ciudades grandes es más típico ir a un supermercado grande para comprar todos los comestibles en un solo sitio. El movimiento "verde", bajo el lema "Piensa globalmente, actúa localmente" ha producido mercados al aire libre donde uno puede comprar productos locales y orgánicos. Los mercados al aire libre y las tiendas especializadas no pueden competir con los precios de los supermercados más grandes, pero sí ofrecen la oportunidad de hablar con los vecinos y los vendedores en un ambiente agradable e íntimo. Formen grupos de cuatro. Contesten las siguientes preguntas y presenten sus respuestas a la clase.

1. ¿Dónde prefieres hacer las compras, en un supermercado, en pequeñas tiendas especializadas o en mercados al aire libre? ¿Por qué?
2. ¿Cuál es el mejor lugar cerca de la universidad para comprar pan? ¿carne? ¿fruta? ¿vegetales?
3. ¿Comes carne? ¿Cuántas veces a la semana comes carne? ¿Dónde?
4. ¿Comes mucha fruta y vegetales? ¿Dónde compras la fruta y los vegetales?
5. ¿Qué te importa más cuando haces las compras, el precio de los productos, su calidad *(quality)*, si son orgánicos o productos locales, la comodidad de comprar todo en un mismo lugar o la amabilidad *(friendliness)* de las personas que trabajan en la tienda?
6. ¿Crees que la idea de ir de compras a varias tiendas especializadas es más común en Estados Unidos o en Europa y otros países? ¿Y la idea de los mercados al aire libre? ¿de productos locales y órganicos?

7 Las compras Formen grupos de cuatro. Cada persona en el grupo debe preparar una lista de las compras que tiene que hacer. Intercambien *(Exchange)* las listas entre el grupo. Túrnense para describir lo que cada persona quiere comprar. Después preparen recomendaciones para cada persona sobre dónde ir de compras.

MODELO *Mark necesita comprar unas salchichas y unos vegetales. Mark debe ir a la carnicería para las salchichas y al mercado al aire libre para los vegetales.*

8 El día de hoy Formen grupos de tres. Cada persona debe preparar una descripción de sus hábitos de consumidor. Intercambien las descripciones y túrnense para leerlas en voz alta. El grupo tiene que adivinar a quién describe cada descripción.

MODELO *Descripción: Nunca voy al supermercado porque prefiero comer en restaurantes de comida rápida (fast food). Cuando invito a amigos a comer en casa, voy a una pizzería y compro todo lo que necesito.*
Grupo: ¡Es Julio!

ESTRATEGIA

Watching facial expressions

As you learned in **Chapter 3,** watching body language aids comprehension. The same is true of watching facial expressions: a smile, a frown, a raised eyebrow, or a laugh. These gestures can give you a better understanding of what the character means.

Antes de ver Estudia las palabras y frases que se usan en el video.

prisa	*hurry*
suerte	*luck*
sueños	*dreams*
Siga derecho...	*Continue straight. . .*
esquina	*corner*
Doble a la derecha...	*Turn to the right. . .*
cuadras	*blocks*

© Cengage Learning 2013

▶ **Ver** Mira el video sin sonido *(without sound)* y pon atencíon en las expresiones faciales.

Después de ver 1 Ahora, mira el video de nuevo con el sonido puesto *(sound on)* y di si las expresiones faciales de estas personas contribuyen al sentido de lo que dicen (**sí o no**).

1. **Javier:** Primero tengo que ir al gimnasio y después al centro estudiantil.
2. **Sergio:** Dicen que el supermercado es el lugar ideal para conocer a la mujer ideal.
3. **Dulce:** ¿A la carnicería? ¿Viene alguna persona especial a cenar?
4. **Chela:** Gracias. Nos vemos luego.
5. **Javier:** Siga derecho hasta aquella esquina.
6. **Sergio:** Algún día, mi amigo, algún día.

Después de ver 2 Mira el video una vez más y pon las actividades de Javier y Chela en el orden correcto.

Javier: _____ ir al banco, _____ ir al gimnasio, _____ ir al centro estudiantil, _____ ir al supermercado

Chela: _____ ir al gimnasio, _____ ir a la carnicería, _____ ir al supermercado

Voces de la comunidad

▶ >> Voces del mundo hispano

En el video para este capítulo Verónica, Ricardo y Paola
hablan de sus barrios, los medios de transporte y los lugares
adónde van frecuentemente. Lee las siguientes oraciones.
Después mira el video una o más veces para decir si las
oraciones son ciertas (**C**) o falsas (**F**).

1. Hay muchos restaurantes y supermercados en el barrio
   de Ricardo.
2. Hay un mercado al aire libre en el barrio de Paola.
3. Verónica frecuentemente usa auto y tren para transportarse.
4. A Ricardo le gusta usar su patineta *(skateboard)* para ir a todas partes.
5. Cuando Verónica usa transporte público es para ir al trabajo.
6. Paola va al centro de la Ciudad de México para comer, caminar y ver películas.

© Cengage Learning 2013

🔊 >> Voces de Estados Unidos

Track 18

Joe Reyna, fundador y director ejecutivo

Courtesy of Viva Markets.

❝Todos los empresarios somos soñadores *(dreamers)*.
Tomamos riesgos *(risks)* y esperamos que den fruto y
hacemos todo lo posible por hacerlos funcionar.❞

Joe Reyna es el fundador y director ejecutivo de Viva! Markets,
una nueva cadena de mercados latinos en el noroeste de
Estados Unidos. Criado en Estados Unidos y México y con
extensa experiencia en el mundo de los negocios, el joven texano
posee las habilidades culturales y profesionales justas para triunfar
en este ambicioso emprendimiento *(undertaking)*. Reyna equipa cada
uno de sus mercados con una panadería, carnicería, restaurante, cremería,
pastelería, tortillería, pescadería y hasta un bazar con otros vendedores.
Además, los mercados ofrecen productos asiáticos y polinesios a modo
de *(as a way to)* atraer a otros consumidores de la zona.

Reyna ha recibido numerosos reconocimientos por sus logros
(achievements) en el mundo de los negocios y contribuciones
filantrópicas. Entre ellos, fue reconocido por *Utah Business Magazine*
como una de las 100 personas más influyentes del estado.

¿Y tú? ¿Qué opinas de los mercados de Reynas? ¿Te interesa visitar uno?
¿Por qué sí o no?

¡Prepárate!

Indicating location: Prepositions of location

En la última cuadra, **frente al** banco, va a ver el centro comercial.

Cómo usarlo

Use prepositions of location to say where something is positioned in relation to other objects, or where it is located in general.

El restaurante está **frente a** la iglesia.

*The restaurant is **facing** the church.*

El café está **dentro del** almacén.

*The café is **inside** the department store.*

Cómo formarlo

1. Commonly used prepositions of location include the following.

al lado de	*next to, on the side of*	La farmacia está **al lado del** hospital.
entre	*between*	La farmacia está **entre el** hospital y la oficina de correos.
delante de	*in front of*	La joyería está **delante del** hotel.
enfrente de	*in front of, opposite*	La joyería está **enfrente del** hotel.
frente a	*in front of, facing, opposite*	La joyería está **frente al** hotel.
detrás de	*behind*	El hotel está **detrás de** la joyería.
debajo de	*below, underneath*	Los libros están **debajo de** la mesa.
encima de	*on top of, on*	El cuaderno está **encima de** los libros.
sobre	*on, above*	La comida está **sobre** la mesa.
dentro de	*inside of*	El libro está **dentro de** la mochila.
fuera de	*outside of*	El pan está **fuera del** refrigerador.
lejos de	*far from*	El súper está **lejos de** la universidad.
cerca de	*close to*	La panadería está **cerca del** hotel.

Usage of **enfrente de, delante de,** and **frente a** varies from country to country. However, they are more or less equivalent to each other.

Some of these prepositions can be used without the **de** as adverbs. For example, **El museo está cerca.**

Remember that when **de** or **a** follows a preposition of location, they combine with **el** to form **del** and **al: frente al hotel, dentro del refrigerador.**

2. Since these prepositions provide information about *location*, they are frequently used with the verb **estar**, which, as you learned in **Chapter 4**, is used to say where something is located.

ACTIVIDADES

1 **¿Dónde está…?** Di dónde están las siguientes cosas. Usa estas preposiciones: **al lado de, debajo de, enfrente de, encima de.** También debes escribir el artículo definido de la segunda cosa, según el modelo.

MODELO   La impresora está _al lado del_ escritorio.

1. Los apuntes están _____ computadora portátil.
2. Los cuadernos están _____ impresora.
3. El diccionario de español está _____ escritorio.
4. El MP3 portátil está _____ computadora portátil.
5. La cámera digital está _____ mesa.
6. La mochila está _____ escritorio.

2 **Treviño**   En grupos de tres, estudien el mapa de Treviño. Luego, túrnense para describir dónde están situados por lo menos diez edificios o sitios. Usen las preposiciones en la página 206.

3 **Nuestro salón de clase**   En grupos de tres, describan dónde están varios objetos en su salón de clase. Usen las preposiciones en la página 206.

4 **Nuestra universidad**   Ahora, trabajen en grupos de tres a cinco para dibujar un mapa de su universidad. Incluyan por lo menos seis edificios principales. Luego, túrnense para describir la posición de uno de los edificios. El grupo tiene que adivinar qué edificio se describe.

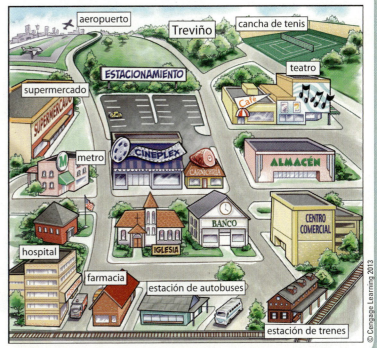

>> Gramática útil 2

Telling others what to do: Commands with **usted** and **ustedes**

Cómo usarlo

1. You have already been seeing command forms in direction lines. In Spanish, there are two sets of singular command forms, since there are two ways to address people directly (**tú** and **usted**). The informal commands, which you will learn in **Chapter 7**, are used with people you would address as tú. In this chapter you will learn formal commands, as well as plural commands with **ustedes**.

2. Command forms are not used as frequently in Spanish as they are in English. For example, in **Chapter 4** you learned that courteous, softening expressions are often used instead of commands: **¿Le importa si uso la computadora?** instead of **Déjeme** (*Let me*) **usar la computadora.**

3. However, one situation in which command forms are almost always used is in giving instructions to someone, such as directions to a specific location.

Siga derecho hasta la esquina. Allí **doble** a la izquierda.

__Continue__ straight ahead until the corner. __Turn__ left there.

Camine tres cuadras hasta llegar a la farmacia. Allí **doble** a la derecha y **cruce** la calle. La carnicería está al lado del banco.

__Walk__ three blocks until you arrive at the pharmacy. There, __turn__ right and __cross__ the street. The butcher shop is next to the bank.

There are three **usted** command forms in this postcard advertising a tour of historic Mexican theaters. What are they?

¡Póngase en escena!

Participe en nuestro tour de los teatros históricos de México, donde las estrellas verdaderas tienen más de 100 años.

Palacio de Bellas Artes, México D.F.　　Teatro Calderón, Zacatecas　　Teatro Juárez, Guanajuato　　Teatro Degollado, Guadalajara

¡Presente esta postal para recibir un descuento de 20%!

EL CONSEJO PARA LA PRESERVACIÓN DE LOS MONUMENTOS NACIONALES

Photos (left to right): Jeri7l/Dreamstime; Rfoxphoto/Dreamstime; Afagundes/Dreamstime; Rfoxphoto/Dreamstime; text: © Cengage Learning 2013

Cómo formarlo

LO BÁSICO

A *command* form, also known as an *imperative* form, is used to issue a direct order to someone you are addressing: **<u>Vaya</u> a la esquina y <u>doble</u> a la derecha.** *(**<u>Go</u>** to the corner and **<u>turn</u>** right.)*

1. The chart below shows the singular formal (**usted**) and plural (**ustedes**) command forms of the verb **seguir** *(to go, to follow).*

	Singular	Plural
affirmative	siga	sigan
negative	no siga	no sigan

2. Here are the rules for forming the usted and ustedes command forms of most verbs. These are true for the affirmative and negative commands.

   ■ Take the **yo** form of the verb in the present indicative. Remove the **o** and add **e** for **-ar** verbs or **a** for **-er / -ir** verbs, to create the **usted** command.

   poner: → pongo → pong- + a → **ponga**

   ■ Add an **n** to the **usted** command form to create the **ustedes** command.

   ponga → **pongan**

> By using the **yo** form of the present indicative, you have already incorporated any irregularities in the verb. Now they automatically carry over into the command form.

infinitive	yo form minus the -o ending	plus e / en for -ar verbs OR a / an for -er / -ir verbs	usted / ustedes command forms
hablar	habl-	+ e / en	**hable / hablen**
pensar	piens-	+ e / en	**piense / piensen**
tener	teng-	+ a / an	**tenga / tengan**
decir	dig-	+ a / an	**diga / digan**
escribir	escrib-	+ a / an	**escriba / escriban**
servir	sirv-	+ a / an	**sirva / sirvan**

3. A few command forms require spelling changes to maintain the original pronunciation of the verb.

   ■ verbs ending in **-car**: change the **c → qu**:

   buscar: → **busco** → **busque / busquen**

   ■ verbs ending in **-zar**: change the **z → c**:

   empezar: → **empiezo** → **empiece / empiecen**

   ■ verbs ending in **-gar**: change the **g → gu**:

   pagar: → **pago** → **pague / paguen**

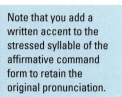

4. A few verbs have irregular **usted** and **ustedes** command forms: **dar (dé / den)**, **estar (esté / estén)**, **ir (vaya / vayan)**, **saber (sepa / sepan)**, and **ser (sea / sean)**.

5. For the command forms of reflexive verbs, attach the reflexive pronoun to the *end* of *affirmative* **usted** / **ustedes** commands and place it *before* *negative* **usted** / **ustedes** commands.

Note that you add a written accent to the stressed syllable of the affirmative command form to retain the original pronunciation.

Prepárese para una sorpresa.	***Prepare yourself*** *for a surprise.*
No se ponga nervioso.	***Don't get*** *nervous.*

6. Here are words and phrases for giving directions.

One commonly used command in Spanish is **¡Vamos!** *(Let's go!)*, which the speaker uses to refer to several people, including himself or herself. Because it includes the speaker in the action, it is used instead of an **ustedes** command form.

¿Me puede decir cómo llegar a...?	*Can you tell me how to get to . . . ?*
¿Me puede decir dónde queda...?	*Can you tell me where . . . is located?*
Cómo no. Vaya...	*Of course. Go . . .*
... a la avenida... / la calle...	*. . . to the avenue . . . / street . . .*
... a la derecha / izquierda / la esquina.	*. . . to the right / the left / the corner.*
... (dos) cuadras.	*. . . (two) blocks.*
... (todo) derecho.	*. . . (straight) ahead.*

bajar (baje)	*to get down from, to get off of (a bus, etc.)*
caminar (camine)	*to walk*
cruzar (cruce)	*to cross*
doblar (doble)	*to turn*
seguir (i) (siga)	*to continue*
subir (suba)	*to go up, to get on*

7. You may soften commands by adding **por favor** or by using these phrases.

Me gustaría / Quisiera (+ infinitive)...	*I'd like (+ infinitive) . . .*
Por favor, **¿(me) puede** (+ infinitive)**?**	*Please, can you (+ infinitive) (me)?*
¿Pudiera / Podría usted (+ infinitive)**?**	*Could you (+ infinitive)?*

—**Me gustaría** comer. **¿Pudiera** recomendarme un restaurante?
—Cómo no. El Farol del Mar es buenísimo.
—¿**Me puede** decir si está lejos?
—Está muy cerca. **¿Quisiera** saber cómo llegar?
—Sí. ¡Muchas gracias! Y también **me gustaría** tener la dirección.

ACTIVIDADES

5 **¿Cómo llego...?** Indica el mandato correcto para completar cada oración.

1. (seguir) usted todo derecho hasta la plaza con la iglesia.
2. (doblar) ustedes aquí en la Calle Federal.
3. (subir) ustedes esta calle todo derecho hasta la esquina con Quinteros.
4. (cruzar) usted aquí y (caminar) dos cuadras.
5. No (ir) ustedes hasta el parque.
6. No (preocuparse) si no llegan inmediatamente. Está un poco lejos.

6 **Los anuncios** El campo de la publicidad hace uso frecuente de los mandatos formales para tratar de convencer al público que compre o use su producto. Completa los anuncios con mandatos, usando la forma de **usted** de los verbos entre paréntesis.

1. (abrir, poner, tener)

> **BANCO MUNDIAL** $
>
> ____ una cuenta en Banco Mundial.
> ____ su dinero en nuestras manos.
> ____ confianza en nuestros profesionales.

2. (venir, cocinar, comprar)

> **SUPERMERCADO CENTRAL**
>
> ____ al Supermercado Central para hacer las compras.
> ____ con la comida más fresca y más natural de la ciudad.
> ____ las comidas favoritas de sus hijos.

3. (esperar, llamar, servir)

> **PIZZERÍA ITALIA**
>
> No ____ .
> ____ al 555-6677 para ordenar su pizza.
> ____ la pizza más fresca y deliciosa en su propia casa en menos de treinta minutos.

4. (trabajar, venir, descubrir)

> **Restaurante París**
>
> Esta noche, no ____ en la cocina.
> ____ al Restaurante París para disfrutar de nuestro ambiente relajante y nuestro excelente servicio.
> ____ nuestra riquísima cocina francesa.

5. (levantar, hacer, recibir)

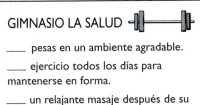

> **GIMNASIO LA SALUD**
>
> ____ pesas en un ambiente agradable.
> ____ ejercicio todos los días para mantenerse en forma.
> ____ un relajante masaje después de su sesión de ejercicios.

6. (usar, navegar, visitar, tomar)

> **CAFÉ CAFÉ**
>
> ¡ ____ nuestro wifi gratis!
> ____ por Internet.
> ____ con amigos.
> ____ un café.

© Cengage Learning 2013

7 **¡Niños!** Los padres también usan los mandatos con frecuencia al hablar con sus hijos. La señora Díaz tiene que salir esta noche. ¿Qué les dice a sus hijos? Indica sus mandatos con la forma de **ustedes**.

1. empezar la tarea al llegar a casa
2. apagar la computadora después de terminar la tarea
3. ser pacientes con la niñera *(babysitter)*
4. no abrir la puerta
5. no jugar fútbol dentro de la casa
6. no salir de la casa
7. no ir a visitar a sus amigos
8. no comer papitas fritas antes de cenar
9. acostarse a las diez
10. cepillarse los dientes antes de acostarse
11. dormir bien
12. estar tranquilos

8 **¡Compre, compre, compre!** Ahora, con un(a) compañero(a), escriban un anuncio comercial para la televisión. Usen el mandato formal con **usted** para convencer a su público. Presenten el anuncio a la clase.

9 **¿Cómo llego?** Tu compañero(a) es turista y te pregunta cómo llegar a varios sitios. Dile cómo llegar y dile qué medio de transporte debe usar. Luego, haz tú el papel *(role)* del (de la) turista; tu compañero(a) te va a dar instrucciones. Pueden usar el mapa de la página 207 y añadir los sitios que no están, o pueden decirse cómo llegar a sitios en su comunidad.

1. el supermercado
2. el centro comercial
3. el metro
4. la estación de trenes
5. la estación de autobuses
6. la cancha de tenis
7. la oficina de correos
8. el banco

10 **La oficina de correos** Escucha la conversación entre un señor y una señorita. La primera vez que escuches la conversación, apunta la información que vas a necesitar. Luego, escribe las instrucciones que le da la señorita al señor para llegar a la oficina de correos. Usa los siguientes verbos en tus oraciones.

Track 19

1. caminar
2. doblar
3. seguir
4. cruzar
5. doblar
6. caminar

Sonrisas

Expresión En grupos de tres o cuatro personas, piensen en las órdenes que les gustaría dar a los profesores de la universidad. Luego, escriban una lista de sus ideas.

MODELO *No den tarea para los fines de semana.*

>> Gramática útil 3

Affirming and negating: Affirmative and negative expressions

Cómo usarlo

¿Viene **alguna** persona especial a cenar?

1. There are a number of words and expressions that are used to express affirmatives and negatives in Spanish. Notice that a double negative form is often used in Spanish, where as it is hardly ever used in English.

No conozco a **nadie** aquí.	*I don't know anyone here.*
¿Conoces **a alguien** aquí?	*Do you know anyone here?*
No quiero ni este libro **ni** ése.	*I don't want this book or that one.*

2. Remember to use the personal **a** that you learned in **Chapter 5** when you refer to people: **No conozco a nadie aquí**.

Cómo formarlo

1. Here are some frequently used affirmative and negative words in Spanish. You have already learned some of these, such as **también, siempre**, and **nunca**.

alguien	*someone*	**nadie**	*no one, nobody*
algo	*something*	**nada**	*nothing*
algún / alguno (a, os, as)	*some, any*	**ningún / ninguno(a)**	*none, no, not any*
siempre	*always*	**nunca / jamás**	*never*
también	*also*	**tampoco**	*neither, not either*
o… o…	*either / or*	**ni… ni…**	*neither / nor*

2. Most of these words do not change, regardless of the number or gender of the words they modify. However, the words **alguno** and **ninguno** can also be used as *adjectives*. In this case, they must change to agree with the nouns they modify. Additionally, when they are used before a masculine noun they shorten to **algún** and **ningún**.

—¿Tienes **algún** libro sobre la informática?	*Do you have **a (any)** book about computer science?*
—No, no tengo **ningún** libro sobre ese tema. Pero tenemos **algunos** libros muy interesantes sobre las redes sociales.	*No, I don't have **a (any)** book on that subject. But we do have **some** very interesting books about social networks.*
—No, gracias, ya tengo **algunas** revistas. ¿No tienes **ninguna** sugerencia sobre otros libros?	*No, thanks, I already have **some** magazines. You don't have **any** suggestions for other books?*

© Cengage Learning 2013

3. **Alguno** and **ninguno** can also be used as *pronouns* to replace a noun already referred to. In this case, they match the number and gender of that noun.

—¿Quieres estos **libros?**   *Do you want these **books?***
—No, gracias, ya tengo **algunos.**   *No, thanks, I already have **some.***
—¿No quieres una **revista?**   *Don't you want a **magazine?***
—No, no necesito **ninguna**.   *No, I don't need **any (one)**.*

The plural forms of **ninguno** and **ninguna**—**ningunos** and **ningunas**—are not frequently used.

4. Notice how in Spanish, unlike English, even when more than one negative expression is used in a sentence, the meaning remains negative.

Nunca hay **nadie** aquí.   *There's **never anyone** here.*
No está **ni** Leo **ni** Ana **tampoco**.   ***Neither** Leo **nor** Ana is here **either**.*

Notice that when a negative word precedes the verb, the word **no** is not used: **Nadie viene.** When the negative word comes after the verb, however, you must use **no** directly before the verb: **No viene nadie.**

ACTIVIDADES

11 **¿Qué pasa?** Escoge la palabra o palabras correctas para completar cada oración.

1. ¡Me encanta el café! (Nunca / Siempre) tomo una taza *(cup)* por la mañana.
2. No tengo (algo / nada) para comer. Voy a ir a mi restaurante favorito.
3. A mis amigos les gusta ese almacén y a mí (también / tampoco).
4. (Alguien / Nadie) hace las compras en ese mercado. Los precios son muy altos.
5. Yo no como carne y mis amigos (también / tampoco) la comen.
6. Necesito unos vegetales. ¿Tienes (algunos / ningunos)?

12 **¡Yo también!** Un(a) amigo(a) está en tu casa y tú le explicas algunas cosas sobre los hábitos de tu familia. Él (Ella) dice que su familia es igual. Con un(a) compañero(a), improvisen esta situación. El (La) amigo(a) siempre usa **también** o **tampoco** en su respuesta.

MODELO   Tú: *Mis tíos nunca cenan antes de las ocho de la noche.*
         Amigo(a): *Mis tíos tampoco.*

1. Mis primos siempre se levantan temprano.
2. Mi abuelo nunca se viste informalmente.
3. Mi abuela siempre se viste elegantemente.
4. A mis padres les encanta salir a comer.
5. Mi hermana es fanática de la música rap.
6. A mis hermanos no les gusta levantarse temprano.
7. Yo siempre me baño y me visto elegantemente si voy a una fiesta.

Ahora describe los hábitos verdaderos de tu familia. Tu compañero(a) te dice si su familia es igual o no.

◀))
Track 20
13 **El visitante** Un visitante pasa el fin de semana en tu casa. Te hace preguntas sobre tu barrio. Contesta sus preguntas en el negativo.

MODELO Escuchas: ¿Hay alguna estación de trenes en el barrio?
Escribes: *No, no hay ninguna estación de trenes en el barrio.*

14 **Encuesta** En parejas, túrnense para hacer y contestar las siguientes preguntas. Contesten primero en afirmativo y luego en negativo. Usen las palabras entre paréntesis en sus respuestas.

MODELO ¿Comes en la cafetería de la universidad? (siempre / nunca)
Sí, siempre como en la cafetería de la universidad.
No, nunca como en la cafetería de la universidad.

1. ¿Algunos de los estudiantes van a la biblioteca (algunos / nadie)
2. ¿Te gusta comer algo antes de clase? (algo / nada)
3. ¿Hay algún cajero automático en la universidad? (algunos / ningún)
4. ¿Vas en metro a la universidad? (siempre / nunca)
5. ¿Hay alguna tienda de video cerca de la universidad? (algunas / ninguna)
6. ¿Estudias antes de clase o después de clase? (o… o… / ni… ni…)

15 **El fin de semana** Vas a pasar el fin de semana en casa de tu compañero(a). Le haces varias preguntas para determinar cómo vas a pasar el fin de semana. Escoge *(Choose)* ideas de la lista o inventa otras. Luego, cambia de papel *(role)* con tu compañero(a). Usa las palabras afirmativas y negativas que acabas de aprender en tus preguntas y tus respuestas.

Ideas posibles: divertido en la tele, comer en el refrigerador, libro de cocina mexicana, escritora mexicana preferida, revista de música popular, juego interactivo, disco compacto de Paulina Rubio, ¿…?

MODELO Tú: *¿Hay algo divertido en la tele?*
Compañero(a): *No, no hay nada divertido en la tele.*

16 **Aquí…** En grupos de tres o cuatro escriban una lista de las preferencias de los estudiantes de su universidad. Usen palabras y expresiones de las tres columnas. Luego, trabajen juntos para escribir un resumen de sus opiniones.

A	B	C
todo el mundo	nunca	comer en…
algunas personas	siempre	comprar algo / nada en…
nadie	jamás	ir a…
		¿…?

Gramática útil 4

Indicating relative position of objects: Demonstrative adjectives and pronouns

Derecho hasta **aquella** esquina...

> In everyday speech **ese** and **aquel** are often used interchangeably.

Cómo usarlo

Demonstrative adjectives and pronouns indicate *relative distance* from the speaker. **Este** is something very close to the speaker, **ese** is something a little farther away, and **aquel** is something at a distance *(over there)*.

1. Demonstrative adjectives:

Esta casa es bonita. También me gusta **esa** casa, pero **aquella** casa es fea.	***This*** *house is pretty. I also like* ***that*** *house but* ***that*** *house (**over there**) is ugly.*

2. Demonstrative pronouns:

De los autos me gusta **éste**, pero **ése** también es bueno. **Aquél** no me gusta.	*Of the cars I like* ***this one***, *but* ***that one*** *is also good. I don't like* ***that one (over there)***.

Cómo formarlo

LO BÁSICO

A demonstrative adjective modifies a noun. A demonstrative pronoun is used instead of a noun.

1. Demonstrative adjectives and pronouns change to reflect gender and number. Demonstrative *adjectives* reflect the gender and number of the nouns they *modify*. Demonstrative *pronouns* reflect the gender and number of the nouns they *replace*.

	Demonstrative adjectives	Demonstrative pronouns
this; these *(close)*	este, esta; estos, estas	éste, ésta; éstos, éstas
that; those *(farther)*	ese, esa; esos, esas	ése, ésa; ésos, ésas
that; those *(at a distance)*	aquel, aquella; aquellos, aquellas	aquél, aquélla; aquéllos, aquéllas

> The only spelling difference between demonstrative adjectives and pronouns is that the pronouns are usually written with an accent. Although accents on demonstrative pronouns were required in the past, the **Real Academia de la Lengua Española** has ruled that they are not necessary. However, most Spanish speakers continue to use these accents. This textbook uses them for the purpose of clarity.

2. Use these words with demonstrative adjectives and pronouns: **aquí** (*here*, often used with **este**), **allí** (*there*, often used with **ese**), and **allá** (*over there*, often used with **aquel**).

3. **Esto** and **eso** are neutral pronouns that refer to a concept or something that has already been said: <u>**Eso** es lo que dijo la profesora. Todo <u>esto</u> es muy interesante.</u>

> **Esto** and **eso** do not change their forms; they are invariable forms.

17 **¡Ayuda, por favor!** Completa las siguientes conversaciones con el pronombre o adjetivo demostrativo apropiado entre paréntesis.

1.   TÚ: Hola, ¿pudiera usted decirme cómo llegar a las canchas de tenis?

   HOMBRE: Cómo no. Siga usted (esta / aquella) calle aquí hasta (esta / esa) esquina allí, la esquina con la avenida Quintana. Luego vaya todo derecho hasta llegar a un parque muy grande. Las canchas de tenis están en (aquel / este) parque.

2.   TÚ: Buenos días. Por favor, ¿pudiera usted decirme cómo ir al aeropuerto?

   MUJER: Claro. Usted debe tomar (ese / aquel) autobús allí en la calle Francisco. A ver, tengo la ruta aquí en (aquella / esta) guía.

    TÚ: Muy bien. Entonces, ¿(ese / este) autobús es el que necesito tomar?

   MUJER: Sí. (Este / Ese) autobús lo lleva directamente al aeropuerto.

3.   TÚ: Perdón. ¿Puede usted recomendar un restaurante bueno?

   HOMBRE: Seguro. (Éste / Aquél) que está aquí cerca es bastante bueno. Pero hay otro allí, mire, al otro lado de la calle, La Criolla. (Ése / Éste) sirve comida muy rica. Creo que (ése, aquél), La Criolla, es mi favorito.

4.   TÚ: Hola, busco la sección de literatura latina.

   MUJER: Muy bien. (Esos / Estos) libros aquí son de autores cubanos. Allí, en la próxima sección, (esos / estos) libros son de autores mexicanos. Y allá, (estos / aquellos) libros son de otros autores latinoamericanos.

    TÚ: ¿Y (esos / estos) libros aquí en la mesa?

   MUJER: ¿(Éstos / Aquéllos) aquí? (Estos / Esos) libros son de autores españoles.

18 **¿Qué pasa aquí?** Completa las oraciones con el adjetivo o pronombre demostrativo correcto.

1. En el cine: Podría ver _____ horario de películas allí?

2. En el dormitorio: ¿Me puedes pasar _____ libro allá?

3. En el mercado: No me gustan esos bistecs. Prefiero _____ aquí.

4. En la pizzería: No quiero una pizza con salchicha. Me gusta más _____ allí con los vegetales.

5. En la papelería: Necesito un cuaderno grande. Ese cuaderno es bueno pero _____ allá es aún mejor.

6. En casa: ¿Dónde pongo _____ silla que tengo aquí — al lado del sofá o al lado de la mesa?

7. En la estación de trenes: ¡ _____ es terrible! ¡Nuestro tren llega muy tarde!

19 En el mercado Con un(a) compañero(a) de clase, miren el dibujo de un mercado en México. ¿Qué quieren comprar para la cena? Escojan tres platos para preparar y hablen de las cosas que necesitan, usando los adjetivos y pronombres demostrativos correctos.

© Cengage Learning 2013

MODELO   Tú: *¿Qué quieres comprar? ¿Compramos ese queso?*
Amigo(a): *Sí, y también estas salchichas. ¿Qué más?*
Tú: *Aquellos huevos, ¿no crees?*

20 Adónde vamos? Con un(a) compañero(a) de clase, hagan una lista de cinco de los siguientes lugares en tu comunidad u otros que prefieren. Incluyan sitios que están muy cerca de la universidad, un poco lejos y muy lejos.

restaurantes   museos   tiendas de música
cafés   tiendas de ropa   pizzerías

Ahora, hablen de los varios sitios de su lista, usando adjetivos y pronombres demostrativos.

MODELO   Tú: *¿Quieres ir al restaurante Chimichangas? Sirven comida mexicana.*
Amigo(a): *No, no me gusta ese restaurante. ¿Por qué no vamos a éste, McMurray's? Sirven comida estadounidense.*

¡Explora y exprésate!

México

Robert Frerck/Getty Images

Información general ▶

Nombre oficial: Estados Unidos Mexicanos

Población: 113,724,226

Capital: México, D.F. (f. 1521) (9.000.000 hab.)

Otras ciudades importantes: Guadalajara (1.600.000 hab.), Monterrey (1.130.000 hab.), Puebla (1.347.000 hab.)

Moneda: peso

Idiomas: español (oficial), náhuatl, maya, zapoteco, mixteco, otomi, totonaca (se hablan aproximadamente 68 idiomas con muchas variaciones)

Mapa de México: Apéndice D

Vale saber…

- La historia de México incluye tres grandes civilizaciones: los olmecas, la primera civilización mesoamérica; los mayas, conocidos por sus avances en las matemáticas, la astronomía, la escritura jeroglífica y también por sus grandes templos y pirámides; y los mexicas (o aztecas), el pueblo que forma la capital de su imperio en Tenochtitlán, ahora la ciudad de México.

- La conquista española de México se refiere a la conquista de los mexicas por Hernán Cortés en México-Tenochtitlán en 1521. México gana la independencia de España en 1810.

- La Revolución Mexicana se considera el conflicto político y social más importante del siglo XX en México

- México tiene una gran diversidad de grupos indígenas: los nahuas, los mayas, los zapotecos, los mixtecos, los otomíes, los totonacas y los tzotziles, entre muchos otros.

El mercado del pueblo, el tianguis

En Estados Unidos, los "farmers' markets" encuentran popularidad en las ciudades hace poco *(recently)*. Pero en México, los tianguis existen desde la época prehispánica. La palabra *tianguis* viene del náhuatl *tianquiztli*, que quiere decir *mercado*. Son mercados al aire libre que se instalan en todas partes de la ciudad para vender frutas y verduras orgánicas, pan, maíz, frijoles, aves *(birds)*, peces *(fish)*, carne, hierbas medicinales, especias *(spices)*, artesanía y mucho más. Hacer las compras en un tianguis es mucho más divertido que hacerlas en los supermercados: hay de todo, y es común escuchar la música de conjuntos musicales tradicionales allí. Aunque se hayan adaptado *(they have adapted)* a los tiempos modernos, los tianguis siguen siendo *(continue being)* el mercado preferido de la gente del pueblo.

Kathrin Ziegler/Getty Images

>> En resumen

La información general

1. ¿Cuáles son tres grandes civilizaciones antiguas de México?
2. ¿Qué gran civilización antigua forma su capital en lo que hoy es la Ciudad de México?
3. ¿En qué año y qué ciudad se realiza *(occurs)* la conquista español?
4. ¿En qué año gana México la independencia de España?
5. ¿Qué conflicto en México se considera el más importante del siglo XX?
6. ¿Cuáles son tres pueblos indígenas de México de hoy?

El tema de la comunidad

1. ¿Qué son los tianguis?
2. ¿Desde cuando existen los tianguis en México?
3. ¿De qué lengua indígen viene la palabra *tianguis*?
4. ¿Cómo son los tianguis diferentes a los supermercados?

🌐 ¿QUIERES SABER MÁS?

Revisa y rellena la tabla que empezaste al principio del capítulo. Luego, escoge un tema para investigar en línea y prepárate para compartir la información con la clase.

Palabras clave: Mesoamérica, la conquista española, Emiliano Zapata, Pancho Villa, la Revolución Mexicana de 1910, Octavio Paz, Diego Rivera, Frida Kahlo, Gael García Bernal

🌐 **Tú en el mundo hispano** Para explorar oportunidades de usar el español para estudiar o hacer trabajos voluntarios o aprendizajes en México, sigue los enlaces en **www.cengagebrain.com**.

🎵 **Ritmos del mundo hispano** Sigue los enlaces en **www.cengagebrain.com** para escuchar música de México.

A leer

ESTRATEGIA

Working with unknown grammatical structures

When you read texts written for native Spanish speakers, you will frequently come across grammatical structures you haven't learned yet. Seeing grammatical endings you don't recognize can be intimidating, but if you focus just on the meaning of the infinitive of the verb, you can usually get its general meaning. Often you can guess the tense (present, past, future, etc.) by looking at the rest of the sentence. If you don't let unknown grammatical structures hold you back, you'll make a great leap forward in understanding authentic Spanish.

1 Aquí hay algunas estructuras gramaticales de la lectura que no sabes. Mira el significado general del verbo para hacer una correspondencia entre las palabras en español y las en inglés.

1. _____ es necesario que **conozca**
2. _____ **podrá** descifrar
3. _____ **esté** todo el día **conectado** al monitor
4. _____ que **se encuentre** ahí
5. _____ **acuda** la gente más "nice"
6. _____ **estar vestido** perfectamente
7. _____ el restaurante que **ofrezca**

a. *you will be able to decipher*
b. *that may be found there*
c. *it's necessary that you know*
d. *the restaurant that offers*
e. *to be dressed perfectly*
f. *he is glued to the screen all day*
g. *the nicest people gather*

2 Ahora, mira las frases de la **Actividad 1.** ¿Cuáles son las formas gramaticales que no sabes? Con un(a) compañero(a), hagan una lista de las siete formas gramaticales. ¿Son del tiempo presente o futuro? Hagan una lista de las formas y sus tiempos.

It's not necessary to understand all the unknown words in the article to do the activities on page 224.

3 Vas a leer un artículo sobre los jóvenes de la Ciudad de México y adónde van para divertirse. Mientras lees, trata de entender los verbos sin pensar demasiado en las estructuras gramaticales que no sabes. Enfoca en las ideas principales del artículo.

LECTURA

Los jóvenes mexicanos se divierten

Alejandro Esquivel

¿Eres telemaníaco(a)...

¿Usted sabe cómo se divierten los "teens"? Las maneras de entretenerse en estos tiempos de revolución electrónica, videojuegos, DVDs, equipos MP3 y antros son tan heterogéneas como la población que ocupa[1] solamente el Distrito Federal... Es necesario que conozca ciertos perfiles de los jóvenes contemporáneos para entender más su manera de ir por la vida. Es así como podrá descifrar algunos de los códigos[2] de la juventud para saber adónde van y qué hacen...

El telemaníaco

Una de las formas de entretenimiento más "ancestrales" es el observar televisión por más de cuatro horas seguidas[3]. A esta joven especie[4] no le interesa ni en lo más mínimo la vida social, pues prefiere observar un maratón entero de Los Simpson a tomar un buen café con sus cuates[5]... Algunos padres prefieren que su "hijito" esté todo el día conectado al monitor, argumentando que es preferible que se encuentre ahí a estar vagabundeando en las calles.

El peace & love

En cuanto a este tipo de jóvenes, les preocupa más lo natural, el amor y la fraternidad entre razas. A diferencia del telemaníaco, éste trata de[6] pasar el menor tiempo posible frente a un televisor. Dentro de sus principales maneras de divertirse está el acudir[7] todos los domingos a la Plaza de Coyoacán, para buscar algún libro y observar los espectáculos culturales que semana a semana ahí se presentan.

El fresa[8]

Este "teen modelo" gusta de asistir a lugares a los cuales acuda la gente más "nice" de la ciudad. Otra forma de diversión son las cenas y los cafés que regularmente se realizan[9] en restaurantes y cafeterías ubicadas[10] en la zona de Bosques de las Lomas y Santa Fe. Al fresa le late[11] bastante asistir a "antros[12]" donde la música comercial sea el hit.

El raver

Los ravers son los encargados de llenar[13] los festivales de música electrónica o raves, ya que éstos sólo son posibles gracias a la asistencia de más de 3 mil personas... La música que se toca es la electrónica y durante los raves se baila sin parar[14] por más de nueve horas continuas y sólo bebiendo agua embotellada. El raver también acude a antros donde solamente se toque electrónica.

El fashion

Otro espécimen fácil de identificar, ya que su preocupación más grande es estar vestido perfectamente. Entre sus grandes pasatiempos está leer revistas de moda[15], pero a la hora de salir trata siempre de asistir al lugar que acaban de inaugurar o al lugar más fashion. También prefiere las cenas en compañía de sus amigos en el restaurante que ofrezca lo último[16] en cocina.

...fresa...u otro tipo?

[1]**vive en** [2]*codes* [3]*continuas* [4]*species* [5]*amigos* [6]**trata...**: *tries to* [7]*ir* [8]*affluent youth* [9]**se...**: *take place* [10]*located* [11]**le...**: *le gusta* [12]*bars or clubs, the "in" places* [13]**encargados...**: *in charge of filling* [14]**sin...**: *without stopping* [15]**revistas...** *fashion magazines* [16]**lo...**: *the latest*

4 Con un(a) compañero(a), escriban el nombre del grupo de jóvenes que va a cada lugar indicado. En algunos casos, más de un grupo va a ese lugar.

Lugar	Grupo
1. antros	
2. raves	
3. la Plaza de Coyoacán	
4. festivales de música electrónica	
5. la zona de Bosques de las Lomas	
6. casa	
7. los lugares más "fashion"	
8. restaurantes	
9. cafés	

5 En el **Capítulo 4** hay una nota sobre los préstamos del inglés al español. Este artículo tiene muchos ejemplos de este tipo de palabra. Trabaja con un(a) compañero(a) de clase. ¿Pueden encontrar seis préstamos del inglés al español?

6 Trabaja en un grupo de tres o cuatro estudiantes. ¿Pueden identificar cinco grupos de "tipos" entre los jóvenes estadounidenses? Escriban una lista de los grupos, unas de sus características y adónde van para divertirse. Luego, compartan su lista con la clase entera.

Diane Diederich/iStockphoto

>> Antes de escribir

ESTRATEGIA

Writing—Adding supporting detail

In **Chapter 5** you wrote topic sentences for paragraphs. Once you have a topic sentence, you have the main idea of your paragraph. But the topic sentence is not enough. You need to include supporting detail—additional information or examples that give your paragraph life and help make it more interesting. If you think of it in terms of a photo, supporting detail is similar to the other items in the photo that are not its focal point—what else can you see and understand from the background?

1 Vas a escribir un párrafo sobre un sitio importante para ti y lo que haces allí. ¿Cuáles son algunos sitios y actividades que puedes describir? Haz una lista con tus ideas.

2 Usa tu lista de la **Actividad 1** y escoge un sitio para describir. Tu oración temática debe identificar el sitio. Después tienes que añadir unos detalles (details) para dar interés a tu descripicón. Sigue el modelo a continuación para escribir tu oración temática y unos detalles sobre el sitio.

Oración temática: *Para mí, el centro de mi comunidad es el café local donde tomo café todos los días.*

Detalles: *el café es bueno, la música es interesante, los empleados son muy amables, tengo wifi, veo a muchas personas y vecinos allí, hablo con todos, conozco a gente nueva, me siento, me relajo, trabajo en la computadora...*

>> Composición

3 Usa la oración temática y los detalles de la **Actividad 2** para escribir un párrafo breve en el que describes el sitio, cómo es y qué haces allí.

>> Después de escribir

4 Mira tu borrador otra vez. Usa la siguiente lista para revisarlo.

- ¿Tiene toda la información necesaria?
- ¿Los detalles relacionan bien con la oración temática?
- ¿Corresponden los sustantivos y adjetivos?
- ¿Corresponden las formas de los verbos y los sustantivos?
- ¿Hay errores de puntuación o de ortografía?

Vocabulario

En la universidad   *At the university*

el apartamento *apartment*
el auditorio *auditorium*
la cancha / el campo de fútbol *soccer field*
la cancha de tenis *tennis court*
el centro estudiantil *student center*
el cuarto *room*

el dormitorio / la residencia estudiantil *dormitory*
el edificio *building*
el estadio *stadium*
la oficina *office*
la piscina *swimming pool*
la pista de atletismo *athletics track*

En la ciudad o en el pueblo   *In the city or in the town*

el aeropuerto *airport*
el almacén *store*
el banco *bank*
el barrio *neighborhood*
el cajero automático *automated teller machine (ATM)*
la casa *house*
el centro comercial *mall*
el cine *cinema*
la estación de trenes / autobuses *train / bus station*
el estacionamiento *parking lot*
la farmacia *pharmacy*
el hospital *hospital*
la iglesia *church*
la joyería *jewelry store*
el mercado... *market*
　　...al aire libre *open-air market; farmer's market*

el museo *museum*
la oficina de correos *post office*
la papelería *stationery store*
el parque *park*
la pizzería *pizzeria*
la plaza *plaza*
el restaurante *restaurant*
el supermercado *supermarket*
el teatro *theater*
la tienda... *store*
　　...de equipo deportivo . . . *sporting goods store*
　　...de juegos electrónicos . . . *electronic games store*
　　...de ropa . . . *clothing store*
el (la) vecino(a) *neighbor*

Hacer las compras...   *Shopping . . .*

En la carnicería   *At the butcher shop*
el bistec *steak*
la chuleta de puerco *pork chop*
el jamón *ham*
el pavo *turkey*
el pollo *chicken*
la salchicha *sausage*

En el supermercado   *At the supermarket*
la comida *food*
las frutas *fruits*
los huevos *eggs*
la leche *milk*
el pan *bread*
las papitas fritas *potato chips*
el queso *cheese*
los refrescos *soft drinks*
los vegetales *vegetables*
el yogur *yogurt*

Medios de transporte   *Means of transportation*

a pie *on foot, walking*
en autobús *by bus*
en bicicleta *on bicycle*
en carro / coche / automóvil *by car*

en metro *on the subway*
en tren *by train*
en / por avión *by plane*

Para decir cómo llegar   *Giving directions*

¿Me puede decir cómo llegar a...?
  Can you tell me how to get to . . . ?
¿Me puede decir dónde queda...?
  Can you tell me where . . . is located?
Cómo no. Vaya... *Of course. Go . . .*
  ...a la avenida... *. . . to the avenue . . .*
  ...a la calle... *. . . to the street . . .*
  ...a la derecha *. . . to the right*
  ...a la esquina *. . . to the corner*

  ...a la izquierda *. . . to the left*
  ...(dos) cuadras *. . . (two) blocks*
  ...(todo) derecho *. . . (straight) ahead*
bajar *to get down from, to get off of (a bus, etc.)*
cruzar *to cross*
doblar *to turn*
seguir (i) *to continue*
subir *to go up, to get on*

Expresiones de cortesía

Me gustaría (+ infinitive)**...**
  I'd like (+ infinitive) . . .
¿Por favor, me puede decir?
  Please, can you tell me . . . ?

¿Pudiera / Podría Ud. (+ infinitive)**...?**
  Could you (+ infinitive) . . . ?
Quisiera (+ infinitive)**...** *I'd like (+ infinitive) . . .*

Expresiones afirmativas y negativas

algo *something*
alguien *someone*
algún, alguno(a, os, as) *some, any*
jamás *never*
nada *nothing*
nadie *no one, nobody*
ni... ni... *neither / nor*

ningún, ninguno(a) *none, no, not any*
nunca *never*
o... o... *either / or*
siempre *always*
también *also*
tampoco *neither, not either*

Preposiciones

al lado de *next to, on the side of*
cerca de *close to*
debajo de *below, underneath*
delante de *in front of*
dentro de *inside of*
detrás de *behind*
encima de *on top of, on*

enfrente de *in front of, opposite*
entre *between*
frente a *in front of, facing, opposite*
fuera de *outside of*
lejos de *far from*
sobre *on, above*

Adjetivos demostrativos

aquel, aquella; aquellos, aquellas *that; those (over there)*
ese, esa; esos, esas *that; those*

este, esta; estos, estas *this; these*

Pronombres demostrativos

aquél, aquélla; aquéllos, aquéllas *that one; those (over there)*
ése, ésa; ésos, ésas *that one; those*
eso *that*

éste, ésta; éstos, éstas *this one; these*
esto *this*

Otras palabras y expresiones

allá *over there*
allí *there*
aquí *here*

>> ## Repaso del Capítulo 6

Prepositions of location (p. 206)

1 Di dónde está el perro, según las ilustraciones.

Preposiciones: debajo de, delante de, dentro de, detrás de, entre, lejos de, sobre

MODELO *El perro está sobre el auto.*

1.
2.
3.
4.
5.
6.

Commands with **usted** and **ustedes** (p. 208)

2 Completa los anuncios *(ads)* con mandatos con **usted** y **ustedes**.

1. _____ (venir) ustedes al Almacén Novomoda. ¡No _____ (perder) nuestras ofertas!

2. _____ (poner) usted su confianza en la Farmacia Benéfica. _____ (hablar) con nuestros farmacéuticos para recibir una consultación de salud gratis.

3. _____ (hacer) su reservación con el Restaurante MundiCultura. _____ (llamar) ahora para recibir un aperitivo complementario.

Affirmative and negative expressions (p. 214)

3 Completa la narración con palabras afirmativas y negativas de la lista.

Palabras afirmativas y negativas: algo, alguien, alguno(a, os, as), nada, nadie, ningún, nunca, siempre, también, tampoco

1. _____ voy al Café Milano para tomar un café con leche. 2. _____ como un pastel y hablo con 3. _____ de los clientes. Después, si no tengo 4. _____ urgente, voy al mercado porque normalmente hay 5. _____ que necesito comprar. Si no veo a 6. _____ que conozco, hago las compras y salgo rápidamente para el parque.

Demonstrative adjectives and pronouns (p. 217)

4 Usa adjetivos y pronombres demostrativos para completar las oraciones.

1. No quiero _____ huevos aquí. Prefiero _____ allí.
2. No quiero _____ leche allá. Prefiero _____ aquí.
3. No quiero _____ vegetales allí. Prefiero _____ allá.
4. No quiero _____ pizza aquí. Prefiero _____ allí.
5. No quiero _____ frutas allá. Prefiero _____ aquí.
6. No quiero _____ yogur aquí. Prefiero _____ allá.

>> Preparación para el Capítulo 7

Irregular-yo verbs in the present indicative (Chapter 5)

5 Tu amiga habla de su rutina diaria. Completa sus comentarios con las formas de yo correctas de los verbos indicados.

Siempre 1. _____ (salir) temprano de casa y 2. _____ (traer) el almuerzo *(lunch)* conmigo. 3. _____ (poner) todo en mi mochila y 4. _____ (conducir) hasta la universidad. Allí 5. _____ (ver) a algunos de mis amigos y hablamos un rato. 6. Como _____ (conocer) a mucha gente, a veces paso media hora hablando. 7. _____ (oír) sus noticias y también 8. _____ (hacer) planes con algunos de ellos para reunirnos después de las clases. Después, ¡a trabajar! Si 9. _____ (decir) la verdad, 10. ¡_____ (saber) que debo estudiar más y hablar menos!

Reflexive verbs (Chapter 5)

6 Completa las oraciones con las formas correctas de los verbos reflexivos. Presta atención a la forma verbal que requiere cada una.

1. Tú _____ (prepararse: *present indicative*) para ir al cine.
2. Yo _____ (acostarse: *present indicative*) tarde después de ir al teatro.
3. Nosotros _____ (preocuparse: *present indicative*) porque el tren llega tarde.
4. Mis amigos _____ (divertirse: *present progressive*) en el parque.
5. Sé que a ustedes no les gusta ir al museo, ¡pero no _____ (quejarse: *command*) tanto, por favor!
6. _____ (sentarse: *command*) usted aquí y _____ (relajarse: *command*) un poco.

Complete these activities to review some previously learned grammatical structures that will be helpful when you learn the new grammar in **Chapter 7**.

Be sure to reread **Chapter 6: Gramática útil 2** before moving on to the new **Chapter 7** grammar sections.

¿Qué pasatiempos prefieres?

TIEMPO PERSONAL

A muchas personas les gusta estar siempre ocupadas y trabajando. Para otras personas los ratos libres (*free time*) son muy importantes.

¿Trabajas para vivir o vives para trabajar? ¿Cuáles son más importantes para ti—los ratos libres o los objetivos profesionales?

Communication

By the end of this chapter you will be able to

- talk about sports and leisure activities
- talk about seasons and the weather
- say how you feel using **tener** expressions
- describe your recent leisure activities
- suggest activities and plans to friends

Gaston Piccinetti/age fotostock

Un viaje por Costa Rica y Panamá

Costa Rica y Panamá comparten una frontera y tienen costas en el mar Caribe y en el océano Pacífico. Costa Rica tiene una geografía más variada que Panamá.

País / Área	Tamaño y fronteras	Sitios de interés
Costa Rica 50.660 km^2	un poco más pequeño que Virginia Occidental; fronteras con Nicaragua y Panamá	sistema grande de parques nacionales, el Teatro Nacional en San José, las plantaciones de café, algunos de los mejores sitios del mundo para navegar en rápidos
Panamá 75.990 km^2	un poco más pequeño que Carolina del Sur; fronteras con Costa Rica y Colombia	el canal de Panamá; las islas de Kuna Yala (antes San Blas) con los kuna, una población indígena; el Parque Nacional de Darién; algunas de las mejores playas centroamericanas para el surfing

¿Qué sabes? Di si las siguientes oraciones son ciertas **(C)** o falsas **(F)**.

1. Costa Rica es un país más pequeño que Virginia Occidental y Carolina del Sur.
2. Panamá es ideal para navegar en rápidos y hacer surfing.
3. Costa Rica y Panamá son países vecinos porque comparten una frontera.
4. El café es un producto importante para Costa Rica.

Lo que sé y lo que quiero aprender Completa la tabla del **Apéndice A**. Escribe algunos datos que **ya sabes** sobre estos países en la columna **Lo que sé**. Después, añade algunos temas que **quieres aprender** a la columna **Lo que quiero aprender**. Guarda la tabla para usarla otra vez en la sección **¡Explora y exprésate!** en la página 259.

Cultures

By the end of this chapter you will have explored

- facts about Costa Rica and Panama
- a special boat race from the Atlantic to the Pacific
- why Costa Rica is a paradise for ecotourism
- whitewater rafting in Costa Rica
- Fahrenheit and Celsius temperatures; seasons and the equator

Globe Art: Adapted from Shutterstock/rtguest

¡Imagínate!

>> Vocabulario útil 1

SERGIO: ¿Viste el **partido de fútbol** entre Argentina y México ayer?

JAVIER: No, llegué tarde a casa.

SERGIO: Pues, te perdiste un partido buenísimo. Yo lo vi en casa de Arturo.

JAVIER: ¿Ah, sí? ¿Quién ganó?

SERGIO: Argentina, 2 a 1.

JAVIER: Me encanta ver los partidos de fútbol internacional por tele.

SERGIO: Y además del fútbol, ¿qué otros deportes te gustan?

JAVIER: Las **competencias de natación**, el **ciclismo** y el **boxeo**.

SERGIO: ¿El boxeo? ¡Guau! Yo prefiero el fútbol nacional, el italiano, el español…

JAVIER: ¿Qué piensas de los deportes de **invierno**?

SERGIO: No sé, hay algunos que me parecen interesantes, como el **hockey sobre hielo** y el **esquí alpino**.

In South America, **correr olas**, literally, "to run waves," is used for surfing.

Remember, as you learned in **Chapter 6, jugar** is used with the preposition **a** in a number of Spanish-speaking countries: **jugar al tenis, jugar al fútbol.** Usage of **a** varies from region to region.

>> Los deportes

el boxeo *boxing*
el esquí acuático *water skiing*
el esquí alpino *downhill skiing*
el golf *golf*
el hockey sobre hielo *ice hockey*
la natación *swimming*
el snowboarding *snowboarding*

>> Actividades deportivas

entrenarse *to train*
esquiar *to ski*
jugar (al) tenis / (al) béisbol / etc. *to play tennis / baseball / etc.*
levantar pesas *to lift weights*
nadar *to swim*
navegar en rápidos *to go whitewater rafting*
patinar sobre hielo *to ice skate*
practicar / hacer alpinismo *to (mountain) climb, hike*
practicar / hacer surfing *to surf*

>> Más palabras sobre los deportes

la competencia *competition*
el equipo *team*
ganar *to win*
el lago *lake*
el partido *game, match*
el peligro *danger*
peligroso(a) *dangerous*
la pelota *ball*
la piscina *pool*
el río *river*
seguro(a) *safe*
la tabla de snowboard *snowboard*

© Cengage Learning 2013

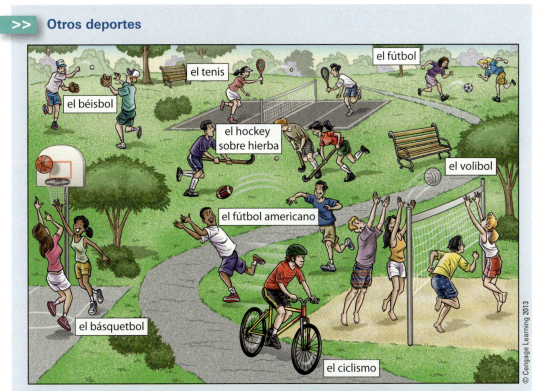

- el fútbol
- el tenis
- el béisbol
- el hockey sobre hierba
- el volibol
- el fútbol americano
- el básquetbol
- el ciclismo

© Cengage Learning 2013

- remar
- pescar
- montar a caballo
- montar en bicicleta
- hacer ejercicio
- patinar en línea

© Cengage Learning 2013

Sports vocabulary in Spanish contains a lot of words that come from English, for example, **jonrón, gol, béisbol, bate, derbi,** and **fútbol.** It is important to remember that the spelling, pronunciation, and grammatical use of these borrowed words follow the rules of Spanish. All the vowels and consonants of *homerun* are adapted to create **jonrón**; it is pronounced with the rolling **r (la erre),** and its plural is **jonrones.**

There are pastimes other than sports that you might be interested in: **el póker en línea** *(online poker),* **jugar a las cartas** *(to play cards),* **los juegos de mesa** *(board games),* **el bridge** *(bridge),* **el ajedrez** *(chess),* **las damas** *(checkers),* **el billar americano** *(pool),* **el billar inglés** *(snooker),* **el solitario** *(solitaire),* **el dominó** *(dominoes),* and **los juegos interactivos** *(interactive games).* If there are other games that you would like to know how to say in Spanish, go to an online word reference forum or a dictionary app and find out their Spanish equivalent.

>> **Las estaciones**

el verano

julio

el invierno

la primavera

abril

el otoño

© Cengage Learning 2013

ACTIVIDADES

1 **En las montañas** Mira la siguiente tabla. Luego, indica qué deportes se pueden practicar en cada lugar. En algunos casos, puede haber varias posibilidades. Limita tus respuestas a un máximo de tres actividades o deportes por cada lugar.

el parque	el océano	el lago	la cancha
las montañas	el gimnasio	la piscina	el río

2 **Atletas famosos** Con un(a) compañero(a) de clase, hagan una lista de atletas y otros jugadores famosos. Luego, digan con qué deporte o juego se asocia cada persona.

MODELOS *Misty May-Treanor*
Misty May-Treanor juega volibol.
Michael Phelps
Michael Phelps practica la natación.

3 **¡Peligro!** Con un(a) compañero(a) de clase, digan qué deportes creen que son peligrosos y cuáles no lo son. Hagan una lista. Luego, intercambien su lista con la de otra pareja. ¿Tienen las mismas opiniones?

4 **El deporte o juego preferido** En grupos de tres o cuatro estudiantes, hagan una lista de sus tres actividades o deportes preferidos. Luego hagan una lista de los tres deportes o actividades que no les gustan mucho. Cada grupo tiene que darle sus resultados a la clase.

MODELO *En nuestro grupo el fútbol, el snowboarding y el surfing son los deportes preferidos.*
En nuestro grupo el golf, la natación y el béisbol son los deportes que menos nos gustan.

5 **Las estaciones** ¿Sabes que los hemisferios norte y sur están en estaciones opuestas durante todo el año? Durante el verano en el hemisferio norte, es invierno en el hemisferio sur. Con un(a) compañero(a) de clase, mira la tabla e indica la estación que corresponde con cada país y mes.

País / mes	Estación
1. Argentina, julio	
2. España, febrero	
3. México, octubre	
4. Uruguay, septiembre	
5. Paraguay, diciembre	
6. Cuba, octubre	
7. Panamá, agosto	
8. Bolivia, octubre	

6 **En el otoño…** Trabaja con un(a) compañero(a) de clase. Digan qué deportes y actividades les gusta hacer en cada estación.

1. en la primavera
2. en el verano
3. en el otoño
4. en el invierno

Vocabulario útil 2

JAVIER: Hola, Beto. Qué milagro verte por aquí.

BETO: Ya sé. ¡Odio el gimnasio! No **tengo ganas** de hacer ejercicio en estas malditas máquinas.

SERGIO: ¡Pobre Beto!… ¿Les **tienes miedo** a las "maquinitas"?

BETO: No, ¡no seas ridículo!

>> **Expresiones con *tener***

tener cuidado *to be careful*
tener ganas de *to feel like (doing)*
tener miedo (de, a) *to be afraid (of)*
tener razón *to be right, correct*
tener vergüenza *to be embarrassed*

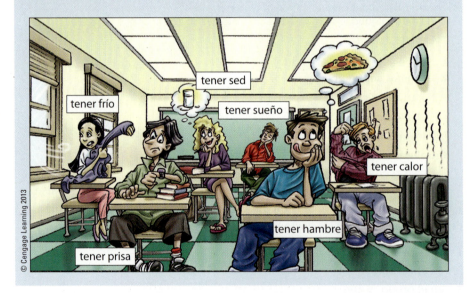

7 **¡Tengo sueño!** Indica cómo te sientes en las siguientes situaciones. En algunos casos hay más de una respuesta posible.

1. Tienes un examen muy difícil.
2. Es el verano y no tienes aire acondicionado.
3. Tienes una nueva raqueta de tenis.
4. Ya son las ocho de la noche y todavía no has cenado (*haven't eaten dinner*).
5. Acabas de jugar básquetbol por tres horas.
6. Ves una película de terror.
7. Son las tres de la mañana y acabas de estudiar.
8. Es el invierno y no llevas chaqueta.
9. Ya son las diez y tu clase de cálculo empieza a las 9:40.
10. Sabes las respuestas correctas a todas las preguntas.

8 **¿Qué tienes?** Usa la siguiente lista. Pasea por la clase y busca una persona que tenga una de las emociones que se describen en la lista. Escribe los nombres al lado de las emociones. Luego escribe un resumen de tu encuesta. (¡Es posible que no encuentres nombres para todas las categorías!)

Esta persona...	Nombre
siempre tiene calor:	
tiene miedo de las serpientes:	
tiene ganas de viajar a Nepal:	
tiene vergüenza cuando tiene que hablar enfrente de mucha gente:	
nunca tiene sueño:	
siempre tiene razón:	
nunca tiene prisa:	
tiene ganas de hacer surfing:	

MODELO *Kelly y Sandra siempre tienen calor. Y Jessie…*

BETO: Yo prefiero jugar tenis, pero hoy no puedo porque **está lloviendo**.

JAVIER: Tienes razón. Y además, **hace mucho viento**. Ayer salí a correr pero hoy no tuve otra opción que venir aquí.

BETO: Sí. ¡**Hace mal tiempo** desde el lunes!

>> **El tiempo**

¿Qué tiempo hace? *What's the weather like?*
Hace buen tiempo. *It's nice weather.*
Hace mal tiempo. *It's bad weather.*
Hace fresco. *It's cool.*
Hace sol. *It's sunny.*

Hace frío.

Hace calor.

Hace viento.

Está nevando. Nieva.

Está nublado.

Está lloviendo. Llueve.

>> **La temperatura**

grados Celsio(s) / centígrados *degrees Celsius*
grados Fahrenheit *degrees Fahrenheit*
La temperatura está a 20 grados Celsio(s) / centígrados. *It's 20 degrees Celsius.*
La temperatura está a 70 grados Fahrenheit. *It's 70 degrees Fahrenheit.*

Note that **grados Celsio(s)** and **centígrados** both refer to measurements on the Celsius scale. **Centígrados** is an older term that has been replaced by **Celsio(s)**. Also notice that whether the plural form of **Celsio** is used varies from country to country.

To convert between Fahrenheit and Celsius:

Grados C → Grados F: (C° × 1,8) + 32 = F°
Ejemplo: (30°C × 1,8) + 32 = 86°F

Grados F → Grados C: (F° − 32) ÷ 1,8 = C°
Ejemplo: (86° F − 32) ÷ 1,8 = 30°C

▬ ACTIVIDADES ▬

9 **El tiempo** Di qué tiempo hace por lo general durante las estaciones o meses indicados.

1. el mes de marzo en tu ciudad
2. el mes de agosto en tu ciudad
3. el mes de enero en tu ciudad
4. el mes de octubre en tu ciudad
5. en invierno en Buenos Aires
6. en invierno en Seattle
7. en verano en Miami
8. en invierno en Chicago

👥 **10** **Prefiero…** Trabaja con un(a) compañero(a) de clase. Identifiquen por lo menos dos actividades que les gusta hacer y dos que no les gusta hacer cuando hace el tiempo indicado. Luego, escriban oraciones completas para hacer un resumen de sus preferencias.

1. cuando hace calor
2. cuando hace frío
3. cuando hace mucho viento
4. cuando nieva
5. cuando llueve

¡Fíjate! ¿Qué tiempo hace?

Cuando hablas del tiempo y de la temperatura en español, hay varias cosas importantes que debes saber. Primero, como viste en la **Actividad 5,** los países al norte y al sur del ecuador están en estaciones opuestas. Es decir, cuando en el norte estamos en invierno, los países al sur están en verano. Cuando es otoño en EEUU, allá es primavera.

Segundo, EEUU y los países de habla española usan dos sistemas diferentes para medir *(to measure)* la temperatura. Aquí usamos el sistema Fahrenheit, mientras que en Latinoamérica y España usan el sistema Celsio.

Finalmente, México, los países del Caribe y varios países de Centroamérica y Sudamérica tienen temporadas de lluvias y temporadas secas *(dry)*. Aunque esto es más común en los países más cerca del ecuador, también puede ocurrir cuando corrientes del océano crean condiciones especiales, como en el noroeste Pacífico de EEUU y en Perú.

Práctica Miren las siguientes tablas y contesten las preguntas sobre el tiempo en las dos ciudades. (**tormenta** = *thunderstorm*, **chaparrón** = *cloudburst, downpour*)

1. ¿Cuál es la temperatura máxima en San José? ¿Y la temperatura mínima?
2. ¿Crees que se dan estas temperaturas en grados Celsio o Fahrenheit?
3. ¿Qué tiempo hace en San José el martes 28 de agosto? ¿Qué tiempo va a hacer el miércoles? ¿Y el sábado?
4. ¿Cuál es la temperatura máxima en la Ciudad de Panamá? ¿Y la temperatura mínima?
5. ¿Hace más calor en la Ciudad de Panamá o en San José?
6. ¿Cuál es el pronóstico para los días entre el jueves y el sábado en la Ciudad de Panamá?
7. ¿Cuándo es la temporada de lluvias en cada país?

ESTRATEGIA

Listening for details

You have learned to listen for the main idea of a video segment. Knowing in advance what to listen for will help you find key information. **Antes de ver 2** will help you focus on this specific information.

Antes de ver 1 Mira las fotos y el texto en las páginas 232, 236 y 238 del **Vocabulario útil**. Luego, completa las siguientes oraciones sobre las personas de las fotos.

1. Javier y Sergio hablan de (los cursos / los deportes).
2. Sergio prefiere (el fútbol nacional / el hockey sobre hielo) sobre el boxeo.
3. Según Beto, él no les tiene (sueño / miedo) a las máquinas del gimnasio.
4. Además, Beto no tiene (ganas / vergüenza) de hacer ejercicio en el gimnasio.
5. Beto no puede jugar tenis porque está (lloviendo / nevando).
6. Hoy también hace mucho (frío / viento).

Antes de ver 2 Ahora mira la siguiente tabla y fíjate en la información que necesites del video para completarla.

	A Javier	A Sergio	A Beto	A Dulce
le gusta...				
no le gusta...				

▶ **Ver** Mira el video para el Capítulo **7** y completa la tabla en **Antes de ver 2**. Si el video no tiene la información necesaria, pon una X.

Después de ver 1 Escribe frases completas para indicar qué le gusta hacer a cada persona que se menciona en **Antes de ver 2**.

MODELO *A Dulce le gusta jugar tenis, pero no le gusta...*

Después de ver 2 Con un(a) compañero(a) de clase, contesta las siguientes preguntas sobre el video.

1. ¿De qué hablan Javier y Sergio al principio de la escena?
2. ¿Va Beto al gimnasio con frecuencia?
3. ¿Qué dice Sergio sobre la condición física de Beto?
4. ¿Por qué empieza Beto a hacer ejercicio con mucho entusiasmo?
5. ¿Qué le dice Beto a Dulce sobre su rutina diaria? ¿Es cierto o falso?
6. ¿Qué hace Dulce cuando hace ejercicio?

Voces de la comunidad

>> Voces del mundo hispano

En el video para este capítulo Essdras, Nicole y Andrés hablan de sus pasatiempos y las estaciones del año. Lee las siguientes oraciones. Después mira el video una o más veces para decir si las oraciones son ciertas (**C**) o falsas (**F**).

1. A Essdras le gusta el invierno porque todo es muy oscuro.
2. Nicole prefiere el otoño porque le gusta el cambio de las hojas *(leaves)*.
3. A Andrés no le gusta la estación lluviosa porque es difícil salir afuera.
4. A Essdras le gusta hacer yoga y levantar pesas.
5. Nicole prefiere bailar y acampar.
6. Andrés no practica ningún deporte.

© Cengage Learning 2013

>> Voces de Estados Unidos

Track 21

Brenda Villa, waterpolista

Cameron Spencer/Getty Images

❝Los medios de comunicación hispanos deben poner de su parte *(do their part)* para dar publicidad a los atletas hispanos en deportes no-tradicionales. Así los padres pueden conocer todas las opciones que hay para sus hijos ❞.

Brenda Villa es la mejor waterpolista femenina de la década 2000–2009, según la Federación Internacional de Natación. Nacida *(Born)* en East L.A. de padres mexicanos, Villa aprendió a jugar polo a los seis años con sus dos hermanos. Después, en Bell Gardens High School, jugó para el equipo masculino porque la escuela no tenía equipo femenino. Villa es graduada de Stanford, donde se especializó en ciencias políticas. Actualmente es entrenadora de polo en Cerritos College en California y también juega para el equipo italiano Orizzonte. Esta súper atleta tiene la distinción de ser la primera latina en el equipo de waterpolo de los EEUU. Sus honores incluyen varias medallas Olímpicas y de campeonatos mundiales y también el **Trofeo Peter J. Cutino** del National Collegiate Athletic Association (NCAA), el más prestigioso honor a nivel *(level)* individual en el waterpolo universitario norteamericano.

¿Y tú? En tu opinión, ¿cuáles son algunos deportes que no reciben la atención o el interés público que merecen *(they deserve)*? ¿Crees que los medios de comunicación deben hacer un esfuerzo para promocionarlos?

> The forms **jugó, aprendió** and **se especializó** are all past-tense forms. You'll learn more about them on page 242.

>> Gramática útil 1

Talking about what you did: The preterite tense of regular verbs

¿Quién **ganó**?

Spanish uses another past tense called the *imperfect* to talk about past actions that were routine or ongoing. You will learn more about this tense in **Chapter 9**.

Cómo usarlo

LO BÁSICO

A *verb tense* is a form of a verb that indicates the time of an action: the past, present, or future. You have already been using the present indicative (**Estudio en la biblioteca**) and the present progressive (**Estoy hablando por teléfono**) tenses.

When you want to talk in Spanish about actions that occurred and were completed in the past, you use the *preterite tense*. The preterite is used to describe

- actions that began and ended in the past;
- conditions or states that existed completely within the past.

Me desperté, leí el periódico y **salí** para el gimnasio.	*I woke up, I read the newspaper, and I left for the gym.*
Fui secretario bilingüe por dos años.	*I was a bilingual secretary for two years.*
Estuve muy cansada ayer.	*I was very tired yesterday.*

Cómo formarlo

1. To form the preterite tense of regular **-ar, -er**, and **-ir** verbs, you remove that ending from the infinitive and add the following endings to the verb stem.

Note that reflexive verbs use the same endings. **Lavarse: me lavé, te lavaste, se lavó, nos lavamos, se lavaron. Reunirse: me reuní, te reuniste, se reunió, nos reunimos, se reunieron.**

	-ar verb: **bailar**		-er and -ir verbs: **comer / escribir**		
yo	**-é**	bail**é**	**-í**	com**í**	escrib**í**
tú	**-aste**	bail**aste**	**-iste**	com**iste**	escrib**iste**
Ud. / él / ella	**-ó**	bail**ó**	**-ió**	com**ió**	escrib**ió**
nosotros / nosotras	**-amos**	bail**amos**	**-imos**	com**imos**	escrib**imos**
vosotros / vosotras	**-asteis**	bail**asteis**	**-isteis**	com**isteis**	escrib**isteis**
Uds. / ellos / ellas	**-aron**	bail**aron**	**-ieron**	com**ieron**	escrib**ieron**

2. Notice that the preterite forms of **-er** and **-ir** verbs are the same.

3. Notice that only the **yo** and **Ud. / él / ella** forms are accented.

4. The **nosotros** forms of the preterite and the present indicative of **-ar** and **-ir** verbs are the same. You can tell which is being used by context.

Bailamos todos los fines de semana.   (present)
Bailamos salsa con Mario ayer.   (past)

5. All stem-changing verbs that end in **-ar** or **-er** are regular in the preterite.

Me desperté a las ocho cuando **sonó** el teléfono.	*I woke up at 8:00 when the telephone **rang**.*
Volví temprano de mis vacaciones porque **perdí** mi pasaporte.	*I returned early from my vacation because **I lost** my passport.*

> Stem-changing verbs that end in **-ir** also have stem changes in the preterite. You will learn these forms in **Chapter 8**.

6. Many of the verbs you have already learned are regular in the preterite tense. A few have some minor changes.

- Verbs that end in **-car, -gar**, and **-zar** have a spelling change in the **yo** form to maintain the correct pronunciation.

  -car: c → qu   sacar: **saqué**, sacaste, sacó, sacamos, sacasteis, sacaron
  -gar: g → gu   llegar: **llegué**, llegaste, llegó, llegamos, llegasteis, llegaron
  -zar: z → c   cruzar: **crucé**, cruzaste, cruzó, cruzamos, cruzasteis, cruzaron

- Verbs that end in **-eer**, as well as the verb **oír**, change **i** to **y** in the two third-person forms. Note the accent on the **-íste, -ímos**, and **-ísteis** endings.

  leer: leí, leíste, leyó, leímos, leísteis, leyeron
  creer: creí, creíste, creyó, creímos, creísteis, creyeron
  oír: oí, oíste, oyó, oímos, oísteis, oyeron

7. You have already learned the word **ayer.** Here are some other useful time expressions to use with the preterite tense: **anoche** *(last night)*, **anteayer** *(the day before yesterday)*, **la semana pasada** *(last week)*, **el mes pasado** *(last month)*, **el año pasado** *(last year)*.

ACTIVIDADES

🔊 **1** **¿Presente o pasado?** Escucha las oraciones e indica si las actividades
Track 22 que se describen ocurren en el presente o el pasado.

	Presente	Pasado
1. Javier y Lidia / esquiar	_____	_____
2. Susana / entrenarse	_____	_____
3. yo / navegar en rápidos	_____	_____
4. mi padre / pescar	_____	_____
5. tú / remar	_____	_____
6. tú / jugar golf	_____	_____
7. yo / patinar sobre hielo	_____	_____
8. yo / nadir	_____	_____

2 El calendario de Rosario Usa el siguiente calendario para decir qué hizo *(did)* Rosario la semana pasada.

lunes 17	martes 18	miércoles 19	jueves 20	viernes 21	sábado 22	domingo 23
A.M.: estudiar con Lalo	A.M.: trabajar en la biblioteca	A.M.: almorzar con Neti	A.M.: leer en la biblioteca	A.M.: correr dos millas	A.M.: desayunar con Sergio	A.M.: ¡descansar!
P.M.: jugar tenis con Fernando	P.M.: salir con Lalo	P.M.: sacar la basura	P.M.: escribir el ensayo para la clase de literatura	P.M.: ¡bailar en la discoteca!	P.M.: entrenarse en el gimnasio	P.M.: comer con Lalo

© Cengage Learning 2013

MODELOS *El lunes por la mañana Rosario estudió con Lalo.*
O: *El lunes por la mañana Rosario y Lalo estudiaron.*

3 Ayer Di qué hicieron *(did)* las siguientes personas ayer.

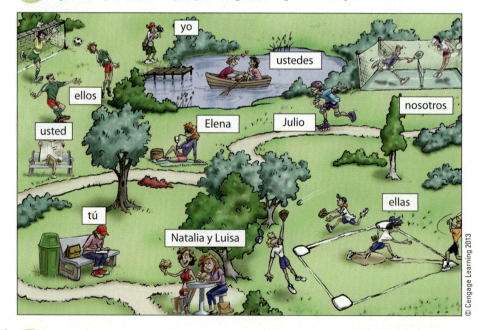

© Cengage Learning 2013

4 La semana pasada Ahora, usa el horario de la **Actividad 2** como modelo y complétalo con tu propia información sobre la semana pasada. Luego, trabaja con un(a) compañero(a) de clase para hablar de sus actividades de la semana pasada.

MODELO Tú: *¿Qué hiciste* (What did you do) *el lunes por la mañana?*
Compañero(a): *Jugué golf. ¿Y tú? ¿Qué hiciste el miércoles por la tarde?*

>> Gramática útil 2

Talking about what you did: The preterite tense of some common irregular verbs

Cómo usarlo

As you learned in **Gramática útil 1,** the preterite is a Spanish past-tense form that is used to talk about actions that occurred and were completed in the past. It describes actions that began and ended in the past and refers to things that happened and are over with, whether they happened just once or over time.

Fuimos al restaurante.
Hicimos deporte todo el día.
¡Estuvimos bien cansados!

We went to the restaurant.
We played sports all day.
We were really tired!

¿**Viste** el partido de fútbol entre Argentina y México ayer?

Cómo formarlo

1. Here are the irregular preterite forms of some frequently used verbs.

	estar	hacer	ir	ser
yo	estuve	hice	fui	fui
tú	estuviste	hiciste	fuiste	fuiste
Ud. / él / ella	estuvo	hizo	fue	fue
nosotros / nosotras	estuvimos	hicimos	fuimos	fuimos
vosotros / vosotras	estuvisteis	hicisteis	fuisteis	fuisteis
Uds. / ellos / ellas	estuvieron	hicieron	fueron	fueron

	dar	ver	decir	traer
yo	di	vi	dije	traje
tú	diste	viste	dijiste	trajiste
Ud. / él / ella	dio	vio	dijo	trajo
nosotros / nosotras	dimos	vimos	dijimos	trajimos
vosotros / vosotras	disteis	visteis	dijisteis	trajisteis
Uds. / ellos / ellas	dieron	vieron	dijeron	trajeron

Ver is irregular only because it does not carry accents in the **yo** and **Ud. / él / ella** forms. **Dar** is irregular because it uses the regular **-er / -ir** endings rather than the **-ar** endings.

2. Verbs that end in **-cir** follow the same pattern as **traer** and **decir**.

conducir: conduje, condujiste, condujo, condujimos, condujisteis, condujeron
producir: produje, produjiste, produjo, produjimos, produjisteis, produjeron
traducir: traduje, tradujiste, tradujo, tradujimos, tradujisteis, tradujeron

3. Notice that although these irregular verbs do for the most part use the regular endings, they have internal changes to the stem that must be memorized.

4. Notice that none of these verbs requires accents in the preterite.

5. Notice that **ser** and **ir** have the same forms in the preterite. But because the verbs have such different meanings, it is usually fairly easy to tell which one is being used.

Fuimos estudiantes durante esos años.	*We **were** students during those years.*
Todos **fuimos** a una fiesta muy alegre.	*We all **went** to a really fun party.*

ACTIVIDADES

5 **¿Qué hicieron?** Haz oraciones completas para decir qué pasó la semana pasada.

MODELO **ir**
　　　　　ellos / al parque a jugar tenis
　　　　　Ellos fueron al parque a jugar tenis.

estar
1. tú y yo / en las montañas para hacer alpinismo
2. Mónica y Sara / en el gimnasio todos los días
3. usted / en la costa para hacer surfing

ir
4. ustedes / al gimnasio a entrenarse
5. yo / a la biblioteca a estudiar
6. Jorge / al parque a jugar básquetbol

ver
7. yo / una película muy buena
8. nosotros / a Mónica y a Sara en el gimnasio
9. tú / una serpiente en el parque

traer
10. Luis / su pelota de béisbol a mi casa para jugar
11. ellos / su equipo (*equipment*) para jugar hockey sobre hierba
12. tú / tus pesas para entrenarte

6 **¿Quién fue?** Con un(a) compañero(a) de clase, digan quiénes fueron las personas indicadas. (En algunos casos, hay más de una respuesta posible.)

MODELO　Abraham Lincoln
　　　　　¿Quién fue Abraham Lincoln?
　　　　　Fue presidente de Estados Unidos.

Respuestas posibles: presidente, futbolista, actor / actriz, cantante, científico(a), político(a), revolucionario(a)

1. Monsieur y Madame Curie
2. Albert Einstein
3. Marilyn Monroe y Natasha Richardson
4. Bill Clinton y George W. Bush
5. Henry Kissinger
6. Che Guevara
7. Michael Jackson
8. Diego Maradona

7 **Las vacaciones** Averigua qué hizo tu compañero(a) de clase durante sus vacaciones del año pasado. Pregúntale si hizo las siguientes cosas y cuánto las hizo.

1. hacer viajes *(trips)* (¿cuántos?)
2. gastar dinero (¿cuánto?)
3. ir a la playa (¿cuántas veces?)
4. ver un partido deportivo (¿cuántas veces?)
5. hacer ejercicio (¿cuántas veces?)

Luego, tu compañero(a) te hace las mismas preguntas. Juntos, determinen la siguiente información.

1. ¿Quién hizo más viajes?
2. ¿Quién gastó más dinero?
3. ¿Quién fue a la playa más?
4. ¿Quién vio más partidos deportivos?
5. ¿Quién hizo más ejercicio?

8 **La reunión** Escucha mientras Cecilia describe qué pasó la semana pasada en la reunión de ex alumnos de su colegio. Primero, completa la tabla con la información necesaria. Luego, escribe oraciones completas según el modelo.

Track 23

Persona	¿Qué dijo?
yo (Cecilia)	
tú (Rosa Carmen)	
José María	
Marcos	*Es periodista.*
Laura y Sebastián	
Leticia	
Pilar y Antonio	

MODELO Marcos
   Marcos dijo que es periodista.

1. yo
2. tú
3. José María
4. Laura y Sebastián
5. Leticia
6. Pilar y Antonio

>> Gramática útil 3

Referring to something already mentioned: Direct object pronouns

LO BÁSICO

A *direct object* is a noun or noun phrase that receives the action of a verb: I buy *a book*. We invite *our friends. Direct object pronouns* are pronouns that replace direct object nouns or phrases: I buy *it*. We invite *them*. Often you can identify the direct object of the sentence by asking *what?* or *whom?:* We buy *what? (a book / it)* / We invite *whom? (our friends / them).*

You use direct object pronouns in both Spanish and English to avoid repetition and to refer to things or people that have already been mentioned. Look at the following passage in Spanish and notice how much repetition there is.

> **Quiero hablar con María. Llamo a María por teléfono e invito a María a visitar a mis padres. Visito a mis padres casi todos los fines de semana.**

Now read the passage after it's been rewritten using direct object pronouns to replace some of the occasions when the nouns **María** and **padres** were used previously. (The direct object pronouns appear underlined.)

> **Quiero hablar con María. <u>La</u> llamo por teléfono y <u>la</u> invito a visitar a mis padres. <u>Los</u> visito casi todos los fines de semana.**

Cómo formarlo

1. Here are the direct object pronouns in Spanish.

Singular		Plural	
me	*me*	**nos**	*us*
te	*you (fam.)*	**os**	*you (fam.)*
lo	*you (form. masc.), him, it*	**los**	*you (form. masc.), them, it*
la	*you (form., fem.), she, it*	**las**	*you (form. fem.), them, it*

2. The third-person direct object pronouns in Spanish must agree in gender and number with the noun they replace.

Compramos **el libro.**	→	**Lo** compramos.
Compramos **la raqueta.**	→	**La** compramos.
Compramos **los libros.**	→	**Los** compramos.
Compramos **las raquetas.**	→	**Las** compramos.

Pues, te perdiste un partido buenísimo. Yo **lo** vi en casa de Arturo.

© Cengage Learning 2013

3. Pay particular attention to the **lo / la** and **los / las** forms, because they can have a variety of meanings. For example, **Lo llamo** can mean *I call you* (formal, male) or *I call him*. **La llamo** can mean *I call you* (formal, female) or *I call her*. Look at the possible meanings for the **los** and **las** forms.

Los llamo. → *I call them. (at least two men, or a man and a woman)*
I call you. (formal, at least two people, at least one male)

Las llamo. → *I call them. (at least two women)*
I call you. (polite form, at least two women)

4. Direct object pronouns always come *before* a *conjugated verb* used by itself.

Me llamas el viernes, ¿no?   *You'll call **me** on Friday, right?*
Te invito a la fiesta.   *I'm inviting **you** to the party.*

5. When a direct object pronoun is used with an *infinitive* or with the *present progressive*, it may come *before* the conjugated verb or it may be *attached* to the infinitive or to the present participle.

Te voy a llamar.   OR: Voy a llamar**te**.
Te estoy llamando.   OR: Estoy llamándo**te**.

6. When a direct object pronoun is used with a *command form*, it *attaches to the end of the affirmative command* but *comes before the negative command* form.

Hágalo ahora, por favor.   BUT: **No lo haga** ahora, por favor.

7. When you use direct object pronouns with *reflexive pronouns*, the *reflexive pronouns come before the direct object pronouns*.

Me estoy lavando **la cara** con jabón.   *I am washing **my face** with soap.*
Me **la** estoy lavando con jabón.   *I am washing **it** with soap.*

Estoy lavándome **la cara** con jabón.   *I am washing **my face** with soap.*
Estoy lavándome**la** con jabón.   *I am washing **it** with soap.*

> Notice that when the direct object pronoun attaches to the present participle, you must add an accent to the next-to-last syllable of the present participle to maintain the correct pronunciation: **llamándote**.

> Again, notice that when the direct object pronoun attaches to the command form, you must add an accent to the next-to-last syllable of command forms of two or more syllables in order to maintain the correct pronunciation: **hágalo**.

ACTIVIDADES

9 **El domingo por la tarde** Tú y tu familia tuvieron una reunión en casa el domingo por la tarde. Todos contribuyeron de diferentes maneras. Escribe lo que hicieron todos usando los complementos directos correctos. Sigue el modelo.

MODELO   Mi mamá y yo compramos <u>la comida</u>.
       La compramos.

1. Mi hermana y yo limpiamos (*cleaned*) <u>la casa</u>.
   _____ limpiamos.

2. Mi papá invitó a <u>los primos</u>.
   _____ invitó.

3. Yo compré <u>los refrescos</u>.
   _____ compré.

4. Mi hermano trajo <u>la música</u>.
   _____ trajo.

5. Mis tíos prepararon <u>la ensalada</u>.
   _____ prepararon.

6. Mi tía hizo <u>las tortillas</u>.
   _____ hizo.

10 **El día horrible de Manuel** Lee sobre el día horrible de Manuel. Sustituye las palabras **en negrilla** *(boldface)* con complementos directos, según el modelo.

MODELO Compré **los libros.**
        Los compré.

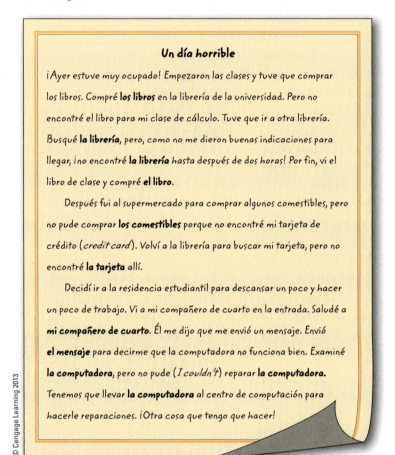

Un día horrible

¡Ayer estuve muy ocupado! Empezaron las clases y tuve que comprar los libros. Compré **los libros** en la librería de la universidad. Pero no encontré el libro para mi clase de cálculo. Tuve que ir a otra librería. Busqué **la librería**, pero, como no me dieron buenas indicaciones para llegar, ¡no encontré **la librería** hasta después de dos horas! Por fin, vi el libro de clase y compré **el libro.**

Después fui al supermercado para comprar algunos comestibles, pero no pude comprar **los comestibles** porque no encontré mi tarjeta de crédito *(credit card)*. Volví a la librería para buscar mi tarjeta, pero no encontré **la tarjeta** allí.

Decidí ir a la residencia estudiantil para descansar un poco y hacer un poco de trabajo. Vi a mi compañero de cuarto en la entrada. Saludé a **mi compañero de cuarto.** Él me dijo que me envió un mensaje. Envió **el mensaje** para decirme que la computadora no funciona bien. Examiné **la computadora**, pero no pude *(I couldn't)* reparar **la computadora.** Tenemos que llevar **la computadora** al centro de computación para hacerle reparaciones. ¡Otra cosa que tengo que hacer!

11 **Pobre Manuel** Contesta las preguntas sobre el día horrible de Manuel (**Actividad 10**). Usa un complemento directo en tu respuesta.

MODELO ¿Encontró Manuel el libro en la librería de la universidad?
        No, no lo encontró.

1. ¿Encontró Manuel la otra librería?
2. ¿Compró los comestibles?
3. ¿Encontró su tarjeta de crédito?
4. ¿Vio a su compañero de cuarto en la residencia estudiantil?
5. Cuando por fin llegó a la residencia estudiantil, ¿pudo hacer su trabajo?
6. ¿Usó la computadora de su cuarto?
7. ¿Llevó la computadora al centro de computaciones?
8. ¿Tuvo un día tranquilo?

12 Natalia El padre de Natalia y Nico es muy exigente *(demanding)*. Les hace muchas preguntas. Haz el papel de Natalia y contesta las preguntas de su padre.

MODELOS   Padre: *¿Limpiaron el baño? (sí)*
           Natalia: *Sí, lo limpiamos.*
           Padre: *¿Limpiaste tu cuarto? (no)*
           Natalia: *No, pero estoy limpiándolo ahora mismo.*

1. ¿Hiciste la tarea? (sí)
2. ¿Prepararon el almuerzo? (no)
3. ¿Hicieron los planes para la fiesta? (no)
4. ¿Leíste la nota de tu mamá? (sí)
5. ¿Viste la lista de comida que debes comprar en el supermercado? (sí)
6. ¿Llamaste a tu abuela? (sí)

13 ¿Lo leíste? Trabaja con un(a) compañero(a) de clase. Háganse preguntas y contéstenlas usando complementos directos. Sigan el modelo.

MODELO   leer / el nuevo libro de James Patterson
           Compañero(a): *¿Leíste el nuevo libro de James Patterson?*
           Tú: *Sí, lo leí. O: No, no lo leí.*

1. ver / la nueva película de Pedro Almodóvar
2. leer / el nuevo libro de Sue Grafton
3. ver / los partidos de básquetbol del WNBA
4. traer / computadora portátil a clase
5. entender / la tarea de la clase de español
6. comprar / las pelotas de tenis
7. descargar / la nueva canción de Calle 13
8. ¿…?

14 ¿Lo tienes? En grupos de tres, túrnense para hacer y contestar preguntas sobre sus actividades recientes. Cuando hacen las preguntas, usen las palabras indicadas con **cuándo** o **dónde**. Cuando contestan, usen un pronombre directo.

MODELOS   comprar tu mochila
           Tú: *¿Dónde compraste tu mochila?*
           Compañero(a): *La compré en la librería de la universidad.*

           hacer la tarea para la clase de español
           Compañero(a): *¿Cuándo hiciste la tarea para la clase de español?*
           Tú: *¡No la hice!*

1. comprar tu computadora
2. hacer la tarea para la clase de ¿…?
3. mirar tus programas favoritos
4. escuchar tu canción favorita
5. llamar a tus padres
6. comer el desayuno *(breakfast)*
7. leer el libro para la clase de ¿…?
8. tomar el café hoy
9. ver a tus amigos
10. lavar la ropa

Sonrisas

👥👥👥 **Expresión** En grupos de tres o cuatro estudiantes, hagan una lista de las reglas (*rules*) de cortesía para el teléfono y el correo electrónico. ¿Qué se debe y no se debe hacer?

MODELO Cuando llamas por teléfono…
No debes llamar muy temprano por la mañana.
Cuando escribes correo electrónico…
Debes escribir mensajes cortos.

Gramática útil 4

Telling friends what to do: **Tú** command forms

¡No lo intentes en casa!

Haz los saltos y trucos más chéveres – habla con nuestros bicilocos profesionales para elegir la mejor bicicleta BMX para ti.

CICLOLOCURA

Calle Eloy Alfaro 27
Casco Antiguo
Ciudad de Panamá
507-516-9997
www.ciclocura.com

Photos (left to right): Rihardzz/Dreamstime; Sampete/Dreamstime; text: © Cengage Learning 2013

> What are the three **tú** command forms used in this ad for a bike shop in Panamá? Which one is a negative form?

Cómo usarlo

1. You have already learned the polite and plural (**usted** and **ustedes**) command forms in **Chapter 6**. Now you will learn the informal command form that you use with people you address as **tú**. (You see these forms in activity direction lines.)

Habla con Claudia.	**Talk** to Claudia.
Pero **no hables** con Leo.	But **don't talk** to Leo.

2. Remember that when you are addressing more than one person informally you use **ustedes** forms, just as you do when you address more than one person formally. In much of the Spanish-speaking world there is no "plural" **tú** command.

3. Because you mostly use informal command forms to address friends, small children, or animals, you don't need to worry about making your requests sound as polite as in formal settings. However, it never hurts to use a softening expression like the ones that follow.

¿Me puedes decir / Me dices…?	*Can you tell me . . . ?*
¿Puedes + *infinitive*…?	*Can you* + infinitive . . . ?
¿Quieres / Quisieras + *infinitive*…?	*Would you like to* + infinitive . . . ?
¿Te importa…?	*Would / Does it matter to you . . . ?*
¿Te molesta…?	*Would / Does it bother you . . . ?*

> The **vosotros** command forms, which are the plural informal command forms used in Spain, are not provided in this textbook because **ustedes** forms are used more universally.

Cómo formarlo

1. Unlike the **usted** and **ustedes** forms that you learned in **Chapter 6**, **tú** commands have one form for affirmative commands and one form for negative commands.

2. To form the affirmative **tú** command form, simply use the **usted / él / ella** present-indicative form of the verb.

Affirmative **tú** command forms		
-ar verb	**-er** verb	**-ir** verb
tomar → **toma**	beber → **bebe**	escribir → **escribe**

3. To form the negative **tú** command form, take the affirmative **tú** command, and replace the final vowel with **es** for **-ar** verbs and with **as** for **-er** / **-ir** verbs.

Notice that the negative **tú** commands are the same as the **usted** command forms, but with an **s** added. **Usted** command: **hable**; negative **tú** command: **no hables.**

Negative **tú** command forms			
	-ar verb **hablar**	**-er** verb **beber**	**-ir** verb **escribir**
affirmative **tú** command	habla	bebe	escribe
negative **tú** command	no **hables**	no **bebas**	no **escribas**

4. These **tú** command forms are irregular and must be memorized.

Notice that the **tú** command for **ser (sé)** is the same as the first person of **saber (sé)**. Context will clarify which is meant: **¡Sé bueno!** vs. **Sé que Manuel es bueno.** The same is true for the command forms of **ir (ve)** and **ver (ve): Ve a clase.** vs. **Ve ese programa.**

	Affirmative **tú** command	Negative **tú**
decir	di	no digas
hacer	haz	no hagas
ir	ve	no vayas
poner	pon	no pongas
salir	sal	no salgas
ser	sé	no seas
tener	ten	no tengas
venir	ven	no vengas

5. As with **usted** command forms, *reflexive pronouns* and *direct object pronouns* attach to affirmative **tú** commands and come before negative **tú** commands. Note that you need to add an accent to the next-to-last syllable of the command form when attaching pronouns.

¡Despiértate, ya es tarde!	***Wake up**, it's late!*
¡No te acuestes ahora!	***Don't go to bed** now!*
Llámame.	***Call me.***
No me llames después de las once.	***Don't call me** after 11:00.*

15 El campamento Tu hermanito va a ir a un campamento de verano. Tú le das algunos consejos. Los primeros cuatro consejos se los das en el afirmativo. Los segundos cuatro consejos se los das en el negativo.

MODELOS (Acostarse) *Acuéstate* temprano.

No (nadar) *nades* solo.

Afirmativo

1. (Usar) tu casco *(helmet)*.
2. (Jugar) con los otros niños.
3. (Ducharse) después de nadar.
4. (Tener) cuidado al nadar.

Negativo

5. No (correr) en la calle.
6. No (caminar) por la noche.
7. No (hacer) deportes peligrosos.
8. No (salir) solo por la noche.

16 ¡Primo! Vas a quedarte en la casa de tu primo. Le haces preguntas sobre la casa y tus quehaceres. Escribe sus respuestas según el modelo.

MODELO ¿Apago las luces antes de acostarme?

Sí, apágalas, por favor.

1. ¿Cierro la puerta del garaje por la noche?
2. ¿Abro las ventanas si hace calor?
3. ¿Pongo los comestibles en el refrigerador?
4. ¿Contesto el teléfono cuando no estás en casa?
5. ¿Apago la computadora antes de acostarme?
6. ¿Saco la basura los lunes por la noche?

Ahora, contesta las preguntas de arriba con un mandato informal negativo.

17 Los consejos Da un consejo (afirmativo o negativo) para cada situación.

MODELO Juan quiere desarrollar sus músculos.

Levanta pesas dos veces por semana.

1. María desea perder cinco kilos.
2. Pedro quiere entrenarse para un maratón.
3. Pablo quiere mejorar su capacidad aeróbica.
4. Margarita quiere correr más rápido.
5. Francisco quiere ponerse en forma pero no tiene mucho tiempo para hacer ejercicio.

18 En la residencia Trabajen en grupos de tres o cuatro personas. Imagínense que un(a) estudiante nuevo(a) acaba de llegar a su residencia estudiantil. Denle consejos para no tener problemas con sus compañeros. Sigan el modelo.

MODELO *No toques música después de las once de la noche.*

Panamá

Gualberto Becerra/Shutterstock

Información general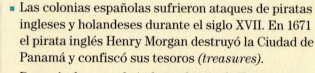

Nombre oficial: República de Panamá

Población: 3.410.676

Capital: Ciudad de Panamá (f. 1519)
(900.000 hab.)

Otras ciudades importantes: San Miguelito
(300.000 hab.), David (128.000 hab.)

Moneda: balboa

Idiomas: español (oficial), inglés

Mapa de Panamá: Apéndice D

Vale saber…

- Vasco Núñez de Balboa y Cristóbal Colón exploraron el país en 1501 y 1502. Buscando el oro y las riquezas de una civilización indígena legendaria, Balboa "descubrió" el océano Pacífico en 1513.

Jim Lipschutz/Shutterstock

- Las colonias españolas sufrieron ataques de piratas ingleses y holandeses durante el siglo XVII. En 1671 el pirata inglés Henry Morgan destruyó la Ciudad de Panamá y confiscó sus tesoros *(treasures)*.

- Después de ganar la independencia de España en 1821, Panamá pasó por mucha turbulencia política. En 1904, Estados Unidos empezó la construcción del canal de Panamá. En 1999, EEUU cedió el canal al gobierno panameño.

- Tal vez los kunas son la tribu más famosa de Panamá, conocidos por la fabricación *(creation)* de sus molas tradicionales de colores vivos que se venden internacionalmente.

Costa Rica

Información general

Nombre oficial: República de Costa Rica

Población: 4.516.220

Capital: San José (f. 1521) (1.500.000 hab.)

Otras ciudades importantes: Alajuela (700.000 hab.), Cártago (450.000 hab.)

Moneda: colón

Idiomas: español (oficial), inglés

Mapa de Costa Rica: Apéndice D

Roberto A Sanchez/iStockphoto

Vale saber…

- Cristóbal Colón fue el primer europeo en llegar a esta área en 1502. Esperando encontrar riquezas naturales y otros metales preciosos, observó los adornos de oro de los indígenas y nombró el país Costa Rica.

- Costa Rica ganó la independencia de España en 1821, y después de unos conflictos políticos, llegó a ser una democracia en 1889.

- La gran mayoría de la población es criolla—mestizos de ascendencia española e indígena. Los grupos indígenas componen menos del 1 por ciento de la población y se distinguen en tres etnias indígenas: chorotega, huetar y brunca.

- Costa Rica es famosa por no tener ejército *(army)*, por el café que se vende a nivel mundial *(worldwide)* y por su diversidad biológica.

McPHOTO/age fotostock

Arnulfo Franco/AP Images

Regata de cayucos *(canoes)* de Océano a Océano

¡En Panamá, puedes remar del océano Atlántico al océano Pacífico a través del canal de Panamá en cayuco! En 1954, un líder de los Boy Scouts que trabajaba para la Compañía del canal de Panamá quiso introducir un grupo de niños exploradores a las tradiciones y cultura de los indígenas panameños que vivían a las orillas *(lived on the shores)* del río Chagres. El principal medio de transporte de los indígenas era el cayuco, una canoa hecha de un tronco de árbol *(tree)* nacional. Pronto, las competencias de cayuco entre los niños exploradores resultan en una regata oficial, la Regata de cayucos de Océano a Océano, tradición que dura 54 años sin interrupción.

Hoy día la regata es organizada por el Club de Remos de Balboa (CREBA). Hay dos categorías: la categoría juvenil (14–21 años) y la categoría abierta (mayores de 22 años) y tres subcategorías: masculina, femenina y mixta. Cada equipo de cuatro deportistas tiene que remar 50 millas en tres días. Maniobrar *(Maneuvering)* un cayuco es un deporte extremo que requiere de los atletas una perseverancia y una exigente *(demanding)* preparación física. ¡Rema de océano a océano! Sólo en Panamá.

El ecoturismo en Costa Rica

DreamPictures/Getty Images

Costa Rica tiene la reputación de practicar una conservación inteligente que atrae *(attracts)* a turistas de todo el mundo. El gobierno ha convertido *(has converted)* los parques nacionales, los bosques y las reservas indígenas en zonas protegidas que cubren 30% del país. El ecoturista puede disfrutar de *(enjoy)* la naturaleza con un impacto mínimo.

En los bosques tropicales puedes observar 850 especies de aves *(birds)*, monos *(monkeys)*, armadillos, jaguares, tapires y diversas especies de mariposas *(butterflies)*. También puedes acampar, hacer alpinismo, montar en bicicleta de montaña o montar a caballo en los parques nacionales como el Poás, el Arenal y el Irazú. Si eres deportista, en las playas y ríos puedes practicar todos los deportes acuáticos: el surfing, la navegación en rápidos, la natación, la pesca, el paseo en bote o en kayak.

Anímate. Transfórmate en ecoturista en Costa Rica, el paraíso del ecoturismo.

La información general

1. ¿Quién descubre el océano Pacífico en 1513?
2. ¿Quién destruye la Ciudad de Panamá?
3. ¿En qué año empieza la construcción del canal de Panamá? ¿Cuándo se hace parte del gobierno panameño?
4. ¿Quién es el primer europeo en llegar a Costa Rica? ¿En qué año?
5. ¿De qué país gana Costa Rica la independencia? ¿Cuándo llega a ser democracia?
6. ¿Por qué se conoce Costa Rica?

El tema de los deportes

1. ¿Qué es el cayuco?
2. ¿Qué tienen que hacer los deportistas en la Regata de cayucos de Océano a Océano?
3. ¿Por qué tiene Costa Rica la reputación de practicar una conservación inteligente que atrae a turistas de todo el mundo?
4. ¿Por qué Costa Rica se puede considerar el paraíso del ecoturismo?

🌐 **¿QUIERES SABER MÁS?**

Revisa y rellena la tabla que empezaste al principio del capítulo. Luego, escoge un tema para investigar en línea y prepárate para compartir la información con la clase.

También puedes escoger de las palabras clave a continuación o en **www.cengagebrain.com.**

Palabras clave: (Panamá) Balboa, los kunas, la construcción del canal de Panamá, la dictadura de Manuel Noriega, Rubén Blades; **(Costa Rica)** las plantaciones de café, Juan Mora Fernández, los ticos, por qué Costa Rica decidió abolir las fuerzas armadas, Óscar Arias.

🌐 **Tú en el mundo hispano** Para explorar oportunidades de usar el español para estudiar o hacer trabajos voluntarios o aprendizajes en Costa Rica y Panamá, sigue los enlaces en **www.cengagebrain.com**.

🎞 **Ritmos del mundo hispano** Sigue los enlaces en **www.cengagebrain.com** para escuchar música de Costa Rica y Panamá.

A leer

ESTRATEGIA

Scanning for detail

In this chapter, you will focus on *scanning*, a complementary skill to *skimming*, which you learned in **Chapter 5.** While skimming is getting the main idea, scanning is looking for specific information. To scan, run your eye over a text while looking for key words about specific pieces of information.

1 Mira el artículo y la foto sobre la navegación en rápidos en Costa Rica y ojea *(scan)* el artículo rápidamente para encontrar la siguiente información.

1. cuántos ríos costarricenses se mencionan
2. los niveles *(levels)* de dificultad que se usan para describir los rápidos de los ríos

2 Las siguientes palabras aparecen *(appear)* en el artículo. Aunque estas palabras no son cognados, tienen una relación semántica con sus equivalentes en inglés. A ver si puedes identificar el equivalente en inglés de cada palabra a la izquierda.

1. _____ media docena
2. _____ principiantes
3. _____ codueño
4. _____ haber pasado
5. _____ poblado
6. _____ trechos
7. _____ apacible

a. *co-owner*
b. *peaceful*
c. *half dozen*
d. *beginners*
e. *stretches*
f. *to have passed (navigated)*
g. *town, village*

3 Ahora, lee el artículo rápidamente para buscar la idea principal. Luego mira la **Actividad 4** en la página 262 para ver qué información necesitas para completarla. Vuelve al artículo y busca esa información. No es necesario entender todas las palabras para hacer las **Actividades 4** y **5**.

Excerpt from "Costa Rica: Adventures in White Water Rafting" by David Dudenhoefer, in Destinos/Miami Aboard, In-Flight magazine, Taca airlines, January/February 1998, pp. 52-60. © HCP/Aboard Publishing, Miami Herald Media Company, 2011. Used with permission.

LECTURA

Costa Rica

Aventuras en los rápidos

Pocos países pueden contar con tan excelentes condiciones para la navegación en rápidos como Costa Rica, donde los retos de este conocido deporte se complementan con la belleza y diversidad de los bosques tropicales.

Michael DeYoung/age fotostock

Quizás[1] las aguas más bravas del país sean aptas sólo para expertos remeros—media docena de equipos olímpicos de kayaks utilizan a Costa Rica como base de entrenamiento—, pero la mayoría de sus ríos rápidos ofrecen condiciones perfectas también para principiantes.

Los navegantes de balsas y kayaks poseen un sistema para evaluar el grado de dificultad de los rápidos y ríos individuales, en una escala que va de la Clase I a la Clase VI —donde el 0 es similar a una piscina y el VII, a las Cataratas del Niágara. Los rápidos de Clase II y III son, por lo general, suficientes para acelerar el ritmo cardíaco. Los de Clase IV pueden ser un poco más peligrosos, mientras que los de Clase V están ya cerca de lo imposible. Los ríos de Clase II y III son magníficos para principiantes. No obstante, resulta recomendable haber pasado, al menos, por un río antes de intentar lanzarse[2] en los de Clase II–IV. Los de Clase IV–V requieren una buena condición física y más experiencia con las balsas.

Las rutas de navegación

El río **Reventazón** posee numerosos tramos[3] navegables. El más popular es la sección Tucurrique (Clase III), que ofrece una excursión segura y emocionante, lo suficientemente fácil para un viaje de primera vez. La sección Peralta (Clase V) es la ruta más difícil de Costa Rica para este tipo de navegación, con rápidos indetenibles y bastante peligro, razón por la cual sólo está abierta para expertos.

El río **Pacuare** (Clase III–IV) es una de las maravillas naturales más impresionantes de Costa Rica. Es un río emocionante de navegar, con numerosos y provocadores rápidos de Clase IV. El Pacuare se navega mejor en un viaje de dos o tres días, lo cual permite un contacto más cercano con el bosque[4] tropical—un área excelente para la observación de pájaros[5].

El **Sarapiquí** (Clase III) es un río hermoso que fluye por el norte de la Cordillera Montañosa Central. La sección de rápidos entre La Virgen y Chilamae proporciona una aventura de navegación en balsa de Clase III, que pasa a través de muchos bosques tropicales y cataratas. La parte más baja del Sarapiquí es un flotador suave que resulta perfecto para niños pequeños.

El **Naranjo** (Clase III–IV) es un río emocionante y provocador que exige[6] cierta experiencia de navegación en balsa. Puede navegarse sólo en meses lluviosos. Queda[7] a un día desde Manuel Antonio y Quepos.

El **Corobicí** (Clase I–II) es un río completamente apacible. Es excelente para los amantes[8] de la naturaleza y puede ser navegado por personas de cualquier edad. En el bosque que viste sus orillas[9] se pueden ver iguanas, monos[10] y una rica variedad de pájaros.

[1]Perhaps [2]**intentar…:** to try to throw oneself [3]sections [4]forest [5]birds [6]demands [7]It is located [8]lovers [9]shores [10]monkeys

4 Completa la siguiente tabla con información del artículo. Si te es necesario, vuelve al artículo para buscarla.

Río	Clase	Una cosa interesante
Reventazón	III–V	
	I–II	
		Una parte es perfecta para los niños pequeños.
Naranjo		
		Se navega mejor en un viaje de dos o tres días.

5 Trabajen en grupos de tres o cuatro estudiantes para hablar de los cinco ríos que se describen en el artículo. ¿Cuál les interesa más? Escojan *(Choose)* un lugar del artículo para ir de vacaciones con el grupo. Para ayudarles con la decisión, contesten las siguientes preguntas.

1. ¿Cuánta experiencia con la navegación en rápidos tienen las distintas personas del grupo?
2. ¿Van a viajar durante la temporada de lluvia (verano) o durante el invierno?
3. ¿A qué distancia de San José están dispuestos *(willing)* a viajar?
4. ¿Cuánto tiempo quieren pasar en el río?
5. ¿Qué les interesa más, la belleza natural o la aventura de los rápidos?

MODELOS *A mí me gusta…*
Yo prefiero… porque…
Vamos a viajar en…

nik wheeler/Alamy

El río Corobicí

steve bly/Alamy

El río Reventazón

>> Antes de escribir

ESTRATEGIA

Writing—Freewriting

Once you are ready to write, freewriting is a useful composition strategy. When you freewrite, you don't worry about spelling, punctuation, grammar, or other errors. Instead, you write rapidly, letting the ideas and words flow as quickly as you can. Once you finish, you go back and revise what you've written.

1 Trabaja con un(a) compañero(a) de clase. Van a escribir un artículo de tres párrafos para el periódico universitario en el que describan un pasatiempo interesante que se puede hacer en su pueblo o ciudad. Para empezar, hagan una lista de actividades posibles.

2 Cuando tengan la lista, escojan *(choose)* el pasatiempo que les guste más. Juntos, escojan tres aspectos específicos para desarrollar *(to develop)* en los tres párrafos del artículo. Escriban una oración temática para cada uno. (Usen el artículo de la página 261 como modelo.)

Párrafo 1:

Párrafo 2:

Párrafo 3:

>> Composición

3 Usando las oraciones temáticas de la **Actividad 2,** escribe los tres párrafos que forman el primer borrador *(draft)* del artículo. Escribe sin detenerte *(freewrite)* y no te preocupes por los errores, la organización, la ortografía ni la gramática.

>> Después de escribir

4 Trabaja con tu compañero(a) otra vez. Intercambien sus borradores y usen las dos versiones para crear un solo artículo.

5 Ahora, miren la nueva versión y revísenla, usando la siguiente lista.

- ¿Tiene el artículo toda la información necesaria?
- ¿Es interesante e informativo también?
- ¿Usaron pronombres de complemento directo para eliminar la repetición?
- ¿Usaron bien el pretérito y otros tiempos gramaticales?
- ¿Hay errores de puntuación o de ortografía?

Vocabulario

Los deportes *Sports*

el básquetbol *basketball*
el béisbol *baseball*
el boxeo *boxing*
el ciclismo *cycling*
el esquí acuático *water skiing*
el esquí alpino *downhill skiing*
el fútbol *soccer*
el fútbol americano *football*
el golf *golf*
el hockey sobre hielo *ice hockey*
el hockey sobre hierba *field hockey*
la navegación en rápidos *whitewater rafting*
la natación *swimming*
el tenis *tennis*
el volibol *volleyball*

Actividades deportivas *Sport activities*

entrenarse *to train*
esquiar *to ski*
hacer ejercicio *to exercise*
jugar (ue) (al) (tenis, béisbol, etc.) *to play (tennis, baseball, etc.)*
levantar pesas *to lift weights*
montar a caballo *to ride horseback*
montar en bicicleta *to ride a bike*
nadar *to swim*
navegar en rápidos *to go whitewater rafting*
patinar en línea *to inline skate (rollerblade)*
patinar sobre hielo *to ice skate*
pescar *to fish*
practicar / hacer alpinismo *to (mountain) climb, hike*
practicar / hacer surfing *to surf*
remar *to row*

Más palabras sobre los deportes *More sports words*

la competencia *competition*
el equipo *team*
ganar *to win*
el lago *lake*
el partido *game, match*
el peligro *danger*
peligroso(a) *dangerous*
la pelota *ball*
la piscina *pool*
el río *river*
seguro(a) *safe*
la tabla de snowboard *snowboard*

Las estaciones *Seasons*

el invierno *winter*
la primavera *spring*
el verano *summer*
el otoño *fall, autumn*

Expresiones con *tener*

tener calor *to be hot*
tener cuidado *to be careful*
tener frío *to be cold*
tener ganas de *to feel like (doing)*
tener hambre *to be hungry*
tener miedo (a, de) *to be afraid (of)*
tener prisa *to be in a hurry*
tener razón *to be right*
tener sed *to be thirsty*
tener sueño *to be sleepy*
tener vergüenza *to be embarrassed, ashamed*

El tiempo *Weather*

¿Qué tiempo hace? *What's the weather like?*
Hace buen / mal tiempo. *It's nice / bad weather.*
Hace calor. *It's hot.*
Hace fresco. *It's cool.*
Hace frío. *It's cold.*
Hace sol. *It's sunny.*
Hace viento. *It's windy.*
Está lloviendo. (Llueve.) *It's raining.*
Está nevando. (Nieva.) *It's snowing.*
Está nublado. *It's cloudy.*

La temperatura *Temperature*

grados Celsio(s) *degrees Celsius*
grados Fahrenheit *degrees Fahrenheit*
La temperatura está a 20 grados Celsio(s). *It's 20 degrees Celsius*
La temperatura está a 68 grados Fahrenheit. *It's 68 degrees Fahrenheit.*

Palabras relativas al tiempo

anoche *last night*
anteayer *the day before yesterday*
el año pasado *last year*
el mes pasado *last month*
la semana pasada *last week*

Repaso y preparación

Complete these activities to check your understanding of the new grammar points in **Chapter 7** before you move on to **Chapter 8**.

The answers to the activities in this section can be found in **Appendix B**.

Preterite tense of regular verbs (p. 242)

1 Completa las oraciones con las formas correctas de los verbos en el pretérito para decir qué hizo cada persona durantes sus vacaciones.

1. Tú _____ (montar) a caballo en las montañas.
2. Marilena _____ (leer) cinco novelas de ciencia ficción.
3. Yo _____ (compartir) una cabaña en la playa con unos amigos.
4. Nosotros _____ (navegar) en rápidos en Costa Rica.
5. Linda y Carmela _____ (correr) en una maratón.

Preterite tense of some common irregular verbs (p. 245)

2 Escribe oraciones completas con las palabras indicadas para decir qué hicieron estas personas ayer.

1. tú y yo / ir al partido de hockey sobre el hielo
2. Marilena / estar en el hospital todo el día con una amiga enferma
3. yo / hacer un poco de ejercicio por la mañana
4. Guille y Paulina / decir que van a casarse
5. mis padres / conducir a la universidad para visitarme
6. tú / traducir tres poemas españoles al inglés

Direct object pronouns (p. 248)

3 Mira las ilustraciones y usa las palabras para decir qué hizo cada persona.

MODELOS Raúl / comprar (sí)
¿La computadora? Raúl la compró.
Marina / leer (no)
¿Los libros? Marina no los leyó.

1. tú / lavar (sí)

2. Victoria / hacer (sí)

3. yo / encontrar (no)

4. nosotros / perder (sí)

5. ustedes / beber (no)

6. Esteban y Federico / levantar (no)

Tú command forms (p. 253)

4 Completa los letreros *(signs)* con mandatos de **tú**.

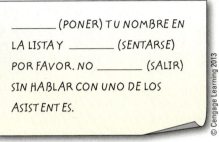

POR FAVOR, NO _____ (PONER)
BEBIDAS CERCA DE LAS COMPUTA-
DORAS. _____ (TENER) MUCHO
CUIDADO Y _____ (LEER) TODAS
LAS INSTRUCCIONES ANTES DE
EMPEZAR.

1

_____ (PONER) TU NOMBRE EN
LA LISTA Y _____ (SENTARSE)
POR FAVOR. NO _____ (SALIR)
SIN HABLAR CON UNO DE LOS
ASISTENTES.

2

© Cengage Learning 2013

>> Preparación para el Capítulo 8

Stem-changing verbs in the present indicative (Chapter 4)

5 Completa las oraciones con las formas correctas de los verbos indicados.

1. Mis amigos _____ (querer) esquiar.
2. Yo _____ (divertirse) en la piscina.
3. Ellos _____ (vestirse) para entrenarse.
4. Ustedes no _____ (poder) pescar hoy.
5. Cuando llueve, yo _____ (dormir) mucho.
6. Tú _____ (pedir) tiempo para descansar.

Gustar with infinitives (Chapter 2) and with nouns (Chapter 4)

6 Haz oraciones completas para decir qué les gusta a las personas indicadas.

1. a mí / remar
2. a usted / nadar
3. a ti / esos esquíes
4. a ellos / el boxeo
5. a nosotros / pescar
6. a ella / la nieve
7. a ti / entrenarse
8. a mi / las vacaciones
9. a nosotros / la primavera

Conocer and saber (Chapter 5), poder and querer (Chapter 4)

7 Completa los comentarios de Lidia con las formas correctas de los verbos indicados.

Yo 1. _____ (saber) hacer muchos deportes diferentes y 2. _____ (conocer) a muchas personas que 3. _____ (saber) hacerlos también. Cuando nieva, nosotros 4. _____ (poder) esquiar. Cuando llueve, mis amigos 5. _____ (poder) venir a mi casa y hacemos ejercicios. Y cuando hace sol, ¡nosotros 6. _____ (conocer) las mejores playas para el surfing! Yo 7. _____ (querer) aprender hacerlo y cuando 8. _____ (poder), voy con ellos porque necesito la práctica.

Complete these activities to review some previously learned grammatical structures that will be helpful when you learn the new grammar in **Chapter 8**.

Be sure to reread **Chapter 7: Gramática útil 2** and **3** before moving on to the **Chapter 8** grammar sections.

¿Cómo defines tu estilo?

ESTILO PERSONAL

Para algunas personas, la ropa es una forma importante de presentarse al mundo e identificarse con los demás. Para otras, solamente sirve para usos prácticos.

¿Tienen mucha importancia para ti la ropa y el estilo personal? ¿Crees que la ropa es una forma de expresión o es solamente para protegerse de los elementos?

Communication

By the end of this chapter you will be able to

- talk about clothing and fashion
- shop for various articles of clothing
- discuss prices
- describe recent purchases and shopping trips
- talk about buying items and doing favors for friends
- make comparisons

AFP/Getty Images

Un viaje por Ecuador y Perú

Ecuador y Perú comparten una frontera y tienen costas en el océano Pacífico. La cordillera *(mountain range)* de los Andes pasa por los dos países.

País / Área	Tamaño y fronteras	Sitios de interés
Ecuador 276.840 km^2	un poco más pequeño que Nevada; fronteras con Colombia y Perú	las islas Galápagos, la selva *(jungle)* amazónica, el volcán Cotopaxi, los baños termales
Perú 1.280.000 km^2	un poco más pequeño que Alaska; fronteras con Bolivia, Brasil, Colombia, Chile y Ecuador	Machu Picchu, las ruinas de Chan-Chan y el Señor de Sipán en la costa pacífica, el lago Titicaca, la selva amazónica

¿Qué sabes? Di si las siguientes oraciones son ciertas **(C)** o falsas **(F)**.

1. Ecuador y Perú son países montañosos.
2. Perú es más de cinco veces más grande que Ecuador.
3. No hay volcanes en estos dos países.
4. La selva amazónica se encuentra en los dos países.

Lo que sé y lo que quiero aprender Completa la tabla del **Apéndice A**. Escribe algunos datos que **ya sabes** sobre estos países en la columna **Lo que sé**. Después, añade algunos temas que **quieres aprender** a la columna **Lo que quiero aprender**. Guarda la tabla para usarla otra vez en la sección **¡Explora y exprésate!** en la página 297.

Cultures

By the end of this chapter you will have explored

- facts about Peru and Ecuador
- organic cotton from Peru
- a colorful fair that sells traditional clothing in Ecuador
- the ancestral tradition of weaving in the Andes
- attitudes towards jeans around the world

¡Imagínate!

DEPENDIENTE:	¿En qué puedo servirle, señor?
JAVIER:	Pues, estoy buscando un regalo para mi madre pero no sé, no veo nada.
DEPENDIENTE:	Pues, si le gusta la **ropa** fina, esta **blusa de seda** es muy bonita y además está rebajada.
JAVIER:	No, no le gusta ese color.
DEPENDIENTE:	¿Quizás este **suéter**?
JAVIER:	No. Tampoco necesita suéter.
DEPENDIENTE:	Y las **joyas**, ¿a quién no le gustan las joyas?… ¿Quizás estos **aretes**? Son de **oro** y le dan ese toque de elegancia a cualquier **vestido.**

>> **Las prendas de ropa**

To say that an item is made of a certain fabric, you need to use **de**: **botas de cuero, abrigo de piel, camiseta de algodón**.

The names for articles of clothing can vary greatly from region to region. For example, *jeans* can also be called **vaqueros, tejanos, bluyines, majones,** or **pantalones de mezclilla**.

>> Las telas

Está hecho(a) de... *It's made (out) of . . .*
Están hechos(as) de... *They're made (out) of . . .*

el algodón *cotton*	**a cuadros** *plaid*
la lana *wool*	**a rayas / rayado(a)** *striped*
el lino *linen*	**bordado(a)** *embroidered*
la mezclilla *denim*	**de lunares** *polka-dotted*
la piel / el cuero *leather*	**de un solo color** *solid, one single color*
la seda *silk*	**estampado(a)** *print*

Other regional variations: In Spain a handbag is **el bolso** and in Mexico it is **la bolsa**; in some places, **la cartera** can also be a handbag, not just a wallet. Other variations are: **los aretes / los pendientes, el anillo / la sortija, la gorra / el gorro,** and **las gafas / los lentes / los anteojos**.

>> Los accesorios

>> Las joyas

la cadena... *chain . . .*	**... (de) plata** *. . . (made of) silver*
... (de) oro *. . . (made of) gold*	

1 **¡Llevo…!** Describe qué ropa llevas hoy. ¡No te olvides de incluir los colores!

MODELO   *Llevo unos pantalones negros, una camiseta azul y unos zapatos negros.*

2 **Me gustan…** Para cada prenda de ropa, indica el tipo de tela y diseño que prefieres. Sigue el modelo.

MODELO   el vestido
Me gustan los vestidos de seda.
O: *Me gustan los vestidos estampados.*

1. el suéter
2. los zapatos de tenis
3. la blusa
4. los pantalones
5. el traje
6. la falda
7. la camiseta
8. la chaqueta

3 **¿Ropa formal o informal?** Trabaja con un(a) compañero(a) de clase. Digan qué les gusta llevar en las siguientes situaciones. Sean tan específicos como puedan.

1. para estudiar
2. para salir a bailar
3. para trabajar en el jardín
4. para visitar a la familia
5. para ir a clases
6. para ir al gimnasio

4 **Las estrellas** Trabajen en grupos de tres o cuatro estudiantes. Primero, hagan una lista de tres personas que son famosas por su manera de vestirse. Luego, usen la imaginación para describir qué llevan en este momento. Incluyan tantos detalles como puedan.

Personas posibles: Lady Gaga, Johnny Depp, Jennifer López, Kanye West, Katy Perry, Beyoncé, etc.

5 **Los accesorios** ¿Quién lleva las siguientes cosas? Para cada accesorio indicado, identifica quién(es) en la clase lo lleva(n). Si nadie lleva el accesorio indicado, di a quién le gusta llevarlo generalmente, o da el nombre de una persona famosa que lo lleva frecuentemente.

MODELOS   una cadena de oro
Stacy lleva una cadena de oro hoy.
O: *Generalmente Stacy lleva una cadena de oro, pero hoy no la lleva.*
unas gafas de sol
Nadie lleva gafas de sol ahora mismo. A Javier Bardem le gusta llevar gafas de sol.

1. una cadena de oro
2. unos guantes
3. un sombrero
4. un reloj
5. un pañuelo de seda
6. un brazalete
7. un cinturón de cuero
8. aretes de plata

6 **¿Qué me pongo?** Descríbele a tu compañero(a) qué ropa y accesorios llevas en las siguientes situaciones. Luego, él o ella hace lo mismo.

1. Es tu primera cita *(date)* con alguien que te gusta mucho.
2. Vas a una recepción para recibir un premio *(prize)*.
3. Vas al gimnasio con tu mejor amigo(a).
4. Vas a un concierto de música hip-hop con un grupo de amigos.
5. Vas a una entrevista para un trabajo de verano.
6. Vas a ir a esquiar en las montañas el fin de semana.

7 **¡Qué anticuado!** Trabajen en parejas. Juntos hagan una lista de ropa y accesorios que están de moda en este momento y otra de los que están pasados de moda. Luego, comparen su lista con la de otra pareja. ¿Incluyeron las mismas prendas?

¡Fíjate! Los tejidos andinos

Sean Sprague/The Image Works

Hoy día puedes ir a los mercados de Perú y Ecuador y comprar prendas de ropa que han sido *(have been)* tejidas a mano usando las técnicas antiguas de los incas, reinterpretadas con nuevas expresiones y tecnologías. Los tejidos pueden verse como un texto histórico, cada sociedad étnica adaptando las técnicas y los diseños para reflejar su estilo, su estética y sus creencias religiosas y sociopolíticas.

Es lógico que vas a encontrar palabras para prendas de ropa en sitios como los Andes que no corresponden a las palabras en tu libro de texto. La gran variedad lingüística de país a país referente a las prendas de ropa se puede notar en la palabra *chompa* de Perú. La chompa es un suéter de lana o algodón de manga larga, pero en Bolivia, Chile, Ecuador y Paraguay es *chomba*, en Argentina y Uruguay es *pulóver*, en Guatemala y Centroamérica es *chumpa* y en España es *jersey*.

¿Tienes alguna prenda de ropa que refleje la cultura de tus antepasados? ¿Qué prendas de ropa varían de nombre a través de Estados Unidos? ¿en otros países de habla inglesa?

Práctica Con un(a) compañero(a), hagan una investigación en Internet sobre uno o dos de los siguientes temas. Compartan su información con la clase.

1. la historia de una prenda de ropa que refleja la cultura de tus antepasados
2. la variedad lingüística de una prenda de ropa en EEUU (escojan una)
3. los símbolos en los diseños de los tejidos andinos

© Cengage Learning 2013

DEPENDIENTE:	Buenas, señorita. **¿En qué puedo servirle?**
CHELA:	La verdad es que estoy buscando un regalo para el cumpleaños de mi mamá pero no tengo ni la menor idea qué comprarle.
DEPENDIENTE:	Su mamá seguro es una mujer de muy buen gusto. Tal vez esta blusa de seda…
CHELA:	Uy, no, ¡a mamá no le gusta ese color!…
DEPENDIENTE:	¡Ya sé exactamente lo que busca!… Estos aretes de oro son preciosos y **están a muy buen precio** hoy.
CHELA:	¡Qué bonitos! Sí, creo que sí le van a gustar a mamá. **Voy a llevármelos.**

In many countries you will hear an alternate female form for **la dependiente: la dependienta**. Both are used interchangeably.

Notice that when you use the phrases **Voy a probármelo(la / los / las)** and **Voy a llevármelo(la / los / las)**, the pronoun that you use must match the object you are referring to: **Me gusta este <u>vestido</u>. Voy a probárme<u>lo</u>. Me encantan estos <u>zapatos</u>. Voy a llevárme<u>los</u>.**

If you want to know if an item is returnable, you can say **¿Puedo devolverlo si hay un problema?**

>> **Ir de compras**

El (La) dependiente

¿En qué puedo servirle? *How can I help you?*
¿Cuál es su talla? *What is your size?*
Está rebajado(a). *It's reduced (on sale).*
Está en venta. *It's on sale.*
Es muy barato(a). *It's very inexpensive.*
Está a muy buen precio. *It's a very good price.*
¿Es un regalo? *Is it a gift?*

de buena (alta) calidad *of good (high) quality*
el descuento *discount*
la oferta especial *special offer*

El (La) cliente

¿Cuánto cuesta(n)? *How much does it (do they) cost?*
¿Lo (La / Los / Las) tiene en una talla…? *Do you have this in a size . . .?*
Voy a probármelo(la / las / los). *I'm going to try it / them on.*
Me queda bien / mal. *It fits nicely / badly.*
Me queda grande / apretado. *It's too big / too tight.*
Voy a llevármelo(la / las / los). *I'm going to take it / them.*
Es (demasiado) caro. *It's (too) expensive.*

>> **La moda**

(no) estar de moda *(not) to be fashionable*

pasado(a) de moda *out of style*

ACTIVIDADES

8 **Por favor...** ¿Qué dices en las siguientes situaciones? Escribe una pregunta o una respuesta para cada situación. En muchos casos, hay más de una respuesta posible.

MODELO Ves una blusa bonita, pero no tiene precio.
¿Cuánto cuesta, por favor?

1. Te pruebas una chaqueta, pero es grande.
2. Decides comprar dos blusas.
3. Ves unos zapatos que te gustan, pero no estás seguro(a) si están rebajados.
4. Te pruebas unos zapatos y decides comprarlos.
5. Quieres probarte un vestido en otra talla y se lo pides a la dependiente.
6. Ves unos pantalones que te gustan, pero quieres otro color.
7. El suéter de vicuña es muy fino, pero no sabes si tienes suficiente dinero para comprarlo.
8. Necesitas una talla más grande.

9 **Situaciones** Trabaja con un(a) compañero(a) de clase. Representen las siguientes situaciones. Túrnense para hacer los papeles del (de la) dependiente y del (de la) cliente.

Situación 1
Buscas un regalo para tu novio(a). Quieres algo de muy alta calidad pero a muy buen precio.

Situación 2
Tienes que ir a una fiesta formal y no sabes qué llevar. Pídele ayuda al (a la) dependiente y compra lo que necesitas.

Situación 3
Eres un(a) estudiante nuevo(a) en la universidad. Vas a un almacén popular para comprar ropa. ¿Qué debes comprar? Pídele consejos al (a la) dependiente y compra por lo menos dos prendas de ropa.

Situación 4
Tu prima acaba de tener un bebé. Quieres comprarle un regalo, pero no sabes qué comprar. Escucha las sugerencias del (de la) dependiente y luego compra el regalo.

10 **¿Qué me voy a poner?** Tú y tu compañero(a) van a una fiesta muy importante y quieren vestirse apropiadamente. Deciden ir a una tienda de ropa para comprarse algo nuevo. Mientras cada uno(a) se prueba diferentes prendas de ropa y accesorios, comenten sus selecciones. ¡Tengan una conversación auténtica!

¿Tú or usted? In some Latin American countries, formal address is used even at home, between parents and children, and husbands and wives. In other countries, it is reserved for the elderly and for differences in social class. To be safe, use the formal address until permission to use the informal is granted. Using the informal when the formal is expected can cause negative reactions.

Notice: In most cases, **bebé** is masculine. You may encounter some native speakers who say **la bebé** for a baby girl.

DEPENDIENTE: Tiene muy buen gusto, señorita. **¿Cómo desea pagar? En efectivo**, ¿verdad?

CHELA: Sí, gracias.

>> **Métodos de pago**

¿Cómo desea pagar? *How do you wish to pay?*
Al contado. / En efectivo. *In cash.*
Con cheque. *By check.*
Con cheque de viajero. *With a traveler's check.*
Con un préstamo. *With a loan.*
Con tarjeta de crédito. *With a credit card.*
Con tarjeta de débito. *With a debit card.*

Cien is used to express the quantity of exactly *one hundred*, as well as before **mil** and **millones**. **Ciento** is used in combination with other numbers to express quantities from 101–199. Note that with numbers using **-cientos**, the number agrees with the noun it modifies: **doscientas tiendas** but **doscientos mercados**.

>> **Los números mayores de 100**

100 cien	**1.000 mil**
101 ciento uno	**2.000 dos mil**
102 ciento dos, etc.	**3.000 tres mil**
200 doscientos(as)	**4.000 cuatro mil**
300 trescientos(as)	**5.000 cinco mil**
400 cuatrocientos(as)	**10.000 diez mil**
500 quinientos(as)	**100.000 cien mil**
600 seiscientos(as)	**1.000.000 un millón**
700 setecientos(as)	**2.000.000 dos millones, etc.**
800 ochocientos(as)	
900 novecientos(as)	

11 **Para pagar** Por lo general, ¿cómo vas a pagar en las siguientes situaciones? Di cuánto crees que te va a costar cada compra.

MODELO   Compras un café grande.
   Dos dólares y treinta centavos.

1. Compras un vestido / un traje nuevo.
2. Compras los libros para las clases.
3. Compras un pasaje *(ticket)* de avión.
4. Compras frutas en el mercado.
5. Compras una cadena de oro.
6. Compras unos recuerdos *(souvenirs)* durante tus vacaciones.

7. Cenas en un restaurante muy elegante.
8. Vas al cine para ver una película.
9. Pagas el alquiler *(rent)* de tu apartamento.
10. Compras una casa nueva.
11. Compras un automóvil nuevo.

12 **De compras** Trabaja con un(a) compañero(a) de clase. Juntos escojan seis objetos del dibujo y representen una escena como la del modelo. Túrnense para hacer el papel del (de la) dependiente y el (la) cliente. Sigan el modelo.

MODELO   el café
   Tú: *Un café grande, por favor.*
   Compañero(a): *Muy bien. Son dos dólares y veinticinco centavos.*
      ¿Cómo desea pagar?
   Tú: *En efectivo. Aquí lo tiene.*

© Cengage Learning 2013

A ver

ESTRATEGIA

Using background knowledge to anticipate content

If you have a rough idea of a video segment's content, you can predict what other information it may contain. Think about the topic and ask yourself what vocabulary you associate with it. By organizing your thoughts in advance, you prepare yourself to understand the content more easily.

Antes de ver En el episodio para este capítulo, Chela y Javier independientemente buscan un regalo para sus madres. Mira las páginas 270, 274 y 276.

1. ¿Para quién buscan un regalo Chela y Javier?
2. ¿Cuáles de los accesorios y prendas de ropa del vocabulario pueden ser un regalo bueno para la mamá de Chela y la de Javier? Y, según ellos, ¿cuáles no son un regalo bueno?
3. ¿Los dos se conocen o no? ¿Crees que van a conocerse en este episodio?

▶ **Ver** Mira el video. Usa la información en **Antes de ver** para entenderlo mejor.

Después de ver 1 Contesta las siguientes preguntas sobre el video.

1. ¿Compró Javier una blusa para su mamá? ¿Y Chela?
2. ¿Compró Javier un suéter para su mamá? ¿Y Chela?
3. ¿Qué compraron Javier y Chela para sus mamás?
4. ¿Por qué no les gustó la blusa a Javier y a Chela? ¿Y el suéter?
5. ¿Sabemos cuánto costaron los aretes?
6. ¿Cómo pagaron Javier y Chela?
7. ¿Qué pensó el dependiente sobre la relación entre Javier y Chela?

Después de ver 2 Escribe un resumen corto de lo que ocurrió en el video para este capítulo. Escribe por lo menos seis oraciones que describan la conversación entre el dependiente y Javier y luego entre el dependiente y Chela. Usa las formas del pretérito que aprendiste en el **Capítulo 7**.

© Cengage Learning 2013

Voces de la comunidad

© Cengage Learning 2013

▶ >> Voces del mundo hispano

En el video para este capítulo José, Bruna, Marcela y Alex hablan de la ropa y la moda. Lee las siguientes oraciones. Después mira el video una o más veces para decir si las oraciones son ciertas (**C**) o falsas (**F**).

1. Cuando José está en Perú, compra su ropa en Marshalls.
2. A Alex no le gusta mucho la ropa artesanal (*handmade*).
3. Las prendas favoritas de José son los suéteres.
4. A Bruna y a Marcela les gustan las faldas.
5. A Marcela le gusta combinar accesorios.
6. A Alex le importa ser original.

🔊 >> Voces de Estados Unidos

Track 24

Nina García, diseñadora

Valerie Macon/Getty Images

❝El primer paso, y el más importante para desarrollar estilo, es proyectar ese tipo de confianza; el tipo de confianza que les dice a los otros que te respetas a ti misma, te amas (*love*) a ti misma y te vistes para ti misma y no para otros. Tú eres tu propia musa.❞

Los fanáticos de Project Runway la conocen como una de los jurados (*judges*) más perspicaces del programa y como una mujer de un gusto impecable. Pero la fama e influencia de Nina García van mucho mucho más allá de este popular programa de televisión. Nina es una autoridad internacional en la industria de la moda. Ha colaborado (*She has collaborated*) con casas de moda tales como Marc Jacobs y Perry Ellis, fue editora de la revista *Elle* y es autora de cuatro libros de moda que figuran entre los libros con mayor éxito de venta (*bestsellers*) del *New York Times*. Actualmente, Nina reside en Nueva York donde trabaja como directora de modas de la revista *Marie Claire*. Nacida en Colombia, es graduada de Boston University, de La Escuela Superior de Moda de París y del Fashion Institute of Technology de la ciudad de Nueva York.

¿Y tú? ¿Te gusta la idea de vestirte con ropa de diseñadores famosos? ¿Te importan las marcas (*brands*) de tus prendas de ropa? ¿Por qué sí o por qué no?

¡Prepárate!

Talking about what you did: The preterite tense of more irregular verbs

Cómo usarlo

1. In Spanish, as in English, many of the verbs you use most are irregular. In this chapter you will learn the preterite forms of **andar, haber, poder, poner, querer, saber, tener**, and **venir.** Notice that most of these verbs are also irregular in the present indicative.

2. The preterite forms of **conocer, saber, poder**, and **querer** can mean something slightly different from their meaning in the present indicative.

	Present indicative meaning	Different preterite meaning
conocer	to know someone, to be acquainted with	to meet
saber	to know a fact	to find out some information
poder	to be able to do something	to accomplish something
no poder	to not be able to	to try to do something and fail
querer	to want; to love	to try to do something
no querer	to not want, love	to refuse to do something

Elena **quiso** llamarme pero **no pudo** encontrar su celular.

*Elena **tried** to call me but **was unable (failed)** to find her cell phone.*

Conocí al padre de Beto y **supe** que Beto está en Colombia.

*I **met** Beto's father and **found out** that Beto is in Colombia.*

Pude completar el trabajo pero **no quise** ir a la oficina.

*I **succeeded in** finishing the work, but I **refused** to go to the office.*

The preterite can be used here because the focus is on the moment or the duration of the action described.

3. When referring to a specific time period in the past, most of these verbs keep their original meaning in the preterite: **Mi ex novio me quiso mucho, pero mi novio actual me quiere más.**

4. Notice that while the rest of these verbs are irregular in the preterite, **conocer** is regular in this tense. Its only irregularity is its **yo** form in the present tense: **conozco.**

Cómo formarlo

Here are the preterite forms of these irregular verbs. Some verbs are somewhat similar in their irregular stems, so they are grouped together to help you memorize them more easily.

andar:	anduv-	anduve, anduviste, anduvo, anduvimos, anduvisteis, anduvieron
tener:	tuv-	tuve, tuviste, tuvo, tuvimos, tuvisteis, tuvieron
poder:	pud-	pude, pudiste, pudo, pudimos, pudisteis, pudieron
poner:	pus-	puse, pusiste, puso, pusimos, pusisteis, pusieron
saber:	sup-	supe, supiste, supo, supimos, supisteis, supieron
hay:		hubo (invariable)
querer:	quis-	quise, quisiste, quiso, quisimos, quisisteis, quisieron
venir:	vin-	vine, viniste, vino, vinimos, vinisteis, vinieron

> **Hubo** is the preterite equivalent of **hay**. Like **hay**, it is a third-person invariable form that is used whether the subject is singular or plural: **Hubo unas ofertas increíbles en las tiendas la semana pasada. Haber** is the infinitive from which **hay** and **hubo** come.

> Notice that although these verbs change their stems, they share the same endings (**-e, -iste, -o, -imos, -isteis, -ieron**).

ACTIVIDADES

1 En el centro comercial Di qué pasó en el centro comercial hoy según el dibujo. Sigue el modelo.

MODELO Mario (beber un refresco grande)
Mario bebió un refresco grande.

1. Adela (comer pizza)
2. Ernesto (andar mucho)
3. Aracely (poder encontrar muchas cosas)
4. Miguel (conocer a Marisa)
5. Leo (poner la mochila en la mesa)
6. Néstor (querer tomar una siesta pero no poder)
7. Beti (saber las últimas noticias)

© Cengage Learning 2013

2 **La vida universitaria** Con un(a) compañero(a) de clase, háganse y contesten las siguientes preguntas.

1. ¿Cómo supiste que te habían aceptado (*you had been accepted*) en la universidad? ¿Cuándo lo supiste?
2. ¿Viniste a la universidad como estudiante nuevo(a), estudiante de intercambio o te transferiste de otra universidad? ¿Te gustó la universidad cuando llegaste por primera vez?
3. ¿Pudiste traer todas tus cosas a la universidad? ¿Qué cosas no pudiste traer?
4. ¿Conociste a muchas personas la primera semana de clases? ¿Cuántas, más o menos?
5. ¿Tuviste que estudiar mucho el semestre / trimestre pasado? ¿Recibiste buenas notas?
6. ¿Aprendiste algo interesante el semestre / trimestre pasado? ¿Qué fue?
7. ¿Tuviste tiempo para hacer mucho ejercicio? ¿Anduviste mucho el semestre / trimestre pasado?
8. ¿Pudiste tomar todas tus clases preferidas?

3 **El semestre o trimestre pasado** Mira el siguiente formulario. Luego, pregúntales a tus compañeros de clase si hicieron las actividades indicadas el semestre o trimestre pasado. Si encuentras a alguien que responde que sí, escribe su nombre en el espacio correspondiente. Sigue el modelo.

MODELO venir a la universidad con mucha ropa nueva
—*¿Viniste a la universidad con mucha ropa nueva?*
—*No, no vine con mucha ropa nueva.*
O: —*Sí, vine con mucha ropa nueva. (Escribe su nombre en el formulario.)*

¿Quién...?	Nombre
tener que estudiar todos los fines de semana	
no conocer a su compañero(a) de cuarto antes de llegar a la universidad	
poner un refrigerador y un televisor en su cuarto	
venir a las clases sin hacer la tarea	
no poder dormir antes de los exámenes importantes	
venir a la universidad con mucha ropa nueva	
tener sueño en las clases	
no querer comer la comida de la cafetería	

Gramática útil 2

Talking about what you did: The preterite tense of -ir stem-changing verbs

Cómo formarlo

1. As you learned in **Chapter 7,** the only stem-changing verbs that also change in the preterite are verbs that end in **-ir.** Present-tense stem-changing verbs that end in **-ar** and **-er** do not change their stem in the preterite.

2. In the preterite, **-ir** stem-changing verbs only experience the stem change in the third-person singular **(usted / él / ella)** and third-person plural **(ustedes / ellos / ellas)** forms.

   ■ Verbs that change **e → ie** in the present change **e → i** in the preterite.

   > **preferir:** preferí, preferiste, **prefirió**, preferimos, preferisteis, **prefirieron**
   > Similar verbs you already know: **divertirse, sentirse**
   > New verb of this kind: **sugerir (ie, i)** *to suggest*

   ■ Verbs that change **e → i** in the present also change **e → i** in the preterite.

   > **pedir:** pedí, pediste, **pidió**, pedimos, pedisteis, **pidieron**
   > Similar verbs you already know: **despedirse, reírse, repetir, seguir, servir, vestir, vestirse**
   > New verbs of this kind: **conseguir (i, i)** *to get, to have;* **sonreír (i, i)** *to smile*

   ■ Verbs that change **o → ue** in the present change **o → u** in the preterite.

   > **dormir:** dormí, dormiste, **durmió**, dormimos, dormisteis, **durmieron**
   > New verb of this kind: **morirse (ue, u)** *to die*

Starting with this chapter, all **-ir** stem-changing verbs will be shown with both of their stem changes in parentheses. The first letter or letters show the present-tense stem change and the second letter shows the preterite stem change.

ACTIVIDADES

4 **Olivia y Belkys** Completa la conversación con la forma correcta del pretérito de los verbos indicados. Después, di si, en tu opinión, Belkys tiene razón en sentirse tan avergonzada *(embarrassed)*.

OLIVIA: ¿Qué tal tu día de compras? ¿ _____ (divertirse)?

BELKYS: No, no _____ (divertirse) ni un poquito y además no compré nada.

OLIVIA: ¡No te lo creo! ¿Tú, sin comprar nada? ¡Imposible!

BELKYS: Pero es la verdad. Yo _____ (ir) con Gerardo porque él _____ (insistir) en acompañarme. Él _____ (sugerir) ir al centro porque le gustan los trajes en una tienda allí.

OLIVIA: ¿Pero ustedes no _____ (conseguir) comprar nada?

BELKYS: No. Los dos _____ (ver) unas cosas bonitas, pero no _____ (poder) encontrar nada a buen precio. Por eso, _____ (preferir) no comprar nada.

OLIVIA: ¡Qué pena!

BELKYS: Y lo peor es que Gerardo _____ (vestirse) con un traje viejo, muy pasado de moda, verde, con rayas amarillas. Yo casi me muero de vergüenza.

OLIVIA: ¡Pobrecita! ¡Imagínate el horror!

BELKYS: Bueno, tú te ríes, ¡pero te digo que yo no _____ (reírse) en toda la tarde! Nosotros _____ (seguir) buscando en todas las tiendas del centro. Por fin _____ (despedirse) y yo _____ (venir) directamente aquí para contarte toda la historia.

OLIVIA: Ay, chica, tranquila. Por lo menos, ¡tú me _____ (hacer) reír un poco!

5 Me sentí… Di cómo se sintieron las siguientes personas en las situaciones indicadas.

MODELO tu tía / después de perder el trabajo
Se sintió desilusionada.

Emociones: aburrido(a), animado(a), cansado(a), contento(a), desilusionado(a), feliz, furioso(a), nervioso(a), ocupado(a), preocupado(a), triste

1. tú / antes de tus exámenes finales
2. tú y tu mejor amigo(a) / al final del semestre o trimestre
3. tu mejor amigo(a) / cuando estuvo enfermo(a)
4. tus padres / cuando saliste para la universidad
5. tu primo(a) / después de perder el partido de fútbol
6. tus amigos / en una película de tres horas y media
7. tu compañero(a) de cuarto / antes de la visita de sus padres
8. tú / después de conocer a una persona simpática

6 En la U Con un(a) compañero(a) de clase, háganse las siguientes preguntas sobre su llegada a la universidad y luego contéstenlas.

1. ¿Cómo te sentiste cuando llegaste a la universidad la primera vez?
2. ¿Qué te sugirió tu familia cuando viniste a la universidad?
3. ¿Le pediste ayuda a tu familia para traer todas tus cosas a la universidad?
4. ¿Te divertiste el primer semestre / trimestre? ¿Qué hiciste?
5. ¿Preferiste vivir en una residencia estudiantil o en un apartamento?
6. ¿Conseguiste un trabajo el primer semestre / trimestre?
7. ¿Siguieron tú y tus amigos la misma carrera de estudios?

Gramática útil 3

Saying who is affected or involved:
Indirect object pronouns

Cómo usarlo

LO BÁSICO

- An *indirect object* is a noun or noun phrase that indicates for whom or to whom an action is done: I bought a gift for *Beatriz*. We asked *the teachers* a question.
- *Indirect object pronouns* are used to replace indirect object nouns: I bought a gift for *her*. We asked *them* a question. Often you can identify the indirect object of the sentence by asking *to* or *for whom*? about the verb: We bought a gift *for whom?* (Beatriz / her) We asked a question *to whom?* (the teachers / them).

1. In **Chapter 7** you learned how to use direct object pronouns to avoid repetition. In this chapter you will learn how you can also use indirect object pronouns to avoid repetition and to clarify to which person you are referring.

2. Look at the following passage and see if you can figure out to whom the boldface indirect object pronouns refer.

> Fui al almacén el miércoles. Tenía una lista larga de compras. **Le** compré unos jeans y una camisa a Miguel. También **le** compré una corbata. A Susana y a Carmen **les** compré unas camisetas. También tuve que comprar**les** calcetines. Además **me** compré una falda bonita y un reloj.

Cómo formarlo

1. Although English uses the same set of pronouns for direct object pronouns and indirect object pronouns, in Spanish there are two slightly different sets.

2. Notice that the only difference between the direct object pronouns and the indirect object pronouns is in the two third-person pronouns. Instead of **lo / la**, the indirect object pronoun is **le**. And instead of **los / las**, the indirect object pronoun is **les**. The indirect object pronouns **le** and **les** do not have to agree in gender with the nouns they replace, as do the direct object pronouns **lo, la, los**, and **las**.

¿En qué puedo **servirle,** señor?

Indirect object pronouns			
me	to / for me	nos	to / for us
te	to / for you	os	to / for you (fam. pl.)
le	to / for you (form. sing) / him / her	les	to / for you (form., pl.) / them

Notice that these are the same pronouns you used with **gustar** and similar verbs in **Chapters 2** and **4**.

3. As with direct object pronouns, indirect object pronouns always come before a conjugated verb used alone.

Te traje el periódico.
*I brought **you** the newspaper.*

Nos dieron un regalo bonito.
*They gave **us** a nice gift.*

4. When an indirect object pronoun is used with an infinitive or with the present progressive, it may come before the conjugated verb, or it may be attached to the infinitive or to the present participle.

Te voy a dar el libro.   OR: Voy a dar**te** el libro.
Te estoy comprando los   OR: Estoy comprándo**te** los
   zapatos.   zapatos.

Notice that when the indirect object pronoun attaches to the present participle, you must add an accent to the next-to-last syllable of the present participle to maintain the correct pronunciation.

5. When an indirect object pronoun is used with a command form, it attaches to the end of the affirmative command but comes before the negative command form.

Cómprame / Cómpreme   BUT: **No me compres / No me compre**
   el libro ahora, por favor.   el libro ahora, por favor.

Again notice that when the indirect object pronoun attaches to the command form, you must add an accent to the next-to-last syllable of command forms of two or more syllables in order to maintain the correct pronunciation.

6. As you learned in **Chapter 4**, if you want to emphasize or clarify to or for whom something is being done, you can use **a** + the person's name, or **a** + prepositional pronoun: **mí, ti, usted, él, ella, nosotros(as), vosotros(as), ustedes, ellos, ellas**. Note that when a pronoun is used, there is sometimes no direct translation in English.

Les escribo una postal **a ustedes**.
*I'm writing **you** a postcard.*

Le doy el regalo **a Lucas**.
*I'm giving the gift **to Lucas**.*

Les traigo el periódico **a mis padres**.
*I bring the newspaper **to my parents**.*

Prepositional pronouns can follow *any* preposition, not just **a**. Other prepositions you know include **con**: *with* (with **con**, **mí** and **ti** change to **conmigo** and **contigo**); **de**: *from, of;* **sin**: *without.*

7. Here are some verbs that are frequently used with indirect object pronouns. Some you already know; others are new: **ayudar** *(to help)*, **comprar, dar, decir, enviar, escribir, gustar** (and verbs like **gustar**), **mandar** *(to send, to order)*, **pedir, prestar** *(to loan or lend)*, **regalar** *(to give a gift)*, **servir**, and **traer**.

ACTIVIDADES

7 **Regalos** Varias personas les regalaron varias cosas a diferentes miembros de su familia. Identifica el pronombre del complemento indirecto en cada oración.

1. Yo _____ regalé una gorra de lana a mi mamá.
2. Ana _____ compró unas pulseras a sus hermanas.
3. Arturo _____ dio unos guantes de cuero a ti.
4. Mi tía _____ trajo unas camisetas del Perú a nosotros.
5. Abuela _____ mandó una tarjeta postal a mis primos.
6. Papá _____ compró unos pantalones cortos a mí y a mi hermano.
7. Andrés _____ trajo una cadena de plata a ti.
8. Nilemy _____ regaló un reloj a su tía.

8 **¡Ay, Hernando!** Completa la siguiente conversación con el complemento indirecto correcto. Después de completarla, léela otra vez para ver si entiendes por qué se usa cada complemento indirecto.

HERNANDO: Oye, tengo que ir al centro. ¿Quieres acompañarme?

SEBASTIÁN: Cómo no. Tengo que (1) comprar_____ un regalo a mi hermanito para el día de su santo.

HERNANDO: Y yo (2) _____ voy a comprar unos jeans y una camiseta nueva.

SEBASTIÁN: ¿Tú con interés en la moda? Hombre, ¿qué (3) _____ pasa?

HERNANDO: Es Lidia. Ahora que salimos juntos los fines de semana (4) _____ dice que toda mi ropa está pasada de moda.

SEBASTIÁN: ¡No (5) _____ digas! A las mujeres… ¡ (6) _____ importa demasiado la ropa!

HERNANDO: Y lo peor es que no tengo mucho dinero. ¿Crees que (7) _____ den un descuento en la tienda donde trabaja Julio?

SEBASTIÁN: Oye, vale la pena *(it's worthwhile)* ir a ver. ¿(8) _____ dijiste a Julio que necesitas comprar ropa?

HERNANDO: Sí. Pero (9) _____ dijo que debemos ir al almacén en el centro. Además dijo que los precios en su tienda son demasiado caros y la calidad no es muy buena.

SEBASTIÁN: Bueno, parece que él no nos puede ayudar. Entonces, ¿vamos directamente al almacén?

HERNANDO: De acuerdo. Oye, ¿no (10) _____ puedes prestar un poco de dinero?

SEBASTIÁN: ¡Hombre! Nunca cambias…

🔊 **9** **De compras** Marisela les compra varias prendas de ropa y accesorios a Track 25 diferentes miembros de su familia y a varias amistades. Escucha mientras ella describe sus compras. Luego, escribe oraciones que expliquen qué le compró a cada quién. Primero estudia el modelo.

MODELO Escuchas: A mi tía le encantan las blusas bordadas. Cuando estaba de vacaciones en Ecuador, le compré una blusa bordada muy bonita.
Escribes: *Le compró una blusa bordada a su tía.*

1. _____ compró una cartera a _____.
2. _____ compró camisetas a _____.
3. _____ compró una pulsera de oro a _____.
4. _____ compró unos guantes de piel (_____).
5. _____ compró unos pantalones cortos a _____.
6. _____ compró unos zapatos de tenis (_____).

10 **De vez en cuando** Con un(a) compañero(a) de clase, digan para quiénes hacen las actividades indicadas. Usen cada verbo por lo menos una vez.

MODELO   comprar un café
          De vez en cuando le compro un café a mi compañero(a) de cuarto.
          O: *Nunca le compro un café a nadie.*

Acción	Objeto directo	Objeto indirecto
escribir	cartas	mi madre / padre
dar	flores	mis padres
comprar	regalos	mi amigo(a)
contar	chismes *(gossip)*	mis amigos
mandar	notas de agradecimiento	mi profesor(a)
pedir	favores	mis profesores
hacer	chistes *(jokes)*	mi novio(a)
traer	ayuda	mi compañero(a) de cuarto
¿…?	ropa	mis compañeros(as) de cuarto
	¿…?	

Frases útiles: de vez en cuando *(sometimes)*, frecuentemente, muchas veces, todas las semanas, todos los días, rara vez *(hardly ever)*, nunca, casi

11 **¿Quién?** Con un(a) compañero(a), háganse preguntas sobre las acciones de sus compañeros de clase. Pueden usar las ideas de la lista o pueden inventar otras. Asegúrense de usar verbos que requieren el uso del objeto indirecto.

MODELO   Tú: *¿Quién le regaló ropa a su novio(a)?*
          Compañero(a): *Dahlia le regaló una chaqueta de cuero a su novio Jesús.*

1. regalar ropa
2. decir siempre la verdad
3. pagar los estudios
4. enviar muchos mensajes de texto
5. ayudar con la tarea
6. ¿…?

12 **¿Y tú?** Con un(a) compañero(a), túrnense para hacer y contestar preguntas sobre las siguientes actividades.

MODELOS   tú enviar a tus padres recientemente: ¿qué?
           Tú: *¿Qué les enviaste recientemente a tus padres?*
           Compañero(a): *Les envié un mensaje de texto la semana pasada.*
           mandar algo a ti por correo recientemente: ¿quién?
           Compañero(a): *¿Quién te mandó algo por correo recientemente?*
           Tú: *Mi abuela me mandó una tarjeta de cumpleaños ayer.*

1. tú regalar a tu mejor amigo(a) para su cumpleaños: ¿qué?
2. ayudar a ti la última vez que mudaste *(you moved)*: ¿quién?
3. tú prestar algo a un(a) amigo(a) o hermano(a) recientemente: ¿qué?
4. tú traer a tus amigos cuando tuvieron una cena en casa: ¿qué?
5. mandar a ti flores u otro regalo durante el año pasado: ¿quién?
6. decir a ti unos chismes súper interesantes recientemente: ¿quién?

>> Gramática útil 4

Making comparisons: Comparatives and superlatives

AR MODA

¡Canasta!

LOS BOLSOS DE MIMBRE, RAFIA Y
CUERDA SON EL ACCESORIO BÁSICO
DEL VERANO, TANTO PARA IR A LA
PISCINA COMO SI SALES DE NOCHE

FOTOS: **GEMA LÓPEZ** ESTILISMO: **JUAN ANTONIO FRÍAS**

Revista de Ana Rosa; Photo de Gema Lopez

> Can you find the comparative words in this text? Are they making an equal or unequal comparison?

Cómo usarlo

LO BÁSICO

Comparatives compare two or more objects. *Superlatives* indicate that one object exceeds or stands above all others. In English we use *more* and *less* with adjectives, adverbs, nouns, and verbs to make comparisons, and we also add *-er* to the end of most one- or two-syllable adjectives: *more expensive, cheaper*. To form superlatives we use *most / least* with adjectives or add *-est* to the end of most one- or two-syllable adjectives: *the most expensive, the cheapest*.

1. Comparatives in Spanish use **más** *(more)* and **menos** *(less)* to make comparisons between people, actions, and things. **Más** and **menos** can be used with nouns, adjectives, verbs, and adverbs.

Nouns:	Hay **más libros** en esta tienda que en aquélla.
	*There are **more books** in this store than in that one.*
Adjectives:	Este libro es **menos interesante** que ése.
	*This book is **less interesting** than that one.*
Verbs:	Yo **leo menos** que él.
	*I **read less** than he (does).*
Adverbs:	Él lee **más lentamente** que yo.
	*He reads **more slowly** than I (do).*

2. **Superlative forms** indicate that something exceeds all others: *extremely, the most, the least.*

Este libro es **interesantísimo**. *This book is **really interesting**.*
Es **el más interesante** de todos. *It's the **most interesting** of all of them.*

Cómo formarlo

1. **Regular comparatives.** Comparisons can be *equal* (as many as) or *unequal* (more than, less than). Comparative forms can be used with nouns, adjectives, adverbs, and verbs.

> Notice that of all the words used in these comparative forms (**tanto, tan, más, menos, como**, and **que**), only **tanto** changes to reflect number and gender.

	Equal comparisons	Unequal comparisons
noun	**tanto** + noun + **como**	**más / menos** + noun + **que**
	(**Tanto** agrees with the noun.)	(**Más / menos** do not agree with the noun.)
	Tengo **tanto dinero como** tú.	Tengo **más dinero que** tú.
	Tengo **tantas tarjetas de crédito como** tú.	Tengo **menos tarjetas de crédito que** tú.
adjective	**tan** + adjective + **como**	**más / menos** + adjective + **que**
	Este reloj es **tan caro como** ése.	Este reloj es **más caro que** ése, pero es **menos caro que** aquél.
verb	verb + **tanto como**	verb + **más / menos** + **que**
	Compro tanto como tú.	Ella **compra menos que** yo, pero él **compra más que** yo.
adverb	**tan** + adverb + **como**	**más / menos** + adverb + **que**
	Pago mis cuentas **tan rápidamente como** tú.	Ella paga sus cuentas **más rápidamente que** yo, pero él paga **menos rápidamente que** yo.

2. **Irregular comparatives.** Some adjectives and adverbs have irregular comparative forms.

- Adjectives

> **Menor** and **mayor** are usually used to refer to people, although they can be used in place of **más grande (mayor)** and **más pequeño (menor)** when referring to objects. If you wish to say that one object is *older* or *newer* than another, use **más viejo** or **más nuevo**.

bueno → mejor:	Este libro es **bueno**, pero ese libro es **mejor**.
malo → peor:	Esta tienda es **mala**, pero esa tienda es **peor**.
joven → menor:	Los dos somos **jóvenes**, pero Remedios es **menor** que yo.
viejo → mayor:	Martín no es **viejo**, pero es **mayor** que Remedios.

- Adverbs

bien → mejor:	Lorena canta muy **bien**, pero Alfonso canta **mejor**.
mal → peor:	Nosotros bailamos **mal**, pero ellos bailan **peor**.

3. Superlatives

- To say that a person or thing is extreme in some way, add **-ísimo** to the end of an adjective. (If the adjective ends in a vowel, remove the vowel first.)

  fácil → **facilísimo** *(very easy)*   contento → **contentísimo** *(extremely happy)*

- To say that a person or thing is the *most . . .* or *the least . . .* use the following formula. (Do not use this formula with the **-ísimo** ending— choose one or the other!)

  article + noun + **más** / **menos** + adjective + **de**

  Roberto es **el estudiante más popular de** la universidad.

  Ellas son **las dependientes más trabajadoras del** almacén.

These superlative forms must change to reflect the gender and number of the nouns they modify: **unos aretes carísimos, unas camisetas baratísimas,** etc.

Notice that the accent is always on the first **í** of **-ísimo**. If the adjective has an accent, it is dropped when you add **-ísimo: difícil → dificilísimo**.

Notice that the article and the adjective must agree with the noun: **el estudiante popular, las dependientes trabajadoras**.

ACTIVIDADES

🔊 **13 El almacén Toneti** Escucha el anuncio sobre Toneti, un almacén grande.
Track 26 Pon una X al lado de cada objeto que se menciona. **¡OJO!** Asegúrate de que la descripción de cada objeto es la correcta.

1. _____ las mochilas más baratas
2. _____ las mochilas más grandes
3. _____ la selección más grande de zapatos
4. _____ los zapatos de tenis más populares
5. _____ los pantalones menos caros del centro
6. _____ los pantalones más caros del centro
7. _____ las camisetas de la más alta calidad
8. _____ las camisetas más bonitas del centro

14 La rebaja Haz comparaciones entre los precios de varias prendas de ropa y accesorios. Sigue el modelo.

MODELO   caro: las botas ($50) / los zapatos de tenis ($40)
Las botas son más caras que los zapatos de tenis.
Los zapatos de tenis son menos caros que las botas.

1. caro: los suéteres ($25) / las camisetas ($15)
2. caro: las camisetas ($15) / los vestidos ($50)
3. caro: las blusas ($30) / las camisetas ($15)
4. caro: las botas ($50) / los vestidos ($50)
5. barato: los vestidos ($50) / los suéteres ($25)
6. barato: las blusas ($30) / las botas ($50)
7. barato: los vestidos ($50) / los zapatos de tenis ($40)
8. barato: las camisetas ($15) / las blusas ($30)

15 **Las personas famosas** Haz comparaciones según el modelo.

MODELO   cantar: Taylor Swift o Rihanna
Taylor Swift canta peor que Rihanna.
O: *Taylor Swift canta mejor que Rihanna.*
O: *Taylor Swift canta tan bien como Rihanna.*

1. cantar: Lady Gaga o Katy Perry
2. bailar: Usher o Jay-Z
3. cocinar: tu mejor amigo(a) o tu madre
4. jugar tenis: Venus Williams o Serena Williams
5. jugar golf: Lorena Ochoa o tus padres
6. patinar sobre hielo: tú o tu mejor amigo(a)
7. nadar: tú o tu hermano(a)
8. jugar béisbol: Albert Pujols o Edgar Rentería
9. hacer esquí acuático: tú o tus amigos
10. tocar la guitarra: Jack White o Keith Richards

16 **En el centro comercial** Trabaja con un(a) compañero(a) de clase. Juntos miren el dibujo y hagan todas las comparaciones que puedan. Usen las palabras y expresiones útiles por lo menos una vez cada una.

Palabras y expresiones útiles: tanto como, más, menos, tan… como, mejor, peor, el (la) más… de todos, el (la) menos… de todos

Comparaciones: alto / delgado; hablar; hacer compras; comer

© Cengage Learning 2013

17 Nuestros amigos Trabaja con un(a) compañero(a) de clase. Primero piensen en seis personas que conozcan los dos. Luego hagan comparaciones según el modelo.

MODELOS   cómico
Sean es más cómico que Jason.
hablar rápido
Sean habla más rápido que Jason.

Palabras y frases útiles: cómico, joven, viejo, alto, extrovertido, introvertido, hablar rápido, comer despacio *(slowly)*, viajar frecuentemente, jugar tenis (u otro deporte) bien, correr rápido, entrenarse frecuentemente

Sonrisas

¿Por qué dice mamá que estoy más loca que un zapato cuando hago algo que no le gusta?

No sé. Es un dicho.

Ya sé, pero la verdad es que los zapatos no tienen nada de loco.

Tienes razón. Es un dicho ridiculísimo.

© Cengage Learning 2013

Expresión En grupos de tres o cuatro estudiantes, trabajen para completar la comparación **"Es más loco(a) que un…"** de una manera diferente. Después de crear una lista de posibilidades, escojan una y hagan una tira cómica semejante a la de arriba.

Perú

Christian Vinces/Shutterstock

Información general ▶

Nombre oficial: República del Perú

Población: 29.907.003

Capital: Lima (f. 1535) (8.000.000 hab.)

Otras ciudades importantes: Callao (2.000.000 hab.), Arequipa (1.300.000 hab.), Trujillo (1.000.000 hab.)

Moneda: nuevo sol

Idiomas: español y quechua (oficiales), aimara y otras lenguas indígenas

----
Mapa de Perú: Apéndice D

Although most reference books and written texts usually use just **Perú** to refer to the country, you will often hear native speakers say **el Perú**. This use of **el** sometimes occurs with **Ecuador** also.

Vale saber…

- La civilización incaica de Perú forma el más grande y poderoso (*powerful*) imperio de Sudamérica en la época prehispánica.

- Otra civilización importante fueron los nazcas, quienes hicieron dibujos en la tierra que sólo se pueden ver desde el aire. El origen y el objetivo de los más de 2000 km. de líneas son un misterio.

Joel Shawn/Shutterstock

- En 1532, Francisco Pizarro captura a Atahualpa, el último emperador inca. Francisco Pizarro funda la ciudad de Lima en 1535. En 1824, Perú gana la independencia de España.

- La mayoría de la población peruana habla español o quechua, las lenguas oficiales, pero también existe una variedad de lenguas nativas, de las cuales el quechua y el aimara son los idiomas más hablados.

Ecuador

Información general

Nombre oficial: República del Ecuador

Población: 14.790.608

Capital: Quito (f. 1556) (2.500.000 hab.)

Otras ciudades importantes: Guayaquil (2.200.000 hab.), Cuenca (460.000 hab.)

Moneda: dólar

Idiomas: español (oficial), quechua

Mapa de Ecuador: Apéndice D

Elena Kalistratova/iStockphoto

Vale saber…

- Ecuador toma su nombre de la línea ecuatorial que divide el globo en dos hemisferios: norte y sur.

- Quito forma parte del imperio incaico hasta la conquista de los españoles en 1533. Al ganar la independencia de España, Quito forma la federación la Gran Colombia con Colombia y Venezuela. En 1830, Quito deja la federación y cambia su nombre a la República del Ecuador.

- A 1.000 kilómetros de la costa ecuatoriana están las islas Galápagos, únicas por su belleza y su flora y fauna. Las condiciones naturales de las islas no han cambiado *(have not changed)* desde hace siglos, resultando en ecosistemas permanentes que permitieron a Charles Darwin desarrollar *(to develop)* su teoría de la evolución.

- Hoy día, los idiomas predominantes son el quechua, la lengua de los incas, y el español, la lengua que enseñan en las escuelas. Muchos ecuatorianos son perfectamente bilingües.

Michael Zysman/Shutterstock

El algodón orgánico

Perú es un país con una industria algodonera importante, un sector principal de la economía del país. Algunos consideran las finas fibras del algodón peruano las mejores del mundo. El cultivo del algodón forma una parte fundamental en la historia de la agricultura peruana. Los agricultores peruanos, localizados en la costa del Pacífico y en los bosques tropicales de la Amazonia, han heredado *(have inherited)* una variedad de técnicas indígenas ancestrales y completamente orgánicas.

El movimiento "verde" ha propulsado el mundo de la moda hacia la producción de materiales orgánicos. El cultivo orgánico del algodón en Perú ha atraído *(has attracted)* la atención de grandes compañías internacionales como Tommy Hilfiger y Nike. Este interés comercial ha abierto *(has opened)* una gran cantidad de posibilidades para aquellos agricultores peruanos que siguen cultivando algodón de una manera natural.

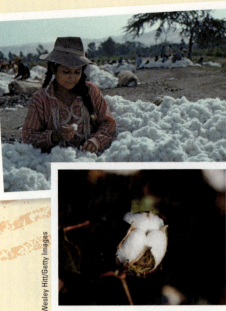

Eye Ubiquitous/Glow Images

Wesley Hitt/Getty Images

Otavalo, el mercado inolvidable

Ecuador es famoso por sus tejidos de lana de llama y alpaca, dos animales de la región andina. En Otavalo, un pueblo a cincuenta millas al norte de Quito, existe un mercado artesanal que se conoce como la "Plaza de los Ponchos".

La gente viene de toda la provincia vestidos en sus trajes típicos indígenas: los hombres en sus pantalones blancos y sombreros negros y las mujeres en sus blusas bordadas, faldas, chales, collares y pulseras. En cientos de puestos *(stalls)*, ponen a la venta sombreros estilo Panamá, suéteres, blusas bordadas, sacos gruesos de lana tejidos a mano, gorros, guantes, vestidos, bufandas y las famosas fajas *(sashes)* que usan los indígenas como cinturones. Igual se venden productos artesanales en madera y cerámica, tejidos de todo tipo, ponchos, piedras semipreciosas, manteles y mucho más.

La feria *(fair)* dura hasta que baja el sol. Es un espectáculo vibrante, colorido y lleno de vida, ¡tal como las prendas de ropa otavaleñas!

Pictor Pictor/Photolibrary

La información general

1. ¿Qué civilización de Perú es una de las más poderosas de Sudamérica en la época prehispánica?
2. ¿Qué civilización deja unas líneas misteriosas que solo se pueden ver desde el aire?
3. ¿Quién es el último emperador inca en Perú? ¿Quién es el español que conquista el imperio incaico en Perú y funda la ciudad de Lima?
4. ¿Con qué otros dos países forma Quito la Gran Colombia?
5. ¿De dónde toma su nombre Ecuador?
6. ¿Qué islas famosas permiten a Charles Darwin desarrollar su teoría de la evolución?

El tema de las compras

1. ¿Qué producto peruano les interesa a los comerciantes internacionales?
2. ¿Qué técnicas han heredado los agricultores peruanos?
3. ¿Por qué producto es famoso Ecuador?
4. ¿Cuáles son tres prendas de ropa que puedes comprar en la Plaza de los Ponchos? ¿Tres accesorios?

🌐 **¿QUIERES SABER MÁS?**

Revisa y rellena la tabla que empezaste al principio del capítulo. Luego, escoge un tema para investigar en línea y prepárate para compartir la información con la clase. También puedes escoger de las palabras clave a continuación o en **www.cengagebrain.com**.

Palabras clave: (Perú) los incas, los aimaraes, el Inti Raymi, Machu Picchu, Mario Vargas Llosa; **(Ecuador)** José de Sucre, la Gran Colombia, la línea ecuatorial, Rosalía Arteaga, Oswaldo Guayasamín

🌐 **Tú en el mundo hispano** Para explorar oportunidades de usar el español para estudiar o hacer trabajos voluntarios o aprendizajes en Perú y Ecuador, sigue los enlaces en **www.cengagebrain.com**.

🎞 **Ritmos del mundo hispano** Sigue los enlaces en **www.cengagebrain.com** para escuchar música de Perú y Ecuador.

A leer

ESTRATEGIA

Using background knowledge to anticipate content

As you learned when watching this chapter's video segment, you can often use prior knowledge to help you understand the content of authentic language, whether it is a video or a reading. When you think about the topic of a piece and compare it with what you already know, you prepare yourself to comprehend more than you might think is possible.

1 Las siguientes palabras están en el artículo de la página 299, que trata de la popularidad de los jeans por todo el mundo. ¿A qué palabras inglesas son similares?

1. overoles
2. cachemira
3. apliques

2 El artículo que vas a leer en este capítulo trata de la influencia de los jeans en la moda internacional. Antes de leer el artículo, escribe de cinco a siete palabras que tú asocies con los jeans y con la mezclilla.

3 Las siguientes frases del artículo contienen palabras que no conoces. A ver si puedes hacer correspondencia entre las frases de las dos columnas para adivinar el sentido de las palabras **en negrilla**.

1. _____ algo moderno, permanente y **novedoso**…
2. _____ El jean es muy dúctil… lo puedes **doblar**…
3. _____ puedes **guardarlo** sin que ocupe mucho espacio
4. _____ Hace ver **varonil** a cualquier hombre.

a. *you can **store** it without it taking up much space*
b. *It makes any man look **manly**.*
c. *something modern, permanent, and **novel**.*
d. *A pair of jeans is very flexible . . . you can **fold** it . . .*

4 Lee el siguiente artículo de un periódico ecuatoriano. ¿Hay palabras que escribiste para la **Actividad 2** en el artículo?

LECTURA

El jean impone su encanto

Los atractivos del jean han sobrepasado[1] los límites del tiempo y de las fronteras. Los clásicos pantalones jeans y los overoles todavía son populares y, además, les dan la posibilidad a sus usuarios de combinarlos de mil maneras. Se pueden usar hasta en ocasiones más elegantes si se usan con una chaqueta o con una blusa de seda o un saco de cachemira. Los beneficios de esta tela son innumerables. Por ejemplo, es común ver carteras de jean, zapatos con tacones de mezclilla y gorras, chalecos, chompas[2], sombreros, mochilas, monederos y otros accesorios de moda que rompen con los diseños tradicionales y se modernizan al usar esta tela tan tradicional y moderna a la vez.

Corbis/Glow Images

Pero, ¿qué es lo que puede ofrecer el jean a los hombres y a las mujeres de esta época? Escuchemos sus testimonios.

"Usar jean es sentirse más joven, a pesar de la edad real que tengas".

"El jean es muy dúctil, por lo que lo puedes doblar y guardarlo sin que ocupe mucho espacio".

"Es resistente a cualquier trato".

"Se lava y sigue como si nada…"

"Puedes llevar libros o bloques de cemento, sabe cuál es su función".

"El cuero es para gente mayor. El jean siempre será[3] joven".

"Hace ver varonil a cualquier hombre".

"Es de los materiales más durables y que además no pasa de moda. Un jean puedes llevarlo años y mientras más rasgado, más en onda[4]".

PhotoNAN/Shutterstock

"Los brazaletes de jean son súper chéveres[5]".

"El jean es discreto cuando debe serlo, pero también sensual cuando le has dado ese papel[6]".

"Sobre el jean puedes poner cualquier tipo de apliques…"

"Es de lo más práctico para vestir. Sólo necesitas un pantalón y falda y la mitad de tus problemas están resueltos[7]".

[1]**han**… *have surpassed* [2]**suéteres** [3]**va a ser** [4]**más rasgado**… *the more ripped, the more in style* [5]*cool*
[6]**le**… *you have given it that role* [7]*solved*

Adapted from "El jean impone su encanto," from El Comercio, Familia Magazine, Numero 643, February 8 1998, Ano XII, pg. 27. Used with approval from El Comercio.

5 Vuelve a la lista de palabras y asociaciones que hiciste para la **Actividad 2.** ¿Te ayudó pensar en este tema antes de leer el artículo? ¿Pudiste predecir algunas de las ideas del texto? ¿Por qué sí o por qué no?

6 Trabaja con un grupo de tres o cuatro estudiantes. Juntos contesten las siguientes preguntas sobre la lectura.

1. ¿Con qué prendas de ropa sugiere el autor combinar los jeans?
2. ¿Qué otras prendas o accesorios son de mezclilla?
3. Hagan una lista de por lo menos cinco aspectos positivos de los jeans que se mencionan en los "testimonios".

7 Haz una encuesta sobre las prendas de ropa y accesorios de mezclilla.

1. Pasa por el salón de clase y pregúntales a tus compañeros las siguientes preguntas.
   - ¿Cuántos pares de jeans tienes? ¿De qué marcas *(brands)*?
   - ¿Tienes otras prendas o accesorios mezclilla? ¿Cuáles?
2. Escribe las respuestas.
3. Después, compara tus resultados con la clase entera. Haz un resumen para decir cuáles son las marcas de jeans más populares y también los accesorios de mezclilla más usados. ¿Son populares los jeans y los accesorios de mezclilla contigo y con tus compañeros de clase?
4. Con un(a) compañero(a) de clase, escriban una cita *(quotation)* como las de la lectura para expresar sus propios sentimientos sobre los jeans.

8 En la opinión de la gente de otros países, los jeans son un símbolo de Estados Unidos (junto con la hamburguesa y los autos grandes). Hablen en grupos sobre las siguientes preguntas. Luego, cada persona debe escribir un resumen corto de la conversación.

1. ¿Hay una diferencia entre una prenda de ropa muy popular y una prenda de ropa "tradicional"? Por ejemplo, en Perú y Ecuador, la ropa tradicional generalmente se refiere a la ropa que usa la gente indígena de la región andina. Los peruanos que viven en las ciudades usan estilos más modernos e internacionales.
2. En la opinión de ustedes, ¿existe una "ropa tradicional" de Estados Unidos"? (Piensen en las regiones geográficas y en los grupos étnicos del país.) Si existe, ¿cómo es?
3. Cuando la gente de otros países piensa en "la ropa típica" de Estados Unidos, ¿a qué tipo de ropa se refieren? En la opinión de ustedes, ¿es correcta o falsa esta imagen del estilo estadounidense?

>> Antes de escribir

ESTRATEGIA

Revising — Editing your freewriting

In **Chapter 7** you learned how to use freewriting as a way of generating a first draft. Once you have written freely, it's important to edit your work to tighten it up, make it more interesting, and make sure it's all relevant. When you edit your freewriting ask yourself: Is this information necessary? Would it be better placed somewhere else? Is there information missing? Can I tighten this up by omitting words and/or sentences?

1 Vas a escribir una descripción de lo que tienes en tu armario, qué artículos te gustan más y por qué. Antes de empezar, escribe tres categorías (o más) de artículos que contiene. Después añade tres artículos para cada categoría. Luego, pon un adjetivo al lado de cada de los nueve artículos (en total).

>> Composición

2 Escribe una descripción de los artículos en tu armario, usando las categorías, artículos y adjetivos que anotaste en la **Actividad 1.** Habla de las categorías y los artículos en cada categoría. ¿Cuál te gusta más y por qué? Escribe sin detenerse y sin pensar demasiado en la gramática, el contenido o la ortografía.

>> Después de escribir

3 Vuelve a tu descripción. Mírala otra vez y contesta las preguntas de la Estrategia. ¿Cómo quieres revisar la información y organización de tu descripción? Analízala con cuidado y escribe la nueva (y probablemente más corta) versión.

4 Mira la nueva versión de tu descripción. Revísala, usando la siguiente lista.

- ¿Está completa la descripción?
- ¿Usaste las formas comparativas y superlativas correctamente?
- ¿Usaste bien los verbos y los tiempos verbales?
- ¿Hay errores de puntuación o de ortografía?

Vocabulario

Las prendas de ropa *Articles of clothing*

el abrigo *coat*
la blusa *blouse*
las botas *boots*
los calcetines *socks*
la camisa *shirt*
la camiseta *t-shirt*
el chaleco *vest*

la chaqueta *jacket (outdoor non-suit coat)*
la falda *skirt*
el impermeable *raincoat*
los jeans *jeans*
los pantalones *pants*
los pantalones cortos *shorts*

el saco *jacket, sports coat*
la sudadera *sweatsuit, track suit*
el suéter *sweater*
el traje *suit*
el traje de baño *bathing suit*
el vestido *dress*

Los zapatos *Shoes*

las botas *boots*
las sandalias *sandals*
los zapatos *shoes*

los zapatos de tacón alto *high-heeled shoes*
los zapatos de tenis *tennis shoes*

Las telas *Fabrics*

Está hecho(a) de... *It's made (out) of . . .*
Están hechos(as) de... *They're made (out) of . . .*
  el algodón *cotton*
  el cuero / la piel *leather*
  la lana *wool*
  el lino *linen*
  la mezclilla *denim*
  la seda *silk*

a cuadros *plaid*
a rayas / rayado(a) *striped*
bordado(a) *embroidered*
de lunares *polka-dotted*
de un solo color *solid (color)*
estampado(a) *print*

Los accesorios *Accessories*

la bolsa *purse*
la bufanda *scarf*
la cartera *wallet*
el cinturón *belt*

las gafas de sol *sunglasses*
la gorra *cap*
los guantes *gloves*
el sombrero *hat*

Las joyas *Jewelry*

el anillo *ring*
los aretes / los pendientes *earrings*
el brazalete / la pulsera *bracelet*
la cadena *chain*

el collar *necklace*
el reloj *watch*
el oro *gold*
la plata *silver*

La moda *Fashion*

(no) estar de moda *(not) to be fashionable*

pasado(a) de moda *out of style*

Ir de compras *Going shopping*

El (La) dependiente *The clerk*
¿Cuál es su talla? *What is your size?*
¿En qué puedo servirle? *How can I help you?*
Es muy barato. *It's very inexpensive.*
Está a muy buen precio. *It's a very good price.*
Está en venta. *It's on sale.*
Está rebajado(a). *It's reduced / on sale.*

¿Es un regalo? *Is it a gift?*
de buena (alta) calidad *of good (high) quality*
el descuento *discount*
la oferta especial *special offer*

El (La) cliente *The customer*

¿Cuánto cuesta(n)? *How much does it (do they) cost?*

Es (demasiado) caro. *It's (too) expensive.*

¿Lo (La / Los / Las) tiene en una talla…? *Do you have it / them in a size . . .?*

Me queda bien / mal. *It fits nicely / badly.*

Me queda grande / apretado(a). *It's too big / too tight.*

Voy a llevármelo(la / los / las). *I'm going to take it / them.*

Voy a probármelo(la / los / las). *I'm going to try it / them on.*

Métodos de pago *Forms of payment*

¿Cómo desea pagar? *How do you wish to pay?*

Al contado. / En efectivo. *In cash.*

Con cheque. *By check.*

Con cheque de viajero. *With a traveler's check.*

Con un préstamo. *With a loan.*

Con tarjeta de crédito. *With a credit card.*

Con tarjeta de débito. *With a debit card.*

Los números mayores de 100 *Numbers above 100*

cien *one hundred*

ciento uno *one hundred and one*

ciento dos, etc. *one hundred and two, etc.*

doscientos(as) *two hundred*

trescientos(as) *three hundred*

cuatrocientos(as) *four hundred*

quinientos(as) *five hundred*

seiscientos(as) *six hundred*

setecientos(as) *seven hundred*

ochocientos(as) *eight hundred*

novecientos(as) *nine hundred*

mil *one thousand*

dos mil *two thousand*

tres mil *three thousand*

cuatro mil *four thousand*

cinco mil *five thousand*

diez mil *ten thousand*

cien mil *one hundred thousand*

un millón *one million*

dos millones, etc. *two million, etc.*

Comparaciones

más [noun / adjective / adverb] **que** *more [noun / adjective / adverb] than*

menos [noun / adjective / adverb] **que** *less [noun / adjective / adverb] than*

[verb] **más / menos que** [verb] *more / less than*

tan [adjective / adverb] **como** *as [adjective / adverb] as*

tanto(a) [noun] **como** *as much [noun] as*

tantos(as) [noun] **como** *as many [noun] as*

[verb] **tanto como** [verb] *as much as*

mayor *older; more*

mejor *better*

menor *younger; less*

peor *worse*

Pronombres de complemento indirecto

me *to / for me*

te *to / for you (fam. sing.)*

le *to / for you (form. sing.), him, her, it*

nos *to / for us*

os *to / for you (fam. pl.)*

les *to / for you (form., pl.), them*

Pronombres preposicionales

mí *me*

ti *you (fam. sing.)*

usted *you (form. sing.)*

él *him*

ella *her*

nosotros(as) *us*

vosotros(as) *you (fam. pl.)*

ustedes *you (form. pl.)*

ellos *them (male or mixed group)*

ellas *them (female)*

conmigo *with me*

contigo *with you*

Verbos

andar *to walk*

ayudar *to help*

conseguir (i, i) *to get, to obtain*

mandar *to send, to order*

morirse (ue, u) *to die*

prestar *to loan, to lend*

regalar *to give a gift*

sonreír (i, i) *to smile*

sugerir (ie, i) *to suggest*

Repaso y preparación

Complete these activities to check your understanding of the new grammar points in **Chapter 8** before you move on to **Chapter 9**.

The answers to the activities in this section can be found in **Appendix B**.

Preterite tense of more irregular verbs (p. 280) and preterite tense of -ir stem-changing verbs (p. 283)

1 Completa las oraciones para saber qué pasó cuando David se reunió con su viejo amigo Ricardo ayer.

1. _____ (saber / yo) ayer que mi viejo amigo Ricardo está aquí de visita por una semana. Lo llamé y nosotros 2. _____ (hacer) planes para hoy a las nueve de la mañana. Él 3. _____ (sugerir) un restaurante para la reunión, pero yo 4. _____ (preferir) ir a un café. Después de que el camarero nos 5. _____ (servir) el café, Ricardo me 6. _____ (decir) que él 7. _____ (querer) llamarme pero no 8. _____ (poder) porque 9. _____ (tener) el viejo número. Entonces me 10. _____ (pedir) el nuevo número y lo 11. _____ (poner) en su lista de contactos.

Salimos del café y 12. _____ (andar) por el centro por unas horas, hablando todo el rato. 13. _____ (reírse) y 14. _____ (divertirse) mucho y el tiempo pasó demasiado rápidamente. Al mediodía 15. _____ (despedirse) y 16. _____ (decir) adiós hasta la próxima vez.

Indirect object pronouns (p. 285)

2 Completa las oraciones con los pronombres indirectos correctos para saber qué recibieron las diferentes personas como regalo.

1. Mis padres _____ regalaron unas botas de cuero a mí y a mi hermana.
2. Tu novio _____ regaló una bufanda de seda y unos aretes de oro.
3. A mis primos sus padres _____ regalaron unas gafas de sol buenísimas.
4. Mi amiga _____ regaló una bolsa de piel.
5. A Manuel sus hermanas _____ regalaron un abrigo nuevo.

Comparatives and superlatives (p. 289)

3 Completa las oraciones con formas comparativas (1–4) y superlativas (5–6), según el contexto.

1. Yo tengo _____ zapatos _____ tú. (=)
2. Ella compra _____ joyas _____ nosotras. (>)
3. Esta camisa es _____ barata _____ ésa. (<)
4. Estas cadenas son _____ caras _____ estas pulseras. (=)
5. Este collar es _____ _____ bonito de todos. (>)
6. Ella es la dependiente _____ popular de la tienda. (>)

Preparación para el Capítulo 9

Complete these activities to review some previously learned grammatical structures that will be helpful when you learn the new grammar in **Chapter 9**.

In addition, be sure to reread **Chapter 8: Gramática útil 1, 2,** and **3** before moving on to the new **Chapter 9** grammar sections.

Preterite tense of regular verbs and some common irregular verbs (Chapter 7)

4 Completa las oraciones con la forma correcta del verbo indicado en el pretérito.

1. Tú _____ (comprar) la falda.
2. Yo _____ (ver) una blusa bonita.
3. El traje _____ (estar) en venta.
4. Ella me _____ (traer) otra talla.
5. Nosotros _____ (ir) a otra tienda de ropa.
6. Tus abuelos te _____ (dar) los aretes.
7. Tú _____ (hacer) esta gorra de lana.
8. Él _____ (escribir) el nombre de la tienda.

Direct object pronouns (Chapter 7)

5 Di si las personas indicadas compraron (o no) la prenda de ropa o accesorio. Sigue el modelo.

MODELO Marta
Marta no las compró.

1.

Delfina

2.

Diego y Eduardo

3.

tú

4.

yo

5.

nosotros

6.

usted

Reflexive verbs (Chapter 4)

6 Di qué se pusieron las personas indicadas ayer.

1. yo / un abrigo
2. ellos / unas sandalias
3. tú / un chaleco
4. nosotros / unos jeans
5. ella / una bufanda
6. ustedes / un impermeable

¿Qué te apetece?

SABORES

La comida da sabor (*flavor*) a las reuniones entre familia y amigos y juega un papel integral en todas las culturas del mundo.

A ti, ¿te importa mucho, bastante o poco lo que comes todos los días? ¿Comes para vivir o vives para comer?

Communication

By the end of this chapter you will be able to

- talk about food and cooking
- shop for food
- order in a restaurant
- talk about what you used to eat and cook
- say what you do for others

Ron Giling/PhotoLibrary/Sabores

Un viaje por Bolivia y Paraguay

Bolivia y Paraguay comparten una frontera. Son los únicos países de Sudamérica que no tienen ni una costa pacífica ni una atlántica. Bolivia es mucho más montañoso que Paraguay, que tiene un clima más tropical y húmedo *(wet)*.

País / Área	Tamaño y fronteras	Sitios de interés
Bolivia 1.084.390 km^2	casi tres veces el área de Montana; fronteras con Argentina, Brasil, Chile, Paraguay y Perú	el lago Titicaca, Tiahuanaco, el salar *(salt flat)* de Uyuni, las ciudades de La Paz y Sucre, los Parques Nacionales Amboró y Noel Kempff
Paraguay 397.300 km^2	un poco más pequeño que California; fronteras con Argentina, Bolivia y Brasil	los ríos Paraguay y Paraná, la presa *(dam)* Itaipú, la región del Chaco, las misiones jesuitas, la ciudad de Asunción

¿Qué sabes? Di si las siguientes oraciones son ciertas (**C**) o falsas (**F**).

1. Bolivia es más grande que California.
2. Paraguay tiene edificios que fueron construidos por los misionarios jesuitas.
3. Paraguay tiene un lago y unos ríos muy grandes.
4. Bolivia y Paraguay son sitios buenos para excursiones al mar.

Lo que sé y lo que quiero aprender Completa la tabla del **Apéndice A**. Escribe algunos datos que **ya sabes** sobre estos países en la columna **Lo que sé**. Después, añade algunos temas que **quieres aprender** a la columna **Lo que quiero aprender**. Guarda la tabla para usarla otra vez en la sección **¡Explora y exprésate!** en la página 335.

Cultures

By the end of this chapter you will have explored

- facts about Bolivia and Paraguay
- **la quinua**, a special food from Bolivia
- **el tereré**, a social tea tradition from Paraguay
- the metric system

>> Vocabulario útil 1

© Cengage Learning 2013

CHELA: Quedamos en vernos a las ocho en punto en el **restaurante**. No llegó hasta las ocho y media. Cuando llegó, no ofreció explicaciones y no se disculpó. El **camarero** nos trajo los **menús** pero en ese momento sonó el celular de Sergio. Habló por teléfono —no sé con quién— por diez minutos enteros mientras yo esperaba. Por fin colgó y **ordenamos**. Yo pedí el **pollo asado** y él pidió el **lomo de res**.

Usage and meaning of **bocadillo** and **sandwich** vary throughout the Spanish-speaking world. In general, a **bocadillo** is made with a crusty bread similar to the French baguette. A **sandwich** is typically made of pre-sliced loaf-style bread.

Food terms vary tremendously from country to country and region to region. For example, *cake* can be **pastel** or **torta**; *pork* can be **puerco** or **cerdo**; *banana* can be **plátano**, **banana**, or **guineo**. When you travel, be prepared to come across a variety of foods that you don't recognize and different names for foods that you do.

>> En el restaurante

Cómo ordenar y pagar

Camarero(a), ¿me puede traer el menú?	*Waiter (Waitress), could you please bring me the menu?*
Soy vegetariano(a) estricto(a).	*I'm a vegan.*
¿Me puede recomendar algo ligero / algo fuerte / algo vegetariano / algo vegano / la especialidad de la casa?	*Can you recommend something light / something filling / something vegetarian / something vegan / the house specialty?*
Para plato principal, voy a pedir…	*For the main course, I would like to order . . .*
Para tomar, quiero…	*To drink, I want . . .*
De postre, voy a pedir…	*For dessert, I would like to order . . .*
¿Me puede traer la cuenta, por favor?	*Can you bring me the check, please?*
¿Cuánto debo dejar de propina?	*How much should I leave as a tip?*

With a partner, go through all the items on the menu on page 309 and decide whether they are masculine or feminine. Check your answers in the **Vocabulario** section on pages 342–343.

Green beans are referred to as **habichuelas** only in the Caribbean. In Spain, they are referred to as **judías verdes**, and in other countries you might see them referred to as **vainas verdes**.

EL MENÚ

Desayuno

cereal	*cereal*
huevos revueltos	*scrambled eggs*
huevos estrellados	*eggs, sunnyside up*
pan tostado	*toast*

Almuerzo

Ensaladas

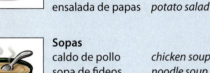

ensalada mixta	*mixed salad*
ensalada de lechuga y tomate	*lettuce and tomato salad*
ensalada de papas	*potato salad*

Sopas

caldo de pollo	*chicken soup*
sopa de fideos	*noodle soup*
gazpacho	*cold, tomato-based soup (Spain)*

Sándwiches (o bocadillos)

sándwich de jamón y queso con aguacate	*ham and cheese sandwich with avocado*
hamburguesa	*hamburger*
hamburguesa con queso	*cheeseburger*
perro caliente	*hot dog*
...con papas fritas	*...with French fries*

Bebidas y refrescos

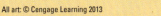

café	*coffee*
té o té helado	*hot or iced tea*
agua mineral	*mineral water*
jugo de fruta	*fruit juice*
leche	*milk*
limonada	*lemonade*
vino blanco / tinto	*white / red wine*
cerveza	*beer*

A la carta

Vegetales

frijoles refritos	*refried beans*
zanahorias	*carrots*
bróculi	*broccoli*
espárragos	*asparagus*
guisantes	*peas*
habichuelas	*green beans*

Postres

flan	*custard*
galletas	*cookies*
pastel	*cake*
helado de vainilla / chocolate	*vanilla / chocolate ice cream*

Frutas

naranja	*orange*
manzana	*apple*
plátano	*banana*
fresas	*strawberries*
uvas	*grapes*
melón	*melon*

Platos principales

Carnes

lomo de res	*prime rib*
bistec	*steak*
chuleta de puerco	*pork chop*
guisado	*beef stew*
pollo asado	*roasted chicken*
pollo frito	*fried chicken*
arroz con pollo	*chicken with rice*

Mariscos

almejas	*clams*
camarones	*shrimp*
langosta	*lobster*

Pescados

atún	*tuna*
salmón	*salmon*
bacalao	*cod*
trucha	*trout*

ACTIVIDADES

1 **¡Tengo hambre!** Tienes mucha hambre. ¿Qué comes y bebes en las siguientes situaciones?

1. Te despertaste tarde y no tienes mucho tiempo para desayunar antes de ir a la oficina.
2. Acabas de correr cinco millas en una carrera para una organización benéfica *(charity)*.
3. Estás en una cita con una persona que es vegetariana y quieres dar una buena impresión.
4. Es tu cumpleaños y estás en un restaurante elegante con varios amigos para celebrarlo.
5. Tu jefe quiere salir a comer contigo para hablar sobre algunos problemas de la oficina.
6. Sales a cenar con tus padres para su aniversario.
7. Estás solo(a) en tu casa o apartamento.

2 **El menú** Con un(a) compañero(a), preparen un menú para las siguientes personas. Incluyan tres comidas y también algunas meriendas *(snacks)* si creen que le hacen falta a esa persona. Incluyan todos los detalles necesarios, incluso lo que debe tomar esa persona con cada comida o merienda.

1. una persona que está a dieta
2. una persona muy activa que necesita muchas calorías
3. una pareja que sale a cenar para celebrar su aniversario
4. un estudiante universitario que no tiene mucho dinero
5. una persona que acaba de despertarse y va a correr un maratón hoy

3 **En el restaurante** En grupos de tres, representen una de las siguientes situaciones. Pueden preparar un guión antes de representar la situación a la clase.

Situación 1: Es el cumpleaños de tu novio(a) y están en un restaurante elegante para la celebración. El (La) camarero(a) es un actor (actriz) a quien no le gusta su trabajo y en realidad no debe servirle comida a la gente.

Situación 2: Tu jefe te invita a cenar. Estás un poco nervioso(a) porque no sabes de lo que quiere hablar. El (La) camarero(a) es un(a) viejo(a) amigo(a) tuyo(a) y te hace muchas recomendaciones, pero tú no tienes hambre y no quieres lo que te sugiere.

¡Fíjate! El sistema métrico

Todos los países de habla española usan el sistema métrico para hacer medidas *(measurements)* como volumen, peso y longitud *(length)*. En el **Vocabulario útil 2**, vas a aprender las palabras **kilo**, **medio kilo** y **litro**. Aquí tienes las palabras para otras medidas métricas. (Nota que las medidas métricas se basan en unidades de un mil.)

Volumen   Para indicar el volumen de algo, como agua en botella u otro líquido.

	cuartos	pintas	tazas	onzas *(ounces)* líquidas
1 **litro** (1.000 **mililitros**)	1,06	2,11	4,23	33,81
medio litro (500 **mililitros**)	0,53	1,06	2,16	16,91
cuarto litro (250 **mililitros**)	0,27	0,53	1,06	8,45

Peso   Para indicar cuánto algo pesa; por ejemplo, doce naranjas o un pedazo de carne.

	libras	onzas
1 **kilo** (kilogramo) (1.000 **gramos**)	2,20	35,27
medio kilo (500 **gramos**)	1,10	17,64
cuarto kilo (250 **gramos**)	0,55	8,82

Longitud de cosas ordinarias   Para indicar las dimensiones lineares, como un mantel para una mesa.

	yardas	pies *(feet)*	pulgadas *(inches)*
1 **metro** (100 **centímetros**, 1.000 **milímetros**)	1,09	3,28	39,37

Distancia y longitud de cosas grandes   Para indicar las distancias y las dimensiones lineares de cosas más grandes.

	millas *(miles)*	yardas	pies
1 **kilómetro** (1.000 **metros**)	0,62	1.083,61	39,37

Práctica   Con un(a) compañero(a), hagan conversiones entre las cantidades indicadas. Usen una calculadora o una aplicación si necesitan ayuda y redondeen *(round up)* al número entero más cercano *(round up to the nearest whole number)*.

1. 2 litros = _____ onzas líquidas
2. 5 litros = _____ pintas
3. 3 kilos = _____ libras
4. 125 gramos = _____ onzas
5. 12 metros = _____ yardas
6. 200 centímetros = _____ pulgadas
7. 5 kilómetros = _____ millas
8. 2 metros = _____ pies

CHELA: Empezamos a comer. Inmediatamente, Sergio llamó al camarero. ¡Pobre camarero! Sergio fue muy descortés con él. Le dijo que la **sopa** estaba **congelada**, que el **bróculi** no estaba **fresco** ¡y que la **carne** estaba **cruda**! Mandó toda la comida a la cocina. ¡Qué vergüenza! No sabía qué hacer. Mientras esperábamos sus platos, **se enfriaron** los míos.

>> Las recetas

Los ingredientes
el aceite de oliva *olive oil*
el ajo *garlic*
el azúcar *sugar*
la cebolla *onion*
la harina *flour*
la mantequilla *butter*
la sal y la pimienta *salt and pepper*
la mayonesa *mayonnaise*
la mostaza *mustard*
el vinagre *vinegar*

Las medidas *Measurements*
un kilo *kilo (approximately 2.2 lbs.)*
medio kilo *half a kilo*
la libra *pound*

el litro *liter*
el galón *gallon*
la cucharada *tablespoonful*
la cucharadita *teaspoonful*
la docena *dozen*
el paquete *package*
el pedazo *piece, slice*
el trozo *chunk, piece*

La preparación
a fuego suave / lento *at low heat*
al gusto *to taste*
al hilo *stringed*
al horno *roasted (in the oven)*
a la parrilla *grilled*
al vapor *steamed*

congelado(a) *frozen*
crudo(a) *raw*
dorado(a) *golden; browned*
fresco(a) *fresh*
frito(a) *fried*
hervido(a) *boiled*
molido(a) *crushed, ground*
picante *spicy*

agregar, añadir *to add*
calentar (ie) (en el microondas) *to heat (in the microwave)*
cocer (ue) *to cook (on the stove)*
enfriarse *to get cold*
freír (i, i) *to fry*
hervir (ie, i) *to boil*
hornear *to bake in the oven*
mezclar *to mix*
pelar *to peel*
picar *to chop, mince*
unir *to mix together, incorporate*

© Cengage Learning 2013

4 **Picadillo boliviano** Lee la siguiente receta para un picadillo boliviano. Con un(a) compañero(a), contesten las siguientes preguntas para ver si entendieron las instrucciones.

PICADILLO

Ingredientes

15 papas peladas y cortadas al hilo
1/2 kg. de cadera de res
5 vainas de ají colorado molido y frito
2 cebollas
1 tomate
1 cucharadita de pimienta
1/4 cucharadita de comino
aceite
sal

Preparación

Pique la carne muy menuda, el tomate en cuadritos y la cebolla finamente picada. En una sartén con poco aceite, fría la cebolla hasta que esté transparente. Añada la pimienta, el comino, la sal al gusto y la carne. Cuando la carne esté dorada, agregue el tomate, deje cocer 5 minutos e incorpore el ají colorado y 1/2 taza de agua. Deje secar a fuego suave el guiso. Aparte fría las papas en abundante aceite caliente. En el momento de servir, una las papas y el guisado de carne. Mezcle bien.

© Cengage Learning 2013

Picadillo is a mincemeat, often spicy, that is typical of Latin America.

1. ¿Qué debes hacer con las quince papas?
2. ¿Qué debes hacer con la carne antes de freírla?
3. ¿Cómo debes cortar el tomate?
4. ¿Qué debes hacer con la cebolla?
5. ¿Qué le vas a añadir a la cebolla después de freírla?
6. ¿Cuándo puedes agregar el tomate?
7. Después de agregar el tomate, ¿qué más le tienes que añadir al guiso?
8. Mientras el guiso se seca a fuego suave, ¿qué debes hacer con las papas?
9. ¿Qué debes hacer al final?

5 **Telecocina** Escoge una receta sencilla, como la del picadillo boliviano, y escríbela en una tarjeta. ¡Vas a explicarle a la clase cómo preparar tu plato favorito! Pero lo vas a tener que hacer sin estufa ni horno. La clase puede hacerte preguntas durante tu demostración. Imagínate que tu presentación se está transmitiendo por televisión.

CHELA: Después de la cena, otro desastre. El camarero
nos servía el café cuando sonó el celular de Sergio
otra vez. Decidió tomar la llamada en privado. Al
levantarse, se pegó en la **mesa** y tiró el café por todo
el **mantel**.

DULCE: ¡Uy, qué horror! ¡Parece de película!

CHELA: Sí, ¡de película de horror! Y no me lo vas a creer, pero
después de todo eso, ¡no le dejó propina al pobre
camarero! ¡Yo tuve que regresar a dejársela!

>> **La mesa**

Cómo poner la mesa   *Setting the table*

el mantel

el tenedor

el cuchillo

el plato hondo

la taza

el vaso

la copa

la servilleta

la cuchara

el plato

━━━━━━┥ ACTIVIDADES ┝━━━━━━

Tomar, not **comer,** is used to refer to eating soup.

6 **¡Necesito un tenedor!** Un(a) amigo(a) da una cena para varios invitados
y te pide que lo (la) ayudes. Al oír los comentarios de los invitados, te das
cuenta de que necesitan ciertos utensilios. ¿Qué le hace falta a cada persona?

1. "No puedo tomar el caldo de pollo".
2. "Me gustaría tomar un té caliente".
3. "Quisiera un poco de agua mineral, por favor".
4. "Voy a abrir una botella de vino".
5. "No puedo cortar este bistec".
6. "Este arroz se ve delicioso".
7. "¿En qué debo servir el gazpacho?"
8. "Necesito algo para limpiarme las manos".

7 **En el comedor** Dile a un(a) compañero(a) cómo poner la mesa, según el dibujo en la página 314. Sigue el modelo. (Vas a usar las preposiciones de locación que aprendiste en el **Capítulo 6**.)

MODELO mantel / mesa
Pon el mantel sobre la mesa.

1. cuchara / plato
2. plato / plato hondo
3. cuchillo / tenedor y plato
4. tenedor y cuchillo / servilleta
5. taza / plato
6. vaso / taza

8 **¡Ayúdame!** Necesitas ayuda para poner la mesa antes de que lleguen tus cuatro invitados. Pídele ayuda a un(a) compañero(a). Dile qué vas a servir y él o ella te dice qué vas a necesitar para poner la mesa. Sigue el modelo.

MODELO Tú: *Primero voy a servir una ensalada mixta.*
Compañero(a): *Vas a necesitar cuatro platos hondos y cuatro tenedores.*
Tú: *Para beber, voy a servir agua mineral y café.*
Compañero(a): *Vas a necesitar cuatro vasos y cuatro tazas.*

9 **La cena** En grupos de cuatro, representen la siguiente situación: Tú y tres amigos van a dar una fiesta para celebrar algo importante. Los cuatro se juntan para planear el menú. No están de acuerdo con varias decisiones:

- dónde va a ser la fiesta
- a quiénes van a invitar
- qué platos van a cocinar
- quién va a preparar qué platos
- cómo los van a preparar
- qué refrescos van a servir

A ver

ESTRATEGIA

Using visuals to aid comprehension

You can learn a lot from just looking at the visuals when you watch video. The scenes and images you see help you understand the language that you hear. Be sure to pay attention to the visuals as well as to the spoken conversation.

Antes de ver 1 En el video de este capítulo Chela describe la cena que tuvo con Sergio. Contesta las preguntas sobre lo que ya sabes de Chela y Sergio.

1. ¿Cómo es Chela? Piensa en tres adjetivos que la describan.
2. ¿Cómo es Sergio? Piensa en tres adjetivos diferentes que lo describan.

Antes de ver 2 Antes de ver el video, mira las fotos. Escoge la oración que exprese la idea principal de cada una.

1. _____ 2. _____ 3. _____

a. Parece que Sergio llegó muy tarde a la cita.
b. A Chela no le gustó nada la conversación telefónica que tuvo Sergio.
c. Sergio fue muy descortés con el camarero.

▶ **Ver** Mira el video. Presta atención a las imágenes mientras lo mires.

Después de ver Pon en el orden correcto estos ejemplos de la descortesía de Sergio.

_____ "Habló por teléfono... por diez minutos enteros mientras yo esperaba".

_____ "... Sergio llamó al camarero. ¡Pobre camarero! Sergio fue muy descortés con él".

_____ "Habló de sí mismo por una eternidad y mientras hablaba no dejaba de arreglarse el pelo".

_____ "... después de todo eso, ¡no le dejó propina al pobre camarero!"

>> Voces del mundo hispano

En el video para este capítulo Michelle, Mariana y Cristina hablan de la comida y los restaurantes. Lee las siguientes oraciones. Después mira el video una o más veces para decir si las oraciones son ciertas (**C**) o falsas (**F**).

© Cengage Learning 2013

1. A Michelle le gusta mucho el saisi, que es un plato típico brasileño.

2. Según Mariana, el silpancho tiene arroz, carne asada, un huevo y una ensalada de cebollas y tomates.

3. El plato favorito de Cristina es la payagua mascada.

4. A Michelle le gustan los restaurantes italianos y tailandeses, pero Mariana prefiere comer en restaurantes árabes.

5. Cristina prefiere las churrasquerías, que son ideales para los vegetarianos.

6. A Michelle le gusta comer en casa y en restaurantes también.

>> Voces de Estados Unidos

Track 27

Aarón Sánchez, especialista en la comida panlatina

Wirelmage/ Getty Images

❝Hay que pensar en la comida latinoamericana en términos de varias superpotencias culinarias: la influencia afro-caribeña; el maíz, el arroz y los frijoles de Centroamérica; de Suramérica tenemos frutos frescos de mar (*seafood*); Perú, la cuna (*cradle*) de las papas, y en Chile y Argentina, la influencia europea ❞

Hijo y nieto de dos prominentes chefs mexicanos, Aarón Sánchez es la personificación del proverbio "de tal palo, tal astilla" ("*a chip off the old block*"). Este joven originario de El Paso, Texas, es dueño (*owner*) de dos restaurantes en la ciudad de Nueva York, Paladar, de inspiración panlatina, y Céntrico, de comida mexicana. Además, es co-animador del programa de televisión "Chef vs. City" del Food Network y autor de *La comida del barrio*. En este libro, Sánchez explora la comida y cultura de La Pequeña Habana, Spanish Harlem, The Mission y otros barrios latinos. Sus recetas se enfocan en platillos caseros (*home-cooked dishes*) tales como la ensalada de nopales y camarones, la sopa de frijoles negros y el fricasé de pollo.

¿Y tú? En tu opinión, ¿es importante mantener las tradiciones culinarias del pasado? ¿Por qué sí o por qué no?

¡Prepárate!

>> **Gramática útil 1**

Talking about what you used to do: The imperfect tense

Habló por teléfono, no sé con quién, por diez minutos enteros mientras yo **esperaba**.

Cómo usarlo

1. You have already learned to talk about completed actions and past events using the *preterite tense* in Spanish.

2. Spanish has another past-tense form known as the *imperfect tense*. The imperfect is used to talk about *ongoing actions* or *conditions* in the past.

3. Use the imperfect tense to talk about the following events or situations in the past.

- to talk about what you habitually did or used to do

  Todos los días, **desayunaba** a las ocho y luego **caminaba** a la escuela.

  *Every day **I used to eat breakfast** at eight and then **I walked** to school.*

- to describe an *action in progress* in the past

  Vivíamos en Asunción con mi prima Enedina y sus padres.

  We were living in Asunción with my cousin Enedina and her parents.

- to *tell the time* in the past

  Por lo general, **eran** las diez de la noche cuando **comíamos.**

  It was usually ten at night when we would eat dinner.

- to describe *emotional or physical conditions* in the past

  Todos **estábamos** muy contentos y nadie se enfermó ese año. **Nos sentíamos** muy afortunados.

  We were all very happy and no one got sick that year. We felt very fortunate.

- to describe *ongoing weather conditions* in the past

  Llovía mucho en Paraguay en esa época.

  It rained a lot in Paraguay during that time.

- to tell someone's *age* in the past

  Enedina **tenía** quince años ese año. *Enedina **was** fifteen that year.*

4. The imperfect tense is generally translated into English in different ways. For example, **comía** can be translated as *I ate* (routinely), *I was eating, I would eat,* or *I used to eat.*

318 Capítulo 9

Cómo formarlo

1. Here are the imperfect forms of regular verbs. Notice that **-er** and **-ir** verbs share the same endings, and that the **yo** and **usted / él / ella** forms are the same.

	cenar	comer	pedir
yo	cen**aba**	com**ía**	ped**ía**
tú	cen**abas**	com**ías**	ped**ías**
usted / él / ella	cen**aba**	com**ía**	ped**ía**
nosotros / nosotras	cen**ábamos**	com**íamos**	ped**íamos**
vosotros / vosotras	cen**abais**	com**íais**	ped**íais**
ustedes / ellos / ellas	cen**aban**	com**ían**	ped**ían**

> Notice the use of accents on the **nosotros / nosotras** form of **-ar** verbs, and on *all* forms of the **-er** and **-ir** verbs.

2. No verbs have stem changes in the imperfect tense, and there are only three verbs that are irregular in the imperfect.

	ir	ser	ver
yo	iba	era	veía
tú	ibas	eras	veías
usted / él / ella	iba	era	veía
nosotros / nosotras	íbamos	éramos	veíamos
vosotros / vosotras	ibais	erais	veíais
ustedes / ellos / ellas	iban	eran	veían

> **Ver** is irregular only in that the **e** is maintained before adding the regular **-er / -ir** imperfect endings.

3. The imperfect form of **hay** is **había**. Like **hay**, it is used with both singular and plural subjects: **Había un restaurante muy bueno allí. / Había algunos restaurantes muy buenos allí.**

ACTIVIDADES

1 **Sergio** Sergio describe su vida cuando tenía catorce años. Cambia los verbos en sus oraciones al imperfecto para saber cómo era su vida.

1. <u>Me levanto</u> a las seis de la mañana todos los días.
2. <u>Tomo</u> el desayuno en casa.
3. <u>Salgo</u> a correr dos millas antes de ir al colegio.
4. <u>Voy</u> al colegio en autobús.
5. <u>Almuerzo</u> en la cafetería del colegio.
6. <u>Tengo</u> clases hasta las cuatro de la tarde.
7. <u>Estudio</u> en la casa de mi novia hasta las ocho y media de la noche.

2 Nuestros hábitos Con un(a) compañero(a), túrnense para hacer oraciones completas con las palabras indicadas para expresar cómo eran sus hábitos con relación a la comida cuando eran niños(as). Sigan el modelo.

MODELO comer (yo) muchos vegetales
Comía muchos vegetales. / No comía muchos vegetales.

1. beber (yo) mucha leche
2. preparar (mis hermanos y yo) el desayuno
3. ir (mi familia) frecuentemente a un restaurante
4. comprar (mis padres) frutas y vegetales orgánicos
5. cocinar (mi madre) muchos platos vegetarianos
6. poner (yo) la mesa para la cena
7. buscar (mis padres) recetas para platos nuevos
8. lavar (mis hermanos y yo) los platos después de comer

3 En la secundaria Entrevista a un(a) compañero(a). Quieres saber más de su vida cuando estaba en la secundaria. Puedes usar las siguientes preguntas para tu entrevista, o puedes hacerle las preguntas que quieras. Túrnense para hacer la entrevista.

1. ¿A qué hora empezaban las clases?
2. ¿A qué hora te levantabas / desayunabas?
3. ¿Comías en la cafetería de la escuela o llevabas tu propia comida?
4. Si llevabas tu propio almuerzo, ¿quién lo preparaba?
5. ¿Qué comías de almuerzo?
6. ¿Trabajabas después de la escuela?
7. ¿Cuántas horas de tarea hacías?
8. ¿Participabas en algún deporte?
9. ¿Ibas a fiestas los fines de semana? ¿Solo(a) o con tus amigos?
10. ¿Eras miembro de algún club u organización en tu escuela?
11. ¿Tenías novio(a)?
12. ¿Qué hacías con tus amigos?

4 Los veranos de mi niñez ¿Cómo pasabas los veranos cuando eras niño(a)? Escribe una descripción de lo que recuerdas de los veranos de tu niñez o de un verano en particular que fue importante u horrible. Léele tu descripción a un(a) compañero(a) y escucha la descripción de él (ella). Usa las siguientes preguntas como guía si quieres.

- ¿Dónde pasabas los veranos? ¿Con quién(es)?
- ¿Qué hacías?
- ¿Qué te gustaba hacer? ¿Por qué?
- ¿Qué no te gustaba hacer? ¿Por qué?
- ¿Cuáles eran tus actividades preferidas del verano?

Gramática útil 2

Talking about the past: Choosing between the preterite and the imperfect tenses

Cómo usarlo

No **sabía** qué hacer. Mientras **esperábamos** sus platos, **se enfriaron** los míos.

1. As you have learned, the preterite tense is generally used in Spanish to express past actions and describe past events that are viewed as completed and over. The imperfect is used to describe past actions or conditions that are viewed as habitual or ongoing.

2. Sometimes the choice between the preterite and the imperfect is not clear-cut. It may depend on the speaker's judgment of the event. However, here are some general guidelines for using the two tenses.

Preterite	Imperfect
1. Relates a *completed past action* or *a series of completed past actions.* **Comimos** en ese restaurante la semana pasada. Ayer, **fuimos** al restaurante, **pedimos** el menú, **comimos** y luego **salimos** para ir al teatro.	1. Describes *habitual or routine past actions.* **Comíamos** en ese restaurante todas las semanas. Siempre **íbamos** al restaurante, **pedíamos** el menú, **comíamos y** luego **salíamos** para ir al teatro.
2. Focuses on the *beginning* or *end* of a past event. La cena **comenzó** a las nueve, pero no **terminó** hasta medianoche.	2. Focuses on the *duration* of the event in the past, rather than its beginning or end. **Cenábamos** desde las nueve hasta medianoche.
3. Relates a *completed past condition* that is viewed as completely over and done with at this point in time (usually gives a time period associated with the condition). Manuel **estuvo** enfermo por dos semanas después de comer en ese restaurante, pero ahora está bien.	3. Describes *past conditions*, such as time, weather, emotional states, age, and location, that were ongoing at the time of description (no focus on beginning or end of condition). El restaurante **era** famoso por su comida latinoamericana y **estábamos** muy contentos con los platos que pedimos.
4. Relates an *action that interrupted* an ongoing action. Ya comíamos el postre cuando por fin Miguel **llegó** al restaurante.	4. Describes *ongoing background events* in the past that were interrupted by another action. Ya **comíamos** el postre cuando por fin Miguel llegó al restaurante.

3. Certain words and phrases related to time may suggest when to use the imperfect or the preterite. These are not hard-and-fast rules, but general indicators.

Preterite	Imperfect
de repente (suddenly)	**generalmente / por lo general**
por fin (finally)	**normalmente**
ayer	**todos los días / meses / años**
la semana pasada	**todas las semanas**
el mes / el año pasado	**frecuentemente**
una vez / dos veces, etc.	**típicamente**

4. In **Chapter 8** you learned that some verbs (**querer, poder, conocer,** and **saber**) sometimes have a different meaning in the preterite tense. This change in meaning does not occur in the imperfect tense.

Cómo formarlo

Review the preterite forms presented in **Chapters 7** and **8**, as well as the imperfect forms presented in **Gramática útil 1** (on page 319 of this chapter).

ACTIVIDADES

5 **¿Qué pasó?** Escoge la forma correcta del verbo para completar cada oración.

1. Mis amigos y yo (comimos / comíamos) en ese restaurante todos los días.
2. Mi amiga me (preparó / preparaba) ese plato ayer.
3. (Estamos / Estábamos) en el café cuando me llamaron.
4. Ese restaurante (fue / era) muy popular por mucho tiempo.
5. Mi hermano (trabajó / trabajaba) como chef por dos años.
6. Siempre (fuimos / estábamos) muy contentos después de comer allí.

6 **Picadillo boliviano** ¡Pobre Amelia! Ella describe lo que le pasó cuando estaba preparando un picadillo boliviano para su familia. Escribe las oraciones según el modelo. Ponle mucha atención al uso del pretérito y el imperfecto.

MODELO   picar la carne / sonar el teléfono
Picaba la carne cuando sonó el teléfono.

1. pelar las papas / empezar a llover
2. freír la cebolla / entrar mi hermano a la cocina empapado *(drenched)*
3. cortar el tomate en cuadritos / llegar papá del trabajo muerto de hambre
4. añadir la sal, la pimienta y el comino / mi hermanito poner la tele
5. agregar el tomate / mi hermanita decidir ayudarme
6. preparar la carne / (ellos) anunciar en la tele que venir un huracán
7. secar el guiso a fuego suave / llegar mamá de la oficina
8. freír las papas en aceite caliente / empezar la tormenta
9. mezclar las papas y el guisado / sentarse todos a la mesa
10. servir el picadillo / cortarse la electricidad

7 **Los veranos de Chela** Escucha mientras Chela describe cómo pasaba los veranos cuando era niña. En un papel aparte, mira los verbos de la lista (abajo) y escríbelos en dos columnas como las siguientes. Mientras escuchas, escribe las formas de los verbos de la siguiente lista que oyes. Escribe las formas del pretérito en la primera columna y las formas del imperfecto en la segunda columna. **¡OJO!** Vas a escuchar más verbos de los que están en la lista. Sólo presta atención a los verbos de la lista.

Acciones: visitar a los abuelos, vivir en un pueblito, llevar su computadora, sorprenderse, levantarse muy temprano, ir a dar una vuelta por el centro, estar triste, la computadora no funcionar, salir juntos, jamás usar la computadora

Completed action in the past	Action in progress or habitual action in the past
	visitaba

8 **¡Qué decepción!** Anoche, Ricardo y Elena fueron a un restaurante a cenar. Elena le describe la cita a su amiga Fernanda. Completa su descripción con las formas correctas del pretérito y del imperfecto de los verbos entre paréntesis.

Anoche Ricardo y yo (1. ir) a un restaurante elegante. No (2. tener) reservación y por eso no (3. sentarse) hasta las diez de la noche. Los dos (4. estar) muertos de hambre. Yo (5. ordenar) una ensalada mixta, pollo asado con habichuelas, flan y un café. Ricardo (6. pedir) una ensalada de papa, lomo de res y un helado de vainilla. Nosotros (7. hablar) de la película que (8. acabar) de ver cuando (9. regresar) el camarero a la mesa. Él nos (10. explicar) que no (11. haber) ni lomo ni pollo y nos (12. preguntar) si (13. querer) una hamburguesa. Ricardo (14. enojarse) mucho y le preguntó si por favor no nos (15. poder) recomendar algo más apetitoso. El camarero (16. sonreír) y (17. decir) que todo lo que (18. quedar) en la cocina (19. ser) ¡hamburguesas y papas fritas! Con el hambre que (20. tener) los dos, (21. decidir) ordenar las hamburguesas. Yo no (22. querer) dejarle buena propina porque había sido *(had been)* un poco descortés, pero Ricardo (23. insistir) en que no (24. ser) su culpa y le (25. dejar) una propina exagerada.

9 **Mi restaurante favorito** Con un(a) compañero(a), túrnense para hacer y contestar las siguientes preguntas sobre la experiencia que tuviste la última vez que comiste en tu restaurante favorito. Pon atención al uso del pretérito y del imperfecto.

1. ¿Con quién fuiste? ¿Qué hora era cuando llegaron al restaurante?
2. ¿Qué platos pidierion? ¿Cómo era la comida?
3. ¿De qué hablaron mientras comían?
4. ¿Comieron un postre? ¿Tomaron café?
5. ¿Cómo era el servicio? ¿Dejaron una propina buena para el (la) camarero(a)?
6. ¿Cómo se sentían al salir del restaurante?

10 **¡Qué horror!** A veces salimos con alguien que no conocemos muy bien y la cita es un desastre. Esto le pasó a Chela cuando salió con Sergio en el video. ¿Has tenido alguna vez una cita desastrosa? Escribe una narración que describa esa cita o una cita imaginaria. Incluye muchos detalles y pon atención al uso del pretérito y del imperfecto.

- ¿Adónde fueron?
- ¿Qué hicieron?
- ¿Qué pasó durante la cita?
- ¿Qué hizo él / ella que te avergonzó *(embarrassed you)* o molestó?
- ¿Cómo te sentías?
- ¿Cómo respondiste?
- ¿…?

>> Gramática útil 3

Avoiding repetition: Double object pronouns

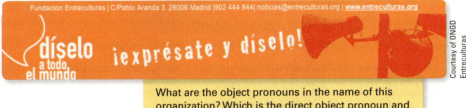

Fundación Entreculturas | C/Pablo Aranda 3. 28006 Madrid |902 444 844| noticias@entreculturas.org | **www.entreculturas.org**

Courtesy of ONGD
Entreculturas

What are the object pronouns in the name of this organization? Which is the direct object pronoun and which is the indirect object pronoun?

Cómo usarlo

1. You studied direct object pronouns (**me, te, lo, la, nos, os, los, las**) in **Chapter 7**. In **Chapter 8** you learned to use indirect object pronouns (**me, te, le, nos, os, les**).

2. Remember that you use direct object pronouns to replace the direct object of a sentence. The direct object receives the action of the verb.

   Preparé **la comida**. → **La** preparé.

3. Remember that you use indirect object pronouns to replace the indirect object of a sentence. The indirect object answers the questions *For whom?* or *To whom?*

   Preparé la comida (para **ti**). → **Te** preparé la comida.

4. When you use direct and indirect object pronouns together, they are called *double object pronouns*.

   Preparé **la comida** (para **ti**). → **Te la** preparé.
   Organicé **un almuerzo** especial (para **ellos**). → **Se lo** organicé.

Cómo formarlo

1. Indirect and direct object pronouns stay the same when used together as double object pronouns, except in the third-person singular and third-person plural (**le** and **les**). In those two cases, the double object pronoun **se** replaces both **le** and **les** when used with the direct objects **lo, la, los,** and **las**.

Indirect object	Direct object
me	me
te	te
le → se	lo / la
nos	nos
os	os
les → se	los / las

2. Follow these rules for using double object pronouns.

- The *indirect object pronoun* always comes *before* the *direct object pronoun*. This is true whether the pronouns are used before a conjugated verb or attached to the end of infinitives, affirmative command forms, and present participles.

  Pedí una sopa. **Me la** sirvieron inmediatamente.
  Le dije al camarero: "Por favor, **tráigamela** con un poco de pan".

- Remember that with *negative command forms*, the double object pronouns must come *before the verb*.

  Quiero un postre, pero **no me lo traiga** inmediatamente.

- When double object pronouns are used with a conjugated verb followed by an infinitive, they may go *before the conjugated verb* or *attach to the infinitive*.

  Me lo van a servir ahora.   O: Van a **servírmelo** ahora.

- When using the direct object pronouns **lo, la, los,** and **las** with the indirect object pronouns **le** or **les,** change **le / les** to **se.** (Notice that you use **se** to replace both **le** and **les.**)

  Susana **le** llevó **los ingredientes** a Elena.

  Susana **se los** llevó (a Elena).

  Ileana y Susana **les** prepararon **la cena** a sus padres.

  Ileana y Susana **se la** prepararon (a sus padres).

> Remember, when pronouns are attached to the end of infinitives, command forms, and present participles, an accent is placed on the verb to maintain the original pronunciation: **tráigamela.**

ACTIVIDADES

11 Escoge los pronombres de doble objeto que mejor completen cada oración.

1. Al señor Martínez le encanta esa sopa. Sírva(sela / selo), por favor.
2. ¡No tienes cuchara! (Te la / Se la) voy a traer ahora mismo.
3. Nuestra abuela hacía un pastel muy rico. Siempre (nos lo / se lo) preparaba cuando veníamos de visita.
4. ¡Este guisado es fabuloso! Quiero la receta. ¿(Me la / Me las) das?
5. Este plato no está listo todavía. No (se lo / te lo) sirvas, por favor.
6. A mí me gusta mucho el flan. ¡Qué bien! Mi mamá esta preparándo(melo / selo) ahora mismo.

12 **Dulce en el restaurante** Dulce fue a un restaurante a comer. Completa su descripción de la cena con los pronombres dobles correctos.

1. Pedí el menú. El camarero _____ _____ trajo inmediatamente.
2. Para plato principal, pedí una chuleta de puerco. _____ _____ sirvieron un poco después.
3. También pedí unos frijoles refritos. _____ _____ prepararon precisamente como me gustan.
4. Para postre, pedí unas galletas de chocolate. _____ _____ trajeron con helado.
5. Para tomar, pedí un té helado. _____ _____ sirvieron bien frío.
6. Por fin pedí la cuenta. El camarero _____ _____ trajo rápidamente.

13 **Miguel** La mamá de Miguel le pregunta si ha hecho varias cosas para los diferentes miembros de su familia. ¿Cómo contesta Miguel? Sigue el modelo.

MODELO ¿Le serviste la leche a tu prima?
Sí, se la serví.

1. ¿Le preparaste el café a tu abuelo?
2. ¿Les compraste las galletas a tus tíos?
3. ¿Le serviste la sopa de fideos a tu hermano?
4. ¿Nos trajiste las servilletas?
5. ¿Te compraste unas galletas en la pastelería?
6. ¿Me imprimiste la receta para el picadillo?
7. ¿Les calentaste las tortillas a tus primos?
8. ¿Les dieron las gracias tus primos a tu hermana y a ti?

14 **Adán y Adelita** El padre de Adán y Adelita cree que sus hijos sólo deben comer comida nutritiva. Nunca les compra comida rápida y no les permite comer postres llenos de azúcar. Primero, haz el papel del padre y contesta las preguntas de sus hijos. Luego, di si les compró o no les compró las comidas que querían.

MODELO **Adán:** Papá, quiero un perro caliente.
Papá: *Hijo, no te lo voy a comprar. O: Hijo, no voy a comprártelo.*
Tú: *Adán quería un perro caliente. Su papá no se lo compró.*

1. **Adelita:** Papá, quiero un helado.
2. **Adán y Adelita:** Papá, queremos unas hamburguesas.
3. **Adán:** Quiero unos plátanos.
4. **Adelita:** Papá, quiero una ensalada mixta.
5. **Adán y Adelita:** Papá, queremos unas papas fritas.
6. **Adelita:** Papá, quiero unas fresas.
7. **Adán:** Papá, quiero una galleta.

◄)) **15 A la hora de comer** Es la hora de comer en casa de Emilia Gutiérrez. La
Track 29 señora Gutiérrez le da instrucciones a Emilia. Escucha lo que le dice y escoge
la frase que mejor complete sus instrucciones.

1. _____   a. Ábremelo, por favor.
2. _____   b. Prepáraselo, por favor.
3. _____   c. Sírvesela, por favor.
4. _____   d. Sírveselo, por favor.
5. _____   e. ¿Nos las calientas, por favor?
6. _____   f. Llévaselas, por favor.
7. _____   g. Dáselo, por favor.
8. _____   h. Tráemelo, por favor.

16 ¿Me lo haces? Con un(a) compañero(a), representen la siguiente
situación. Un(a) de ustedes está enfermo(a) y le pide unos favores al (a la)
otro(a). Sigan el modelo y túrnense para representar los dos papeles.

MODELO   preparar una sopa de pollo
Tú: *¿Me preparas una sopa de pollo?*
Compañero: *Claro. Te la estoy preparando / estoy preparándola
ahora mismo.*

1. traer un suéter   4. preparar mis platos favoritos
2. pasar el control-remoto   5. lavar los platos
3. escribir una nota para la farmacia 6. mandar un e-mail al profesor

17 ¿Qué quieres para tu cumpleaños? Con un(a) compañero(a), túrnense
para representar la siguiente situación. Usen los pronombres dobles por lo
menos dos veces en su conversación. Pueden practicar antes de representarle
la situación a la clase. (Nota que los verbos **dar, traer, servir, preparar** y
comprar frecuentemente requieren dos pronombres porque indican una acción
hacia otra persona.)

Es tu cumpleaños y tus amigos quieren saber qué regalos quieres. Te van a dar
una fiesta y también quieren saber qué comidas quieres. Eres muy exigente
(demanding): quieres muchas cosas y te gusta una variedad de cosas. Pide
todo lo que te apetezca *(you desire)*.

MODELO   Amigo(a): *¿Qué quieres para tu cumpleaños?*
Tú: *Me gustaría tener la nueva versión de Banda de Rock.*
Amigo(a): *Vamos a comprártela. ¿Y qué quieres comer?*
Tú: …

>> Gramática útil 4

Indicating for whom actions are done and what is done routinely: The uses of **se**

Cómo usarlo

You have used the pronoun **se** in several different ways. Here's a quick review of the uses you already know (items 1 and 2 in the chart), and one new use (item 3).

Al levantarse, **se** pegó en la mesa y tiró el café por todo el mantel.

Use **se** . . .	
1. to replace **le** or **les** when used with a direct object pronoun.	Marta **le** dio un regalo a Selena. Marta **se** lo dio.
2. with reflexive verbs, when using **usted / ustedes** and **él / ella / ellos / ellas** forms.	Ustedes **se** vistieron y salieron para la oficina. Ella **se** vistió después de ducharse.
3. to give general and impersonal information about "what is done."	**Se sirve** comida paraguaya en ese restaurante. **¡Se come** muy bien allí!

Cómo formarlo

Se can be used to express actions with no specific subject and to say what "one does" in general. **Se** is always used with a third-person form of the verb.

- If a noun immediately follows the **se** + verb construction, the verb agrees with the noun.

  Se sirve el desayuno todo el día.   ***Breakfast is served*** *all day.*
  Se venden empanadas aquí.   ***Empanadas are sold*** *here.*

- If no noun immediately follows **se** + verb, the third-person singular form of the verb is used.

  Se come muy bien aquí.   ***One eats*** *well here.*
  Se duerme mal después de una comida fuerte.   ***One sleeps*** *badly after a heavy meal.*

18 **Recomendaciones** Escoge la expresión que mejor complete cada oración.

1. (Se sirve / Se sirven) la cena a las 8:00 hasta las 11:00.
2. (Se habla / Se hablan) el español en ese restaurante.
3. (Se come / Se comen) muy bien en esa cafetería.
4. (Se vende / Se venden) frutas muy frescas en ese mercado.
5. (Se compra / Se compran) bastante barato en Tienda La Oferta.
6. (Se duerme / Se duermen) mal en esos hoteles.
7. (Se relaja / Se relajan) mucho en el Spa Oasis.
8. (Se busca / Se buscan) cocineros con cinco años de experiencia.

19 **Observaciones** Usando la construcción impersonal con **se**, di cómo es la experiencia de uno en las siguientes situaciones.

MODELO (Ver) muy bien desde aquí.
Se ve muy bien desde aquí.

1. (Trabajar) muy duro en la clase de física.
2. (Dormir) muy bien en ese hotel.
3. (Ver) mucho de la ciudad desde esa ventana.
4. (Aprender) mucho en esa clase.
5. (Cenar) muy bien en el restaurante Paraíso.
6. (Oír) muy bien con esos audífonos.

20 **Los anuncios clasificados** Vas a escribir unos anuncios clasificados para el periódico universitario. Algunas personas te describen lo que necesitan o buscan. Escribe la primera línea de cada anuncio según lo que te dicen.

MODELO —Me voy a graduar este año y tengo muchos libros usados que quiero vender.
Se venden libros usados.

1. —Soy director y quiero montar *(put together)* una obra de teatro. Busco tres actores y una actriz.
2. —Vamos a hacer un Festival Boliviano y necesitamos voluntarios para ayudar con todos los detalles.
3. —Voy a estudiar al extranjero este semestre y quiero alquilar mi apartamento.
4. —Para las Navidades queremos darles ropa y juguetes a los niños pobres. Aceptamos donaciones de ropa y juguetes usados.

Sonrisas

👥👥 **Expresión** En grupos de tres o cuatro estudiantes, contesten las siguientes preguntas sobre la tira cómica.

1. ¿Por qué se usa un verbo singular con los dos primeros letreros?
2. ¿Por qué se usa un verbo plural con los dos últimos letreros?
3. ¿Crees que el niño va a recibir dinero de la gente que ve su letrero? ¿Por qué?
4. Piensen en unos letreros cómicos para los siguientes lugares. Luego, compartan sus ideas con otro grupo. ¿Qué grupo tiene los letreros más creativos?

   a. restaurante
   b. tienda
   c. hospital
   d. consultorio *(office)* de un dentista
   e. taller de un mecánico
   f. la pizarra en la clase de español

Bolivia

Celso Diniz/Shutterstock

Información general ▶

Nombre oficial: Estado Plurinacional de Bolivia

Población: 9.947.418

Capitales: Sucre (poder judicial) (350.000 hab.)
y La Paz (sede del gobierno) (f. 1548)
(900.000 hab.)

Otras ciudades importantes: Santa Cruz de
la Sierra (1.800.000 hab.), Cochabamba
(1.200.000 hab.), El Alto (900.000 hab.)

Moneda: peso (boliviano)

Idiomas: español, quechua, aimara

Mapa de Bolivia: Apéndice D

Image Asset Management/age fotostock

Vale saber…

- Hay varias civilizaciones prehispánicas en Bolivia. Las más importantes son las culturas Chiripa y Wankarani en el altiplano y la de Tiahuanaco cerca del lago Titicaca.

- La colonización española empieza en 1535 y termina en 1826 cuando el libertador Simón Bolívar presenta la primera Constitución al país. Bolivia recibe su nombre del héroe de la independencia de cinco países sudamericanos.

- Es el único país en Latinoamérica con dos capitales. La Paz es la capital administrativa del gobierno y Sucre es la capital constitucional.

- Con la promesa de la justicia social para todos, Evo Morales es el primer miembro de la mayoría indígena elegido presidente en 2005. Fue reelegido en 2009.

Paraguay

Información general

Nombre oficial: República del Paraguay

Población: 6.375.830

Capital: Asunción (f. 1537) (690.000 hab.)

Otras ciudades importantes: Ciudad del Este (320.000 hab.), San Lorenzo (300.000 hab.)

Moneda: guaraní

Idiomas: español y guaraní (oficiales)

Mapa de Paraguay: Apéndice D

Christopher Pillitz/Getty Images

Vale saber…

- Los españoles empiezan a llegar a Paraguay en el siglo XVI. Asunción se funda en 1536 por el explorador español Juan de Salazar de Espinosa.

- Las misiones jesuitas de Latinoamérica fueron construidas *(were constructed)* por la orden religiosa Compañía de Jesús entre 1609 y 1678. Estos misioneros jesuitas españoles y portugueses viajaron a las áreas más remotas de Sudamérica donde establecieron misiones, convirtieron a los indígenas al catolicismo y les enseñaron su idioma.

- Paraguay declara la independencia de España en 1813, siendo el primer país latinoamericano que se proclama república.

Kevin Moloney/Getty Images

- Paraguay siempre ha sido *(has been)* un país bilingüe y bicultural. Se calcula que el 90% de sus habitantes hablan español y guaraní, el idioma de sus pobladores antes de la llegada de los españoles. Las escuelas, las oficinas del gobierno y los medios de comunicación se comunican con el pueblo paraguayo en los dos idiomas.

La quinua boliviana

Bolivia es el primer productor mundial de la quinua, una planta alimenticia que se ha cultivado *(has been grown)* en los Andes desde hace cinco mil años. Para los incas, la quinua era un alimento sagrado *(sacred)*, segundo en importancia solo a la papa. La quinua tiene un gran valor nutricional por varias razones: su contenido de proteína es muy alto; contiene aminoácidos esenciales para el desarrollo humano que no ofrecen ni el arroz ni el trigo *(wheat)*; es pobre en grasas; no contiene gluten; y es fácil de digerir *(digest)*. Por todas sus propiedades nutricionales, NASA está examinando la posibilidad de mandar la quinua al espacio en vuelos *(flights)* de larga duración. De los incas a los astronautas, la quinua sigue alimentando al humano de una manera sabrosa y saludable.

El tereré paraguayo

El tereré es mucho más que un té, es toda una tradición paraguaya. El tereré se prepara con yerba mate y agua fría. Si hace mucho calor, se añade hielo *(ice)*. Hay muchas maneras de preparar el tereré, hasta se pueden añadir hierbas naturales como la menta para darle distintos sabores. El tereré no es sólo delicioso, refrescante, sano y natural, sino también calma la sed, no contiene azúcar y es una buena alternativa al agua natural para mantenerse hidratado, especialmente en épocas de mucho calor. El tereré se prepara en la guampa, un tipo de vaso de madera *(wood)* o de cuerno de vaca *(cow's horn)*. El rito *(ritual)* de pasar la guampa entre la ronda de amigos es la parte más importante de la costumbre paraguaya, porque el tereré no sólo es un té, es un evento social.

La información general

1. ¿En qué capacidad funcionan las dos capitales de Bolivia?
2. ¿Qué heroe de la independencia sudamericana le da su nombre a Bolivia?
3. ¿Cómo se distingue Evo Morales de todos los presidentes bolivianos?
4. ¿Qué orden religiosa tuvo un gran impacto en el idioma de los indígenas paraguayos?
5. ¿Qué hace Paraguay en 1813 que lo distingue de otros países latinoamericanos?
6. El gobierno paraguayo usa dos idiomas para comunicarse con la gente. ¿Cuáles son?

El tema de los alimentos

1. ¿De qué planta alimenticia es Bolivia el primer productor mundial?
2. ¿Por qué la quinua tiene un gran valor nutricional?
3. ¿Por qué el tereré es bueno en épocas de mucho calor?
4. ¿Qué parte del rito de tomar el tereré es la más importante?

🌐 ¿QUIERES SABER MÁS?

Revisa y rellena la tabla que empezaste al principio del capítulo. Luego, escoge un tema para investigar en línea y prepárate para compartir la información con la clase.

También puedes escoger de las palabras clave a continuación o en **www.cengagebrain.com**.

Palabras clave: (Bolivia) los incas, los aimaraes, Carnaval de Oruro, Festival de la Virgen de Urkupiña, Jaime Escalante, Evo Morales; **(Paraguay)** guaraníes, misiones jesuitas, la Guerra del Paraguay, Augusto Roa Bastos, Olga Bliner

🌐 **Tú en el mundo hispano** Para explorar oportunidades de usar el español para estudiar o hacer trabajos voluntarios o aprendizajes en Bolivia y Paraguay, sigue los enlaces en **www.cengagebrain.com**.

🎵 **Ritmos del mundo hispano** Sigue los enlaces en **www.cengagebrain.com** para escuchar música de Bolivia y Paraguay.

A leer

ESTRATEGIA

Setting a time limit

You have learned strategies to help you focus on getting the main idea without becoming too bogged down in the details. Another good way to do this is to set a time limit. Reading under deadline pressure forces you to focus on what's important, rather than on trying to understand every single word.

There are two irregular future tense forms in the reading: **habrá** and **podrán**. Can you guess what they mean? (Hint: they are two irregular verbs used frequently in Spanish.) You will learn more about the future tense in **Chapter 13**.

Recognizing word families helps expand your vocabulary. The word **cría** is used twice in the reading with two different meanings: the raising of a crop and the young trout. Based on this, can you guess what **un criadero** and the phrase **el pescado criado** mean?

1 Vas a leer un artículo sobre la piscicultura, o el cultivo de peces, en una laguna cerca del pueblo boliviano de Botijlaca. La piscicultura da esperanza *(hope)* a los pobladores *(residents)* de Botijlaca, quienes ganan más bolivianos–la moneda nacional de Bolivia–por sus cosechas *(harvests)* de trucha que por el trabajo en las otras industrias de la región.

2 El artículo describe la vida de los residentes de Botijlaca y la región cercana. Para familiarizarte con el vocabulario desconocido, haz correspondencia entre las palabras de la izquierda y la derecha.

1. el centro paceño
2. el nivel del mar
3. el pastoreo de llamas y ovejas
4. las familias madrugan
5. en cuyas orillas se llevará a cabo la feria
6. una decena de truchas
7. son resbalosas y sin escamas
8. la siembra fue en noviembre pasado
9. anclar redes y cosechar todos los peces
10. fueron degustados por un centenar de visitantes

a. *the families get up early*
b. *the stocking (of fish) was last November*
c. *the center of La Paz*
d. *they are slippery and without scales*
e. *sea level*
f. *the shepherding of llamas and sheep*
g. *they were tasted by about 100 visitors*
h. *to anchor the nets and harvest all the fish*
i. *on whose shores the fair will take place*
j. *(a unit of) ten trout*

3 En el artículo se usan varias palabras para describir la carne de trucha, según el método de criarla. Basándote en palabras que ya conoces, ¿puedes adivinar el significado de estas palabras?

- Características positivas: sabrosa, suave
- Características negativas: seca, dura

4 Ahora, vas a leer el artículo por primera vez. Trata de entender sólo las ideas principales y leer el artículo completo en 15 o 20 minutos.

LECTURA

Botijlaca

El pueblo se abre al turismo gracias a la trucha

por Aleja Cuevas Pacohuanca

La producción piscícola devuelve la esperanza a Botijlaca, una pequeña comunidad del Valle de Zongo. En particular, la cría de trucha entusiasma a los pobladores de este lugar, que después de mucho tiempo advierten la posibilidad de mejorar su economía.

Además de consumirlo y venderlo, el pescado de carne rosada promete[1] ser un atractivo para la región. La trucha nada en las aguas frías de la laguna Viscachani.

Botijlaca se encuentra a una hora y media de viaje del centro paceño, es la primera comunidad de las 13 que tiene el Valle de Zongo. Está situada a 3.492 metros sobre el nivel del mar.

La población cuenta con[2] 60 familias. Mientras las mujeres se dedican al pastoreo de llamas y ovejas, los hombres trabajan de manera eventual en una de las plantas hidroeléctricas de la Compañía Boliviana de Energía Eléctrica (Cobee) que se encuentra en el lugar, al norte de la ciudad de La Paz.

La Feria de la Trucha

Muy temprano, las familias madrugan para ser parte de la Primera Feria Productiva y de la Trucha. Domitila Alaña, cargada[3] de su pequeño hijo, camina hacia la laguna Viscachani, en cuyas orillas se llevará a cabo la feria. Dice que allá habrá muchos platos preparados con trucha.

Aurelio Vargas, vicepresidente de la Asociación de Piscicultura de Botijlaca, que cuenta con

Aleja Cuevas

25 socios[4], acaba de pescar una decena de truchas, agarra[5] una y la muestra, son resbalosas y sin escamas. "Hace dos semanas —cuenta— que empezamos a sacar los pescados y ahora estamos promocionando la primera cosecha".

Alaña recuerda que antes no había mucho pescado en la zona, pero gracias a un proyecto piscícola impulsado por el municipio se introdujeron más de 5.000 alevines (crías de truchas) en Viscachani. Ahora, siete meses después, están listos para el consumo. [...]

Así, la producción masiva de truchas abre la posibilidad de desarrollar[6] proyectos turísticos en la comunidad. Por ejemplo, se pretende[7] construir cabañas para dar hospedaje y alimentación[8] a los visitantes. Éstos también podrán pescar. "Mi esposo gana al mes 800 bolivianos en Cobee, ya no conviene, por eso vamos a dedicarnos al turismo", cuenta Domitila. [...]

Según la alcadesa[9] [de Zongo, Erlinda Quispe], un próximo proyecto se orienta a la producción de otros pescados, como las carpas, en la población de Huaylipaya. "En Zongo existe constantemente agua y se tiene que aprovechar[10]".

---

[1]*promises* [2]*includes* [3]*weighed down with* [4]*associates* [5]*grabs* [6]*to develop* [7]*esperan* [8]**hospedaje:** *lodging and food* [9]*mayor* [10]*to take advantage*

Aleja Cuevas

El grande devora al chico

El técnico del Centro de Investigación y Desarrollo Acuícola Boliviano (CIDAB) Santos Saavedra, encargado de hacer la reproducción de la trucha en Botijlaca, indica que en la laguna se colocaron[11] 5.000 alevines de cinco gramos, los que fueron traídos[12] desde las aguas del lago Titicaca.

En ocho meses, la trucha alcanza[13] un peso de 300 gramos, ideal para el consumo y la venta, refiere el técnico. La siembra fue en noviembre pasado. Los peces de los criaderos del lago deben llegar a pesar 700 gramos.

Pero según explica, el pescado criado en una laguna que contiene alimento natural (pequeñas larvas, por ejemplo), como es el caso de Viscachani, alcanza un mejor desarrollo, al menos es más sano. "Con alimento natural, la trucha llega a ser más sabrosa y suave, mientras que en un criadero la carne es seca y dura".

Por su experiencia, lo que corresponde hacer con las truchas de la laguna Viscachani es anclar redes y cosechar todos los peces. "Hay que sacarlas a todas (truchas) —explica Saavedra— para volver a introducir alevines; si colocamos los peces pequeños, los grandes se los devoran, porque las truchas son carnívoras".

En la feria, Aurelio Vargas y otros socios de la Asociación pescaron cerca de dos arrobas[14] de trucha. El pescado fue preparado en diversas formas: frito, ahumado[15], a la parrilla... En tanto, los platos fueron degustados por un centenar de visitantes, quienes, a su vez, disfrutaron de[16] un paisaje de montañas rocosas en medio de las cuales se advierten hilos de agua cristalina.

[11]were placed [12]were brought [13]reaches [14]a unit of measurement that varies between 11 and 16 kilograms; in this region the number is approximately 11.5 kilos [15]smoked [16]enjoyed

5 Di si las siguientes oraciones sobre la lectura son ciertas o falsas.

_____ 1. Botijlaca es una comunidad situada al norte de La Paz.

_____ 2. Antes de la llegada de la industria piscícola, la mayoría de los hombres en Botijlaca trabajaban como pastores *(shepherds)*.

_____ 3. La Primera Feria Productiva y de la Trucha se celebró cerca de la laguna Viscachani.

_____ 4. Siempre había mucho pescado en la laguna, porque es un sitio tradicional para la pesca.

_____ 5. La carne de las truchas de los criaderos es más sabrosa porque las truchas comen alimento natural.

_____ 6. Los pescadores tienen que sacar todas las truchas al mismo tiempo, porque si no lo hacen, las truchas grandes comen los alevines que se introducen en la laguna más tarde.

6 Escoge la respuesta que mejor complete cada oración. Vuelve a la lectura para buscar la respuesta, si es necesario.

1. Los pescadores sacaron la primera cosecha de truchas hace _____.
   a. diez días   b. dos semanas

2. El proyecto piscícolo fue una iniciativa _____.
   a. de Cobee   b. del municipio

3. Los alevines están listos para el consumo _____ después de su introducción a la laguna.
   a. dos semanas   b. siete meses

4. Los hombres ganan 800 bolivianos al mes _____.
   a. en Cobee   b. como parte de este proyecto

5. En el futuro, el próximo proyecto va a ser la producción de _____
   a. otros pescados   b. otros centros para el turismo

6. El peso ideal para el consumo y la venta de la trucha es _____.
   a. 300 gramos   b. 700 gramos

> **Hace** plus a unit of time means *...ago*. Here, **hace diez días** is *ten days ago* and **hace dos semanas** is *two weeks ago*. You will learn more about this structure in **Chapter 10**.

7 En un grupo de tres o cuatro estudiantes, hablen de otros pueblos, ciudades, regiones o países que tengan ferias dedicadas a la comida o la bebida. ¿Conocen algunas de las siguientes? ¿Qué otras conocen? ¿Les gustan las ferias de la comida y la bebida? ¿Por qué sí o no?

- La Feria de la Ostra *(Oyster)*, Galway, Irlandia
- La Feria del Mango, Nuevo Delhi, India
- La Tomatina, Buñol, España
- El Campeonato Mundial del Pastel de Crema, Coxheath, UK
- La Feria de la Hamburguesa, Seymour, Wisconsin
- La Feria del Ajo, Gilroy, California

A escribir

ESTRATEGIA

Writing—Writing a paragraph

You have learned that a paragraph's topic sentence (**oración temática**) tells the reader its main idea. That sentence is followed by examples and details that illustrate it, as you learned in **Chapter 6**. Think of a paragraph as a separate composition that contains a main idea followed by supporting facts and examples. When you move on to a new idea, you create a new paragraph.

1 Trabaja con un(a) compañero(a) de clase. Van a escribir tres párrafos cortos que describan una experiencia con la comida. Escojan uno de los siguientes temas y piensen en una historia que quieren contar:

1. la primera vez que cociné
2. la primera vez que fui a un restaurante elegante
3. mis experiencias culinarias en un país extranjero

2 Después de establecer su tema, miren la tabla y complétenla, usando las oraciones modelo como guía.

	Oración temática (que comunica la idea principal del párrafo)	Detalles y ejemplos que ilustran la oración temática
Párrafo 1: Comienzo / fondo *(background)* de la historia (Recuerden que se usa el imperfecto para describir.)	*Yo tenía trece años y tenía una familia muy grande.*	*Era el menor de seis hijos y a veces me sentía un poco tímido en la presencia de mis hermanos mayores...*
Párrafo 2: La acción de la historia (Por lo general se usa el pretérito para relatar la acción de una historia. Se usa el imperfecto para describir las emociones de los participantes y los estados del pasado.)	*Un día tuve que preparar la cena para mi familia entera.*	*Tenía miedo porque no sabía cocinar muy bien y creía que no podía hacerlo. Miraba los libros de recetas...*
Párrafo 3: El fin de la historia y el resultado	*Aunque la cena estaba muy rica, el postre salió crudo.*	*Mis hermanos se rieron, pero no se burlaron de mí* (they didn't make fun of me).

>> Composición

3 Ahora, escriban su historia. Usen palabras y expresiones de la siguiente lista mientras escriban.

Pretérito
de repente (*suddenly*)
por fin (*finally*)
ayer
la semana pasada
el mes / el año pasado
una vez / dos veces, etc.

Imperfecto
generalmente / por lo general
normalmente
todos los días / meses / años
todas las semanas
frecuentemente
típicamente

John Burke/Photolibrary

La primera vez que preparé la cena para mi familia, no salió muy bien...

>> Después de escribir

4 Intercambien su borrador con el de otra pareja de estudiantes. Usen la siguiente lista para revisarlo.

- ¿Tiene su historia toda la información necesaria?
- ¿Es interesante?
- ¿Usaron bien las formas del pretérito? ¿Y las del imperfecto?
- ¿Usaron complementos directos e indirectos para eliminar la repetición?
- ¿Hay errores de puntuación o de ortografía?

Vocabulario

En el restaurante   *At the restaurant*

el menú *menu*

El desayuno   *Breakfast*

el cereal *cereal*
los huevos estrellados *eggs sunnyside up*
los huevos revueltos *scrambled eggs*
el pan tostado *toast*

El almuerzo   *Lunch*

Las ensaladas   *Salads*

la ensalada de fruta *fruit salad*
la ensalada de lechuga y tomate
    lettuce and tomato salad
la ensalada de papa *potato salad*
la ensalada mixta *tossed salad*

Las sopas   *Soups*

el caldo de pollo *chicken soup*
el gazpacho *cold, tomato-based soup (Spain)*
la sopa de fideos *noodle soup*

Los sándwiches (los bocadillos)   *Sandwiches*

con papas fritas *with french fries*
la hamburguesa *hamburger*
la hamburguesa con queso *cheeseburger*
el perro caliente *hot dog*
el sándwich de jamón y queso con aguacate
    ham and cheese sandwich with avocado

Los platos principales   *Main dishes*

Las carnes   *Meats*

el arroz con pollo *chicken with rice*
el bistec *steak*
la chuleta de puerco *pork chop*
el guisado *beef stew*
el lomo de res *prime rib*
el pollo asado *roasted chicken*
el pollo frito *fried chicken*

Los mariscos   *Shellfish*

las almejas *clams*
los camarones *shrimp*
la langosta *lobster*

Los pescados   *Fish*

el atún *tuna*
el bacalao *cod*
el salmón *salmon*
la trucha *trout*

A la carta   *À la carte*

Los vegetales   *Vegetables*

el bróculi *broccoli*

los espárragos *asparagus*
los frijoles (refritos) *(refried) beans*
los guisantes *peas*
las habichuelas *green beans*
las zanahorias *carrots*

Los postres   *Desserts*

él flan *custard*
la galleta *cookie*
el helado de vainilla / chocolate *vanilla / chocolate
    ice cream*
el pastel *cake*

Las frutas   *Fruit*

las fresas *strawberries*
la manzana *apple*
el melón *melon*
la naranja *orange*
el plátano *banana*
las uvas *grapes*

Las bebidas y los refrescos   *Beverages*

el agua mineral *sparkling water*
el café *coffee*
la cerveza *beer*
el jugo de fruta *fruit juice*
la leche *milk*
la limonada *lemonade*
el té / té helado *hot / iced tea*
el vino blanco / tinto *white / red wine*

Cómo ordenar y pagar   *How to order and pay*

Camarero(a), ¿me puede traer el menú? *Waiter
    (Waitress), could you please bring me the menu?*
Soy vegetariano(a) estricto(a). *I'm a vegan.*
**¿Me puede recomendar algo ligero /
    algo fuerte / algo vegetariano / algo vegano /
    la especialidad de la casa?** *Can you
    recommend something light / something filling /
    something vegetarian / something vegan / the
    house specialty?*

Para plato principal, voy a pedir... *For the main
    course, I would like to order . . .*
Para tomar, quiero... *To drink, I want . . .*
De postre, voy a pedir... *For dessert, I would like
    to order . . .*

¿Me puede traer la cuenta, por favor? *Can you
    bring me the check, please?*
¿Cuánto debo dejar de propina? *How much
    should I leave as a tip?*

Las recetas   *Recipes*

Los ingredientes   *Ingredients*
el aceite de oliva *olive oil*
el ajo *garlic*
el azúcar *sugar*
la cebolla *onion*
el comino *cumin*
la harina *flour*
la mantequilla *butter*
la mayonesa *mayonnaise*
la mostaza *mustard*
la sal y la pimienta *salt and pepper*
el vinagre *vinegar*

Las medidas   *Measurements*
la cucharada *tablespoonful*
la cucharadita *teaspoonful*
la docena *dozen*
el galón *gallon*
el kilo *kilo*
la libra *pound*
el litro *liter*
medio kilo *half a kilo*
el paquete *package*
el pedazo *piece, slice*
el trozo *chunk, piece*

La preparación   *Cooking preparation*
a fuego suave / lento *at low heat*
al gusto *to taste*
al hilo *stringed*
al horno *roasted (in the oven)*
a la parrilla *grilled*
al vapor *steamed*
congelado(a) *frozen*
crudo(a) *raw*
dorado(a) *golden; browned*
fresco(a) *fresh*
frito(a) *fried*
hervido(a) *boiled*
molido(a) *crushed, ground*
picante *spicy*
agregar *to add*
añadir *to add*
calentar (ie) *to heat*
cocer (ue) *to cook*
enfriarse *to get cold*
freír (i, i) *to fry*
hervir (ie, i) *to boil*
mezclar *to mix*
pelar *to peel*
picar *to chop, mince*
unir *to mix together; incorporate*

La mesa   *The table*

Cómo poner la mesa   *Setting the table*
la copa *wine glass*
la cuchara *spoon*
el cuchillo *knife*
el mantel *tablecloth*
el plato *plate*

el plato hondo *bowl*
la servilleta *napkin*
la taza *cup*
el tenedor *fork*
el vaso *glass*

Otras palabras y expresiones

Expresiones para usar con el imperfecto
frecuentemente *frequently*
generalmente / por lo general *generally*
normalmente *normally*
típicamente *typically*
todas las semanas *every week*
todos los días / meses / años *every day / month / year*

Expresiones para usar con el pretérito
ayer *yesterday*
de repente *suddenly*
el mes / el año pasado *last month / year*
por fin *finally*
la semana pasada *last week*
una vez / dos veces, etc. *once, twice, etc.*

Complete these activities to check your understanding of the new grammar points in **Chapter 9** before you move on to **Chapter 10**.

The answers to the activities in this section can be found in **Appendix B**.

The imperfect tense (p. 318)

1 Di qué hacía cada persona con relación a la comida.

1. la señora Muñoz / preparar unas galletas
2. yo / freír un huevo
3. nosotros / pelar zanahorias para una ensalada
4. Manolito / poner la mesa
5. Sarita y Carmela / picar cebollas para una sopa
6. tú / hervir agua para preparar el té

Choosing between the preterite and the imperfect (p. 321)

2 Escribe la forma correcta (pretérito o imperfecto) de cada verbo para completar la oración.

1. _____ (Ser) las tres de la tarde y yo 2. _____ (querer) tomar un café en la cafetería. Cuando 3. _____ (llegar) allí, 4. _____ (ver) a mi amiga Lucía. Ella 5. _____ (estar) muy cansada y 6. _____ (tener) ganas de descansar un rato en la cafetería. Yo 7. _____ (sentarse) en su mesa y nosotros 8. _____ (empezar) a hablar. Mientras 9. _____ (hablar), ella me 10. _____ (decir) que tenemos examen mañana en la clase de cálculo. "¡No me digas!" yo 11. _____ (exclamar). "No lo 12. _____ (saber). ¡Tengo que estudiar!" 13. _____ (Despedirme) de ella y 14. _____ (salir) corriendo. 15. _____ (Estar) muy nervioso por el exámen y 16. _____ (querer) pasar todo el día estudiando.

Double object pronouns (p. 325)

3 Usa cada ilustración y las palabras indicadas para hacer mandatos informales afirmativos y negativos, según la situación. Sigue los modelos.

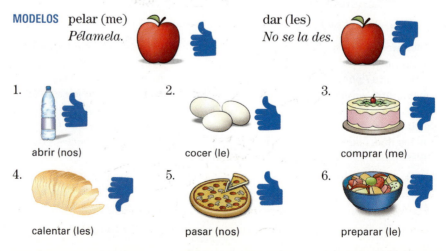

MODELOS   pelar (me)
Pélamela.

dar (les)
No se la des.

1. abrir (nos)
2. cocer (le)
3. comprar (me)
4. calentar (les)
5. pasar (nos)
6. preparar (le)

All art: © Cengage Learning 2013

The uses of se (p. 329)

4 Complete the sentences with the correct form of the verb indicated.

1. Se _____ (comer) bien en esa taquería.
2. Se _____ (vender) tacos riquísimos.
3. Se _____ (hablar) el español y el inglés.
4. Se _____ (servir) la cena hasta las diez.
5. Se _____ (cerrar) entre las tres y las cinco.
6. Se _____ (dormir) en este hotel.

>> Preparación para el Capítulo 10

Article, noun, and adjective agreement (Chapters 1 and 2)

5 Haz oraciones completas con el artículo definido, el verbo **ser** o **estar** y la forma correcta del adjetivo indicado. Sigue el modelo.

MODELO   copa (ser) / bonito
          La copa es bonita.

1. manteles (ser) / rojo
2. flan (ser) / bueno
3. almejas (estar) / fresco
4. café (estar) / caliente
5. carne (estar) / frito
6. huevos (ser) / blanco
7. pescado (estar) / crudo
8. té (estar) frío
9. limonada (ser) / dulce
10. platos (estar) / limpio
11. langosta (ser) / caro
12. fresas (ser) / barato

> Complete these activities to review some previously learned grammatical structures that will be helpful when you learn the new grammar in **Chapter 10**.
>
> Be sure to reread **Chapter 9: Gramática útil 1** before moving on to the new **Chapter 10** grammar sections.

Simple possessive adjectives (Chapter 3)

6 Escribe el adjetivo posesivo correcto para cada cosa indicada.

1. _____ servilleta (yo)
2. _____ galletas (tú)
3. _____ pan (nosotros)
4. _____ uvas (ellos)
5. _____ vasos (usted)
6. _____ mantel (ella)
7. _____ platos (ustedes)
8. _____ menú (él)
9. _____ tazas (nosotros)
10. _____ cuchillos (tú)

Forms of hacer (Chapters 5 and 7)

7 Completa las oraciones con formas de **hacer** en el presente o el pretérito, según el caso.

1. Oye, Maite, ¿qué _____ para la cena anoche?
2. Yo _____ las compras en el supermercado todos los lunes.
3. El año pasado, mi madre _____ un pastel de chocolate para mi cumpleaños.
4. Ustedes ya _____ las reservaciones en el restaurante, ¿verdad?
5. Nosotros _____ una excursión al mercado al aire libre esta tarde.

¿Dónde vives?

LOS SITIOS

Los sitios y sus ambientes *(atmospheres)* juegan un papel muy importante en nuestras vidas y en nuestras memorias.

¿Tienes recuerdos de la casa o sitio donde te criaste *(you were raised)*? ¿Cómo son?

Communication

By the end of this chapter you will be able to

- talk about your childhood
- describe homes and their furnishings
- talk about household tasks
- indicate numerical order
- express possession
- talk about the duration of past and present events

Maxine Bessieres/Alamy

Un viaje por Guatemala y Nicaragua

Guatemala y Nicaragua son países centroamericanos. Nicaragua es el país más grande de Centroamérica. Los dos países tienen costas en el Atlántico y el Pacífico, pero la costa atlántica de Guatemala es muy pequeña. Guatemala es más montañoso que Nicaragua.

País / Área	Tamaño y fronteras	Sitios de interés
Guatemala 108.430 km²	un poco más pequeño que Tennessee; fronteras con Belice, El Salvador, Honduras y México	el lago Atitlán, la ciudad de Antigua, las ruinas mayas de Tikal, la Reserva de la Biosfera de la Sierra de las Minas con su bosque nuboso *(cloud forest)*
Nicaragua 120.254 km²	un poco más pequeño que Nueva York; fronteras con Costa Rica y Honduras	el lago de Nicaragua y sus tiburones *(sharks)*, Bluefields y la Costa de los Mosquitos, la catedral de Santo Domingo en Managua, muchos volcanes (incluso el más alto, San Cristóbal)

¿Qué sabes? Di si las siguientes oraciones son ciertas **(C)** o falsas **(F)**.

1. Aunque hay muchos volcanes en Nicaragua, Guatemala es más montañoso.
2. Guatemala es más pequeño que el estado de Nueva York.
3. Hay ruinas mayas en Nicaragua.
4. Los tiburones en Nicaragua están en el lago de Bluefields.

Lo que sé y lo que quiero aprender Completa la tabla del **Apéndice A**. Escribe algunos datos que **ya sabes** sobre estos países en la columna **Lo que sé**. Después, añade algunos temas que **quieres aprender** a la columna **Lo que quiero aprender**. Guarda la tabla para usarla otra vez en la sección **¡Explora y exprésate!** en la página 369.

Cultures

By the end of this chapter you will have explored

- facts about Guatemala and Nicaragua
- ancient and modern sites in Guatemala and Nicaragua
- a unique recycling program in Guatemala
- Alter Eco: "green" furniture and home decor
- some Hispanic proverbs
- Nicaragua's poetic tradition

¡Imagínate!

>> Vocabulario útil 1

© Cengage Learning 2013

BETO: Cuando era niño, me gustaba preparar la comida para mi familia.

DULCE: ¿En serio? Yo creía que a los chicos no les gustaba hacer nada en la casa. Mis hermanos siempre decían que el trabajo de casa era para las mujeres.

BETO: ¡Qué anticuado! Yo no pienso así. Me crié en **el centro de la ciudad**. Somos muy modernos los hombres de la ciudad.

DULCE: ¿De veras? Qué bueno. En mi casa, mis hermanas y yo teníamos que hacer los quehaceres domésticos, mis hermanos sólo hacían lo que tenía que ver con **el garaje** o **el jardín**.

Ordinal numbers must agree in gender with the nouns they modify: **el segundo piso, la tercera oficina**. They are usually used in front of the noun. **Primero** and **tercero** shorten to **primer** and **tercer** when used before a masculine singular noun: **primer piso, tercer dormitorio** (but **primera casa, tercera ciudad**).

Ordinal numbers can be used without nouns when it is clear what they are referring to: **Mi casa es *la cuarta* de la calle. Primero** and **tercero** are not shortened when used without a noun: **Este piso *es el tercero*, pero vamos *al primero*.**

>> Áreas de la ciudad

las afueras *the outskirts*
el apartamento *apartment*
el barrio *neighborhood*
...comercial *business district*
...residencial *residential neighborhood*
el centro de la ciudad *downtown*
los suburbios *suburbs*
los vecinos *neighbors*

>> La casa

el garaje *garage*
el jardín *garden, yard*
la lavandería *laundry room*
el pasillo *hallway*
el patio *patio*
el sótano *basement, cellar*

>> Números ordinales

primer(o) *first*
segundo *second*
tercer(o) *third*
cuarto *fourth*
quinto *fifth*
sexto *sixth*
séptimo *seventh*
octavo *eighth*
noveno *ninth*
décimo *tenth*

el techo

el dormitorio
(la recámara / el cuarto /
la habitación)

la pared

el clóset

el baño

el segundo piso

la cocina

el comedor

la sala

el primer piso

las escaleras

la chimenea

© Cengage Learning 2013

In most Spanish-speaking countries, people refer to the ground floor (what we consider the first floor) as **la planta baja**. What we call the second floor is then referred to as **el primer piso**, the third as **el segundo piso**, etc. In Spain, speakers may use the word **planta** instead of **piso** to refer to the floor of a building, because there, **piso** also means *apartment*.

ACTIVIDADES

1 **¿En qué cuarto estás?** Di en qué cuarto o lugar de la casa está tu compañero(a) de clase basándote en lo que él (ella) te dice que está haciendo.

MODELO Compañero(a): Estoy preparando la comida.
Tú: *Estás en la cocina.*

1. Estoy lavando la ropa.
2. Estoy mirando la tele.
3. Estoy cenando con mi familia.
4. Me estoy lavando los dientes.
5. Estoy subiendo al segundo piso.
6. Estoy cambiándole el aceite al carro.
7. Estoy regando (*watering*) las plantas.
8. Estoy en la computadora.

2 **¿Dónde vives?** En grupos de cuatro, describan el barrio donde viven, qué tipo de casa o apartamento tienen y cómo llegan a la universidad de su casa. Añadan todos los detalles personales que quieran. Tus compañeros pueden hacerte preguntas si no les das suficiente información.

MODELO *Yo vivo en un barrio residencial en las afueras de la ciudad. Hay apartamentos y también casas individuales. Vivo en un aparta-mento en el segundo piso. Manejo para llegar a la universidad.*

Al final, informen a otro grupo o a la clase quién vive más lejos de la universidad y cuál es el modo de transporte más común.

If you or any members of your group live on campus, describe the neighborhood where you grew up.

3 **Mi casa** En grupos de tres, háganse preguntas y describan su casa o apartamento. Averigüen cómo es, cuántos cuartos tiene, si hay jardín y garaje, etc. Pueden describir la casa de su niñez o donde vive su familia ahora.

MODELOS Compañero(a): *¿Cuántos dormitorios hay en tu casa?*
Tú: *Hay tres dormitorios, dos en el segundo piso y uno en el primero.*

▶ >> Vocabulario útil 2

BETO: No me parece justo. Yo **tendía las camas, pasaba la aspiradora, lavaba los platos** igual que mis hermanas.

DULCE: Pues eres único.

BETO: Sí, mi mamá decía que yo era su ayudante preferido. **Barría el piso, sacaba la basura, ponía la mesa, limpiaba los baños, planchaba, sacudía las alfombras...**

DULCE: Oye, me estás tomando el pelo, ¿verdad? Yo no conozco a ningún niño tan trabajador.

>> Los quehaceres domésticos

Dentro de la casa

arreglar el dormitorio

limpiar el baño

hacer la cama

lavar los platos

sacudir los muebles

barrer el suelo / el piso

Dentro de la casa

- lavar la ropa
- planchar
- guardar la ropa
- trapear el piso
- pasar la aspiradora
- poner y quitar la mesa
- poner sus juguetes en su lugar
- preparar la comida

© Cengage Learning 2013

Fuera de la casa

- darle de comer al perro y al gato
- regar (ie) las plantas
- sacar la basura
- sacar a pasear al perro
- cortar el césped
- hacer el reciclaje

© Cengage Learning 2013

el tocador / la cómoda

la alfombra

el cuadro

el sillón

la persiana

la cama

la mesita de noche

la silla

la lámpara

la mesa

el espejo

las cortinas

el sofá

© Cengage Learning 2013

ACTIVIDADES

4 **¿Dónde pongo esto?** Un(a) amigo(a) acaba de mudarse *(has just moved)* a un nuevo apartamento. Tú le vas a ayudar a poner todos sus muebles y decoraciones en su lugar. Pregúntale dónde van ciertas cosas. Él (Ella) va a decirte dónde quiere cada cosa.

MODELO Tú: *¿Dónde pongo el sillón?*
Compañero(a): *Pon el sillón en la sala, por favor.*

1.

2.

3.

4.

5.

6.

© Cengage Learning 2013

5 **Los quehaceres** Ves que hay un problema en casa. ¿Qué quehacer le pides a tu hermano(a) que haga? Sigue el modelo.

MODELO   Hay muchos juguetes en el piso.
         ¿Puedes poner los juguetes en su lugar?

1. Es hora de comer.
2. Estamos listos para cenar.
3. Acabamos de llegar del gimnasio y hay mucha ropa sucia *(dirty)*.
4. La cama necesita sábanas limpias *(clean sheets)*.
5. Hay varias botellas plásticas en la cocina que están vacías *(empty)*.
6. Hay ropa, zapatos y libros por todo el dormitorio.
7. La blusa está arrugada *(wrinkled)*.
8. El césped está demasiado alto.

6 **¿A quién le toca?** En grupos de tres, representen la siguiente situación. Ustedes tres son compañeros(as) de cuarto ¡y su apartamento es un desastre! Decidan entre sí *(among yourselves)* quién va a hacer cada quehacer. Pueden negociar si quieren.

MODELO   No hay platos limpios para la cena.
         Compañero(a) #1: *¿Quién va a lavar los platos?*
         Compañero(a) #2: *Yo los puedo lavar si [Compañero(a) #3] hace las compras.*
         Compañero(a) #3: *Estás loco(a). Prefiero sacar la basura.*
         Compañero(a) #1: *Bueno, los lavo yo.*

Problema	Nombre / Tarea
No hay platos limpios para la cena.	[Nombre] va a lavar los platos.
El perro tiene mucha hambre.	
Las plantas están secas.	
El suelo de la cocina está sucio *(dirty)*.	
Hay mucho polvo *(dust)* en los muebles.	
Mañana es día de reciclaje.	
Hay varias bolsas de basura.	
El perro tiene que salir.	
La alfombra está sucia.	
El baño es un desastre.	

▶ >> Vocabulario útil 3

© Cengage Learning 2013

BETO: Pues, exagero un poco, pero sí me gustaban algunos de los quehaceres.

DULCE: ¿Como cuáles?

BETO: Pues, a ver, me gustaba limpiar **el refrigerador**…

>> Los electrodomésticos

el abrelatas eléctrico *electric can opener*
la aspiradora *vacuum cleaner*
el congelador *freezer*
la estufa *stove*
la lavadora *washer*
el lavaplatos *dishwasher*
la licuadora *blender*

el microondas *microwave*
la plancha *iron*
el procesador de comida *food processor*
el refrigerador *refrigerator*
la secadora *dryer*
el televisor *television set*
la tostadora *toaster*

┤ ACTIVIDADES ├

7 **¿Qué necesitas?** Identifica el electrodoméstico que necesitas en cada situación.

1. Tienes que lavar ropa esta noche porque no tienes nada que ponerte mañana.
2. Tienes que abrir una lata *(can)* de atún.
3. Tu ropa está muy arrugada *(wrinkled)* porque la acabas de sacar de la maleta.
4. Quieres pan tostado con los huevos revueltos.
5. Tienes ganas de tomar un batido de frutas *(smoothie)*.
6. No tienes mucho tiempo para preparar la cena, así que decides comer un paquete de comida preparada.
7. Quieres enfriar la botella de vino.
8. Quieres limpiar la alfombra.

8 **La casa nueva** En grupos de tres, representen la siguiente situación a la clase. Pueden preparar un guión si quieren: Tres amigos(as) van a ser compañeros(as) de casa. Tienen que comparar qué tienen y qué necesitan para la casa nueva. La casa tiene tres dormitorios, una sala grande, una cocina y dos baños.

- ¿Qué muebles y electrodomésticos tienen entre los tres?
- ¿Qué necesitan comprar?
- ¿En qué cuartos quieren poner los distintos muebles y electrodomésticos?

¡Fíjate! Los refranes en español

Los refranes *(proverbs)* reflejan las actitudes psicológicas, religiosas, espirituales, prácticas, tradicionales y humorísticas de la cultura originaria. Sin embargo, hay unos refranes universales que se conocen por todo el mundo y no pertenecen *(don't belong)* a una cultura en particular. Un refrán que se oye por dondequiera en Estados Unidos y que probablemente conoces es **Mi casa es tu casa**. Aquí están otros refranes que usan como metáfora el hogar, los muebles y los quehaceres:

Si quieres que te vengan a ver, ten la casa sin barrer.
(Expect a surprise visit if the house is a mess.)

Con promesas no se cubre la mesa.
(You can't eat promises!)

El amigo viejo es el mejor espejo.
(An old friend is the best reflection.)

Las paredes oyen.
(The walls have ears.)

© Cengage Learning 2013

Práctica En grupos de tres o cuatro personas, hablen de los siguientes temas.

1. ¿Qué actitud refleja cada refrán?
2. Escriban un refrán de su cultura que usa el hogar cómo metáfora; o un refrán que usan entre familia o amigos con frecuencia. Escriban el refrán en su lengua original; tradúzcanlo al español si está en otro idioma.
3. Compartan los refranes más interesantes con la clase.

ESTRATEGIA

Listening to tone of voice

Listening carefully to a speaker's tone of voice (**el tono de voz**) helps you understand what lies beneath their surface commentary. In this chapter's video segment, pay particular attention to Dulce and Beto's tone of voice. In many cases, what they say may contradict what they are actually thinking and feeling!

Antes de ver Piensa en lo que ya sabes de Beto y Dulce. ¿Cómo es la personalidad de Beto? ¿Cómo es la personalidad de Dulce?

▶ **Ver** Mientras ves el video, presta atención al tono de voz de Beto y Dulce.

Después de ver 1 Lee los siguientes comentarios del video y mira el video otra vez. Si crees que el tono contradice (*contradicts*) el comentario, escribe **C**; si crees que añade más información, marca **A**. Si crees que el tono no afecta el comentario, no escribas nada.

1. _____ Dulce: Hace mucho tiempo que no voy de picnic.
2. _____ Beto: Sí, mi mamá decía que yo era su ayudante preferido.
3. _____ Dulce: ¡Vas a ser un padre excelente!
4. _____ Beto: Mira, prueba éstos, los compré en el supermercado.
5. _____ Dulce: ¡Planchabas! ¡Limpiabas los baños! ¡Cocinabas! ¡Súper-Chico!

Después de ver 2 Di si los siguientes comentarios sobre el video son ciertos (**C**) o falsos (**F**).

1. _____ Beto dice que preparaba la comida para su familia.
2. _____ En la familia de Dulce, los hijos también preparaban la comida.
3. _____ Beto se crió (*was raised*) en el centro de la ciudad y se considera un hombre moderno.
4. _____ En realidad, Beto sí hacía las camas, pasaba la aspiradora y lavaba los platos.
5. _____ Dulce cree que Beto está exagerando.
6. _____ Beto está nervioso y confiesa que no preparó la comida.

© Cengage Learning 2013

Voces de la comunidad

▶ >> Voces del mundo hispano

En el video para este capítulo Winnie y Carlos hablan de dónde viven ahora y qué quehaceres hacían de niño(a). Lee las siguientes oraciones. Después mira el video una o más veces para decir si las oraciones son ciertas **(C)** o falsas **(F)**.

1. Winnie tiene una casa en la Ciudad de Guatemala y vive con su hermana.

2. Carlos vive en un apartamento de dos cuartos.

3. En el cuarto de Winnie hay muchos recortes *(clippings)* de artistas y deportistas.

4. Carlos tiene cuadros de cultura de Nicaragua en las paredes de su habitación.

5. A Carlos le gustaba hacer todos los mandados (quehaceres) de la casa cuando era niño.

6. De niña Winnie compartía los quehaceres con su prima.

> Carlos uses the words **mandados** and **quehaceres** interchangeably. **Mandados** can also be used more specifically to mean errands.

🔊 >> Voces de Estados Unidos

Track 30

César y Rafael Pelli, arquitectos

❝Lo que importa es la ciudad. Los edificios son secundarios. Los arquitectos no entienden esto. Creen que su edificio es el más importante en el mundo. Pero un edificio es parte de una ciudad.❞

El World Financial Center en Nueva York, la Torre de Carnegie Hall y las Torres Gemelas Petronas de Kuala Lumpur (Malasia). Estos edificios, que figuran entre los más altos del mundo, son algunas de las obras maestras del famoso arquitecto argentino César Pelli. Después de licenciarse *(earned a degree)* en arquitectura en su país natal, Pelli vino a Estados Unidos a seguir sus estudios y luego decidió quedarse. Considerado uno de los arquitectos vivos *(living)* más importantes, ha recibido más de 200 premios por la excelencia en diseño y se han publicado numerosos libros y artículos sobre su obra. Fue decano de la escuela de arquitectura de Yale, ha sido premiado con la medalla de oro del American Institute of Architects (Instituto Estadounidense de Arquitectos) y tiene una de las firmas de arquitectura más solicitadas del mundo (Pelli Clarke Pelli), donde colabora con su hijo, Rafael, que también es un arquitecto de renombre *(renowned)*, y que ha enseñado arquitectura en la Universidad de Harvard, Parsons The New School of Design en Nueva York, y el Instituto de Arquitectura del Sur de California.

> The forms **ha recibido, se han publicado,** and **ha sido premiado** are all forms of the present perfect tense, which you will learn in **Chapter 14.** Their English equivalents are *has received, has published,* and *has been awarded.*

¿Y tú? ¿Te interesa la arquitectura? ¿Hay unos ejemplos de casas o edificios históricos o únicos en tu comunidad?

¡Prepárate!

Emphasizing ownership: Stressed possessives

Cómo usarlo

1. You have already learned how to express possession in Spanish using possessive adjectives and phrases with **de**.

   Es **tu** habitación.   It's *your* bedroom.
   Es la habitación **de Nati**.   It's *Nati's* bedroom.

2. When you wish to emphasize, contrast, or clarify who owns something, you can also use stressed possessives.

Stressed possessives		Unstressed possessive	
Es la casa **mía**.	*It's **my** house.*	Es **mi** casa.	*It's **my** house.*
¡La casa es **mía**!	*The house is **mine**!*		
La casa es **mía**, no **suya**.	*The house is **mine**, not **yours / his / hers**.*		

3. Stressed possessives must agree in number and gender with the noun they modify: **un libro mío, la calculadora mía, los platos míos, las mochilas mías**.

4. Stressed possessives may be used as adjectives with a noun, in which case they follow the noun: **Es el coche <u>mío</u>**. If it's clear what is being referred to, the noun may be dropped: **—¿De quién es el coche? —Es <u>mío</u>**.

5. Stressed possessives can also be used as pronouns that replace the noun. Notice that the article is maintained: **Le gusta <u>el coche mío</u>. Le gusta <u>el mío</u>**.

Cómo formarlo

English uses inflection and vocal stress to emphasize something: *These are **my** books.* In Spanish, inflection and vocal stress are not used the way they are in English. Instead, stressed possessive forms play this role. For example, if you want to emphasize ownership in Spanish, you would say **Estos libros son <u>míos</u>**, but never **Estos son <u>mis</u> libros**.

Here are the stressed possessive forms in Spanish.

	Singular	Plural	
yo	**mío, mía**	**míos, mías**	*my, mine*
tú	**tuyo, tuya**	**tuyos, tuyas**	*your, yours*
usted / él / ella	**suyo, suya**	**suyos, suyas**	*your, yours, his, her, hers, its*
nosotros / nosotras	**nuestro, nuestra**	**nuestros, nuestras**	*our, ours*
vosotros / vosotras	**vuestro, vuestra**	**vuestros, vuestras**	*your, yours*
ustedes / ellos / ellas	**suyo, suya**	**suyos, suyas**	*your, yours, their, theirs*

ACTIVIDADES

1 **Organizando la casa** Sigue el modelo para decir qué pertenece *(belongs)* a cada persona indicada.

MODELO él
Es suya.

1. yo

2. nosotros

3. usted

4. tú

5. ellos

2 **María, Elena y yo** Un amigo quiere saber de quién son ciertos muebles y decoraciones. Contesta sus preguntas según el modelo.

Track 31

MODELO Ves: *yo*
Escuchas: ¿De quién es esta lámpara?
Escribes: *Es mía.*

1. María
2. Elena
3. tú
4. Elena
5. María
6. yo

3 **La fiesta** Después de la fiesta, el anfitrión *(host)* encuentra algunas cosas de los invitados. Contesta sus preguntas con **no**, según el modelo.

MODELO Anfitrión: ¿Es éste el impermeable de Martín? (gris)
Tú: *No, no es suyo. El suyo es gris.*

1. ¿Es éste tu abrigo? (negro)
2. ¿Es ésta la bufanda de María? (azul)
3. ¿Son éstos los guantes de Miguel? (de piel)
4. ¿Son éstas las botas de ustedes? (de otra marca)
5. ¿Son éstas las bolsas de Ana y Adela? (verdes)

4 **¿De quién es?** En grupos de cuatro, hagan lo siguiente.

1. Cada persona escribe una descripción corta de su posesión favorita en un trocito de papel *(slip of paper)*.
2. Júntense con otro grupo para intercambiar los trocitos de papel. Túrnense para elegir un trocito del otro grupo y tratar de adivinar de quién es.

MODELO mi chaqueta de cuero negro, estilo motocicleta
Tú: *Sean, ¿es tuya?*
Compañero: *Sí, es mía.* O: *No, no es mía.*

© Cengage Learning 2013

>> Gramática útil 2

Hace mucho tiempo que no voy de picnic.

Expressing ongoing events and duration of time: Hace / Hacía with time expressions

Cómo usarlo

1. **Hace** and **hacía** are used to talk about ongoing actions and their duration. They can also be used to say how long it has been since someone has done something or since something has occurred. Look carefully at the following formulas and model sentences.

- To express *an action that has been occurring over a period of time and is still going on*

> **hace** + period of time + **que** + present indicative

Hace tres años que vivimos en este barrio.	*We've been living in this neighborhood for three years.*

- To say *how long it has been since you have done something*

> **hace** + period of time + **que** + **no** + present indicative

Hace seis meses que no salimos de la ciudad.	*We haven't left the city in six months.*

- To express *how long ago an event took place*

> preterite + **hace** + period of time

Vine aquí **hace tres años.**	*I came here three years ago.*

- To say *how long an action had been going on in the past* before another more recent past event

> **hacía** + period of time + **que** + imperfect

Cuando nos mudamos a esta nueva casa, **hacía cinco años que vivíamos** en ese apartamento.	*When we moved to this new house, we had been living in that apartment for five years.*

> You can also say **Hace tres años que vine aquí.** Notice that **que** precedes the verb in this case.

2. Use the following formulas to ask *questions* with **hace** and **hacía**.

- To ask *how long an action or event has been going on* (**hace** + present indicative)

¿Cuánto tiempo hace que vives aquí?	*How long have you been living here?*

- To ask *how long it has been since an action or event last occurred* (**hace** + **no** + present)

¿Cuánto tiempo hace que no hablas con tus abuelos?	*How long has it been since you spoke to your grandparents?*

Image copyright: © Cengage Learning 2013

- To ask *how long ago an action took place* (**hace** + preterite)

¿Cuánto tiempo hace que hablaste con tus abuelos?

How long ago did you speak to your grandparents?

- To ask *how long an action or event had been going on in the past* (**hacía** + imperfect)

¿Cuánto tiempo hacía que no podías ir a las clases cuando decidiste ir al médico?

How long had you not been able to go to classes when you decided to go to the doctor?

> Notice that in all these examples only the forms **hace** and **hacía** are used.

ACTIVIDADES

5 **¡Odio los quehaceres!** Odias los quehaceres. Di cuánto tiempo hace que no haces ciertos quehaceres en tu casa.

MODELO ...no pasar la aspiradora (dos meses)
Hace dos meses que no paso la aspiradora.

1. ...no limpiar el baño (tres semanas)
2. ...no preparar la comida en casa (una semana)
3. ...no cortar el césped (seis semanas)
4. ...no trabajar en el jardín (un mes)
5. ...no lavar el auto (tres meses)
6. ...no arreglar el sótano (dos años)
7. ...no trapear el piso (un mes)

6 **Hacía cinco años que…** Manuel y su familia se mudaron de Guatemala a Estados Unidos hace muchos años. Manuel recuerda cuando él se graduó del colegio. ¿Qué dice?

MODELO nosotros / vivir en Estados Unidos (5)
Cuando me gradué del colegio, hacía cinco años que vivíamos en Estados Unidos.

1. yo / estudiar inglés (10)
2. mamá / estudiar computación (3)
3. mi novia y yo / conocerse (1)
4. nosotros / alquilar nuestra casa (2)

7 **¿Y tú?** Túrnense para preguntarle a un(a) compañero(a) cuánto tiempo hace que él o ella no hace los quehaceres de la **Actividad 5**.

MODELO Tú: *¿Cuánto tiempo hace que no pasas la aspiradora?*
Compañero(a): *Hace dos semanas que no paso la aspiradora.*

8 **¿Cuánto tiempo hace?** Túrnense para preguntarle a un(a) compañero(a) cuánto tiempo hace que participó en ciertas actividades. Puedes usar ideas de la lista o puedes inventar tus propias preguntas.

Ideas: estudiar español en…, comprar tu carro, hablar con tus abuelos, mudarte a tu apartamento, conocer a tu novio(a), ¿…?

MODELO Tú: *¿Cuánto tiempo hace que estudiaste español en Nicaragua?*
Compañero(a): *Estudié español en Nicaragua hace cinco años.*

Sonrisas

Pasé los últimos diez años en un monasterio budista en Nepal.

Hace diez años que no viajo en avión.

Hace diez años que no leo una novela moderna.

Como dicen los budistas: Lo único que no cambia es que ¡TODO cambia!

© Cengage Learning 2013

Expresión En grupos de tres o cuatro estudiantes, imaginen que pasaron los últimos diez años en un sitio donde el mundo tecnológico no existe como existe hoy en sus vidas diarias. Vuelvan a escribir *(Rewrite)* la tira cómica con las cosas que les sorprende cuando vuelven al mundo de hoy.

¿Conoces a alguien como el hombre en la tira, que no sabe mucho del mundo de hoy? ¿Qué cosas le sorprenden?

Gramática útil 3

Expressing yourself correctly: Choosing between por and para

Cómo usarlo

1. You have already learned some expressions that use the prepositions **por** (**por favor, por lo general**) and **para** (**Para plato principal, voy a pedir…**).

2. **Por** and **para** are often translated with the same words in English, but they are not used interchangeably in Spanish. Here are some guidelines to help you use them correctly.

por dentro ...

y por fuera

por dentro la belleza y elegancia de las maderas nobles naturales de roble o sapelly barnizadas.

por fuera el acabado y la dureza del aluminio lacado al fuego.

Can you figure out why **por** is used in this ad and not **para**?

Use **por**...	
to describe the *method by which an action is carried out*.	Viajamos **por** avión. Hablamos **por** teléfono. Nos comunicamos **por** Internet.
to give a *cause or reason*.	Miguel está preocupado **por** su salud. Elena está nerviosa **por** el examen.
to give a *time of day*.	Vamos al café **por** la tarde. **Por** las noches, comemos en casa.
to describe *motion through or around* a place.	Pasamos **por** la playa todas las mañanas. Vas **por** el centro de la ciudad y luego doblas a la izquierda.
to express the idea of an *exchange*.	Pagué doce dólares **por** el espejo. ¡Gracias **por** todo!
to say that something was done on *behalf of someone else*.	Lo hice **por** mi hermano porque estaba enfermo. Puedo hablar **por** ellos.
to express *units of measurement*.	Venden las naranjas **por** kilo. Venden la harina **por** gramos.
to express *duration of time*.	Estuvimos en el restaurante **por** dos horas. Fuimos a Bolivia **por** tres semanas.
in certain *fixed expressions*.	**por ejemplo** (*for example*) **por eso** (*so, that's why*) **por favor** (*please*) **por fin** (*finally*) **por lo menos** (*at least*) **por supuesto** (*of course*)

Use **para**...	
to indicate *destination*.	Salimos **para** un parque en las afueras y nos perdimos.
to indicate a *recipient* of an object or action.	El cuadro es **para** Angélica. Limpié la casa **para** mis padres.
to indicate a *deadline or specific time in the future*.	Hicimos reservaciones en el restaurante **para** la próxima semana.
to express *intent or purpose*.	Estas lámparas son **para** la sala. Vinieron temprano **para** limpiar la casa.
to indicate an *employer*.	Trabajo **para** la universidad.
to make a *comparison* or state an *opinion*	**Para** estudiante, tiene mucho dinero. **Para** mí, la sopa de ajo es la mejor de todas.

3. To aid your understanding of these two prepositions, here are some ways they are translated into English.

Por	Para
(in exchange) for	*for* (deadline)
during, in	*toward, in the direction of*
through, along	*for* (recipient or purpose)
on behalf of	*in order to* + verb
for (duration of an event)	*for . . .* (in comparison with others)
by (transportation)	*for* (employer)

ACTIVIDADES

🔊 Track 32

9 **¿Por qué?** Escucha las oraciones. Indica si usan **por** o **para** y escoge la razón correcta.

1. _____ Razón: ☐ cause or reason   ☐ deadline
2. _____ Razón: ☐ employer   ☐ time of day
3. _____ Razón: ☐ duration of time   ☐ destination
4. _____ Razón: ☐ method   ☐ state opinion
5. _____ Razón: ☐ recipient   ☐ fixed expression
6. _____ Razón: ☐ intent or purpose   ☐ exchange

10 **¡Vamos a Nicaragua!** Ernesto va a viajar a Nicaragua. Completa su descripción con **por** o **para** para saber más de su viaje con su familia.

1. Vamos a ir a Nicaragua _____ las vacaciones.
2. Vamos principalmente _____ visitar a mis tíos.
3. Hicimos las reservaciones _____ Internet.
4. Pagamos muy poco _____ los boletos.
5. Mi tío trabaja _____ una compañía de telecomunicaciones en Nicaragua.
6. Nos vamos a quedar en Managua _____ un mes.

11 **Preguntas personales** Túrnense para hacer y contestar las siguientes preguntas.

1. ¿Qué cosas necesitas para tu cuarto, apartamento o casa? ¿Por qué? ¿Para qué los vas a usar?

2. ¿A qué hora normalmente regresas a tu cuarto, apartamento o casa? ¿Por la tarde? ¿Por la noche?

3. Piensa en cuatro de tus posesiones favoritas. ¿Recuerdas cuánto pagaste por cada una?

4. Para ti, ¿cuál es la cosa más importante que necesitas cuando buscas un apartamento o casa? ¿Por qué?

5. ¿Qué quehaceres domésticos necesitas hacer? ¿Para cuándo debes hacerlos?

6. Si tienes compañero(a) de cuarto, ¿qué haces para ayudarle a él o ella? ¿Qué hace él o ella para ayudarte a ti?

7. Durante un día normal, ¿por cuántas horas estás en tu cuarto, apartamento o casa?

12 **¿Por o para?** Vas a hacerle cinco preguntas a tu compañero(a). Usa elementos de las cuatro columnas para formar las preguntas. Luego, él o ella te va a hacer cinco preguntas a ti. Sé creativo(a) con tus preguntas y sincero(a) con tus respuestas.

MODELOS *¿Te gusta hacer compras por Internet?*
Cuando haces reservaciones, ¿prefieres hacerlas por Internet o por teléfono?
Cuando termines la universidad, ¿quieres trabajar para una compañía internacional o nacional?

Columna A	Columna B	Columna C	Columna D
¿Te gusta...?	hacer compras	por	Internet o en persona
¿Vas a...?	hacer reservaciones	para	un restaurante, el cine, etc.
¿Quieres...?	esperar a un amigo		media hora, una hora, dos horas, etc.
¿…?	viajar		avión (autobús, tren, etc.)
	comprar un regalo		[nombre de persona]
	trabajar		una compañía (de..., multinacional, etc.)
	comunicarte		teléfono (correo electrónico, mensaje de texto, etc.)
	¿…?		¿...?

Guatemala

De Agostini/Getty Images

Información general ▶

Nombre oficial: República de Guatemala

Población: 13.550.440

Capital: Guatemala (f. 1775) (1.104.890 hab.)

Otras ciudades importantes: Mixco (410.000 hab.), Villa Nueva (400.000 hab.)

Moneda: quetzal

Idiomas: español (oficial), lenguas mayas y otras lenguas amerindias

Mapa de Guatemala: Apéndice D

Vale saber…

- La gran civilización maya florece en grandes ciudades como Tikal, Uaxactún y Dos Pilas. Cuando llega el explorador español Pedro de Alvarado a Guatemala en 1524, la civilización maya ya está en declive *(decline)*.

Craig Chiasson/iStockphoto

- Guatemala gana la independencia de España en 1821. Guatemala pasa por una guerra civil en los años 1960–1996. La guerra termina con un acuerdo de paz facilitado por las Naciones Unidas.

- La gran mayoría de la población o es de ascendencia maya (más del 40%), o es mestiza (59%). Hoy día en el país se hablan más de veinte lenguas de la familia maya-quiché.

- "La biblia" de los maya-quiché es el *Popol Vuh*. Este libro sagrado describe la creación de los hombres, las mujeres y el mundo entero.

Nicaragua

Información general

Nombre oficial: República de Nicaragua

Población: 5.995.928

Capital: Managua (f. 1522) (2.000.000 hab.)

Otras ciudades importantes: León (200.000 hab.), Chinandega (180.000 hab.)

Moneda: córdoba

Idiomas: español (oficial), mosquito, inglés y lenguas indígenas en la costa atlántica

Mapa de Nicaragua: Apéndice D

Andoni Canela/Photolibrary

Vale saber…

- Antes de la llegada de Cristóbal Colón, varios grupos indígenas vivían en Nicaragua: los nicaraos, los chorotegas, los chontales y los mosquitos (llamados también 'misquitos' en otras partes de Centroamérica). Hoy día, el 69% de la población de Nicaragua es mestiza.

- Cristóbal Colón llega a la región en 1502, aunque las primeras colonizaciones españolas no se fundan hasta 1524. En 1838, Nicaragua se hace república independiente.

- Nicaragua ha tenido *(has had)* varios dictadores, pero la de la dinastía de Anastasio Somoza entre 1926–1979 fue la más larga. La Revolución Sandinista ocurre en 1978 y resulta en ponerle fin a la dictadura de la familia Somoza.

- En 1990, Violeta Barrios Chamorro fue la primera mujer presidenta elegida democráticamente en las Américas.

- En Acahualinca, a orillas *(on the shores)* del lago de Managua, hay unas famosas huellas *(footprints)* antiguas que tienen más de seis mil años. Una hipótesis de su origen sugiere que se formaron cuando unas personas pisaron *(they stepped on)* la lava caliente mientras escapaban de una erupción volcánica.

Nik Wheeler/Photolibrary

Bruno Domingos/Reuters/Landov

Construcciones creativas

Cuando Mateo Paneitz, un voluntario del Cuerpo de Paz, llegó a San Juan Comalapa, en Guatemala, se encontró con una situación desagradable: todos echaban la basura al río, incluso él. Para resolver dos problemas a la vez, la contaminación y el desempleo, tuvo la idea de usar la basura como materia prima *(raw material)* para la construcción de edificios. Su proyecto de reciclaje ha recibido *(has received)* atención internacional por su innovación y su doble objetivo de preservar el medio ambiente *(environment)* y crear puestos de trabajo para la gente de la comunidad. La idea central de la organización *Long Way Home*, empezada por Paneitz en 2004, es construir edificios con desechos *(waste)* reciclados. En seis años, han construido una escuela, una casa, una cocina y tienen planes para construir más hogares y edificios con llantas *(tires)*, botellas, bolsas y tubos de plástico. Su primera obra, La Escuela Técnica Maya, existe como testimonio de lo que se puede hacer con una buena idea, mucha cooperación y bastante pasión.

Hogar, verde hogar *(home)*

Las ocho mujeres superpoderosas *(powerful)* que formaron el conglomerado Alter Eco decidieron que querían crear una sinergía entre sus pequeños negocios *(businesses)* para ofrecer una nueva alternativa verde y nacional. Las seis tiendas forman un mini-centro comercial y tienen un compromiso *(obligation)* con la mujer, la naturaleza y los artesanos nicaragüenses. El lema de Alter Eco, "alianza hecha a mano *(handmade)*", lo dice todo. Carla Fjeld, una de las propietarias, explica: "…en los malls te venden cosas de todas partes del mundo y jamás conoces a las personas que las elaboran, mientras que aquí las cosas están hechas a mano, por artesanos que los clientes pueden conocer…". Puedes hacer de tu casa un hogar verde al comprar una lámpara o un bello mueble hecho de madera *(wood)* de fuentes sostenibles, o puedes decorar tu cocina con cerámicas sin plomo *(lead-free)* diseñadas por pintores nicaragüenses. El que hace sus compras en Alter Eco invita la armonía con la naturaleza a su propio hogar.

LA PRENSA/DIANA NIVIA. Used with permission.

>> En resumen

La información general

1. ¿Qué gran civilización está en declive cuando llegan los españoles a Guatemala en 1524?
2. ¿En qué año gana Guatemala la independencia de España?
3. ¿Cómo termina la guerra civil de Guatemala?
4. ¿Cuándo se hace república independiente Nicaragua?
5. ¿Qué revolución le pone fin a la dictadura de la familia Somoza?
6. ¿Quién fue la primera mujer presidenta elegida democráticamente en las Américas?

El tema de la vivienda

1. ¿Cuál es la idea central del proyecto de reciclaje de *Long Way Home?*
2. ¿Qué dos problemas intenta resolver el programa de reciclaje de *Long Way Home?*
3. ¿Qué es Alter Eco?
4. Al crear Alter Eco, ¿qué tres cosas son importantes para las propietarias?

🌐 ¿QUIERES SABER MÁS?

Revisa y rellena la tabla que empezaste al principio del capítulo. Luego, escoge un tema para investigar en línea y prepárate para compartir la información con la clase. También puedes escoger de las palabras clave a continuación o en **www.cengagebrain.com**.

Palabras clave: (Guatemala) los dialectos maya-quiché, *Popol Vuh*, Efraín Ríos Montt, la familia de Rigoberta Menchú Tum, Augusto Monterroso, Miguel Ángel Asturias, Carlos Mérida; **(Nicaragua)**; Mosquitos, Anastasio Somoza, Sandino, Revolución Sandinista; el modernismo, Rubén Darío, Ernesto Cardenal, Violeta Chamorro

---

🌐 **Tú en el mundo hispano** Para explorar oportunidades de usar el español para estudiar o hacer trabajos voluntarios o aprendizajes en Guatemala y Nicaragua, sigue los enlaces en **www.cengagebrain.com**.

🎵 **Ritmos del mundo hispano** Sigue los enlaces en **www.cengagebrain.com** para escuchar música de Guatemala y Nicaragua.

A leer

ESTRATEGIA

Understanding poetry

Many poems feature rhyme **(la rima)**. Words rhyme when they share similar sounds, for example, **pino** and **fino**. Blank verse **(El verso libre)** is a kind of poetry that does not follow the usual rules of rhyme. Instead, it relies on the sounds of words and the division of lines to create its own sense of rhythm and motion.

AFP/Getty Images

Valga in this context loosely means *let this (page) serve*. **Intentar** means *to try*.

1 Vas a leer un poema de Rubén Darío (1867–1916), considerado el poeta más importante de Nicaragua, y un poema en dos partes de un poeta nicaragüense vanguardista, José Coronel Urtecho (1906–1994). Estos poemas, entre otros, aparecen en un sitio web que se llama "Dariana". Lee el siguiente comentario del sitio web sobre Darío y contesta las preguntas a continuación.

"Se ha dicho que el mejor producto de exportación de Nicaragua es su poesía. Y toda nuestra mejor poesía y, por qué no, nuestra misma nicaraguanidad nacen *(are born)* y se fundamentan en Rubén Darío… Darío pronosticó que un día su poesía, indefectiblemente, iría a las muchedumbres *(would reach the masses)*. Valga esta humilde página y esta todo-abarcante *(all-encompassing)* tecnología para intentarlo".

1. Según este comentario, ¿cuál es el mejor producto de exportación de Nicaragua?
2. ¿Creía Darío que muchas o pocas personas leerían *(would read)* su poesía?

2 Lee las siguientes preguntas. Después, lee los poemas de la página 371 rápidamente para buscar las respuestas. (Luego vas a leer los poemas otra vez.)

1. ¿Cuál(es) de los poemas se escribe(n) en rima? ¿Se escribe uno en verso libre?
2. Busca un ejemplo de dos palabras que riman.
3. Busca el uso de la repetición de palabras en los dos poemas. Escribe dos ejemplos de la repetición de una palabra o de palabras semejantes.
4. ¿Cuál es el tema principal de los dos poemas?

3 Ahora lee los poemas con más detalle. Escucha los sonidos *(sounds)* de las palabras y trata de entender la idea principal de cada poema.

LECTURA

Dos canciones de amor para el otoño
José Coronel Urtecho

I Cuando ya nada pido
y casi nada espero
y apenas puedo nada[1]
es cuando más te quiero.

II Basta[2] que estés, que seas
Que te pueda llamar, que te llame María
Para saber quién soy y conocer quién eres
Para saberme tuyo y conocerte mía
Mi mujer entre todas las mujeres.

Amo, amas
Rubén Darío

Amar[3], amar, amar siempre, con todo
el ser y con la tierra y con el cielo[4],
con lo claro del sol y lo oscuro del lodo[5]:
amar por toda ciencia y amar por todo anhelo[6].

Y cuando la montaña de la vida
nos sea dura y larga y alta y llena de abismos,
amar la inmensidad que es de amor encendida[7]
¡y arder[8] en la fusión de nuestros pechos[9] mismos!

[1]**apenas…:** *There's nothing to be done, I can do no more.* [2]**Basta…:** Es bastante [3]*to love* [4]**con la tierra…:** *with the earth and with the sky* [5]*mud* [6]*wish, desire* [7]*burning, on fire* [8]*to burn* [9]*hearts (literally, chests)*

>> Después de leer

4 Trabaja con un(a) compañero(a) para contestar las preguntas de comprensión.

"Dos canciones de amor para el otoño, I, II" de Coronel Urtecho

1. ¿Cuál de las siguientes oraciones mejor expresa la idea central del primer poema?
   a. Cuando el autor no tiene esperanza es cuando está más enamorado.
   b. El autor no pide ni espera el amor, porque no lo quiere.
   c. El autor no puede querer a nadie porque no tiene esperanza.

2. ¿Es optimista o pesimista la actitud del poeta? ¿Por qué?

3. ¿Cuál de los poemas les gustó más? ¿Por qué?

"Amo, amas" de Darío

4. ¿Cuál de las siguientes oraciones mejor expresa la idea central del poema?
   a. El amor es duro *(hard)* y difícil.
   b. El amor es como una montaña alta que es difícil escalar.
   c. El amor verdadero es eterno, como la naturaleza.

5. ¿Es optimista o pesimista la actitud del poeta? ¿Por qué?

6. ¿Están de acuerdo con el mensaje del poema?

A escribir

ESTRATEGIA

Writing—Adding transitions between paragraphs

You have learned how to write paragraphs that contain a topic sentence and supporting detail. Often the shift from one paragraph to another may sound choppy without transition words and phrases that make a thematic link (**enlace**) between the content of the two paragraphs. In that case you may need to write an opening transition sentence for a new paragraph that is then followed by the topic sentence, or add a transitional phrase to the beginning of your topic sentence.

1 Vas a escribir una descripción de tres párrafos. Escoge tu sitio preferido en tu cuarto, residencia estudiantil, apartamento o casa y descríbelo. Después, habla de lo que haces allí y explica por qué es tu sitio preferido. Organiza la información según la siguiente tabla.

Párrafo 1: ¿Cómo es el sitio?	Párrafo 2: ¿Qué haces allí?	Párrafo 3: ¿Por qué es tu sitio preferido?
Oración temática:	Oración temática:	Oración temática:
Detalles interesantes:	Detalles interesantes:	Detalles interesantes:

Marcos Welsh /age fotostock

>> Composición

2 Escribe el borrador de tu composición, escribiendo sin detener *(freewriting)* y sin preocuparte por el momento por las transiciones entre párrafos.

>> Después de escribir

3 Ahora vas a crear las transiciones entre los párrafos. Mira tu composición y copia las oraciones indicadas en otra hoja de papel.

1. Última oración del Párrafo 1:
2. Primera oración del Párrafo 2:
3. Última oración del Párrafo 2:
4. Primera oración del Párrafo 3:

4 Mira las oraciones que escribiste para la **Actividad 3** y añade las transiciones entre los párrafos. Aquí tienes algunas palabras y expresiones que pueden servir como enlaces.

a pesar de que	*in spite of*
afortunadamente	*fortunately*
al contrario	*on the contrary*
como resultado	*as a result*
de esta manera / de este modo	*(in) this way*
de igual importancia	*of equal importance*
de la misma manera / del mismo modo	*in the same way*
desgraciadamente	*unfortunately*
por un lado	*on one hand*
por el otro lado	*on the other hand*
por esta razón	*for this reason*
sin decir más / demasiado	*without saying more / too much*
sin embargo	*nevertheless*

1. Enlace entre Párrafo 1 y Párrafo 2:
2. Enlace entre Párrafo 2 y Párrafo 3:

5 Revisa la composición y añade tus nuevos enlaces. Usa la siguiente lista para ayudarte a revisar la composición entera otra vez.

- ¿Ayudan los enlaces a clarificar la transición entre los párrafos?
- ¿Usaste algunas de las palabras y expresiones de la lista para los enlaces?
- ¿Hay algo que no es necesario? ¿Hay algo que falta *(is missing)*?
- ¿Usaste bien las formas posesivas?
- ¿Usaste **por** y **para** correctamente?
- ¿Hay errores de puntuación o de ortografía?

Vocabulario

Áreas de la ciudad   *Parts of the city*

las afueras *the outskirts*
el apartamento *apartment*
el barrio *neighborhood*
…comercial *business district*
…residencial *residential neighborhood*

el centro de la ciudad *downtown*
los suburbios *suburbs*
los vecinos *neighbors*

La casa   *The house*

el baño *bathroom*
la chimenea *fireplace*
el clóset *closet*
la cocina *kitchen*
el comedor *dining room*
el dormitorio (el cuarto, la habitación, la recámara) *bedroom*
las escaleras *stairs*
el garaje *garage*
el jardín *garden, yard*

la lavandería *laundry room*
la oficina *office*
la pared *wall*
el pasillo *hallway*
el patio *patio*
el primer piso (segundo, etc.) *first floor (second, etc.)*
la sala *living room*
el sótano *basement, cellar*
el techo *roof*

Números ordinales   *Ordinal numbers*

primer(o) *first*
segundo *second*
tercer(o) *third*
cuarto *fourth*
quinto *fifth*

sexto *sixth*
séptimo *seventh*
octavo *eighth*
noveno *ninth*
décimo *tenth*

Los quehaceres domésticos   *Household chores*

Dentro de la casa   *Inside the house*
arreglar el dormitorio *to straighten up the bedroom*
barrer el suelo (el piso) *to sweep the floor*
guardar la ropa *to put away the clothes*
hacer la cama *to make the bed*
lavar los platos (la ropa) *to wash the dishes (the clothes)*
limpiar el baño *to clean the bathroom*
pasar la aspiradora *to vacuum*
planchar *to iron*
poner los juguetes en su lugar *to put the toys away*
poner y quitar la mesa *to set and to clear the table*
preparar la comida *to prepare the food*
sacudir los muebles *to dust the furniture*
trapear el piso *to mop the floor*

Fuera de la casa   *Outside the house*
cortar el césped *to mow the lawn*
darle de comer al perro (gato) *to feed the dog (cat)*

hacer el reciclaje *to do the recycling*
regar (ie) las plantas *to water the plants*
sacar a pasear al perro *to take the dog for a walk*
sacar la basura *to take out the garbage*

Los muebles y decoraciones   *Furniture and decorations*
la alfombra *rug, carpet*
la cama *bed*
las cortinas *curtains*
el cuadro *painting, print*
el espejo *mirror*
la lámpara *lamp*
la mesa *table*
la mesita de noche *night table*
la persiana *Venetian blind*
la silla *chair*
el sillón *armchair*
el sofá *sofa*
el tocador (la cómoda) *dresser*

Los electrodomésticos *Appliances*

el abrelatas eléctrico *electric can opener*
la aspiradora *vacuum cleaner*
el congelador *freezer*
la estufa *stove*
la lavadora *washer*
el lavaplatos *dishwasher*
la licuadora *blender*

el microondas *microwave*
la plancha *iron*
el procesador de comida *food processor*
el refrigerador *refrigerator*
la secadora *dryer*
el televisor *television set*
la tostadora *toaster*

Adjetivos posesivos

mío, mía, míos, mías *my, mine*
tuyo, tuya, tuyos, tuyas *your, yours*
suyo, suya, suyos, suyas *your, yours, his, her, hers, its, their, theirs*
nuestro, nuestra, nuestros, nuestras *our, ours*
vuestro, vuestra, vuestros, vuestras *your, yours*

Otras palabras y expresiones

para *for; by* (a deadline); *toward, in the direction of; for* (a specific recipient, employer, or purpose); *in order to* (+ verb); *for. . .* (in comparison with others)
por (in exchange) *for; during; through, along; on behalf of; for* (duration of an event); *by* (a means of transportation)
por ejemplo *for example*
por eso *so, that's why*
por favor *please*
por fin *finally*
por lo menos *at least*
por supuesto *of course*

Repaso y preparación

>> ## Repaso del Capítulo 10

Complete these activities to check your understanding of the new grammar points in **Chapter 10** before you move on to **Chapter 11**.

The answers to the activities in this section can be found in **Appendix B**.

Stressed possessives (p. 358)

1 Escribe oraciones con posesivos enfáticos según el modelo.

MODELO yo (no) / tú (sí)
¿La licuadora? No es mía. Es tuya.

1.
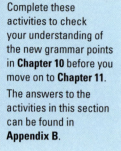
tú (no) / ellos (sí)

2.
usted (no) / yo (sí)

3.

nosotros (no) / ustedes (sí)

4.
yo (no) / ella (sí)

5.
él (no) / nosotros (sí)

6.
ellos (no) / tú (sí)

Hace / Hacía with time expressions (p. 360)

2 Contesta las preguntas con oraciones que contengan **hace** o **hacía** para expresar la duración de un evento o situación. Presta atención al contexto para ver si se refiere al momento presente o al pasado.

1. ¿Cuánto tiempo hace que Sarita no va de vacaciones? (un año)
2. ¿Cuánto tiempo hace que ellos viven en esa casa? (seis meses)
3. ¿Cuánto tiempo hace que ellos limpiaron el baño? (dos semanas)
4. ¿Cuánto tiempo hacía que Luis no podía trabajar en la casa? (tres meses)
5. ¿Cuánto tiempo hace que los abuelos vinieron de visita? (dos años)

Por and para (p. 363)

3 Completa las oraciones con **por** o **para**, según el caso.

1. ¡Pagué sólo cuarenta dólares _____ ese sillón!
2. _____ mí, es importante tener una casa limpia.
3. ¡_____ fin arreglaste tu dormitorio!
4. Limpiamos la casa _____ tres horas ayer.
5. Compré esta lámpara _____ Angelita.
6. _____ la mañana, normalmente lavo la ropa.
7. ¡Tenemos que organizar y limpiar la sala _____ mañana!
8. Mi madre trabaja _____ una tienda que vende muebles.

Preparación para el Capítulo 11

>>

Complete these activities to review some previously learned grammatical structures that will be helpful when you learn the new grammar in **Chapter 11**.

In addition, be sure to reread **Chapter 10: Gramática útil 1** before moving on to the new **Chapter 11** grammar sections.

Regular and stem-changing present-indicative **yo** forms (Chapters 2, 3, and 4)

4 Completa las oraciones con las formas correctas de **yo** de los verbos indicados.

Todas las semanas, tengo mucho que hacer en casa.

1. _____ (lavar) los platos.
2. _____ (planchar) la ropa.
3. _____ (barrer) el suelo.
4. _____ (sacudir) los muebles.
5. _____ (hervir) el agua para el café.
6. _____ (regar) las plantas.
7. _____ (servir) la comida a la familia.
8. _____ (volver) a lavar los platos.
9. Les _____ (pedir) ayuda a los hijos.
10. Al final del día, ¡_____ (dormir) muy bien!

Irregular-**yo** forms and **yo** forms of irregular verbs (Chapters 1, 3, 4, and 5)

5 Completa las oraciones con la forma **yo** del verbo indicado.

1. _____ (estar) en el jardín.
2. _____ (conducir) al centro.
3. A las seis, le _____ (dar) de comer al perro.
4. Le _____ (decir) "Hola" a mi vecino.
5. _____ (oír) el tono de la secadora.
6. _____ (venir) para cortar el césped.
7. _____ (ver) al jardinero los lunes.
8. _____ (saber) reparar la tostadora.
9. _____ (poner) la mesa para la cena.
10. _____ (tener) una sofá y dos sillones.

Negative tú commands (Chapter 7)

6 Completa las oraciones con los mandatos negativos informales correctos.

1. Por favor, no _____ (lavar) los platos ahora mismo.
2. ¡Ay, no _____ (planchar) esa blusa de seda!
3. No _____ (sacar) a pasear al perro cuando hace mucho frío.
4. No _____ (pasar) la aspiradora mientras los niños están durmiendo.
5. ¡No _____ (poner) la mesa con esas copas sucias!
6. No _____ (usar) ese microondas; está roto.
7. No _____ (trapear) el piso cuando estoy preparando la comida.
8. No _____ (sacudir) los muebles con ese trapo sucio.
9. ¡No _____ (comer) dulces antes de la cena!
10. No _____ (insistir) en ver ese programa; ya es tarde.

Reference Materials

Appendix A: KWL Chart

Lo que sé	Lo que quiero saber	Lo que aprendí

Capítulo 1 (pp. 40–41)

Act. 1: 1. la 2. X 3. la 4. X 5. X 6. X 7. unos 8. una 9. los

Act. 2: 1. Tú 2. Nosotros 3. Yo 4. es 5. son 6. somos

Act. 3: 1. Hay dos chicas. 2. Hay un hombre. 3. Hay una mujer. 4. No hay niño. 5. No hay computadora. 6. No hay mochila. 7. Hay una serpiente. 8. No hay elefante.

Act. 4: 1. tienes 2. tiene 3. tengo 4. tenemos 5. tienen 6. tienes

Act. 5: 1. tengo que 2. tienen que 3. tenemos que 4. tiene que 5. tienes que 6. tienen que

Act. 6: *Answers will vary depending on current year.* 1. Tú tienes... años. 2. Ellos tienen... años. 3. Usted tiene... años. 4. Ella tiene... años. 5. Yo tengo... años. 6. Nosotros tenemos... años. 7. Ustedes tienen... años. 8. Tú y yo tenemos... años.

Capítulo 2 (pp. 80–81)

Act. 1: 1. Esteban y Carolina caminan. 2. Usted pinta. 3. Loreta levanta pesas. 4. Yo saco fotos. 5. Nosotros tomamos el sol. 6. Tú cocinas. 7. Ustedes hablan por teléfono. 8. Tú y yo patinamos.

Act. 2: 1. A mí me gusta estudiar. 2. A ti te gusta mirar televisión. 3. A usted le gusta visitar a amigos. 4. A nosotras nos gusta pintar. 5. A ustedes les gusta practicar deportes.

Act. 3: 1. Gretchen y Rolf son alemanes. Son muy sinceros. 2. Brigitte es francesa. Es muy divertida. 3. Nosotras somos españolas. Somos simpáticas. 4. Yo soy estadounidense. Soy muy generosa. 5. Usted es japonesa. Es muy interesante. 6. Tú eres italiano. Eres muy activo.

Act. 4: 1. las 2. El 3. la 4. unos 5. la 6. una 7. un 8. la 9. la 10. las

Act. 5: 1. f, es 2. d, es 3. a, es 4. g, son 5. b, somos 6. e, eres 7. c, soy

Capítulo 3 (pp. 118–119)

Act. 1: 1. qué 2. Por qué 3. Cuál 4. cuándo 4. Cuántas 5. Quién

Act. 2: 1. escribe 2. debemos 3. como 4. viven 5. lee

Act. 3: 1. mis 2. tus 3. nuestra 4. sus 5. sus 6. mi

Act. 4: 1. voy, van 2. va, vamos 3. vas

Act. 5: 1. A mí me gusta leer. 2. A nosotros nos gusta comer. 3. A ustedes les gusta bailar. 4. A ti te gusta cocinar. 5. A él le gusta patinar. 6. A mí me gusta cantar.

Act. 6: 1. estudia 2. cocina 3. toca 4. canta 5. levantan 6. practican 7. miramos 8. alquilamos 9. trabajo 10. visito 11. paso

Act. 7: 1. Rogelio y Mauricio son muy egoístas. 2. Tú eres muy impaciente. 3. Nosotros somos muy perezosos. 4. Yo soy muy activo(a). 5. Sandra es muy generosa. 6. Néstor y Nicolás son muy tímidos.

Capítulo 4 (pp. 158–159)

Act. 1: 1. les gustan 2. me encanta 3. le molesta 4. nos interesan 5. te importa 6. le gusta

Act. 2: 1. estás 2. estamos 3. soy 4. son 5. Estoy 6. Está 7. es 8. es 9. está 10. son 11. es 12. están

Act. 3: 1. Tú duermes mucho. 2. Yo cierro la computadora portátil. 3. Ella entiende las instrucciones. 4. Nosotras jugamos el juego interactivo. 5. Usted repite la contraseña. 6. Ellos quieren un MP3 portátil. 7. Yo puedo instalar el programa. 8. Nosotros preferimos ir a un café con wifi.

Act. 4: 1. lentamente 2. rápidamente 3. Generalmente 4. fácilmente

Act. 5: debe, envias, recibes, grabas, instalas, llevas, trabajas, hablan, funciona, bajo, subo, pesa, saco, accedo, leo, usamos, comentan, ofrecemos, vendemos, debes

Capítulo 5 (pp. 194–195)

Act. 1: *Answers will vary for **Sí/No** column.* 1. Sé 2. Conozco 3. Conduzco 4. Hago 5. Salgo 6. Veo

Act. 2: 1. Tú conoces Buenos Aires. 2. Ellos saben jugar golf. 3. Yo sé todas las respuestas. 4. Usted conoce a mis primos. 5. Nosotras conocemos al chef. 6. Ella sabe cocinar bien.

Act. 3: 1. se maquilla 2. me acuesto 3. se reunen 4. te levantas 5. nos enfermamos 6. se pelean

Act. 4: 1. Ella está hablando con un paciente. 2. Yo estoy escribiendo un artículo. 3. Ellos están preparando la comida. 4. Nosotros estamos pintando. 5. Usted está sirviendo la comida. 6. Él está trabajando en la computadora.

Act. 5: 1. grande 2. extrovertidas 3. simpáticas 4. tonto 5. contentos 6. nerviosos 7. viejos 8. divertidos 9. triste

Act. 6: 1. Mi tío lava su auto todas las semanas. 2. Mis abuelos no duermen mucho. 3. Mis primas prefieren estudiar en la residencia estudiantil. 4. Mi hermano y yo corremos en el parque los sábados. 5. Tú manejas todos los días. 6. Mi madre viste a mi hermanita por las mañanas. 7. Yo miro una película. 8. Mi madre y yo vivimos en un apartamento grande.

Act. 7: 1. La mujer de negocios está en la oficina. 2. Tú y yo estamos en el salón de clase. 3. El Doctor Méndez está en el hospital. 4. Los programadores están en el centro de computación. 5. La policía está en el parque. 6. Yo estoy en la biblioteca. 7. Los cocineros están en el restaurante. 8. Tú estás en el gimnasio.

Capítulo 6 (pp. 228–229)

Act. 1: El perro está lejos del auto. 2. El perro está delante del auto. 3. El perro está detrás del auto. 4. El perro está debajo del auto. 5. El perro está dentro del auto. 6. El perro está entre los autos.

Act. 2: 1. Vengan, pierdan 2. Ponga, Hable 3. Haga, Llame

Act. 3: 1. Siempre, 2. También, 3. algunos 4. nada 5. algo 6. nadie

Act. 4: 1. estos, ésos 2. aquella, ésta 3. esos, aquéllos 4. esta, ésa 5. aquellas, éstas 6. este, ése

Act. 5: 1. salgo 2. traigo 3. Pongo 4. conduzco 5. veo 6. conozco 7. Oigo 8. hago 9. digo 10. sé

Act. 6: 1. te preparas 2. me acuesto 3. nos preocupamos
4. se están divirtiendo / están divirtiéndose 5. se quejen
6. Siéntese, relájese

Capítulo 7 (pp. 266–267)

Act. 1: 1. montaste 2. leyó 3. compartí 4. navegamos
5. corrieron

Act. 2: 1. Tú y yo fuimos... 2. Marilena estuvo... 3. Yo hice...
4. Guille y Paulina dijeron... 5. Mis padres condujeron...
6. Tú tradujiste...

Act. 3: 1. ¿Los perros? Tú los lavaste. 2. ¿El surfing? Victoria
lo hizo. 3. ¿La pelota (de golf)? Yo no la encontré. 4. ¿Las
mochilas? Nosotros las perdimos. 5. ¿Los refrescos? Ustedes
no los bebieron. 6. ¿Las pesas? Esteban y Federico no las
levantaron.

Act. 4: 1. pongas, Ten, lee 2. Pon, siéntate, salgas

Act. 5: 1. quieren 2. me divierto 3. se visten 4. pueden
5. duermo 6. pides

Act. 6: 1. A mí me gusta remar. 2. A usted le gusta nadar.
3. A ti te gustan esos esquíes. 4. A ellos les gusta el boxeo.
5. A nosotros nos gusta pescar. 6. A ella le gusta la nieve.
7. A ti te gusta entrenarte. 8. A mí me gustan las vacaciones.
9. A nosotros nos gusta la primavera.

Act. 7: 1. sé 2. conozco 3. saben 4. podemos 5. pueden
6. conocemos 7. quiero 8. puedo

Capítulo 8 (pp. 304–305)

Act. 1: 1. Supe 2. hicimos 3. sugirió 4. preferí 5. sirvió 6. dijo
7. quiso 8. pudo 9. tuvo 10. pidió 11. puso 12. anduvimos 13. Nos
reímos 14. nos divertimos 15. nos despedimos 16. dijimos

Act. 2: 1. nos 2. te 3. les 4. me 5. le

Act. 3: 1. tantos, como 2. más, que 3. menos, que 4. tan, como
5. el más 6. más

Act. 4: 1. compraste 2. vi 3. estuvo 4. trajo 5. fuimos 6. dieron
7. hiciste 8. escribió

Act. 5: 1. Delfina lo compró. 2. Diego y Eduardo no la
compraron. 3. Tú no los compraste. 4. Yo los compré.
5. Nosotros las compramos. 6. Usted no lo compró.

Act. 6: 1. Yo me puse un abrigo. 2. Ellos se pusieron unas
sandalias. 3. Tú te pusiste un chaleco. 4. Nosotros nos
pusimos unos jeans. 5. Ella se puso una bufanda. 7. Ustedes
se pusieron un impermeable.

Capítulo 9 (pp. 344–345)

Act. 1: 1. La señora Muñoz preparaba unas galletas. 2. Yo freía
un huevo. 3. Nosotros pelábamos zanahorias para una ensalada.
4. Manolito ponía la mesa. 5. Sarita y Carmela picaban cebollas
para una sopa. 6. Tú hervías agua para preparar el té.

Act. 2: 1. Eran 2. quería 3. llegué 4. vi 5. estaba 6. tenía 7. me
senté 8. empezamos 9. hablábamos 10. dijo 11. exclamé
12. sabía 13. Me despedí 14. salí 15. Estaba 16. quería

Act. 3: 1. Ábrenosla. 2. Cuéceselos. 3. No me lo compres.
4. No se lo calientes. 5. Pásanosla. 6. No se la prepares.

Act. 4: 1. come 2. venden 3. hablan 4. sirve 5. cierra
6. duerme

Act. 5: 1. Los manteles son rojos. 2. El flan es bueno. 3. Las
almejas están frescas. 4. El café está caliente. 5. La carne
está frita. 6. Los huevos son blancos. 7. El pescado está
crudo. 8. El té está frío. 9. La limonada es dulce. 10. Los
platos están limpios. 11. La langosta es cara. 12. Las fresas
son baratas.

Act. 6: 1. mi 2. tus 3. nuestro 4. sus 5. sus 6. su 7. sus 8. su
9. nuestras 10. tus

Act. 7: 1. hiciste 2. hago 3. hizo 4. hicieron 5. hacemos

Capítulo 10 (pp. 376–377)

Act. 1: 1. ¿La aspiradora? No es tuya. Es suya. 2. ¿Las
licuadoras? No son suyas. Son mías. 3. ¿Las planchas?
No son nuestras. Son suyas. 4. ¿La tostadora? No es mía.
Es suya. 5. ¿Los microondas? No son suyos. Son nuestros.
6. ¿El lavaplatos? No es suyo. Es tuyo.

Act. 2: 1. Hace un año que Sarita no va de vacaciones.
2. Hace seis meses que ellos viven en esa casa. 3. Ellos
limpiaron el baño hace dos semanas. 4. Hacía tres meses que
Luis no podía trabajar en la casa. 5. Los abuelos vinieron de
visita hace dos años.

Act. 3: 1. por 2. Para 3. Por 4. por 5. para 6. Por 7. para
8. para

Act. 4: 1. Lavo 2. Plancho 3. Barro 4. Sacudo 5. Hiervo
6. Riego 7. Sirvo 8. Vuelvo 9. pido 10. duermo

Act. 5: 1. Estoy 2. Conduzco 3. doy 4. digo 5. Oigo 6. Vengo
7. Veo 8. Sé 9. Pongo 10. Tengo

Act. 6: 1. laves 2. planches 3. saques 4. pases 5. pongas
6. uses 7. trapees 8. sacudas 9. comas 10. insistas

Regular Verbs
Simple Tenses

Infinitive	Past participle / Present participle	Indicative					Subjunctive	
		Present	Imperfect	Preterite	Future	Conditional	Present	Imperfect*
cantar *to sing*	cantado cantando	canto	cantaba	canté	cantaré	cantaría	cante	cantara
		cantas	cantabas	cantaste	cantarás	cantarías	cantes	cantaras
		canta	cantaba	cantó	cantará	cantaría	cante	cantara
		cantamos	cantábamos	cantamos	cantaremos	cantaríamos	cantemos	cantáramos
		cantáis	cantabais	cantasteis	cantaréis	cantaríais	cantéis	cantarais
		cantan	cantaban	cantaron	cantarán	cantarían	canten	cantaran
correr *to run*	corrido corriendo	corro	corría	corrí	correré	correría	corra	corriera
		corres	corrías	corriste	correrás	correrías	corras	corrieras
		corre	corría	corrió	correrá	correría	corra	corriera
		corremos	corríamos	corrimos	correremos	correríamos	corramos	corriéramos
		corréis	corríais	corristeis	correréis	correríais	corráis	corrierais
		corren	corrían	corrieron	correrán	correrían	corran	corrieran
subir *to go up, to climb up*	subido subiendo	subo	subía	subí	subiré	subiría	suba	subiera
		subes	subías	subiste	subirás	subirías	subas	subieras
		sube	subía	subió	subirá	subiría	suba	subiera
		subimos	subíamos	subimos	subiremos	subiríamos	subamos	subiéramos
		subís	subíais	subisteis	subiréis	subiríais	subáis	subierais
		suben	subían	subieron	subirán	subirían	suban	subieran

*In addition to this form, another one is less frequently used for all regular and irregular verbs: cantase, cantases, cantase, cantásemos, cantaseis, cantasen; corriese, corrieses, corriese, corriésemos, corrieseis, corriesen; subiese, subieses, subiese, subiésemos, subieseis, subiesen.

Commands

Person	Affirmative	Negative	Affirmative	Negative	Affirmative	Negative
tú	canta	no cantes	corre	no corras	sube	no subas
usted	cante	no cante	corra	no corra	suba	no suba
nosotros	cantemos	no cantemos	corramos	no corramos	subamos	no subamos
vosotros	cantad	no cantéis	corred	no corráis	subid	no subáis
ustedes	canten	no canten	corran	no corran	suban	no suban

Stem-Changing Verbs: -ar and -er Groups

Type of change in the verb stem	Subject	Indicative Present	Subjunctive Present	Commands Affirmative	Commands Negative	Other -ar and -er stem-changing verbs
-ar verbs e > ie pensar *to think*	yo	pienso	piense	—	—	atravesar *to go through, to cross;* cerrar *to close;* despertarse *to wake up;* empezar *to start;* negar *to deny;* sentarse *to sit down*
	tú	piensas	pienses	piensa	no pienses	
	él/ella, Ud.	piensa	piense	piense	no piense	
	nosotros/as	pensamos	pensemos	pensemos	no pensemos	
	vosotros/as	pensáis	penséis	pensad	no penséis	
	ellos/as, Uds.	piensan	piensen	piensen	no piensen	Nevar *to snow* is only conjugated in the third-person singular.
-ar verbs o > ue contar *to count, to tell*	yo	cuento	cuente	—	—	acordarse *to remember;* acostarse *to go to bed;* almorzar *to have lunch;* colgar *to hang;* costar *to cost;* demostrar *to demonstrate, to show;* encontrar *to find;* mostrar *to show;* probar *to prove, to taste;* recordar *to remember*
	tú	cuentas	cuentes	cuenta	no cuentes	
	él/ella, Ud.	cuenta	cuente	cuente	no cuente	
	nosotros/as	contamos	contemos	contemos	no contemos	
	vosotros/as	contáis	contéis	contad	no contéis	
	ellos/as, Uds.	cuentan	cuenten	cuenten	no cuenten	
-er verbs e > ie entender *to understand*	yo	entiendo	entienda	—	—	encender *to light, to turn on;* extender *to stretch;* perder *to lose*
	tú	entiendes	entiendas	entiende	no entiendas	
	él/ella, Ud.	entiende	entienda	entienda	no entienda	
	nosotros/as	entendemos	entendamos	entendamos	no entendamos	
	vosotros/as	entendéis	entendáis	entended	no entendáis	
	ellos/as, Uds.	entienden	entiendan	entiendan	no entiendan	
-er verbs o > ue volver *to return*	yo	vuelvo	vuelva	—	—	mover *to move;* torcer *to twist*
	tú	vuelves	vuelvas	vuelve	no vuelvas	
	él/ella, Ud.	vuelve	vuelva	vuelva	no vuelva	
	nosotros/as	volvemos	volvamos	volvamos	no volvamos	
	vosotros/as	volvéis	volváis	volved	no volváis	
	ellos/as, Uds.	vuelven	vuelvan	vuelvan	no vuelvan	Llover *to rain* is only conjugated in the third-person singular.

Stem-Changing Verbs: -ir Verbs

Type of change in the verb stem	Subject	Indicative		Subjunctive		Commands	
		Present	Preterite	Present	Imperfect	Affirmative	Negative
-ir verbs e > ie or i Infinitive: sentir *to feel* Present participle: sintiendo	yo	siento	sentí	sienta	sintiera	—	—
	tú	sientes	sentiste	sientas	sintieras	siente	no sientas
	él/ella, Ud.	siente	sintió	sienta	sintiera	sienta	no sienta
	nosotros/as	sentimos	sentimos	sintamos	sintiéramos	sintamos	no sintamos
	vosotros/as	sentís	sentisteis	sintáis	sintierais	sentid	no sintáis
	ellos/as, Uds.	sienten	sintieron	sientan	sintieran	sientan	no sientan
-ir verbs o > ue or u Infinitive: dormir *to sleep* Present participle: durmiendo	yo	duermo	dormí	duerma	durmiera	—	—
	tú	duermes	dormiste	duermas	durmieras	duerme	no duermas
	él/ella, Ud.	duerme	durmió	duerma	durmiera	duerma	no duerma
	nosotros/as	dormimos	dormimos	durmamos	durmiéramos	durmamos	no durmamos
	vosotros/as	dormís	dormisteis	durmáis	durmierais	dormid	no durmáis
	ellos/as, Uds.	duermen	durmieron	duerman	durmieran	duerman	no duerman

Other similar verbs: advertir *to warn;* arrepentirse *to repent;* consentir *to consent, pamper;* convertir(se) *to turn into;* divertir(se) *to amuse (oneself);* herir *to hurt, wound;* mentir *to lie;* morir *to die;* preferir *to prefer;* referir *to refer;* sugerir *to suggest*

Type of change in the verb stem	Subject	Indicative		Subjunctive		Commands	
		Present	Preterite	Present	Imperfect	Affirmative	Negative
-ir verbs e > i Infinitive: pedir *to ask for, to request* Present participle: pidiendo	yo	pido	pedí	pida	pidiera	—	—
	tú	pides	pediste	pidas	pidieras	pide	no pidas
	él/ella, Ud.	pide	pidió	pida	pidiera	pida	no pida
	nosotros/as	pedimos	pedimos	pidamos	pidiéramos	pidamos	no pidamos
	vosotros/as	pedís	pedisteis	pidáis	pidierais	pedid	no pidáis
	ellos/as, Uds.	piden	pidieron	pidan	pidieran	pidan	no pidan

Other similar verbs: competir *to compete;* despedir(se) *to say good-bye;* elegir *to choose;* impedir *to prevent;* perseguir *to chase;* repetir *to repeat;* seguir *to follow;* servir *to serve;* vestir(se) *to dress, to get dressed*

Verbs with Spelling Changes

Verb type	Ending	Change	Verbs with similar spelling changes
1 **buscar** *to look for*	**-car**	• Preterite: yo busqué • Present subjunctive: busque, busques, busque, busquemos, busquéis, busquen	comunicar, explicar *to explain*, indicar *to indicate*, sacar, pescar
2 **conocer** *to know*	*vowel* + **-cer** or **-cir**	• Present indicative: conozco, conoces, conoce, and so on • Present subjunctive: conozca, conozcas, conozca, conozcamos, conozcáis, conozcan	nacer *to be born*, obedecer, ofrecer, parecer, pertenecer *to belong*, reconocer, conducir, traducir
3 **vencer** *to win*	*consonant* + **-cer** or **-cir**	• Present indicative: venzo, vences, vence, and so on • Present subjunctive: venza, venzas, venza, venzamos, venzáis, venzan	convencer, torcer *to twist*
4 **leer** *to read*	**-eer**	• Preterite: leyó, leyeron • Imperfect subjunctive: leyera, leyeras, leyera, leyéramos, leyerais, leyeran • Present participle: leyendo	creer, poseer *to own*
5 **llegar** *to arrive*	**-gar**	• Preterite: yo llegué • Present subjunctive: llegue, llegues, llegue, lleguemos, lleguéis, lleguen	colgar *to hang*, navegar, negar *to negate, to deny*, pagar, rogar *to beg*, jugar
6 **escoger** *to choose*	**-ger** or **-gir**	• Present indicative: escojo, escoges, escoge, and so on • Present subjunctive: escoja, escojas, escoja, escojamos, escojáis, escojan	proteger, *to protect*, recoger *to collect, gather*, corregir *to correct*, dirigir *to direct*, elegir *to elect, choose*, exigir *to demand*
7 **seguir** *to follow*	**-guir**	• Present indicative: sigo, sigues, sigue, and so on • Present subjunctive: siga, sigas, siga, sigamos, sigáis, sigan	conseguir, distinguir, perseguir
8 **huir** *to flee*	**-uir**	• Present indicative: huyo, huyes, huye, huimos, huís, huyen • Preterite: huí, huiste, huyó, huimos, huisteis, huyeron • Present subjunctive: huya, huyas, huya, huyamos, huyáis, huyan • Imperfect subjunctive: huyera, huyeras, huyera, huyéramos, huyerais, huyeran • Present participle: huyendo • Commands: huye (tú), huya usted, huyamos (nosotros), huid (vosotros), huyan (ustedes), (negative) no huyas (tú), no huya (usted), no huyamos (nosotros), no huyáis (vosotros), no huyan (ustedes)	concluir, contribuir, construir, destruir, disminuir, distribuir, excluir, influir, instruir, restituir, substituir
9 **abrazar** *to embrace*	**-zar**	• Preterite: yo abracé • Present subjunctive: abrace, abraces, abrace, abracemos, abracéis, abracen	alcanzar *to achieve*, almorzar, comenzar, empezar, gozar *to enjoy*, rezar *to pray*

Compound Tenses

	Indicative					Subjunctive	
	Present perfect	Past perfect	Preterite perfect	Future perfect	Conditional perfect	Present perfect	Past perfect
	he	había	hube	habré	habría	haya	hubiera
	has	habías	hubiste	habrás	habrías	hayas	hubieras
	ha	había	hubo	habrá	habría	haya	hubiera
cantado	hemos	habíamos	hubimos	habremos	habríamos	hayamos	hubiéramos
corrido	habéis	habíais	hubisteis	habréis	habríais	hayáis	hubierais
subido	han	habían	hubieron	habrán	habrían	hayan	hubieran

All verbs, both regular and irregular, follow the same formation pattern with **haber** in all compound tenses. The only thing that changes is the form of the past participle of each verb. (See the chart below for common verbs with irregular past participles.) Remember that in Spanish, no word can come between **haber** and the past participle.

Common Irregular Past Participles

Infinitive	Past participle	
abrir	**abierto**	*opened*
caer	caído	*fallen*
creer	creído	*believed*
cubrir	**cubierto**	*covered*
decir	**dicho**	*said, told*
descubrir	**descubierto**	*discovered*
escribir	**escrito**	*written*
hacer	**hecho**	*made, done*
leer	leído	*read*
morir	**muerto**	*died*
oír	oído	*heard*
poner	**puesto**	*put, placed*
resolver	**resuelto**	*resolved*
romper	**roto**	*broken, torn*
(son)reír	(son)reído	*(smiled) laughed*
traer	traído	*brought*
ver	**visto**	*seen*
volver	**vuelto**	*returned*

Reflexive Verbs

Regular and Irregular Reflexive Verbs: Position of the Reflexive Pronouns in the Simple Tenses

Infinitive	Present participle	Reflexive pronouns	Indicative						Subjunctive	
			Present	Imperfect	Preterite	Future	Conditional		Present	Imperfect
lavarse	lavándome	me	lavo	lavaba	lavé	lavaré	lavaría		lave	lavara
to wash oneself	lavándote	te	lavas	lavabas	lavaste	lavarás	lavarías		laves	lavaras
	lavándose	se	lava	lavaba	lavó	lavará	lavaría		lave	lavara
	lavándonos	nos	lavamos	lavábamos	lavamos	lavaremos	lavaríamos		lavemos	laváramos
	lavándoos	os	laváis	lavabais	lavasteis	lavaréis	lavaríais		lavéis	lavarais
	lavándose	se	lavan	lavaban	lavaron	lavarán	lavarían		laven	lavaran

Regular and irregular reflexive verbs: Position of the reflexive pronouns with commands

Person	Affirmative	Negative	Affirmative	Negative	Affirmative	Negative
tú	lávate	no te laves	ponte	no te pongas	vístete	no te vistas
usted	lávese	no se lave	póngase	no se ponga	vístase	no se vista
nosotros	lavémonos	no nos lavemos	pongámonos	no nos pongamos	vistámonos	no nos vistamos
vosotros	lavaos	no os lavéis	poneos	no os pongáis	vestíos	no os vistáis
ustedes	lávense	no se laven	pónganse	no se pongan	vístanse	no se vistan

Regular and irregular reflexive verbs: Position of the reflexive pronouns in compound tenses*

Reflexive Pronoun	Indicative										Subjunctive			
	Present Perfect		Past Perfect		Preterite Perfect		Future Perfect		Conditional Perfect		Present Perfect		Past Perfect	
me	he		había		hube		habré		habría		haya		hubiera	
te	has	lavado	habías	lavado	hubiste	lavado	habrás	lavado	habrías	lavado	hayas	lavado	hubieras	lavado
se	ha	puesto	había	puesto	hubo	puesto	habrá	puesto	habría	puesto	haya	puesto	hubiera	puesto
nos	hemos	vestido	habíamos	vestido	hubimos	vestido	habremos	vestido	habríamos	vestido	hayamos	vestido	hubiéramos	vestido
os	habéis		habíais		hubisteis		habréis		habríais		hayáis		hubierais	
se	han		habían		hubieron		habrán		habrían		hayan		hubieran	

*The sequence of these three elements—the reflexive pronoun, the auxiliary verb **haber**, and the present perfect form—is invariable and no other words can come in between.

Regular and irregular reflexive verbs: Position of the reflexive pronouns with conjugated verb + infinitive**

Reflexive Pronoun	Indicative										Subjunctive			
	Present		Imperfect		Preterite		Future		Conditional		Present		Imperfect	
me	voy a		iba a		fui a		iré a		iría a		vaya a		fuera a	
te	vas a	lavar	ibas a	lavar	fuiste a	lavar	irás a	lavar	irías a	lavar	vayas a	lavar	fueras a	lavar
se	va a	poner	iba a	poner	fue a	poner	irá a	poner	iría a	poner	vaya a	poner	fuera a	poner
nos	vamos a	vestir	íbamos a	vestir	fuimos a	vestir	iremos a	vestir	iríamos a	vestir	vayamos a	vestir	fuéramos a	vestir
os	vais a		ibais a		fuisteis a		iréis a		iríais a		vayáis a		fuerais a	
se	van a		iban a		fueron a		irán a		irían a		vayan a		fueran a	

The reflexive pronoun can also be placed after the infinitive: voy a lavarme**, voy a poner**me**, voy a vestir**me**, and so on. Use the same structure for the present and the past progressive: **me** estoy lavando / estoy lavándo**me**; **me** estaba lavando / estaba lavándo**me**.

Irregular Verbs

andar, caber, caer

Infinitive	Past participle / Present participle	Indicative					Subjunctive	
		Present	Imperfect	Preterite	Future	Conditional	Present	Imperfect
andar *to walk; to go*	andado / andando	ando andas anda andamos andáis andan	andaba andabas andaba andábamos andabais andaban	anduve anduviste anduvo anduvimos anduvisteis anduvieron	andaré andarás andará andaremos andaréis andarán	andaría andarías andaría andaríamos andaríais andarían	ande andes ande andemos andéis anden	anduviera anduvieras anduviera anduviéramos anduvierais anduvieran
caber *to fit; to have enough space*	cabido / cabiendo	**quepo** cabes cabe cabemos cabéis caben	cabía cabías cabía cabíamos cabíais cabían	cupe cupiste cupo cupimos cupisteis cupieron	**cabré** **cabrás** **cabrá** **cabremos** **cabréis** **cabrán**	**cabría** **cabrías** **cabría** **cabríamos** **cabríais** **cabrían**	**quepa** **quepas** **quepa.** **quepamos** **quepáis** **quepan**	cupiera cupieras cupiera cupiéramos cupierais cupieran
caer *to fall*	caído / cayendo	**caigo** caes cae caemos caéis caen	caía caías caía caíamos caíais caían	caí caíste **cayó** caímos caísteis **cayeron**	caeré caerás caerá caeremos caeréis caerán	caería caerías caería caeríamos caeríais caerían	caiga caigas caiga caigamos caigáis caigan	cayera cayeras cayera cayéramos cayerais cayeran

Commands

Person	andar		caber		caer	
	Affirmative	Negative	Affirmative	Negative	Affirmative	Negative
tú	anda	no andes	cabe	no quepas	cae	no caigas
usted	ande	no ande	**quepa**	no quepa	**caiga**	no caiga
nosotros	andemos	no andemos	**quepamos**	no quepamos	**caigamos**	no caigamos
vosotros	andad	no andéis	cabed	no quepáis	caed	no caigáis
ustedes	anden	no anden	**quepan**	no quepan	**caigan**	no caigan

dar, decir, estar

Infinitive	Past participle / Present participle	Indicative					Subjunctive	
		Present	Imperfect	Preterite	Future	Conditional	Present	Imperfect
dar *to give*	dado dando	doy das da damos dais dan	daba dabas daba dábamos dabais daban	di diste dio dimos disteis dieron	daré darás dará daremos daréis darán	daría darías daría daríamos daríais darían	dé des dé demos deis den	diera dieras diera diéramos dierais dieran
decir *to say,* *to tell*	dicho diciendo	digo dices dice decimos decís dicen	decía decías decía decíamos decíais decían	dije dijiste dijo dijimos dijisteis dijeron	diré dirás dirá diremos diréis dirán	diría dirías diría diríamos diríais dirían	diga digas diga digamos digáis digan	dijera dijeras dijera dijéramos dijerais dijeran
estar *to be*	estado estando	estoy estás está estamos estáis están	estaba estabas estaba estábamos estabais estaban	estuve estuviste estuvo estuvimos estuvisteis estuvieron	estaré estarás estará estaremos estaréis estarán	estaría estarías estaría estaríamos estaríais estarían	esté estés esté estemos estéis estén	estuviera estuvieras estuviera estuviéramos estuvierais estuvieran

Commands

Person	dar		decir		estar	
	Affirmative	Negative	Affirmative	Negative	Affirmative	Negative
tú	da	no des	di	no digas	está	no estés
usted	dé	no dé	diga	no diga	esté	no esté
nosotros	demos	no demos	digamos	no digamos	estemos	no estemos
vosotros	dad	no deis	decid	no digáis	estad	no estéis
ustedes	den	no den	digan	no digan	estén	no estén

haber*, hacer, ir

Infinitive	Past participle / Present participle	Indicative					Subjunctive	
		Present	Imperfect	Preterite	Future	Conditional	Present	Imperfect
haber* *to have*	habido habiendo	he has ha hemos habéis han	había habías había habíamos habíais habían	hube hubiste hubo hubimos hubisteis hubieron	habré habrás habrá habremos habréis habrán	habría habrías habría habríamos habríais habrían	haya hayas haya hayamos hayáis hayan	hubiera hubieras hubiera hubiéramos hubierais hubieran
hacer *do*	hecho haciendo	hago haces hace hacemos hacéis hacen	hacía hacías hacía hacíamos hacíais hacían	hice hiciste hizo hicimos hicisteis hicieron	haré harás hará haremos haréis harán	haría harías haría haríamos haríais harían	haga hagas haga hagamos hagáis hagan	hiciera hicieras hiciera hiciéramos hicierais hicieran
ir *to go*	ido yendo	voy vas va vamos vais van	iba ibas iba íbamos ibais iban	fui fuiste fue fuimos fuisteis fueron	iré irás irá iremos iréis irán	iría irías iría iríamos iríais irían	vaya vayas vaya vayamos vayáis vayan	fuera fueras fuera fuéramos fuerais fueran

*__Haber__ also has an impersonal form, __hay.__ This form is used to express "There is, There are." The imperative of __haber__ is not used.

Commands

Person	hacer		ir	
	Affirmative	Negative	Affirmative	Negative
tú	haz	no hagas	ve	no vayas
usted	haga	no haga	vaya	no vaya
nosotros	hagamos	no hagamos	vamos	no vayamos
vosotros	haced	no hagáis	id	no vayáis
ustedes	hagan	no hagan	vayan	no vayan

jugar, oír, oler

Infinitive	Past participle / Present participle	Indicative					Subjunctive	
		Present	Imperfect	Preterite	Future	Conditional	Present	Imperfect
jugar *to play*	jugado / jugando	**juego** / **juegas** / **juega** / jugamos / jugáis / **juegan**	jugaba / jugabas / jugaba / jugábamos / jugabais / jugaban	**jugué** / jugaste / jugó / jugamos / jugasteis / jugaron	jugaré / jugarás / jugará / jugaremos / jugaréis / jugarán	jugaría / jugarías / jugaría / jugaríamos / jugaríais / jugarían	**juegue** / **juegues** / **juegue** / **juguemos** / **juguéis** / **jueguen**	jugara / jugaras / jugara / jugáramos / jugarais / jugaran
oír *to hear, to listen*	oído / oyendo	**oigo** / **oyes** / **oye** / oímos / oís / **oyen**	oía / oías / oía / oíamos / oíais / oían	oí / oíste / **oyó** / oímos / oísteis / **oyeron**	oiré / oirás / oirá / oiremos / oiréis / oirán	oiría / oirías / oiría / oiríamos / oiríais / oirían	**oiga** / **oigas** / **oiga** / **oigamos** / **oigáis** / **oigan**	oyera / oyeras / oyera / oyéramos / oyerais / oyeran
oler *to smell*	olido / oliendo	**huelo** / **hueles** / **huele** / olemos / oléis / **huelen**	olía / olías / olía / olíamos / olíais / olían	olí / oliste / olió / olimos / olisteis / olieron	oleré / olerás / olerá / oleremos / oleréis / olerán	olería / olerías / olería / oleríamos / oleríais / olerían	**huela** / **huelas** / **huela** / olamos / oláis / **huelan**	oliera / olieras / oliera / oliéramos / olierais / olieran

Commands

Person	jugar		oír		oler	
	Affirmative	Negative	Affirmative	Negative	Affirmative	Negative
tú	juega	no juegues	oye	no oigas	huele	no huelas
usted	juegue	no juegue	oiga	no oiga	huela	no huela
nosotros	juguemos	no juguemos	oigamos	no oigamos	olamos	no olamos
vosotros	jugad	no juguéis	oíd	no oigáis	oled	no oláis
ustedes	jueguen	no jueguen	oigan	no oigan	huelan	no huelan

poder, poner, querer

Infinitive	Past participle / Present participle	Indicative					Subjunctive	
		Present	Imperfect	Preterite	Future	Conditional	Present	Imperfect
poder *to be able to, can*	podido pudiendo	puedo puedes puede podemos podéis pueden	podía podías podía podíamos podíais podían	pude pudiste pudo pudimos pudisteis pudieron	podré podrás podrá podremos podréis podrán	podría podrías podría podríamos podríais podrían	pueda puedas pueda podamos podáis puedan	pudiera pudieras pudiera pudiéramos pudierais pudieran
poner* *to put*	puesto poniendo	pongo pones pone ponemos ponéis ponen	ponía ponías ponía poníamos poníais ponían	puse pusiste puso pusimos pusisteis pusieron	pondré pondrás pondrá pondremos pondréis pondrán	pondría pondrías pondría pondríamos pondríais pondrían	ponga pongas ponga pongamos pongáis pongan	pusiera pusieras pusiera pusiéramos pusierais pusieran
querer *to want, to wish; to love*	querido queriendo	quiero quieres quiere queremos queréis quieren	quería querías quería queríamos queríais querían	quise quisiste quiso quisimos quisisteis quisieron	querré querrás querrá querremos querréis querrán	querría querrías querría querríamos querríais querrían	quiera quieras quiera queramos queráis quieran	quisiera quisieras quisiera quisiéramos quisierais quisieran

*Similar verbs to poner: imponer, suponer.

Commands**

Person	poner		querer	
	Affirmative	Negative	Affirmative	Negative
tú	pon	no pongas	quiere	no quieras
usted	ponga	no ponga	quiera	no quiera
nosotros	pongamos	no pongamos	queramos	no queramos
vosotros	poned	no pongáis	quered	no queráis
ustedes	pongan	no pongan	quieran	no quieran

Note: The imperative of **poder is used very infrequently and is not included here.

saber, salir, ser

Infinitive	Past participle / Present participle	Indicative					Subjunctive	
		Present	Imperfect	Preterite	Future	Conditional	Present	Imperfect
saber *to know*	sabido / sabiendo	sé	sabía	supe	sabré	sabría	sepa	supiera
		sabes	sabías	supiste	sabrás	sabrías	sepas	supieras
		sabe	sabía	supo	sabrá	sabría	sepa	supiera
		sabemos	sabíamos	supimos	sabremos	sabríamos	sepamos	supiéramos
		sabéis	sabíais	supisteis	sabréis	sabríais	sepáis	supierais
		saben	sabían	supieron	sabrán	sabrían	sepan	supieran
salir *to go out, to leave*	salido / saliendo	salgo	salía	salí	saldré	saldría	salga	saliera
		sales	salías	saliste	saldrás	saldrías	salgas	salieras
		sale	salía	salió	saldrá	saldría	salga	saliera
		salimos	salíamos	salimos	saldremos	saldríamos	salgamos	saliéramos
		salís	salíais	salisteis	saldréis	saldríais	salgáis	salierais
		salen	salían	salieron	saldrán	saldrían	salgan	salieran
ser *to be*	sido / siendo	soy	era	fui	seré	sería	sea	fuera
		eres	eras	fuiste	serás	serías	seas	fueras
		es	era	fue	será	sería	sea	fuera
		somos	éramos	fuimos	seremos	seríamos	seamos	fuéramos
		sois	erais	fuisteis	seréis	seríais	seáis	fuerais
		son	eran	fueron	serán	serían	sean	fueran

Commands

Person	saber		salir		ser	
	Affirmative	Negative	Affirmative	Negative	Affirmative	Negative
tú	sabe	no sepas	sal	no salgas	sé	no seas
usted	sepa	no sepa	salga	no salga	sea	no sea
nosotros	sepamos	no sepamos	salgamos	no salgamos	seamos	no seamos
vosotros	sabed	no sepáis	salid	no salgáis	sed	no seáis
ustedes	sepan	no sepan	salgan	no salgan	sean	no sean

sonreír, tener*, traer

Infinitive	Past participle / Present participle	Indicative					Subjunctive	
		Present	Imperfect	Preterite	Future	Conditional	Present	Imperfect
sonreír *to smile*	sonreído sonriendo	sonrío sonríes sonríe sonreímos sonreís sonríen	sonreía sonreías sonreía sonreíamos sonreíais sonreían	sonreí sonreíste sonrió sonreímos sonreísteis sonrieron	sonreiré sonreirás sonreirá sonreiremos sonreiréis sonreirán	sonreiría sonreirías sonreiría sonreiríamos sonreiríais sonreirían	sonría sonrías sonría sonriamos sonriáis sonrían	sonriera sonrieras sonriera sonriéramos sonrierais sonrieran
tener* *to have*	tenido teniendo	tengo tienes tiene tenemos tenéis tienen	tenía tenías tenía teníamos teníais tenían	tuve tuviste tuvo tuvimos tuvisteis tuvieron	tendré tendrás tendrá tendremos tendréis tendrán	tendría tendrías tendría tendríamos tendríais tendrían	tenga tengas tenga tengamos tengáis tengan	tuviera tuvieras tuviera tuviéramos tuvierais tuvieran
traer *to bring*	traído trayendo	traigo traes trae traemos traéis traen	traía traías traía traíamos traíais traían	traje trajiste trajo trajimos trajisteis trajeron	traeré traerás traerá traeremos traeréis traerán	traería traerías traería traeríamos traeríais traerían	traiga traigas traiga traigamos traigáis traigan	trajera trajeras trajera trajéramos trajerais trajeran

*Many verbs ending in -tener are conjugated like tener: contener, detener, entretener(se), mantener, obtener, retener.

Commands

sonreír

Person	Affirmative	Negative
tú	sonríe	no sonrías
usted	sonría	no sonría
nosotros	sonriamos	no sonriamos
vosotros	sonreíd	no sonriáis
ustedes	sonrían	no sonrían

tener

Person	Affirmative	Negative
tú	ten	no tengas
usted	tenga	no tenga
nosotros	tengamos	no tengamos
vosotros	tened	no tengáis
ustedes	tengan	no tengan

traer

Person	Affirmative	Negative
tú	trae	no traigas
usted	traiga	no traiga
nosotros	traigamos	no traigamos
vosotros	traed	no traigáis
ustedes	traigan	no traigan

valer, venir*, ver

Infinitive	Present participle / Past participle	Indicative					Subjunctive	
		Present	Imperfect	Preterite	Future	Conditional	Present	Imperfect
valer *to be worth*	Past participle: valido Present participle: valiendo	valgo vales vale valemos valéis valen	valía valías valía valíamos valíais valían	valí valiste valió valimos valisteis valieron	valdré valdrás valdrá valdremos valdréis valdrán	valdría valdrías valdría valdríamos valdríais valdrían	valga valgas valga valgamos valgáis valgan	valiera valieras valiera valiéramos valierais valieran
venir* *to come*	Past participle: venido Present participle: viniendo	vengo vienes viene venimos venís vienen	venía venías venía veníamos veníais venían	vine viniste vino vinimos vinisteis vinieron	vendré vendrás vendrá vendremos vendréis vendrán	vendría vendrías vendría vendríamos vendríais vendrían	venga vengas venga vengamos vengáis vengan	viniera vinieras viniera viniéramos vinierais vinieran
ver *to see*	Past participle: visto Present participle: viendo	veo ves ve vemos veis ven	veía veías veía veíamos veíais veían	vi viste vio vimos visteis vieron	veré verás verá veremos veréis verán	vería verías vería veríamos veríais verían	vea veas vea veamos veáis vean	viera vieras viera viéramos vierais vieran

*Similar verb to venir: prevenir

Commands

Person	valer Affirmative	valer Negative	venir Affirmative	venir Negative	ver Affirmative	ver Negative
tú	vale	no valgas	ven	no vengas	ve	no veas
usted	valga	no valga	venga	no venga	vea	no vea
nosotros	valgamos	no valgamos	vengamos	no vengamos	veamos	no veamos
vosotros	valed	no valgáis	venid	no vengáis	ved	no veáis
ustedes	valgan	no valgan	vengan	no vengan	vean	no vean

AMÉRICA DEL SUR

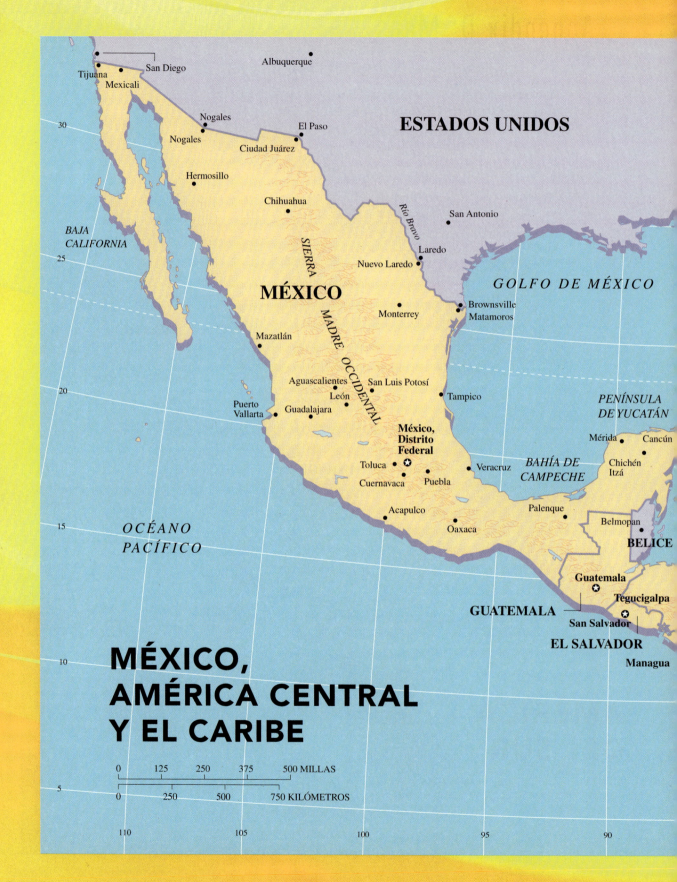

ESTADOS UNIDOS

Albuquerque

San Diego
Tijuana
Mexicali

Nogales
Nogales
El Paso
Ciudad Juárez

Hermosillo

Chihuahua

San Antonio

Río Bravo

**BAJA
CALIFORNIA**

SIERRA

Laredo
Nuevo Laredo

MÉXICO

MADRE OCCIDENTAL

Monterrey
Brownsville
Matamoros

GOLFO DE MÉXICO

Mazatlán

Aguascalientes
San Luis Potosí
León
Tampico

*PENÍNSULA
DE YUCATÁN*

Puerto
Vallarta
Guadalajara

**México,
Distrito
Federal**

Mérida
Cancún

Veracruz
Chichén
Itzá

*BAHÍA DE
CAMPECHE*

Toluca
Cuernavaca
Puebla

Acapulco

Oaxaca

Palenque

Belmopan

BELICE

*OCÉANO
PACÍFICO*

Guatemala

Tegucigalpa

GUATEMALA

San Salvador

EL SALVADOR

Managua

MÉXICO,
AMÉRICA CENTRAL
Y EL CARIBE

0   125   250   375   500 MILLAS

0   250   500   750 KILÓMETROS

OCÉANO
ATLÁNTICO

Miami

Nassau

BAHAMAS

La Habana

CUBA

MAR CARIBE

Santiago
de Cuba

Puerto Príncipe

REPÚBLICA
DOMINICANA

San Juan

Santo
Domingo

HAITÍ

PUERTO
RICO

GUADALUPE

Kingston

JAMAICA

MARTINICA

HONDURAS

NICARAGUA

Lago de
Nicaragua

San José

CANAL DE
PANAMÁ

Colón

Panamá

Caracas

PANAMÁ

COSTA
RICA

GOLFO
DE
PANAMÁ

VENEZUELA

COLOMBIA

Bogotá

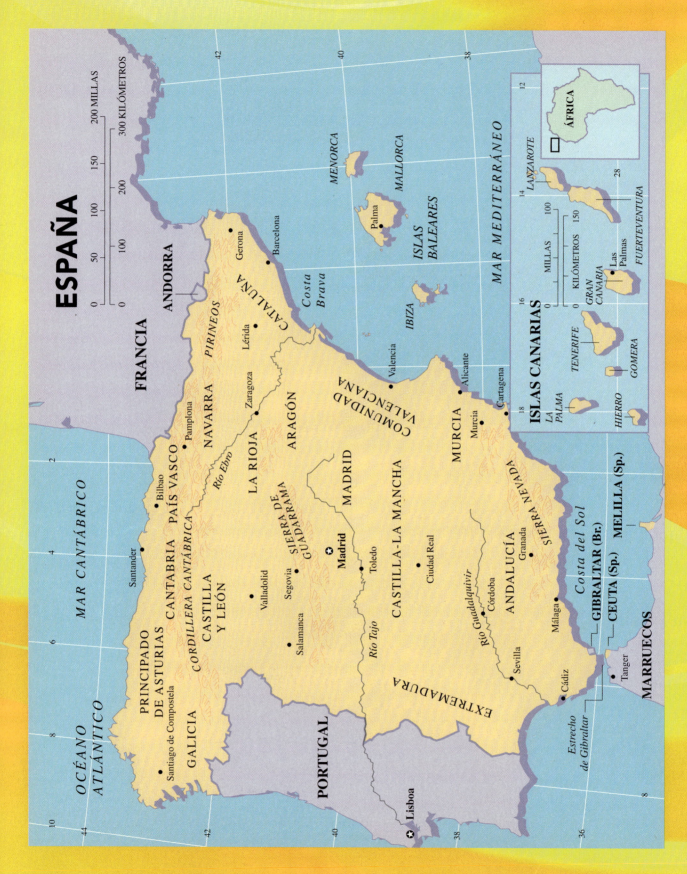

ESPAÑA

FRANCIA

ANDORRA

OCÉANO ATLÁNTICO

MAR CANTÁBRICO

FRANCIA

PIRINEOS

CATALUÑA

Gerona

Barcelona

Costa Brava

MENORCA

MALLORCA

Palma

ISLAS BALEARES

MAR MEDITERRÁNEO

IBIZA

Santander

Bilbao

Pamplona

Lérida

Zaragoza

Río Ebro

NAVARRA

PAÍS VASCO

CANTABRIA

CORDILLERA CANTÁBRICA

PRINCIPADO DE ASTURIAS

GALICIA

Santiago de Compostela

CASTILLA Y LEÓN

Valladolid

Salamanca

Segovia

SIERRA DE GUADARRAMA

LA RIOJA

ARAGÓN

COMUNIDAD VALENCIANA

Valencia

Alicante

Cartagena

MURCIA

Murcia

MADRID

Madrid

Toledo

CASTILLA-LA MANCHA

Ciudad Real

Río Tajo

EXTREMADURA

PORTUGAL

Lisboa

Río Guadalquivir

Sevilla

Córdoba

Granada

SIERRA NEVADA

ANDALUCÍA

Málaga

Costa del Sol

Cádiz

Estrecho de Gibraltar

Tánger

MARRUECOS

GIBRALTAR (Br.)

CEUTA (Sp.)

MELILLA (Sp.)

200 MILLAS

300 KILÓMETROS

150

100

50

0

200

100

0

ISLAS CANARIAS

LANZAROTE

FUERTEVENTURA

Las Palmas

GRAN CANARIA

TENERIFE

GOMERA

LA PALMA

HIERRO

MILLAS

KILÓMETROS

100

150

0

ÁFRICA

Appendix E: Grammar Review

Chapter 1

>> ## Gramática útil 1

Identifying people and objects: Nouns and articles

Cómo usarlo

Nouns identify people, places, and things: **señora Velasco, calle,** and **teléfono** are all nouns. *Articles* supply additional information about the noun.

1. *Definite* articles refer to a specific person, place, or thing.

La Avenida Central es **la** calle más importante de **la** universidad. *(You already know which avenue and university you are talking about.)*

*Central Avenue is **the** most important street in **the** university.*

2. *Indefinite* articles refer to a noun without identifying a specific person, place, or thing.

Un amigo es **una** persona que te gusta. *(You are making a generalization, true of any friend.)*

*A friend is **a** person you like.*

Cómo formarlo

LO BÁSICO

- *Number* indicates whether a word is singular or plural: **la calle** *(sing.),* **las calles** *(pl.),* **un escritorio** *(sing.),* **unos escritorios** *(pl.)*
- *Gender* indicates whether a word is masculine or feminine: **una avenida** *(fem.),* **el teléfono** *(masc.)*

The idea of gender for non-person nouns and for articles does not exist in English, although it is a feature of Spanish and other languages. When learning new Spanish words, memorize the article with the noun to help remember gender.

3. Noun gender and number

- **Gender:** Often you can tell the gender of a Spanish noun by looking at its ending. Here are some general guidelines.

Masculine	Feminine
1. Nouns ending in **-o: el amigo, el muchacho**	Exception to rule #1: **la mano** *(hand)*
Exceptions to rule #2: words ending in **-ma: el sistema, el problema, el tema, el programa;** also **el día, el mapa**	2. Nouns ending in **-a: la compañera de cuarto, una chica**
Exceptions to rule #3: **el avión, el camión**	3. Nouns ending in **-ión, -dad, -tad,** and **-umbre** are usually feminine: **la información, una universidad, una costumbre** *(custom)*

When nouns ending in **-ión** become plural, they lose the accent on the o: **la corporación,** but **las corporaciones.**

Nouns referring to people often reflect gender by changing a final **o** to an **a** (**chico / chica, amigo / amiga**) or adding an **a** to a final consonant (**profesor / profesora**). For nouns ending in **-e, -ista,** or **-a** that refer to people, the article or context indicates gender (**el estudiante / la estudiante, el guitarrista / la guitarrista, Juan / Juanita es atleta**).

■ **Number:** Spanish nouns form their plurals in several ways.

Singular	Plural
Ends in vowel: **calle**	Add **s: calles**
Ends in consonant: **universidad**	Add **es: universidades**
Ends in **-z: lápiz**	Change **z** to **c** and add **es: lápices**

4. Definite and indefinite articles

■ Here are the Spanish definite articles, which correspond to the English article *the*.

	Singular	Plural
Masculine	**el amigo** *the friend (male)*	**los amigos** *the friends (male or mixed group)*
Feminine	**la amiga** *the friend (female)*	**las amigas** *the friends (female)*

■ Here are the Spanish indefinite articles, which correspond to the English articles *a, an,* and *some*.

	Singular	Plural
Masculine	**un amigo** a friend *(male)*	**unos amigos** some friends *(male or mixed group)*
Feminine	**una amiga** a friend *(female)*	**unas amigas** some friends *(female)*

In the past, **los** and **unos**, rather than **las** and **unas**, were used to refer to groups containing one or more males. The **Real Academia de la Lengua Española** recently ruled that the feminine forms should be used for groups with more females than males, but usage is changing slowly.

■ Remember that you use masculine articles with masculine nouns and feminine articles with feminine nouns. When a noun is in the plural, the corresponding plural article (masculine or feminine) is used: **el hombre, los hombres.**

■ When referring to a person's *profession*, the article is omitted: **Liana es profesora y Ricardo es dentista.**

- ■ However, when you use a *title* to refer to someone, the article is used: **Es el profesor Gómez.** When you address that person directly, using their title, the article is not used: **Buenos días, profesor Gómez.**

When the noun is modified, the article is used: **Liana es una profesora excelente.**

The following titles are typically used with the article when referring to a person, and without the article when addressing that person directly.

señor (Sr.)	*Mr.*	**señorita (Srta.)**	*Miss / Ms.*
señora (Sra.)	*Mrs. / Ms.*	**profesor / profesora**	*professor*

>> Gramática útil 2

Identifying and describing: Subject pronouns and the present indicative of the verb **ser**

Cómo usarlo

The Spanish verb **ser** can be used to identify people and objects, to describe them, to make introductions, and to say when something will take place. It is one of two Spanish verbs that are the equivalents of the English verb *to be*.

Mi teléfono **es** el 2-39-71-49.	*My telephone number **is** 2-39-71-49.*
Yo **soy** Mariela y ella **es** Elena.	*I **am** Mariela and this **is** Elena.*
La fiesta **es** el miércoles.	*The party **is** on Wednesday.*

> **Estar**, which you have already used in the expression **¿Cómo estás?**, also means *to be*. You will learn other ways to use **estar** in **Chapter 4.**

Cómo formarlo

LO BÁSICO

- *Pronouns* are words used to replace nouns. (Some English pronouns are *it, she, you, him*, etc.)
- Verbs change form to reflect *number* and *person*. *Number* refers to singular versus plural. *Person* refers to different subjects.
- A verb's *tense* indicates the time frame in which an event takes place (for example, *talk, talked, will talk*). The *present indicative tense* refers to present-time events or conditions (*I talk, I am talking*).

1. Subject pronouns

- Subject pronouns are pronouns that are used as the subject of a sentence. Here are the subject pronouns in Spanish.

Singular		Plural	
yo	*I*	**nosotros / nosotras**	*we*
tú	*you (fam.)*	**vosotros / vosotras**	*you (fam.)*
usted (Ud.)	*you (form.)*	**ustedes (Uds.)**	*you (fam., form.)*
él, ella	*he, she*	**ellos, ellas**	*they*

> In Spanish, it is not always necessary to use the subject pronoun with the verb, as long as the subject is understood. For example, it's less common to say **Yo soy Rafael**, because **Soy Rafael** is clear enough on its own.

- The **vosotros / vosotras** forms are primarily used in Spain. They allow speakers to address more than one person informally. In most other places, Spanish speakers use **ustedes** to address several people, regardless of the formality of the relationship. The **vosotros** forms of verbs are provided in *Cuadros* so that you can recognize them, but they are not included for practice in activities.

2. Formal vs. familiar

English has a single word—*you*—to address people directly, regardless of how well you know them. As you have already seen, Spanish has two basic forms of address: the **tú** form and the **usted** form.

- **Tú** is used to address a family member, a close friend, a child, or a pet.
- **Usted** (often abbreviated **Ud.**) is a more formal means of address used with older people, strangers, acquaintances, and sometimes with colleagues.
- Remember that the **ustedes** form is normally used to address more than one person in both *informal* and *formal* contexts (except in Spain, where **vosotros**(as) is used in informal contexts).

Levels of formality vary throughout the Spanish-speaking world, so it's important when traveling to listen to how **tú** and **usted** are used and to follow the local practice.

In some countries, you will hear **vos** forms (Argentina and parts of Uruguay, Chile, and Central America). This is a variation of **tú** that is used only in these regions.

To show respect, you sometimes hear the titles **don** and **doña** used with people you address as **usted**. **Don** and **doña** are used with the person's first name: **don Roberto, doña Carmen**.

3. The present tense of the verb **ser**

The present indicative forms of the verb **ser** are as follows. Note the subject pronouns associated with each form.

ser *(to be)*	
Singular	
yo soy	*I am*
tú eres	*you (s. fam.) are*
usted es	*you (s. form.) are*
él es	*he is*
ella es	*she is*
Plural	
nosotros / nosotras somos	*we are*
vosotros / vosotras sois	*you (pl. fam.) are*
ustedes son	*you (pl. form. or pl. fam.) are*
ellos son	*they (masc. or mixed) are*
ellas son	*they (fem.) are*

Gramática útil 3

Expressing quantity: **Hay** + nouns

Cómo usarlo

1. **Hay** is the Spanish equivalent of *there is* or *there are* in English.

Hay una reunión en la cafetería.	***There is*** *a meeting in the cafeteria.*
Hay tres estudiantes en la clase.	***There are*** *three students in the class.*
Hay unos libros en la mesa.	***There are*** *some books on the table.*
Hay una fiesta el viernes.	***There is*** *a party on Friday.*

2. **Hay** is used with both singular and plural nouns, and in both affirmative and negative contexts.

   Hay un bolígrafo, pero no **hay** lápices en la mesa.

3. **Hay** can be used with numbers or with indefinite articles (**un, una, unos, unas**), but it is never used with definite articles (**el, la, los, las**).

¡**Hay** tres profesores en la clase, pero sólo **hay** una estudiante!	***There are*** *three professors in the class, but* ***there is*** *only one student!*

4. With a plural noun or negative, typically no article is used with **hay** unless you are providing extra information.

Hay papeles en la mesa.	***There are papers*** *on the table.*
No hay libros en el escritorio.	***There aren't (any) books*** *on the desk.*
Hay quince personas en la clase.	***There are fifteen people*** *in the class.*

   BUT:

Hay unas personas interesantes en la clase.	***There are some interesting people*** *in the class.*

Cómo formarlo

Hay is an *invariable verb form* because it never changes to reflect number or person. That is why **hay** can be used with both singular and plural nouns.

>> # Gramática útil 4

Expressing possession, obligation, and age: **Tener, tener que, tener + años**

Cómo usarlo

1. The verb **tener** means *to have*. It is used in Spanish to express possession and to give someone's age. You can also use it with **que** and another verb to say what you have to do: **Tengo que irme.** *(I have to go.)*

Tengo dos teléfonos en casa.	*I **have** two telephones in my house.*
Elena **tiene** veinte años. ¿Cuántos años **tienen** Sergio y Dulce?	*Elena **is** twenty years old. How old **are** Sergio and Dulce?*
Tengo que irme porque **tengo** clase.	*I **have to** go because I **have** class.*

2. When **tener** is used to express possession, the article is usually omitted, unless number is emphasized or you are referring to a specific object.

3. Note that where Spanish uses **tener... años** to express age, the English equivalent is *to be . . . years old*.

Cómo formarlo

1. Here are the forms of the verb **tener** in the present indicative tense.

> Remember, it's better to use the verb without a subject pronoun unless the subject is unclear or you want to emphasize it.

tener *(to have)*			
yo	**tengo**	nosotros / nosotras	**tenemos**
tú	**tienes**	vosotros / vosotras	**tenéis**
Ud., él, ella	**tiene**	Uds., ellos, ellas	**tienen**

2. When talking about age, it's helpful to know the months of the year so that you can say when people's birthdays are celebrated.

¿Cuándo es tu cumpleaños? *When is your birthday?*

enero	julio
febrero	agosto
marzo	septiembre
abril	octubre
mayo	noviembre
junio	diciembre

> In Spanish the word for birthday is **cumpleaños**, which literally means "completes **(cumple)** years **(años)**." Many Spanish speakers celebrate their saint's day **(el día de su santo)**, which is the birthday of the saint whose name is the same as or similar to their own. For example: **El 19 de marzo es el día de San José.**

3. When giving dates in Spanish, the day of the month comes first: **el quince de abril** = *April 15th.* When writing the date with numbers, the day always comes before the month: 15/4/10 = **el quince de abril de 2010.**

Chapter 2

 ## Gramática útil 1

**Describing what you do or are doing:
The present indicative of regular -ar verbs**

Cómo usarlo

In English we use a variety of structures to express different present-tense concepts. In Spanish many of these are communicated with the same grammatical form. The present indicative tense in Spanish can be used. . .

- to describe routine actions:

  ¡Estudias mucho!　　　　　　　*You study a lot!*

- to say what you are doing now:

  Estudias matemáticas hoy.　　*You are studying
  　　　　　　　　　　　　　　　　mathematics today.*

- to ask questions about present events:

  ¿Estudias con Enrique todas
  　las semanas?　　　　　　　　*Do you study with Enrique
  　　　　　　　　　　　　　　　every week?*

- to indicate plans in the immediate future:

  Estudias con Enrique el viernes, ¿no?　*You're going to study with
  　　　　　　　　　　　　　　　　　　　Enrique on Friday, right?*

> The use of the present tense to talk about future plans is used more in some regions of the Spanish-speaking world than others.

Notice how the same form in Spanish, **estudias**, can be translated four different ways in English.

Cómo formarlo

LO BÁSICO

- An *infinitive* is a verb before it has been conjugated to reflect person and tense. **Bailar** *(To dance)* is an infinitive.
- A *verb stem* is what is left after you remove the **-ar, -er,** or **-ir** ending from the infinitive. **Bail-** is the verb stem of **bailar.**
- A *conjugated verb* is a verb whose endings reflect person *(I, you, he/she, we, you, they)* and tense *(present, past, future, etc.).* **Bailas** *(You dance)* is a conjugated verb (person: *you familiar singular;* tense: *present*).

1. Spanish infinitives end in **-ar**, **-er**, or **-ir**. For now, you will learn to form the present indicative tense of verbs ending in **-ar**. To form the present indicative tense of a regular **-ar** verb, simply remove the **-ar** and add the following endings.

bailar *(to dance)*			
yo	bail**o**	nosotros / nosotras	bail**amos**
tú	bail**as**	vosotros / vosotras	bail**áis**
Ud., él, ella	bail**a**	Uds., ellos, ellas	bail**an**

2. Remember, as you learned in **Chapter 1**, you do not need to use the subject pronouns (**yo, tú, él, ella**, etc.) unless the meaning is not clear from the context of the sentence, or you wish to clarify, add emphasis, or make a contrast.

Camino en el parque todos los días.   *I walk in the park every day.*
But:
Yo camino en el parque, pero Lidia camina en el gimnasio.   *I walk in the park, but Lidia walks in the gymnasium.*

3. You may use certain conjugated present-tense verbs with infinitives. However, do not use two conjugated verbs together unless they are separated by a comma or the words **y** *(and)*, **pero** *(but)*, or **o** *(or)*.

> Notice that in this usage, Spanish infinitives are often translated into English as *-ing* forms: *I stop working.*

Necesitamos trabajar el viernes.   *We have to work on Friday.*
Los sábados, **trabajo, practico** deportes y **visito** a amigos.   *On Saturdays I work, play sports, and visit friends.*
Los domingos, **dejo de trabajar**.   *On Sundays I stop working.*
¡**Bailo, canto** o **escucho** música!   *I dance, sing, or listen to music!*

4. To say what you don't do or aren't planning to do, use **no** before the conjugated verb.

¡**No estudio** los fines de semana!   *I don't study on the weekends!*

5. Add question marks to turn a present-tense sentence into a *yes/no* question.

¿**No estudias** los fines de semana?   *Don't you study on the weekends?*
¿**Tienes que estudiar** este fin de semana?   *Do you have to study this weekend?*

6. Other regular **-ar** verbs:

> The expression **acabar de** can be used with any infinitive to say what activity you and others have just completed: **Acabo de llegar.** *(I just arrived.)* **Acabamos de cenar.** *(We just ate dinner.)*

apagar	*to turn off*	llegar	*to arrive*
acabar de (+ infinitive)	*to have just done something*	necesitar (+ infinitive)	*to need (to do something)*
buscar	*to look for*	pasar	*to pass (by); to happen*
cenar	*to eat dinner*	preparar	*to prepare*
comprar	*to buy*	regresar	*to return*
dejar de (+ infinitive)	*to leave; to stop (doing something)*	usar	*to use*
descansar	*to rest*	viajar	*to travel*
llamar	*to call*		

Gramática útil 2

Saying what you and others like to do: **Gustar** + infinitive

Cómo usarlo

The Spanish verb **gustar** can be used with an infinitive to say what you and your friends like to do. Note that **gustar**, although often translated as *to like*, is really more similar to the English *to please*. **Gustar** is always used with pronouns that indicate *who is pleased* by the activity mentioned.

—**Me gusta bailar** salsa.	***I like to dance*** *salsa.* ***(Dancing*** *salsa* ***pleases me.)***
—¿**Te gusta bailar** también?	***Do you like to dance****, too?* ***(Does dancing please you****, too?)***
—No, pero a **Luis le gusta** mucho.	*No, but **Luis likes it** a lot. (No, but **it pleases Luis** a lot.)*

Cómo formarlo

LO BÁSICO

The pronouns used with **gustar** are indirect object pronouns. They show the person who is being pleased or who likes something. You will learn more about them in **Chapter 8**.

1. When **gustar** is used with one or more infinitives, it is always used in its third-person singular form **gusta**. Sentences with **gusta** + *infinitive* can take the form of statements or questions without a change in word order.

—**Nos gusta cocinar** y **cenar** en restaurantes.	***We like to cook*** *and* ***to eat*** *dinner in restaurants.*
—¿**Te gusta cocinar** también?	***Do you like to cook*** *also?*

2. **Gusta** + *infinitive* is used with the following pronouns.

gusta + infinitive	
Me gusta cantar. *I like to sing.*	**Nos** gusta cantar. *We like to sing.*
Te gusta cantar. *You like to sing.*	**Os** gusta cantar. *You (fam. pl.) like to sing.*
Le gusta cantar. *You (form.) / He / She like (s) to sing.*	**Les** gusta cantar. *You (pl.) / They like to sing.*

¡OJO! Do not confuse **me, te, le, nos, os,** and **les** with the subject pronouns **yo, tú, él, ella, Ud., nosotros, vosotros, ellos, ellas,** and **Uds.** that you have already learned.

3. When you use **gusta**, you can also use **a** + *person* to emphasize or clarify *who* it is who likes the activity mentioned. Clarification is particularly important with **le** and **les,** because they can refer to several people.

Le gusta navegar por Internet.	*He/She likes to browse the Internet. (Who does?)*
A Beto / A él le gusta navegar por Internet.	*Beto / He likes to browse the Internet.*
A ellos les gusta cantar.	*They like to sing.*
A nosotros nos gusta conversar.	*We like to talk.*
A Sergio y a Anilú les gusta bailar.	*Sergio and Anilú like to dance.*

Notice that **mí** has an accent, but **ti** does not.

4. If you want to emphasize or clarify what you or a close friend like, use **a mí** (with **me gusta**) and **a ti** (with **te gusta**).

A mí me gusta alquilar películas, pero **a ti te gusta** mirar televisión.	*I like to rent movies, but you like to watch television.*

5. To create negative sentences with **gusta** + *infinitive*, place **no** before the *pronoun* + **gusta.**

No nos gusta trabajar.	*We don't like to work.*
A Roberto **no le gusta cocinar**.	*Roberto doesn't like to cook.*

6. To express agreement with someone's opinion, use **también**. If you want to disagree, use **no** or **tampoco**. If you want to ask a friend if they like an activity you've already mentioned, ask **¿Y a ti?**

—¿Te gusta cocinar?	*Do you like to cook?*
—**A mí, no.** No me gusta. Me gusta comer en restaurantes. **¿Y a ti?**	*No, not me. I don't like it. I like to eat in restaurants. And you?*
—**A mí también.** Pero no me gusta comer en restaurantes elegantes.	*Me too. But I don't like to eat in fancy restaurants.*
—**¡A mí tampoco!**	*Me neither!*

>> Gramática útil 3

Describing yourself and others: Adjective agreement

Cómo usarlo

As you learned in **Chapter 1,** Spanish nouns must agree with definite and indefinite articles in both gender and number. This agreement is also necessary when using Spanish adjectives. Their endings change to reflect the number and gender of the nouns they modify.

Anilú es **delgada**.	*Anilú is **thin**.*
Sergio y Beto son **inteligentes**.	*Sergio and Beto are **intelligent**.*
Sergio es un hombre **alto**.	*Sergio is a **tall** man.*
Dulce y Anilú son mujeres **jóvenes**.	*Dulce and Anilú are **young** women.*

Notice that in these cases the adjectives go *after* the noun, rather than before, as in English.

Cómo formarlo

LO BÁSICO

A *descriptive adjective* is a word that describes a noun. It answers the question *What is . . . like?*

To modify is to limit or qualify the meaning of another word. A descriptive adjective *modifies* a noun by specifying characteristics that apply to that noun: **un estudiante** vs. **un estudiante inteligente**.

1. **Gender**: If an adjective is used to modify a masculine noun, the adjective must have a masculine ending. If it is used to modify a feminine noun, it must have a feminine ending.

   - The masculine ending for adjectives ending in **-o** is the **o** form.
   - The feminine ending for adjectives ending in **-o** is the **a** form.
   - Adjectives ending in **-e** or most consonants don't change to reflect gender.
   - Adjectives ending in **-or** add **a** to the ending for the feminine form.

Un professor	Una profesora
simpátic**o**	simpátic**a**
interesant**e**	interesant**e**
trabajad**or**	trabajad**ora**

2. **Number**: If an adjective is used to modify a plural noun or more than one noun, it must be used in its plural form.

   - To create the plural of an adjective ending in a vowel, add **s**.
   - To create the plural of an adjective ending in a consonant, add **es**.
   - To create the plural of an adjective ending in **-or**, add **es** to the masculine form and **as** to the feminine form.
   - To create the plural of an adjective ending in **-z**, change the **z** to **c** and add **es**.

El profesor	Los profesores	Las profesoras
simpático	simpático**s**	simpática**s**
interesante	interesante**s**	interesante**s**
trabajador	trabajador**es**	trabajador**as**
feli**z**	feli**ces**	feli**ces**

Numbers do not change to match the number or gender of the nouns they describe. They go *before* the noun, rather than after.

3. As with articles and subject pronouns, adjectives that apply to mixed groups of males and females typically use the masculine form.

4. Most descriptive adjectives are used *after* the noun, rather than before.

Note that Spanish does not use a serial comma, as English does optionally. In the following English sentence, the comma after *generous* can be kept or omitted: *My friends are active, generous, and funny.* In Spanish, you do not use a comma after **generosos**: **Mis amigos son activos, generosos y cómicos.**

5. If you want to use more than one adjective, you can use **y** *(and)* or **o** *(or)*.

El estudiante es simpático **y** trabajador.
¿Es el profesor alto **o** bajo?
Mis amigos son activos, generosos **y** cómicos.
¿Son ellas extrovertidas **o** introvertidas?

- If **y** appears before a word that begins with an **i**, it changes to **e**.
  La instructora es divertida **e** interesante.

- If **o** appears before a word that begins with an **o**, it changes to **u**.
  Hay siete **u** ocho estudiantes buenos en la clase.

6. Adjectives of nationality follow slightly different rules. These adjectives add **a / as** feminine endings for nationalities whose names end in **-l, -s,** and **-n**. See the nationalities in the following group for examples. Adjectives of nationality are always used after the noun.

Nacionalidades		
África		
ecuatoguineano(a) Guinea Ecuatorial		
Asia		
chino(a) China	**indio(a)** India	
coreano(a) Corea	**japonés, japonesa** Japón	
Australia		
australiano(a) Australia		
Centroamérica y el Caribe		
costarricense Costa Rica	**guatemalteco(a)** Guatemala	**panameño(a)** Panamá
cubano(a) Cuba	**hondureño(a)** Honduras	**puertorriqueño(a)** Puerto Rico
dominicano(a) República Dominicana	**nicaragüense** Nicaragua	**salvadoreño(a)** El Salvador
Europa		
alemán, alemana Alemania	**francés, francesa** Francia	**italiano(a)** Italia
español, española España	**inglés, inglesa** Inglaterra	**portugués, portuguesa** Portugal
Norteamérica		
canadiense Canadá	**estadounidense** Estados Unidos	**mexicano(a)** México
Sudamérica		
argentino(a) Argentina	**colombiano(a)** Colombia	**peruano(a)** Perú
boliviano(a) Bolivia	**ecuatoriano(a)** Ecuador	**uruguayo(a)** Uruguay
chileno(a) Chile	**paraguayo(a)** Paraguay	**venezolano(a)** Venezuela

Notice the umlaut on the **ü** in **nicaragüense**. It is called a **diéresis** in Spanish. The **diéresis** is placed on the **u** in the syllables **gue** and **gui** to indicate that the **u** needs to be pronounced. Compare: **bilingüe, pingüino** and **guerra, Guillermo.**

Estados Unidos is often abbreviated as **EEUU** or **EE.UU.** in Spanish. Some native speakers do not use the article **los** with **EEUU: en Estados Unidos** or **en EEUU.**

Remember that Puerto Ricans are U.S. citizens.

7. Several adjectives in Spanish may be used *before* or *after* the noun they modify. Three common adjectives of this type are **bueno** *(good)*, **malo** *(bad)*, and **grande** *(big, large)*. When **bueno** and **malo** are used before a singular masculine noun, they have a special shortened form. Whenever **grande** is used before any singular masculine or feminine noun, its shortened form **gran** is used. Note that **grande** has different meanings when used *before* the noun *(great, famous)* and *after* the noun *(big, large)*.

un estudiante bueno **una estudiante buena**	BUT:	un **buen** estudiante una buena estudiante
un día malo **una semana mala**	BUT:	un **mal** día una mala semana
un hotel grande	BUT:	un **gran** hotel
una universidad grande	BUT:	una **gran** universidad

Chapter 3

>> Gramática útil 1

Asking questions: Interrogative words

Cómo usarlo

You have already seen, learned, and used a number of interrogative words to ask questions. **¿Cómo te llamas?**, **¿Cuál es tu dirección electrónica?**, **¿Dónde vives?**, and **¿Qué tal?** are all questions that begin with interrogatives: **cómo, cuál, dónde, qué.**

As in English, we use interrogatives in Spanish to ask for specific information. Here are the Spanish interrogatives.

¿Cuál(es)?	*What? Which one(s)?*	**¿Dónde?**	*Where?*
¿Qué?	*What? Which?*	**¿Adónde?**	*To where?*
¿A qué hora?	*(At) What time?*	**¿De dónde?**	*From where?*
¿De qué?	*About what? Of what?*	**¿Quién(es)?**	*Who?*
¿Cuándo?	*When?*	**¿De quién(es)?**	*Whose?*
¿Cuánto(a)?	*How much?*	**¿Cómo?**	*How?*
¿Cuántos(as)?	*How many?*	**¿Por qué?**	*Why?*

1. ¿Qué? and **¿cuál?** may appear interchangeable at first sight, but they are used in very specific ways.

¿Qué? is . . .

- used to ask for a definition: **¿Qué es el reloj de veinticuatro horas?**
- used to ask for an explanation or further information: **¿Qué vas a estudiar este semestre?**

- generally used when the next word is a noun: **¿Qué libros te gustan más? ¿Qué clase tienes a las ocho?**

¿Cuál? is . . .

- used to express a choice between specified items: **¿Cuál de los libros prefieres?**
- used when the next word is a form of **ser** but the question is *not* asking for a definition: **¿Cuál es tu número de teléfono? ¿Cuáles son tus clases favoritas?**

2. **¿Dónde?** is used to ask where something is.

  ¿**Dónde** está la biblioteca?   *Where is the library?*

Notice that **dónde** and **adónde** are both translated the same way into English.

3. **¿Adónde?** is used to ask where someone is going.

  ¿**Adónde** vas ahora?   *Where are you going now?*

4. **¿De quién es?** and **¿De quiénes son?** are used to ask about possession. You answer using **de**.

  —¿**De quién** es la computadora?   *Whose computer is this?*
  —**Es de** Miguel.   *It's Miguel's.*

  —¿**De quiénes** son los libros?   *Whose books are these?*
  —**Son de** Anita y Manuel.   *They're Anita's and Manuel's.*

Note that the interrogative is two separate words with an accent on **qué. Porque** is one single word with no accent.

5. Questions using **¿por qué?** can be answered using **porque** *(because).*

  —¿**Por qué** tienes que trabajar?   *Why do you have to work?*
  —¡**Porque** necesito el dinero!   *Because I need the money!*

Cómo formarlo

1. Interrogatives are always preceded by an inverted question mark (¿). The question requires a regular question mark (?) at the end.

2. Notice that in a typical question the subject *follows* the verb.

  ¿Dónde **estudia Marcos**?   *Where does **Marcos study**?*
  ¿Qué instrumento **tocan** ustedes?   *What instrument do **you play**?*

3. **¿Quién?** and **¿cuál?** change to reflect number.

  ¿**Quién** es el hombre alto? / ¿**Quiénes** son los hombres altos?
  ¿**Cuál** de los libros tienes? / ¿**Cuáles** son tus idiomas favoritos?

4. **¿Cuánto?** changes to reflect both number and gender.

  ¿**Cuánto** dinero tienes?   *How much money do you have?*
  ¿**Cuánta** comida compramos?   *How much food should we buy?*
  ¿**Cuántos** años tienes?   *How many years old are you? / How old are you?*

  ¿**Cuántas** personas hay?   *How many people are there?*

5. When you want to ask *how much* in a general way, use **¿cuánto?**

  ¿**Cuánto** es?   ¿**Cuánto** necesitamos?

6. Note that interrogatives always require an accent.

7. You have already learned how to form simple *yes/no* questions by adding **no** to a sentence.

¿**No escribes** e-mails hoy?

Aren't you writing *any e-mails today?*

8. You can also form simple *yes/no* questions by adding a tag question, such as ¿**verdad?** *(Isn't that right?)* and ¿**no?** to the end of a statement.

Cantas en el coro con Ana, ¿**no?**

*You sing in the chorus with Ana, **right?***

Enrique baila salsa muy bien, ¿**verdad?**

*Enrique dances salsa very well, **right?***

> When a Spanish speaker adds ¿**verdad?** or ¿**no?** to a question, he or she is expecting an affirmative answer.

>> Gramática útil 2

Talking about daily activities: The present indicative of regular -er and -ir verbs

Cómo usarlo

In **Chapter 2,** you learned how to use the present indicative of regular **-ar** verbs to talk about daily activities. The present indicative of **-er** and **-ir** verbs are used in the same contexts.

Remember:

1. The present indicative, depending on how it is used, can correspond to the following English usages: *I read* (in general), *I am reading, I am going to read, I do read,* and, if used as a question, *Do you read?*

2. You can often omit the subject pronoun when the subject is clear from the verb ending used or from the context of the sentence.

Leo en la biblioteca todos los días.

I read *in the library every day.*

Lees en la residencia estudiantil, ¿no?

You read *in the dorm, right?*

3. You may use an infinitive after certain conjugated verbs.

¿**Tienes que imprimir** esto?

Do you have to print *this?*

¿**Necesitas leer** este libro?

Do you need to read *this book?*

¡**Dejo de leer** después de medianoche!

I stop reading *after midnight!*

4. However, do not use two verbs conjugated in the present tense together unless they are separated by a comma or the words **y** *(and)* or **o** *(or)*.

Leo, estudio y **escribo** composiciones en la biblioteca.

I read, study, *and **write** compositions in the library.*

5. Remember that you can negate sentences in the present indicative tense to say what you don't do or aren't planning to do.

No comemos en la cafetería hoy.

We're not eating *in the cafeteria today.*

No leo todos los días.

I don't read *every day.*

To form the present indicative tense of **-er** and **-ir** verbs, simply remove the **-er** or **-ir** and add the following endings.

comer *(to eat)*			
yo	**como**	nosotros / nosotras	**comemos**
tú	**comes**	vosotros / vosotras	**coméis**
Ud. / él / ella	**come**	Uds. / ellos / ellas	**comen**

Notice that the present indicative endings for **-er** and **-ir** verbs are identical except for the **nosotros** and **vosotros** forms.

vivir *(to live)*			
yo	**vivo**	nosotros / nosotras	**vivimos**
tú	**vives**	vosotros / vosotras	**vivís**
Ud. / él / ella	**vive**	Uds. / ellos / ellas	**viven**

Here are some commonly used **-er** and **-ir** verbs.

-er verbs			
aprender a (+ infinitive)	*to learn to (do something)*	**creer (en)**	*to believe (in)*
beber	*to drink*	**deber** (+ infinitive)	*should, ought (to do something)*
comer	*to eat*	**leer**	*to read*
comprender	*to understand*	**vender**	*to sell*
correr	*to run*		

-ir verbs			
abrir	*to open*	**escribir**	*to write*
asistir a	*to attend*	**imprimir**	*to print*
compartir	*to share*	**recibir**	*to receive*
describir	*to describe*	**transmitir**	*to broadcast*
descubrir	*to discover*	**vivir**	*to live*

>> Gramática útil 3

Talking about possessions: Simple possessive adjectives

1. You already have learned to express possession using **de** + a noun or name.

Es la computadora portátil **de la profesora**.

*It's **the professor's** laptop computer.*

2. You can also use possessive adjectives to describe your possessions, other people's possessions, or items that are associated with you. You are already familiar with some possessive adjectives from the phrases **¿Cuál es <u>tu</u> dirección?** and **Aquí tienes <u>mi</u> número de teléfono**.

—¿Cuándo es **tu** clase de historia?   *When is **your** history class?*

—A las dos. Y **mi** clase de español   *At two. And **my** Spanish class*
    es a las tres.   *is at three.*

3. When you use **su** (which can mean *your, his, her, its,* or *theirs*), the context will usually clarify who is meant. If not, you can follow up with **de** + name.

Es **su** libro. Es **de la profesora**.   *It's **her** book. It's **the professor's**.*

Cómo formarlo

LO BÁSICO

Possessive adjectives modify nouns in order to express possession. In other words, they tell who owns the item.

1. Here are the simple possessive adjectives in Spanish.

mi mis	*my*	nuestro / nuestra nuestros / nuestras	*our*
tu tus	*your (fam.)*	vuestro / vuestra vuestros / vuestras	*your (fam. pl.)*
su sus	*your (form.), his, her, its*	su sus	*your (pl.), their*

> The subject pronoun **tú** *(you)* has an accent on it to differentiate it from the possessive adjective **tu** *(your)*.
>
> **Tú** trabajas los lunes, ¿verdad?
>
> **Tu** libro está en mi casa.

2. Notice that . . .

- all possessive adjectives change to reflect number: **mi clase, mis clases; nuestro compañero de cuarto, nuestros compañeros de cuarto.**
- **mi, tu,** and **su** do not change to reflect gender, but **nuestro** and **vuestro** do: **nuestro libro, nuestros amigos, vuestras clases,** but **mi libro, mi clase.**
- unlike other adjectives, which often go after the noun they modify, simple possessive adjectives always go before the noun: **su profesora, nuestras amigas.**

>> Gramática útil 4

Indicating destination and future plans: The verb **ir**

Cómo usarlo

You can use the Spanish verb **ir** to say where you and others are going. You can also use it to say what you and others are going to do in the near future.

Vamos a la biblioteca mañana.   *We're going to the library tomorrow.*
Vamos a estudiar.   *We're going to study.*

Cómo formarlo

LO BÁSICO

An *irregular verb* is one that does not follow the normal rules, such as **tener**, which you learned in **Chapter 1**.

A *preposition* links nouns, pronouns, or noun phrases to the rest of the sentence. Prepositions can express location, time sequence, purpose, or direction. *In, to, after, under,* and *for* are all English prepositions.

> You have already used similar expressions: **necesitar** + infinitive *(to need to do something),* **tener que** + infinitive *(to have to do something),* and **dejar de** + infinitive *(to stop doing something).*

1. Here is the verb **ir** in the present indicative tense. **Ir**, like the verbs **ser** and **tener** that you have already learned, is an irregular verb.

ir *(to go)*			
yo	**voy**	nosotros / nosotras	**vamos**
tú	**vas**	vosotros / vosotras	**vais**
Ud. / él / ella	**va**	Uds. / ellos / ellas	**van**

2. Use the preposition **a** with the verb **ir** to say where you are going.

   Voy a la cafetería.   *I'm going to the cafeteria.*

3. When you want to use the verb **ir** to say what you are going to do, use this formula: **ir** + **a** + *infinitive.*

   Vamos a comer a las cinco hoy.   *We're going to eat at 5:00 today.*
   Después, **vamos a ir** al   *Afterward, we're going to go to*
       concierto.   *the concert.*

4. When you use **a** together with **el**, it contracts to **al**. The same holds true for **de** + **el**: **del**.

   a + el = **al**   de + el = **del**

   Voy **a la** biblioteca y luego **al** gimnasio. Después, **al** mediodía, voy a estudiar en la biblioteca **del** centro de comunicaciones.

Chapter 4

>> Gramática útil 1

Expressing likes and dislikes: **Gustar** with nouns and other verbs like **gustar**

Cómo usarlo

As you learned in **Chapter 2,** you can use **gustar** with an infinitive to say what activities you and other people like to do.

Me gusta estudiar en la biblioteca, pero **a Vicente le gusta estudiar** en la cafetería.	*I like to study* in the library, but *Vicente likes to study* in the cafeteria.

You can also use **gustar** with nouns, to say what thing or things you (and others) like or dislike. In this case, you use **gusta** with a single noun and **gustan** with plural nouns or a series of nouns.

—¿**Te gusta** esta **computadora?**	*Do you like* this *computer?*
—Sí, ¡pero **me gustan** más estas **portátiles**!	*Yes, but I like* these *laptops more!*

When you make negative sentences with **gusta** and **gustan,** you use **no** before the pronoun + **gusta / gustan.**

Nos gustan los programas de diseño gráfico, pero **no nos gustan** los programas de arte.	*We like* the graphic design programs, *but we don't like* the art programs.

> Remember that when you use **gustar** + infinitive you only use **gusta: Les gusta comer en la cafetería.**

Cómo formarlo

LO BÁSICO

- In Spanish, an *indirect object pronoun* is used with **gustar** to say who likes something. Because **gustar** literally means to *please*, the indirect object answers the question: *Pleases whom?*

- A *prepositional pronoun* is a pronoun that is used after a preposition, such as **a** or **de**.

1. As you have already learned, you must use forms of **gustar** with the correct indirect object pronoun.

Me gusta	el foro.	**Nos gusta**	el foro.
Me gustan	los foros.	**Nos gustan**	los foros.
Te gusta	el foro.	**Os gusta**	el foro.
Te gustan	los foros.	**Os gustan**	los foros.
Le gusta	el foro.	**Les gusta**	el foro.
Le gustan	los foros.	**Les gustan**	los foros.

> You will learn more about Spanish indirect object pronouns in **Chapter 8.**

2. As you have learned, if you want to *emphasize* or *clarify* who likes what, you can use **a** + name or noun, or **a** + prepositional pronoun. Note that when **a** + prepositional pronoun is used, there is often no direct translation in English. Notice that except for **mí** and **ti**, the prepositional pronouns are the same as the subject pronouns you already know.

Notice that while **mí** takes an accent, **ti** does not.

Prepositional pronoun	Indirect object pronoun	Form of gustar + noun
A mí	me	gustan los videojuegos.
A ti	te	gustan los videojuegos.
A Ud. / a él / a ella	le	gustan los videojuegos.
A nosotros / a nosotras	nos	gustan los videojuegos.
A vosotros / a vosotras	os	gustan los videojuegos.
A Uds. / a ellos / a ellas	les	gustan los videojuegos.

A mí me gustan los MP3 portátiles pero **a Elena** no le gustan.

A ella le gustan los teléfonos inteligentes que también tocan MP3s.

*I like MP3 players, but **Elena** doesn't like them.*

***She** likes smartphones that also play MP3s.*

3. A number of other Spanish verbs are used like **gustar.** These verbs are usually just used in two forms, as is **gustar.**

—**Me interesan** mucho estos celulares.

—¿No **te molesta** la recepción mala aquí?

I'm interested in these cell phones.

*Doesn't the bad reception here **bother you**?*

Other verbs like gustar	
encantar *to like a lot*	¡Me encanta la tecnología!
fascinar *to fascinate*	A Ana le fascinan esos sitios web.
importar *to be important to someone; to mind*	Nos importa tener acceso a Internet. ¿Te importa si usamos la computadora?
interesar *to interest, to be interesting*	A ellos les interesan las redes sociales.
molestar *to bother*	Nos molestan las computadoras viejas.

In Spanish-speaking cultures, courtesy is of utmost importance. It is very common to use phrases like ¿**Le importa?** or ¿**Le molesta?** to ask someone a question. ¿**Le importa si uso la computadora?** would be more likely heard than **Voy a usar la computadora** or ¿**Puedo usar la computadora?** It's also common to use **por favor** when asking a question and **gracias** upon receiving the answer. Other common expressions of courtesy are:

¡**Perdón!** / ¡**Disculpe!** / ¡**Lo siento!** *Pardon me! / Excuse me! / I'm sorry!*

No hay de qué. / **No se preocupe.**
No problem. / Not to worry.

Con permiso. *Excuse me. . . / With your permission. . .*

Cómo no. *Of course. / Certainly.*

>> Gramática útil 2

Describing yourself and others and expressing conditions and locations: The verb estar and the uses of ser and estar

Cómo usarlo

You already know that the verb **ser** is translated as *to be* in English. You have already used the verb **estar**, which is also translated as *to be*, in expressions such as **¿Cómo estás?** While both these Spanish verbs mean *to be*, they are used in different ways.

1. Use estar . . .

- to express location of people, places, or objects.

La profesora Suárez **está** en la biblioteca.	*Professor Suárez **is** in the library.*
Los libros **están** en la mesa.	*The books **are** on the table.*

- to talk about a physical condition.

—¿Cómo **está** usted?	*How **are** you?*
—**Estoy** muy bien, gracias.	*I'm well, thank you.*
—Yo **estoy** un poco cansada.	*I'm a little tired.*

- to talk about emotional conditions.

El señor Albrega **está** un poco nervioso hoy.	*Mr. Albrega **is** a little nervous today.*
Estoy muy ocupada esta semana.	*I'm very busy this week.*

2. Use ser . . .

- to identify yourself and others.

Soy Ana y ésta **es** mi hermana Luisa.	*I'm Ana and this **is** my sister Luisa.*

- to indicate profession.

Pablo Picasso **es** un artista famoso.	*Pablo Picasso **is** a famous artist.*

- to describe personality traits and physical features.

Somos altos y delgados.	*We **are** tall and thin.*
Somos estudiantes buenos.	*We **are** good students.*

- to give time and date.

Es la una. Hoy **es** miércoles.	*It **is** one o'clock. Today **is** Wednesday.*

- to indicate nationality and origin.

—**Eres** española, ¿no?	*You **are** Spanish, right?*
—Sí, **soy** de España.	*Yes, I **am** from Spain.*

- to express possession with **de**.

Este celular **es de Anita.**	*This **is** Anita's cell phone.*

- to give the location of an event.

La fiesta **es** en la residencia estudiantil.	*The party **is** in the dorm.*

> Notice that expressing the location of people, places, and things (other than events) requires the use of **estar. Ser** is used only to indicate *where an event will take place.*

Cómo formarlo

1. Here are the forms of the verb **estar** in the present indicative tense.

estar *(to be)*			
yo	**estoy**	nosotros / nosotras	**estamos**
tú	**estás**	vosotros / vosotras	**estáis**
Ud. / él / ella	**está**	Uds. / ellos / ellas	**están**

2. In the **¡Imagínate!** section you learned some adjectives that are commonly used with **estar** to describe physical and emotional conditions.

aburrido(a)	nervioso(a)
cansado(a)	ocupado(a)
contento(a)	preocupado(a)
enfermo(a)	seguro(a)
enojado(a)	triste
furioso(a)	

Don't forget that when you use adjectives with **estar,** as with any other verb, they need to agree with the person or thing they are describing in both gender and number.

Los estudiantes están preocupados por Miguel.	*The students are worried about Miguel.*
Elena está nerviosa a causa del examen.	*Elena is nervous because of the exam.*

>> Gramática útil 3

Talking about everyday events: Stem-changing verbs in the present indicative

Cómo usarlo

In **Chapters 1** and **2** you learned the present indicative forms of regular **-ar, -er,** and **-ir** verbs in Spanish. There are other Spanish verbs that use the same endings as regular **-ar, -er,** and **-ir** verbs in this tense, but they also have a small change in their stem. (Remember that the stem is the part of the infinitive that is left after you remove the **-ar / -er / -ir** ending.)

—¿Qué **piensas** de este MP3 portátil?	*What **do you think** of this MP3 player?*
—Me gusta, pero **prefiero** éste.	*I like it, but I **prefer** this one.*
—¿Verdad? Bueno, ¿por qué no le **pides** el precio al dependiente?	*Really? Well, why don't **you ask** the sales clerk the price?*

Cómo formarlo

1. There are three categories of stem-changing verbs in the present indicative.

	o → ue: encontrar (to find)	e → ie: preferir (to prefer)	e → i: pedir (to ask for)
yo	encuentro	prefiero	pido
tú	encuentras	prefieres	pides
Ud. / él / ella	encuentra	prefiere	pide
nosotros / nosotras	encontramos	preferimos	pedimos
vosotros / vosotras	encontráis	preferís	pedís
Uds. / ellos / ellas	encuentran	prefieren	piden

2. Note that the stem changes in all forms except the **nosotros / nosotras** and **vosotros / vosotras** forms.

3. Remember, all the endings for the present indicative are the same for these verbs as for the other regular verbs you've learned: **-o, -as, -a, -amos, -áis, -an** for **-ar** verbs; **-o, -es, -e, -emos / -imos, -éis / -ís, -en** for **-er** and **-ir** verbs. The only thing that is different here is the change in the stem.

4. Here are some commonly used Spanish verbs that experience a stem change in the present indicative tense.

e → ie

cerrar	to close
comenzar (a)	to begin (to)
empezar (a)	to begin (to)
entender	to understand
pensar de	to think (of), have an opinion about
pensar en	to think about, to consider
perder	to lose
preferir	to prefer
querer	to want, to love
sentir	to feel

o → ue

contar	to tell, to relate; to count
dormir	to sleep
encontrar	to find
jugar*	to play
poder	to be able to
sonar	to ring, to go off (phone, alarm clock, etc.)
soñar (con)	to dream (about)
volver	to return

e → i

pedir	to ask for something
repetir	to repeat
servir	to serve

***Jugar** is the only **u → ue** stem-changing verb in Spanish. It's grouped with the **o → ue** verbs, because its change is most similar to those.

Gramática útil 4

Describing how something is done: Adverbs

Cómo usarlo

When you want to say how an activity is carried out (slowly, thoroughly, generally, etc.), you use an adverb.

Generalmente, prefiero usar una contraseña secreta.
Generally, I prefer to use a secret password.

Escribo más **rápido / rápidamente** en computadora que con bolígrafo.
*I write more **rapidly** on the computer than I do with a pen.*

Este programa es **muy** lento.
*This program is **very** slow.*

Cómo formarlo

LO BÁSICO

An adverb is a word that modifies a verb, an adjective, or another adverb. (Sometimes adjectives can also be used as adverbs—for example, *fast*). *Generally, rapidly,* and *very* are all adverbs. You can identify an adverb by asking the question, *"How?"*

1. To form an adverb from a Spanish adjective, it is often possible to add the ending **-mente** to the adjective: **fácil → fácilmente**. If the adjective ends in an **-o**, change it to **-a** before adding **-mente**: **rápido → rápidamente**.

> **Lento** and **rápido** can also be used with **muy** for the same effect: **Esta computadora se conecta a Internet muy rápido / muy lento / rápidamente / lentamente.**

2. Here are some frequently used Spanish adjectives that can be turned into **-mente** adverbs.

fácil *(easy)*	→ **fácilmente**
difícil *(difficult)*	→ **difícilmente**
lento *(slow)*	→ **lentamente**
rápido *(fast)*	→ **rápidamente**

3. The following **-mente** adverbs are also useful to talk about your routine and what you normally do.

frecuentemente	*frequently*	**normalmente**	*normally*
generalmente	*generally*		

4. Here are some other common Spanish adverbs.

> Remember, adverbs can be used to modify other adverbs, so it's perfectly acceptable to use **muy** with **frecuentemente** or **mal**, for example!

bastante	*somewhat, rather*	Este sistema es **bastante** lento.
bien	*well*	Tu computadora funciona **bien**.
demasiado	*too much*	Navego **demasiado** por Internet.
mal	*badly*	¡Mi cámara web funciona muy **mal**!
mucho	*a lot*	Me gustan **mucho** los juegos interactivos.
muy	*very*	Guardo archivos **muy** frecuentemente.
poco	*little*	Chateo **poco** por Internet.

Chapter 5

Gramática útil 1

Describing daily activities: Irregular-**yo** verbs in the present indicative, **saber** vs. **conocer**, and the personal **a**

Cómo usarlo

1. You have already learned the present indicative tense of many verbs. These include regular **-ar, -er,** and **-ir** verbs (**hablar, comer, vivir,** etc.), some irregular verbs (**ser, tener, ir**), and some stem-changing verbs (**pensar, poder, dormir,** etc.).

2. Now you will learn some verbs that are regular in all forms of the present indicative except the **yo** form. Like other verbs in the present indicative tense, these verbs can be used to say what you routinely do, what you are doing at the moment, or what you plan to do in the future.

Todos los días **salgo** para la universidad a las ocho.	*Every day **I leave** for the university at 8:00.*
Ahora mismo, **pongo** mis libros en la mochila y **digo** "hasta luego" a mi compañera de cuarto.	*Right now, **I put / I'm putting** my books in my backpack and **I say / I'm saying**, "See you later" to my roommate.*
Esta noche, **traigo** mis libros a casa otra vez y **hago** la tarea.	*Tonight, **I bring / I'll bring** my books home again and **I do / I'll do** my homework.*

Cómo formarlo

Irregular-**yo** verbs

Many irregular-**yo** verbs in the present indicative fall into several recognizable categories. Others have to be learned individually.

1. -go endings:

hacer	*to make; to do*	**hago**, haces, hace, hacemos, hacéis, hacen
poner	*to put*	**pongo**, pones, pone, ponemos, ponéis, ponen
salir	*to leave, to go out (with)*	**salgo**, sales, sale, salimos, salís, salen
traer	*to bring*	**traigo**, traes, trae, traemos, traéis, traen

2. -zco endings:

conducir	*to drive; to conduct*	**conduzco**, conduces, conduce, conducimos, conducís, conducen
conocer	*to know a person; to be familiar with*	**conozco**, conoces, conoce, conocemos, conocéis, conocen
traducir	*to translate*	**traduzco**, traduces, traduce, traducimos, traducís, traducen

Conducir is used more frequently in Spain to talk about driving. In most of Latin America, the verbs **manejar** and **guiar** (both regular -ar verbs) are used. (**Guiar** uses an accent on the i in these forms: **guío, guías, guía, guían**.)

3. Other irregular-**yo** verbs:

dar	to give	**doy,** das, da, damos, dais, dan
oír	to hear	**oigo,** oyes, oye, oímos, oís, oyen
saber	to know a fact; to know how to	**sé,** sabes, sabe, sabemos, sabéis, saben
ver	to see	**veo,** ves, ve, vemos, veis, ven

Note that **oír** requires a **y** in the **tú, él / ella / Ud.,** and **ellos / ellas / Uds.** forms.

4. Two irregular-**yo** verbs (-**go** verbs) with a stem change:

decir	to say, to tell	**digo,** dices, dice, decimos, decís, dicen
venir	to come, to attend	**vengo,** vienes, viene, venimos, venís, vienen

5. Remember that most of these verbs are irregular only in the **yo** form. Otherwise, they follow the rules for regular -**ar, -er**, and -**ir** verbs that you have already learned. **Oír** uses the regular endings but includes a spelling change: the addition of **y** to all forms except the **yo** form. **Decir** and **venir** also have a stem change in addition to the irregular-**yo** form, but they still use -**ir** present-tense endings.

Saber vs. conocer

Saber and **conocer** both mean *to know*. It's important to know when to use each one.

- Use **saber** to say that you know a fact or information, or that you know how to do something.

Eduardo **sabe** hablar alemán, jugar tenis y bailar flamenco. Además **sabe** dónde están todos los restaurantes buenos de la ciudad.	*Eduardo **knows how** to speak German, play tennis, and dance flamenco. He also **knows** where all the good restaurants in the city are.*

- Use **conocer** to say that you know a person or are familiar with a thing.

—¿**Conocen** a Sandra?	*Do you **know** Sandra?*
—No, pero **conocemos** a su hermana.	*No, but we **know** her sister.*
—¿**Conoces** bien Tegucigalpa?	*Do you **know** Tegucigalpa well?*
—Sí, pero no **conozco** las otras ciudades de Honduras.	*Yes, but I don't **know** the other cities in Honduras.*

One way to remember the difference between **saber** and **conocer** is that **saber** is usually followed by either a verb or a phrase, while **conocer** is often followed by a noun and is never followed by an infinitive.

The personal **a** can also be used with pets: **Adoro a mi perro.**

The personal a

When you use **conocer** to say that you know a person, notice that you use the preposition **a** before the noun referring to the person. This preposition is known as the personal **a** in Spanish and it must be used whenever a person receives the action of any verb (not just **conocer**). It has no equivalent in English.

In **Chapter 3** you learned that **a + el = al.** The personal **a** is no exception: **Veo al profesor.**

Conocemos **a** Nina y **a** Roberto.	*We know Nina and Roberto.*
¿Ves **a** tus amigos frecuentemente?	*Do you see your friends frequently?*

Gramática útil 2

Describing daily activities: Reflexive verbs

Cómo usarlo

1. So far, you have learned to use Spanish verbs to say what actions people are doing or to describe people and things.

Elena **habla** por teléfono.	Elena **talks** on the phone.
Tu hermano **está** cansado.	Your brother **is** tired.

2. Spanish has another category of verbs, called *reflexive* verbs, where the action of the verb *reflects back* on the person who is doing the action. When you use reflexive verbs in Spanish, they are often translated in English as *with* or *to myself, yourself, himself, herself, ourselves, yourselves, themselves*.

Lidia **se maquilla**.	Lidia **puts makeup on (herself)**.
Antes de ir a clase, yo **me ducho,**	Before going to class, **I shower,**
me visto y **me peino**.	**get dressed**, and **comb my hair**.

3. Notice how a reflexive verb is always used with a reflexive pronoun. These pronouns always match the subject of the sentence. The action of the verb *reflects back* on the person when the pronoun is used.

Yo me acuesto a las once.	**I go to bed (put myself to bed)** *at eleven*.
Tú te despiertas a las diez los fines de semana.	**You get up (wake yourself up)** *at ten on the weekends*.
Nosotros nos bañamos antes de salir de casa.	**We bathe (ourselves) before** *we leave the house*.
Ellos se afeitan todos los días.	**They shave (themselves)** *every day*.

> The reflexive pronoun and verb must always match the subject of the sentence: **Nosotros nos bañamos, Ellos se afeitan, Mateo se lava,** etc.

4. Most reflexive verbs can also be used without the reflexive pronoun to express non-reflexive actions, that is, actions that are performed on someone other than oneself.

Mateo **se baña** todos los días.	Mateo **bathes** every day.
Mateo **baña** a su perro.	Mateo **bathes (washes)** his dog.

5. Reflexive pronouns can also be used to indicate *reciprocal actions*.

Leo y Ali **se cortan** el pelo.	Leo and Ali **cut each other's** hair.

Cómo formarlo

LO BÁSICO

- A *reflexive verb* is one in which the action described reflects back on the subject.
- A *reflexive pronoun* is a pronoun that refers back to the subject of the sentence. English reflexive pronouns are *myself, herself, ourselves,* etc.

1. You conjugate reflexive verbs the same way you would any other verb. The only difference is that you must always include the reflexive pronoun.

2. Here is the reflexive verb **lavarse** conjugated in the present indicative tense.

lavarse (to wash oneself)	
yo	**me lavo**
tú	**te lavas**
Ud. / él / ella	**se lava**
nosotros(as)	**nos lavamos**
vosotros(as)	**os laváis**
Uds. / ellos / ellas	**se lavan**

3. The only difference in the way that reflexive and non-reflexive verbs are conjugated is the addition of the reflexive pronoun to the verb form. Verbs that are irregular or stem-changing when used non-reflexively have the same irregularities or stem changes when used with a reflexive pronoun.

Me despierto a las seis y media.   *I wake (myself) up at 6: 30.*
Despierto a mi esposo a las siete.   *I wake my husband up at 7: 00.*

4. When you use a reflexive verb in its infinitive form, the reflexive pronoun may attach at the end of the infinitive (most commonly) or go at the beginning of the entire verb phrase.

Voy a acostarme a las once.   OR: **Me voy a acostar** a las once.
Necesito acostarme a las once.   **Me necesito acostar** a las once.
Tengo que acostarme a las once.   **Me tengo que acostar** a las once.

> Remember that when you use a reflexive verb as an infinitive, you still need to change the pronoun to match the subject of the sentence: **Voy a acostar<u>me</u> a las once, pero tú vas a acostar<u>te</u> a medianoche**.

Notice that with **gustar** (and similar verbs), the reflexive pronoun *must* be attached at the end of the infinitive.

Me gusta acostar<u>me</u> a las once.

5. Here are some common reflexive verbs, many of which refer to daily routine. Many reflexive verbs have a stem change, which is indicated in parenthesis.

acostarse (ue) *to go to bed*	**levantarse** *to get up*
afeitarse *to shave oneself*	**maquillarse** *to put on makeup*
bañarse *to take a bath*	**peinarse** *to brush / comb one's hair*
cepillarse el pelo *to brush one's hair*	**ponerse (la ropa)** *to put on (clothing)*
cepillarse los dientes *to brush one's teeth*	**prepararse** *to get ready*
despertarse (ie) *to wake up*	**quitarse (la ropa)** *to take off (clothing)*
ducharse *to take a shower*	**secarse el pelo** *to dry one's hair*
lavarse *to wash oneself*	**sentarse (ie)** *to sit down*
lavarse el pelo *to wash one's hair*	**vestirse (i)** *to get dressed*
lavarse los dientes *to brush one's teeth*	

6. Some Spanish verbs are used with reflexive pronouns to emphasize a change in state or emotion. Spanish has many more verbs that are used this way than English does. Note that some of these verbs (**casarse, comprometerse,** etc.) are usually used to express reciprocal actions, due to the nature of their meaning.

> Reflexive actions always carry the meaning to *oneself*. Reciprocal actions always carry the meaning *to each other*.

casarse *to get married*	**irse** *to leave, to go away*
comprometerse *to get engaged*	**pelearse** *to have a fight*
despedirse (i) *to say goodbye*	**preocuparse** *to worry*
divertirse (ie) *to have fun*	**quejarse** *to complain*
divorciarse *to get divorced*	**reírse (i)** *to laugh*
dormirse (ue) *to fall asleep*	**relajarse** *to relax*
enamorarse *to fall in love*	**reunirse** *to meet, to get together*
enfermarse *to get sick*	**separarse** *to separate*

> **Reunirse** carries an accent on the **u** when conjugated: **se reúnen.**

7. Here are some common words and phrases to use with these verbs.

a veces *sometimes*	**siempre** *always*
antes *before*	**todas las semanas** *every week*
después *after*	**todos los días** *every day*
luego *later*	**...veces al día /** *. . . times a day /*
nunca *never*	**por semana** *per week*

>> Gramática útil 3

Describing actions in progress: The present progressive tense

Cómo usarlo

1. The present progressive tense is used in Spanish to describe actions that are in progress at the moment of speaking. It is equivalent to the *is / are + -ing* structure in English.

En este momento **estamos llamando** a los abuelos.	*Right now, **we are calling** the (our) grandparents.*
Están comiendo ahora.	***They are eating** right now.*

2. Note that the present progressive tense is used *much* more frequently in English than it is in Spanish. Whereas in English it is used to describe future plans, in Spanish the present indicative or the **ir** + **a** + infinitive structure is used instead.

Salimos con la familia este viernes.	***We are going out** with the family this Friday.*
Vamos a salir con la familia este viernes.	***We are going to go out** with the family this Friday.*

3. Use the present progressive in Spanish only to describe actions in which people are engaged at the moment. Do not use it to describe routine ongoing activities (use the present indicative), to describe generalized action (use the infinitive), or to describe future actions.

Right now:	No puedo hablar. **Estamos estudiando.**	*I can't talk. **We're studying** (right now).*
BUT:		
Routine:	**Estudio** español, biología, historia e informática.	***I am studying / I study** Spanish, biology, history, and computer science.*
Generalized action:	**Estudiar** es importante.	***Studying** is important.*
Future:	**Estudio** con Mario el lunes.	***I will study** with Mario on Monday.*

Cómo formarlo

LO BÁSICO

A *present participle* is the verb form that expresses a continuing or ongoing action. In English, present participles end in *-ing: laughing, reading.*

1. Form the present progressive tense by using the present indicative forms of the verb **estar** (which you learned in **Chapter 4**) and the present participle.

estoy / estás / está / estamos / estáis / están + present participle

2. Here's how to form the present participle of regular **-ar**, **-er**, and **-ir** verbs.

-ar verbs	-er / -ir verbs
Remove the **-ar** from the infinitive and add **-ando**.	Remove the **-er** / **-ir** from the infinitive and add **-iendo**.
caminar → **caminando**	ver → **viendo**
	escribir → **escribiendo**

Estamos caminando al centro.   ***We're walking*** *downtown.*
Estoy viendo la televisión.   ***I'm watching*** *television.*
Chali **está escribiendo** su trabajo.   *Chali **is writing** her paper.*

3. A few present participles are irregular.

leer: **leyendo**   oír: **oyendo**

4. All **-ir** stem-changing verbs show a stem change in their present participle as well.

e → i			
despedirse	**despidiéndose**	reírse	**riéndose**
divertirse	**divirtiéndose**	repetir	**repitiendo**
pedir	**pidiendo**	servir	**sirviendo**
o → u			
dormir	**durmiendo**	morir	**muriendo**

5. As you may have noticed in the list above, to form the present participle of reflexive verbs, you may attach the reflexive pronoun to the end of the present participle, or place it before the entire verb phrase, the same as when you use reflexive verbs in the infinitive. Note that when the pronoun is attached, the new present participle form requires an accent to maintain the correct pronunciation.

Lina **está levantándose** ahora mismo. /   *Lina **is getting up** right now.*
Lina **se está levantando** ahora mismo.

Estoy divirtiéndome mucho. /   *I'm **having** a lot of **fun**.*
Me estoy divirtiendo mucho.

Spanish–English Glossary

The vocabulary includes the active vocabulary presented in the chapters and many receptive words. Exceptions are verb conjugations, regular past participles, adverbs ending in **-mente,** superlatives, diminutives, and proper names of individuals and most countries. Active words are followed by a number that indicates the chapter in which the word appears as an active item. **P** refers to the opening pages that precede Chapter 1.

The gender of nouns is indicated except for masculine nouns ending in **-o** and feminine nouns ending in **-a.** Stem changes and spelling changes are shown for verbs, e.g., **dormir (ue, u); buscar (qu).**

The following abbreviations are used. Note that the *adj., adv.,* and *pron.* designations are used only to distinguish similar or identical words that are different parts of speech.

adj.	adjective	*fam.*	familiar	*irreg.*	irregular verb	*p.p.*	past participle
adv.	adverb	*form.*	formal	*m.*	masculine	*pron.*	pronoun
f.	feminine	*inf.*	infinitive	*pl.*	plural	*s.*	singular

A

a to; **~ cambio de** in exchange for; **~ nivel mundial** worldwide; **~ pesar de** in spite of; **~ pie** on foot, walking, 6; **~ través de** across, throughout
abogado(a) lawyer, 5
abrelatas eléctrico (*m. s.*) electric can opener, 10
abrigo coat, 8
abril April, 1
abrir to open, 3; **Abran los libros.** Open your books. P
abuelo(a) grandfather (grandmother), 5
abundancia abundance
aburrido(a) boring, 2; bored, 4
aburrimiento boredom
acabar de (+inf.) to have just (*done something*), 2
académico(a) academic
acceder to access, 4
accesorio accessory, 8
acción (*f.*) action, 5
aceite (*m.*) **de oliva** olive oil, 9
acero steel
aconsejar to advise, 10
acostarse (ue) to go to bed, 5
acrecentar (ie) to strengthen; to increase
actividad (*f.*) activity, P; **~ deportiva** sports activity, 7
activo(a) active, 2
actor (*m.*) actor, 5
actriz (*f.*) actress, 5

actualidad (*f.*): **en la ~** at the present time
acudir to go; to attend
adelantar to get ahead, to promote
adelante ahead
además besides
adinerado(a) rich, wealthy
adiós goodbye, 1
adivinar to guess; **Adivina.** Guess. P
administración (*f.*) **de empresas** business administration, 3
¿adónde? (to) where?
adquisición (*f.*) acquisition
aeropuerto airport, 6
afán (*m.*) desire
afeitarse to shave oneself, 5
afueras (*f. pl.*) outskirts, 10
agosto August, 1
agregar (gu) to add, 9
agrícola agricultural
agua (*f.*) (*but:* **el agua**) water; **~ dulce** fresh water; **~ mineral** sparkling water, 9
aguacate avocado, 9
ajedrez (*m.*) chess
ajo garlic, 9
al (a + el) to the, 3
albergar (gu) to shelter
albóndiga meatball
alcalde (alcaldesa) mayor
alcanzar (c) to achieve
alemán (alemana) German, 2
alemán (*m.*) German language, 3
alfabeto alphabet

alfombra rug, carpet, 10
algo something, 6
algodón (*m.*) cotton, 8
alguien someone, 6
algún, alguno(a)(s) some, any, 6
alistar to recruit; to enroll
allá over there, 6
allí there, 6
alma (*f.*) (*but:* **el alma**) soul
almacén (*m.*) store, 6
almeja clam, 9
almohada pillow
almuerzo lunch, 9
¿Aló? hello (*on the phone*), 1
alpinismo: practicar / hacer ~ to hike, to (mountain) climb, 7
alquilar videos / películas to rent videos / movies, 2
alquiler (*m.*) rent
alrededor de around
altitud (*f.*) altitude, height
altivo(a) arrogant
alto(a) tall, 2
altoparlante (*m., f.*) speaker, 4
altura height
amanecer (zc) to dawn
amante (*m., f.*) lover
amar to love
amarillo(a) yellow, 4
ambiente (*m.*) atmosphere; **medio ~** (*m.*) environment
ambigüedad (*f.*) ambiguity
ambos(as) both
amenaza threat
amigo(a) friend, P
amor (*m.*) love
anaranjado(a) orange (*in color*), 4
andar (*irreg.*) to walk, 8

anexo attachment

anfitrión (*m.*) host

anhelo wish, desire

anillo ring, 8

anoche last night, 7

anónimo(a) anonymous

Antártida Antarctica

anteayer the day before yesterday, 7

antecesor(a) ancestor

anteojos (*m. pl.*) eyeglasses

antepasado(a) ancestor

anteponer to give preference

antes before, 5

anticuado(a) antiquated, old-fashioned

antipático(a) unpleasant, 2

antros bar or club; the "in" place

anuncio personal personal ad

añadir to add, 9

año year, 3; ~ **pasado** last year, 7; **tener** (*irreg.*) ... ~ to be . . . years old, 1

apacible mild, gentle

apagar (gu) to turn off, 2

aparatos electrónicos electronics, 4

aparecer (zc) to appear

apariencia física physical appearance

apartamento apartment, 6

apenas scarcely

apetecer (zc) to long for

aplicación (*f.*) application, 4

apodo nickname

apoyar to support

apreciar to appreciate

aprender to learn, 3

aprendizaje (*m.*) learning

apropiado(a) appropriate

apto(a) apt, fit

apuntes (*m.*) notes, P

aquel / aquella(s) (*adj.*) those (over there), 6

aquél / aquélla(s) (*pron.*) those (over there), 6

aquí here, 6

árbol (*m.*) tree; ~ **genealógico** family tree

archivar to file, 4

archivo file, 4; ~ **PDF** PDF file, 4

arder to burn

arete (*m.*) earring, 8

argentino(a) Argentinian, 2

arquitecto(a) architect, 5

arquitectura architecture, 3

arreglar el dormitorio to straighten up the bedroom, 10

arroz (*m.*) **con pollo** chicken with rice, 9

arrugado(a) wrinkled

arte (*m.*) art, 3

artesanía handicrafts

artículo article, 1

artista (*m., f.*) artist, 5

asado(a) grilled

asco disgusting

asegurarse to make sure

asistente (*m., f.*) assistant, 5; ~ (*m.*) **electrónico** electronic notebook, 4

asistir a to attend, 3

aspiradora vacuum cleaner, 10

ataque (*m.*) attack

atardecer (*m.*) late afternoon

atún (*m.*) tuna, 9

audiencia audience

audífonos (*m. pl.*) earphones, 4

audio audio, P

auditorio auditorium, 6

aumentar to increase

aun even

aún yet (*in negative contexts*); still

australiano(a) Australian, 2

autobús: en ~ by bus, 6

automóvil: en ~ by car, 6

avenida avenue, 1

avergonzado(a) embarrassed

avergonzar (ue) (c) to embarrass

avión (*m.*) airplane; **en ~** by airplane, 6

aviso warning

ayer yesterday, 3

ayuda help

ayudar to help, 8

azúcar (*m., f.*) sugar, 9; **caña de ~** sugar cane

azul blue, 4

B

bacalao codfish, 9

bailar to dance, 2

baile (*m.*) dance, 3

bajar to get down from, to get off of (*a bus, etc.*), 6; to download, 4

bajo(a) short (*in height*), 2

balay large basket

baldosa paving stone

banco (commercial) bank, 6

bañador(a) bather

bañar to swim; to give someone a bath, 5; **bañarse** to take a bath, 5

baño bathroom, 10

barato: Es muy ~. It's very inexpensive. 8

barco boat

barrer el suelo / el piso to sweep the floor, 10

barrio neighborhood, 1; ~ **residencial** residential neighborhood, suburbs, 10; ~ **comercial** business district, 10

básquetbol (*m.*) basketball, 7

basta it is enough

bastante somewhat, rather, 4

Bastante bien. Quite well. 1

basura garbage, 10; **sacar la ~** to take out the garbage, 10

basurero wastebasket

batir to beat; to break

beber to drink, 3

bebida beverage, 9

béisbol (*m.*) baseball, 7

belleza beauty

bello(a) beautiful

berro watercress

besar to kiss

bicicleta: en ~ on bicycle, 6; **montar en ~** to ride a bike, 7

bien well, 4; ~, **gracias.** Fine, thank you. 1; **(no) muy ~** (not) very well, 1

bienestar (*m.*) well-being

bienvenido(a) welcome

bilingüe bilingual

biología biology, 3

bistec (*m.*) steak, 6

blanco(a) white, 4

blog blog, 4

blusa blouse, 8

bocadillo sandwich, 9

boda wedding

bodegón (*m.*) tavern

bolígrafo ballpoint pen, P

boliviano(a) Bolivian, 2

bolsa purse, 8

bombero(a) fire fighter, 5

bondadoso(a) kind; good

bonito(a) pretty

bordado(a) embroidered, 8

borrador (*m.*) rough draft

bosquejo outline
bota boot, 8
botar to throw out
bote (*m.*) boat
boxeo boxing, 7
brazalete (*m.*) bracelet, 8
breve brief
bróculi (*m.*) broccoli, 9
broma joke
bueno(a) good, 2; **Buenas noches.** Good night. Good evening. 1; **Buenas tardes.** Good afternoon. 1; **Buenos días.** Good morning. 1
bufanda scarf, 8
buscador (*m.*) search engine, 4
buscar (qu) to look for, 2
buzón (*m.*) **electrónico** electronic mailbox, 4

C

caballo: montar a ~ to ride horseback, 7
cable (*m.*) cable, 4
cabo end
cacao chocolate
cachemira cashmere
cadena chain, 8
caer (*irreg.*) to fall
café (*m.*) coffee, 9; (*adj.*) brown, 4
cafetería cafeteria, 3
caimán (*m.*) alligator (*cayman*)
cajero automático automated bank teller, ATM, 6
cajón (*m.*) large box; drawer
calcetín (*m.*) sock, 8
calculadora calculator, P
cálculo calculus, 3
caldo de pollo chicken soup, 9
calentar (ie) to heat, 9
calidad (*f.*) quality; **de buena (alta) ~** of good (high) quality, 8
calificación (*f.*) evaluation
calle (*f.*) street, 1
calor: Hace ~. It's hot., 7; **tener** (*irreg.*) **~** to be hot, 7
caluroso(a) warm
cama bed, 10; **hacer la ~** to make the bed, 10
cámara: ~ digital digital camera, 4; **~ web** webcam, 4

camarero(a) waiter (waitress), 5
camarón (*m.*) shrimp, 9
cambio change; exchange rate; **a ~ de** in exchange for
caminar to walk, 2
camisa shirt, 8
camiseta t-shirt, 8
campestre rural
campo: ~ de estudio field of study, 3; **~ de fútbol** soccer field, 6
caña de azúcar sugar cane
canadiense (*m., f.*) Canadian, 2
canasta basket
cancha soccer field, 6; **~ de tenis** tennis court, 6
canela cinnamon
cansado(a) tired, 4
cantante (*m., f.*) singer
cantar to sing, 2
capítulo chapter, P
característica trait; **~ de la personalidad** personality trait, 2; **~ física** physical trait, 2
Caribe (*m., f.*) Caribbean (sea)
cariño love, fondness, affection
carne (*f.*) meat, 9
cargar to upload, 4
carnicería butcher shop, 6
caro: Es (demasiado) caro(a). It's (too) expensive. 8
carpintero(a) carpenter, 5
carrera career, 5
carreta wooden cart
carro: en ~ by car, 6
carta: a la ~ à la carte, 9
cartera wallet, 8
cartón (*m.*) cardboard
casa house, 6
casarse to get married, 5
casco helmet
casero(a) homemade
castaño brown, 2
catarata waterfall
catorce fourteen, P
cebolla onion, 9
celebración (*f.*) celebration
celos: tener (*irreg.*) **~** to be jealous
celosamente jealously
celoso(a) jealous
cena dinner
cenar to eat dinner, 2
censo census
centavo cent

centro center; **~ comercial** mall, 6; **~ de computación** computer center, 3; **~ de comunicaciones** media center, 3; **~ de la ciudad** downtown, 10; **~ estudiantil** student center, 6
Centroamérica Central America
cepillarse el pelo to brush one's hair, 5
cepillo brush, 5; **~ de dientes** toothbrush, 5
cerca de close to, 6
cereal (*m.*) cereal, 9
cero zero, P
cerrar (ie) to close, 4; **Cierren los libros.** Close your books. P
cerveza beer, 9
chaleco vest, 8
champú (*m.*) shampoo, 5
chaparrón (*m.*) cloudburst, downpour
chaqueta jacket (*outdoor, non-suit coat*), 8
chatear to chat online, 4
Chau. Bye, Goodbye, 1
cheque (*m.*) check; **pagar con ~ / con ~ de viajero** to pay by check / with a traveler's check, 8
chévere terrific, great, cool (*Cuba, Puerto Rico*)
chico(a) boy (girl), P
chileno(a) Chilean, 2
chimenea fireplace, 10
chino Chinese language, 3
chino(a) Chinese, 2
chisme (*m.*) gossip
chismoso(a) gossiping
chompa sweater
chuleta de puerco pork chop, 6
ciberespacio cyberspace, 4
ciclismo cycling, 7
ciego(a) blind; **cita a ciegas** blind date
cien one hundred, P; **~ mil** one hundred thousand, 8
ciencias (*f. pl.*) science, 3; **~ políticas** political science, 3
científico(a) scientific
ciento uno one hundred and one, 8
cierto(a) certain
cinco five, P; **~ mil** five thousand, 8
cincuenta fifty, P

cine (*m.*) cinema, 6
cinturón (*m.*) belt, 8
cita quotation; **~ a ciegas** blind date
ciudad (*f.*) city, 6
claridad (*f.*) clarity
clase (*f.*) class, P; **~ baja** lower class
clic: hacer ~ / doble ~ to click / double click, 4
cliente (*m., f.*) customer, 8
clóset (*m.*) closet, 10
cobre (*m.*) copper
cocer (-z) (ue) to cook, 9
coche: en ~ by car, 6
cocina kitchen, 10
cocinar to cook, 2
cocinero(a) cook, chef, 5
código code
colectivo bus
cólera anger
collar (*m.*) necklace, 8
colombiano(a) Colombian, 2
colonia neighborhood, 1
color (*m.*) color, 4; **de un solo ~** solid (colored), 8
coma comma
comedor (*m.*) dining room, 10
comenzar (ie) (c) to begin, 4
comer to eat, 3; **darle de ~ al perro / gato** to feed the dog / cat, 10
cómico(a) funny, 2
comida food, 6
comino cumin, 9
¿cómo? how? 3; **¿~ desea pagar?** How do you wish to pay? 8; **¿~ es?** What's he / she / it like? 2; **¿~ está (usted)?** (*s. form.*) How are you? 1; **¿~ están (ustedes)?** (*pl.*) How are you? 1; **¿~ estás (tú)?** (*s. fam.*) How are you? 1; **¿~ te / le / les va?** How's it going with you? 1; **~ no.** Of course. 6; **¿~ se dice…?** How do you say . . . ? P; **¿~ se llama?** (*s. form.*) What's your name? 1; **¿~ te llamas?** (*s. fam.*) What's your name? 1
cómoda dresser, 10
compañero(a) de cuarto roommate, P
comparación (*f.*) comparison, 8
compartir to share, 3
competencia competition, 7

competir (i, i) to compete
complicidad (*f.*) complicity
comportamiento behavior
comprar to buy, 2
compras: hacer las ~ to go shopping, 6
comprender to understand, 3
comprensión (*f.*) understanding
comprometerse to get engaged, 5
computación (*f.*) computer science, 3
computadora computer, P; **~ portátil** laptop computer, P
común common
comunicación (*f.*) **pública** public communications, 3
con with
concordancia agreement
concurso contest
conducir (zc) to drive, to conduct, 5
conectar to connect, 4
conexión (*f.*) connection, 4; **hacer una ~** to go online, 4
confección (*f.*) confection
conferencista (*m., f.*) speaker
congelado(a) frozen, 9
congelador freezer, 10
conjunto group; **en ~** as a group
conmigo with me, 8
conocer (zc) to meet; to know a person, to be familiar with, 5
conseguir (i, i) to get, to obtain, 8
contabilidad (*f.*) accounting, 3
contado: al ~ in cash, 8
contador(a) accountant, 5
contar (ue) to tell, to relate, 4; to count; **~ con** to be certain of
contento(a) happy, 4
contestar to answer; **Contesten.** Answer. P
contigo with you (*fam.*), 8
contracción (*f.*) contraction, 3
contrario: al ~ on the contrary
contraseña password, 4
conversación (*f.*) conversation
convertir (ie, i) to change
copa wine glass, goblet, 9
coraje (*m.*) courage
cordillera mountain range
coreano(a) Korean, 2
corregir (i, i) (j) to correct
correo electrónico e-mail, 4
correr to run, 3
to mow the lawn, 10; **~ la conexión** to go offline, 4

cortesía courtesy, 4
cortina curtain, 10
corto(a) short (*in length*)
costarricense (*m., f.*) Costa Rican, 2
cotidiano(a) daily
crear to create
creativo(a) creative
crecimiento growth
creer (en) to believe (in); to think, 3
cronología chronology
crucero cruise ship
crudo(a) raw, 9
cruzar (c) to cross, 6
cuaderno notebook, P
cuadra (city) block, 6
cuadro painting; print, 10
cuadros: a ~ plaid, 8
¿cuál? what? which one? 3; **¿~ es tu / su dirección (electrónica)?** (*s. fam. / form.*) What's your (e-mail) address? 1; **¿~ es tu / su número de teléfono?** (*s. fam. / form.*) What is your phone number? 1
¿cuáles? what? which ones? 3
cualquier whatever
¿cuándo? when? 3; **¿~ es tu cumpleaños?** When is your birthday? 1
¿cuánto(a)? how much? 3; **¿Cuánto cuesta(n)?** How much does it (do they) cost? 8
¿cuántos(as)? how many? 3
cuarenta forty, P
cuarto room, P; bedroom, 10
cuarto(a) fourth, 10
cuate(a) friend, buddy
cuatro four, P
cuatrocientos(as) four hundred, 8
cubano(a) Cuban, 2
cuchara spoon, 9
cucharada tablespoonful, 9
cucharadita teaspoonful, 9
cuchillo knife, 9
cuenta check, bill, 9
cuento de hadas fairy tale
cuero leather, 8
cuestionario questionnaire
cuidado: tener (*irreg.*) **~** to be careful, 7; **¡~!** careful!
cuidadoso(a) cautious, 2
culinario(a) culinary

cultura culture
cuna cradle
cuñado(a) brother- in-law (sister-in-law), 5
curso básico basic course, 3
cuy (*m.*) guinea pig
cuyo(a) whose

D

dar (*irreg.*) to give, 5; ~ **información personal** to give personal information, 1; ~ **la hora** to give the time, 3; ~ **un papel** to give (play) a role; ~**le de comer al perro / gato** to feed the dog / cat, 10; ~**le mucha dicha** to give one a lot of happiness
dato fact; piece of information
De nada. You're welcome. 1
debajo de below, underneath, 6
deber (+ *inf.*) should, ought to (*do something*), 2
décimo(a) tenth, 10
decir (*irreg.*) to say, to tell, 5; ~ **cómo llegar** to give directions, 6; ~ **la hora** to tell the time, 3; **Se dice...** It's said . . . , P
decoración (*f.*) decoration, 10
definido(a) definite, 1
dejar to leave, to stop, 2; ~ **de** (+ *inf.*) to stop (*doing something*), 2
del (**de** + **el**) from the, of the, 3
delante de in front of, 6
delgado(a) thin, 2
demasiado(a) too much, 4
demostrar (**ue**) to demonstrate, to show
demostrativo(a) demonstrative, 6
dentista (*m., f.*) dentist, 5
dentro de inside of, 6; ~ **la casa** inside the house, 10
dependiente (*m., f.*) salesclerk, 5
deporte (*m.*) sport, 7
derecha: a la ~ to the right, 6
derecho: (todo) ~ (straight) ahead, 6
desarrollar to develop
desayuno breakfast, 9
descalificar (**qu**) to disqualify
descalzo(a) barefoot
descansar to rest, 2
descargar to download, 4

descortés rude
describir to describe, 2
descubrir to discover, 3
descuento discount, 8
desear to want; to wish, 10
desempeñarse to manage; to work (as)
desengaño disillusionment
desilusión (*f.*) disappointment
desodorante (*m.*) deodorant, 5
despachar to dispatch; to wait on; to work (from a home office)
despacio (*adv.*) slowly; (*adj.*) slow
despedido(a) fired (*from a job*)
despedirse (**i, i**) to say good-bye, 1
despertar (**ie**) to wake someone up, 5; **despertarse** (**ie**) to wake up, 5
después after, 5
destacar (**qu**) to emphasize
detalle (*m.*) detail
detrás de behind, 6
día (*m.*) day, 3; ~ **de la semana** day of the week, 3; ~ **de las Madres** Mother's Day, 3; **todos los días** every day, 3
dialecto dialect
dibujo drawing, P
    diccionario dictionary, P
dicha happiness
dicho saying
diciembre December, 1
diecinueve nineteen, P
dieciocho eighteen, P
dieciséis sixteen, P
diecisiete seventeen, P
diez ten, P; ~ **mil** ten thousand, 8
diferencia difference
difícil difficult, 4
dinero money
director(a) de social media social media director, 5
dirección (*f.*) address
disco duro hard drive, 4
Disculpe. Excuse me. 4
diseñador(a) gráfico(a) graphic designer, 5
diseño design; ~ **gráfico** graphic design, 3
disfrutar (**la vida**) to enjoy (life)
disponibilidad (*f.*) availability
dispuesto(a) willing

diversidad (*f.*) diversity
diversión (*f.*) amusement
divertido(a) fun, entertaining, 2
divertirse (**ie, i**) to have fun, 5
dividir to divide
divorciarse to get divorced, 5
doblar to turn, 6; to fold
doce twelve, P
docena dozen, 9
doctor(a) doctor
dólar (*m.*) dollar
domesticado(a) tame, tamed
domingo Sunday, 2
dominicano(a) Dominican, 2
don (doña) title of respect used with male (female) first name, 1
¿dónde? where? 3; **¿** ~ **tienes la clase de... ?** Where does your . . . class meet? 3; **¿** ~ **vives / vive?** (*s. fam. / form.*) Where do you live? 1
dondequiera: por ~ everywhere
dorado(a) golden, browned, 9
dormir (**ue, u**) to sleep, 4; **dormirse** (**ue, u**) to fall asleep, 5
dormitorio bedroom, 10; ~ **estudiantil** dormitory, 6
dos two, P; ~ **mil** two thousand, 8
doscientos(as) two hundred, 8
ducharse to take a shower, 5
duelo pain
dueño(a) owner, 5
dulce (*adj.*) sweet
duro(a) hard

E

economía economics, 3
ecuador (*m.*) equator
ecuatoriano(a) Ecuadoran, 2
edad (*f.*) age
edificio building, 6
educación (*f.*) education, 3
efectivo: en ~ in cash, 8
egoísta selfish, egotistic, 2
ejemplo example, 10; **por** ~ for example, 10
ejercicio: hacer ~ to exercise, 7
el (*m.*) the, 1
él he, 1; him, 8
electricidad (*f.*) electricity
electrodoméstico appliance, 10
elefante (*m.*) elephant

ella she, 1; her, 8

ellos(as) they, 1; them, 8

e-mail (*m.*) e-mail, P

embajador(a) ambassador

emoción (*f.*) emotion, 4

empapado(a) drenched

emparejar to match

empezar (ie) (c) to begin, 4

empresas (*pl.*) business

en in, on, at; **~ autobús / tren** by bus / train, 6; **~ bicicleta** on bicycle, 6; **~ carro / coche / automóvil** by car, 6; **~ línea** online, 4; **~ metro** on the subway, 6; **~ realidad** actually

enamorarse to fall in love, 5

Encantado(a). Delighted to meet you. 1

encargado de in charge of

encendida burning, on fire

encima de on top of, on, 6

encontrar (ue) to find, 4

encuentro encounter; meeting

encuesta survey

enero January, 1

enfatizar (c) to emphasize

enfermarse to get sick, 5

enfermero(a) nurse, 5

enfermo(a) sick, 4

enfrente de in front of, opposite, 6

enfriarse to get cold, 9

engañar to fool

engaño hoax

enlace (*m.*) link, 4

enojado(a) angry, 4

ensalada salad, 9; **~ de fruta** fruit salad, 9; **~ de lechuga y tomate** lettuce and tomato salad, 9; **~ de papa** potato salad, 9; **~ mixta** tossed salad, 9

ensayo essay

enseñar to teach

entender (ie) to understand, 4

entonces then

entre between, 6

entregar (gu) to turn in; **Entreguen la tarea.** Turn in your homework. P

entrenador(a) trainer

entrenarse to train, 7

entresemana during the week, on weekdays, 3

entretener (*like* **tener**) to entertain

enviar to send, 4

equilibro: poner en ~ to balance

equipo team, 7

erupción (*f.*) **volcánica** volcanic eruption

escaleras (*f. pl.*) stairs, 10

esclavo(a) slave

escoger (j) to choose

esconder to hide

escribir to write, 3; **Escriban en sus cuadernos.** Write in your notebooks. P

escritorio desk, P

escuchar to listen; **~ música** to listen to music, 2; **Escuchen el audio / el CD.** Listen to the tape / CD. P

escuela school, 3

ese (esa) (*s. adj.*) that, 6

ése (ésa) (*s. pron.*) that one, 6

eso that, 6; **por ~** so, that's why, 10

esos (esas) (*pl. adj.*) those, 6

ésos (ésas) (*pl. pron.*) those (ones), 6

España Spain

español (a) Spanish, 2

español (*m.*) Spanish language, 3

espárragos (*m.pl.*) asparagus, 9

especialidad de la casa house special, 9

especie (*f.*) species

espejo mirror, 10

esperanza wish, hope

esperar to hope, 10

esposo(a) husband (wife), 5

esquí (*m.*) ski, skiing; **~ acuático** water skiing, 7; **~ alpino** downhill skiing, 7

esquiar to ski, 7

esquina corner, 6

estación (*f.*) season, 7 **de trenes / autobuses** train / bus station, 6

estacionamiento parking lot, 6

estadio stadium, 6

estadística statistics, 3

estado state, 5; **~ civil** marital status

Estados Unidos United States

estadounidense (*m., f.*) U. S. citizen, 2

estampado(a) print, 8

estancia ranch

estar (*irreg.*) to be, 1;

estatura height (*of a person*)

este (esta) (*s. adj.*) this, 6

éste (ésta) (*s. pron.*) this one, 6

estilo style

estos(as) (*pl. adj.*) these, 6

éstos(as) (*pl. pron.*) these (ones), 6

estrategia strategy

estudiante (*m., f.*) student, P

estudiar to study; **~ en la biblioteca (en casa)** to study at the library (at home), 2; **Estudien las páginas... a...** Study pages . . . to . . . P

estudio studio, 3

estufa stove, 10

etapa era

Europa Europe

evitar to avoid

exhibir to exhibit

exigir (j) to demand

éxito success

exótico(a) exotic, strange

expresar preferencias to express preferences, 2

expresión (*f.*) expression, 1

extrovertido(a) extroverted, 2

F

fácil easy, 4

falda skirt, 8

falso(a) false

familia family; **~ nuclear** nuclear family, 5; **~ política** in-laws, 5

fantasía fantasy

farmacia pharmacy, 6

fascinar to fascinate, 4

fatal terrible, awful, 1

favor: por ~ please, 1

febrero February, 1

fecha date, 3; **¿A qué ~ estamos?** What is today's date? 3

felicidad (*f.*) happiness

femenino(a) feminine

feo(a) ugly, 2

ferrocarril (*m.*) railroad

filantrópico(a) philanthropic

filosofía philosophy, 3

fin (*m.*) end; intention; **~ de semana** weekend, 2; **por ~** finally, 9

final final
financiero(a) financial
física physics, 3
físico(a) physical, 5
flan (*m.*) custard, 9
flor (*f.*) flower
florecer (zc) to flower, to flourish
flotador(a) floating
fondo background
fortaleza fortress
foro forum, 4
foto (*f.*) photo, P; **sacar fotos** to take photos, 2
francés (francesa) French, 2
francés (*m.*) French language, 3
frecuentemente frequently, 4
freír (i, i) to fry, 9
frente a in front of, facing, opposite, 6
fresa strawberry, 9
fresco(a) fresh, 9; **Hace fresco.** It's cool. 7
frijoles (*m.*) **(refritos)** (refried) beans, 9
frío(a) cold; **Hace frío.** It's cold. 7; **tener** (*irreg.*) **frío** to be cold, 7
frito(a) fried, 9
frontera border
fruta fruit, 6
fuego fire; **a ~ suave / lento** at low heat, 9
fuente (*f.*) source
fuera de outside of, 6; **~ de la casa** outside the house, 10
fuerte strong, filling (*e.g., a meal*), 9
funcionar to function, 4
funciones (*f. pl.*) **de la computadora** computer functions, 4
fundador(a) founder
fungir to work
furioso(a) furious, 4
fútbol (*m.*) soccer, 7; **~ americano** football, 7

G

gafas (*f. pl.*) **de sol** sunglasses, 8
galleta cookie, 9
galón (*m.*) gallon, 9
ganadería cattle, livestock
ganado cattle
ganar to win, 7

ganas: tener (*irreg.*) **~ de** to have the urge to, to feel like, 7
garaje (*m.*) garage, 10
gato(a) cat, 2
gazpacho cold tomato soup (*Spain*), 9
general: por lo ~ generally, 9
género genre
generoso(a) generous, 2
gente (*f.*) people
geografía geography, 3
gerente (*m., f.*) manager, 5
gimnasio gymnasium, 3
gobernador(a) (*m.*) governor
golf (*m.*) golf, 7
gordo(a) fat, 2
gorra cap, 8
gozar (c) to enjoy
grabador (*m.*) **de discos compactos / DVD** CD / DVD recorder, 4
grabar to record, 4
gracias: Muchas ~. Thank you very much. 1
grado degree; **~ Celsio(s)** Celsius degree, 7; **~ Fahrenheit** Fahrenheit degree, 7
gráfica graph
grande big, great, 2
grano: al ~ to the point
gris gray, 4
gritar to shout, to scream
grito scream
grupo group; **~ de conversación** chat room, 4; **~ de noticias** news group, 4
guagua bus (*Cuba, Puerto Rico*)
guante (*m.*) glove, 8
guapo(a) handsome, attractive, 2
guardar to store; **~ la ropa** put away the clothes, 10; to save, 4
guatemalteco(a) Guatemalan, 2
guión (*m.*) script
guionista (*m., f.*) script writer
guisado beef stew, 9
guisante (*m.*) pea, 9
guitarra guitar, 2
gustar: A mí / ti me / te gusta . . . I / You like . . . , 2; **A . . . le gusta . . .** He / She likes . . . , 2; **A . . . les gusta . . .** They / You (*pl.*) like . . . , 2; **Me gustaría** (*+ inf.*) **. . .** I'd like (*+ inf.*) . . ., 6

gusto taste; **al ~** to individual taste, 9; **El ~ es mío.** The pleasure is mine. 1; **Mucho ~.** My pleasure. 1; **Mucho ~ en conocerte.** A pleasure to meet you. 1

H

haba (*f.*) (*but:* **el haba**) bean
habichuela green bean, 9
habitación (*f.*) bedroom, 10
habitante (*m., f.*) inhabitant
hablar por teléfono to talk on the telephone, 2
hacer (*irreg.*) to make, to do, 5; **Hace buen / mal tiempo.** It's nice / bad weather. 7; **Hace calor / fresco / frío.** It's hot / cool / cold. 7; **Hace sol / viento.** It's sunny / windy. 7; **~ alpinismo** to hike, 7; **~ caso** to pay attention, to obey; **~ clic / doble clic** to click / double click, 4; **~ ejercicio** to exercise, 7; **~ el reciclaje** to do the recycling, 10; **~ la cama** to make the bed, 10; **~ las compras** to go shopping, 6; **~ preguntas** to ask questions, 3; **~ surfing** to surf, 7; **~ una conexión** to go online, 4; **Hagan la tarea para mañana.** Do the homework for tomorrow. P
hambre (*f.*) (*but:* **el hambre**) hunger; **tener** (*irreg.*) **~** to be hungry, 7
hamburguesa hamburger, 9; **~ con queso** cheeseburger, 9
hardware (*m.*) hardware, 4
harina flour, 9
hasta until; **~ luego.** See you later, 1; **~ mañana.** See you tomorrow. 1; **~ pronto.** See you soon. 1
hay there is, there are, 1
hecho fact
hecho(a) (*p. p.*): **Está ~ de...** It's made out of . . . , 8
helado de vainilla / chocolate vanilla / chocolate ice cream, 9
herencia heritage
hermanastro(a) stepbrother (stepsister), 5

hermano(a) (menor, mayor) (younger, older) brother (sister), 5

hermoso(a) handsome, beautiful

hervido(a) boiled, 9

hervir (ie, i) to boil, 9

hierro iron

hijo(a) son (daughter), 5

hilo: al ~ stringed, 9

himno hymn

hispano(a) Hispanic

hispanohablante Spanish-speaking

historia history, 3

hockey (*m.*) **sobre hielo / hierba** ice / field hockey, 7

hogar (*m.*) home; **sin ~** homeless

hoja de papel sheet of paper, P

hola hello, 1

hombre (*m.*) man, P; **~ de negocios** businessman, 5

hondureño(a) Honduran, 2

honesto(a) honest

hora hour; time; **dar** (*irreg.*) **la ~** to give the time, 3; **decir la ~** to tell the time, 3

horario schedule

horno oven; **al ~** roasted (in the oven), 9

hospital (*m.*) hospital, 6

hoy today, 3; **~ es martes treinta.** Today is Tuesday the 30th. 3; **¿Qué día es ~?** What day is today? 3

huella footprint

huevo egg, 6; **~ estrellado** egg sunny-side up, 9; **~ revuelto** scrambled egg, 9

humanidades (*f. pl.*) humanities, 3

húmedo(a) humid

humilde humble

I

ícono del programa program icon, 4

identidad (*f.*) identity

idioma (*m.*) language, 3

iglesia church, 6

Igualmente. Likewise. 1

impaciente impatient, 2

impermeable (*m.*) raincoat, 8

importar to be important to someone; to mind, 4

impresionante impressive

impresora printer, 4

imprimir to print, 3

impulsivo(a) impulsive, 2

incendio forestal forest fire

increíble incredible

indefinido(a) indefinite, 1

índice (*m.*) index

indio(a) Indian, 2

indígena indigenous

influencia influence

influir (y) to influence

informática computer science, 3

informe (*m.*) report

ingeniería engineering, 3

ingeniero(a) engineer, 5

inglés (inglesa) English, 2

inglés (*m.*) English language, 3

ingrediente (*m.*) ingredient, 9

ingreso revenue

inmigración (*f.*) immigration

insistir to insist, 10

instalar to install, 4

instructor(a) instructor, P

inteligente intelligent, 2

intentar to attempt

intercambiar to exchange

interesante interesting, 2

interesar to interest, to be interesting, 4

Internet (*m.* or *f.*) Internet

intérprete (*m., f.*) interpreter

íntimo(a) intimate

introvertido(a) introverted, 2

invertir to invest

invierno winter, 7

ir (*irreg.*) to go, 3; **~ a** (+ *inf.*) to be going to (*do something*), 3; **~ de compras** to go shopping, 8; **irse** to leave, to go away, 5

irresponsable irresponsible, 2

italiano(a) Italian, 2

italiano (*m.*) Italian language

izquierda: a la ~ to the left, 6

J

jabón (*m.*) soap, 5

jamás never, 6

jamón (*m.*) ham, 6

japonés (japonesa) Japanese, 2

japonés (*m.*) Japanese language, 3

jardín (*m.*) garden, 10

jeans (*m. pl.*) jeans, 8

jornada laboral workday

joven young, 2

joyas (*f. pl.*) jewelry, 8

joyería jewelry store, 6

juego interactivo interactive game, 4

jueves (*m.*) Thursday, 3

jugar (ue) (gu) to play, 4; **~ tenis (béisbol, etc.)** to play tennis (baseball, etc.), 7

jugo de fruta fruit juice, 9

juguete (*m.*) toy, 10

juguetón (juguetona) playful

julio July, 1

junio June, 1

juntar to group

juntarse to join

juventud (*f.*) youth

K

kilo kilo, 9; **medio ~** half a kilo, 9

L

la (*f.*) the, 1

labio lip

lado side; **al ~ de** next to, on the side of, 6

ladrillo brick

lago lake, 7

lámpara lamp, 10

lana wool, 8

langosta lobster, 9

lanzarse (c) to throw oneself

lápiz (*m.*) pencil, P

lavadora washer, 10

lavandería laundry room, 10

lavaplatos (*m. s.*) dishwasher, 10

lavar to wash, 5; **~ los platos (la ropa)** to wash the dishes (the clothes), 10

lavarse to wash oneself, 5; **~ el pelo** to wash one's hair, 5; **~ los dientes** to brush one's teeth, 5

le to / for you (*form. s.*), to / for him, to / for her, 8

lección (*f.*) lesson, P

leche (*f.*) milk, 6

lector (*m.*) **de CD-ROM / DVD** DVD / CD-ROM drive, 4

leer (y) to read, 3; **Lean el Capítulo 1.** Read Chapter 1. P

lejos de far from, 6

lema (*m.*) slogan

lentes (*m. pl.*) eyeglasses

lento(a) slow, 4

les to / for you (*form. pl.*), to / for them, 8

letrero sign

levantar to raise, to lift, 5; **~ pesas** to lift weights, 2

levantarse to get up, 5

libra pound, 9

libre free

librería bookstore, 3

libro book, P; **~ electrónico** e-book, P

licencia de manejar driver's license

licuado de fruta fruit shake, smoothie

licuadora blender, 10

ligero(a) light, lightweight, 9

limonada lemonade, 9

limpiar el baño to clean the bathroom, 10

lindo(a) pretty, 2

línea: en ~ online, 4

lingüístico(a) linguistic

lino linen, 8

literatura literature, 3

litro liter, 9

llamar to call, 2; **llamarse** to name, 2; **Me llamo . . .** My name is . . . , 1

llano(a) flat

llanura plain

llegar (gu) to arrive, 2

llenar to fill

llevar to take, to carry **llover** to rain; **Está lloviendo. (Llueve.)** It's raining. 7

lobo wolf

lodo mud

lograr to achieve

lomo de res prime rib, 9

los (las) (*pl.*) the, 1

luego later, 5

lugar (*m.*) place; **~ de nacimiento** birthplace

lujoso(a) luxurious

lunares: de ~ polka-dotted, 8

lunes (*m.*) Monday, 3

luz (*f.*) light; **~ solar** sunlight

M

madera wood

madrastra stepmother, 5

madre (*f.*) mother, 5

maestro(a) teacher, 5

maíz (*m.*) corn

mal badly, 4

malo(a) bad, 2

mamá mother, 5

mañana morning, 3; tomorrow, 3; **de la ~** in the morning (*with precise time*), 3; **por la ~** during the morning, 3

mandar to send; to order, 8

mandato command

manejar to drive, 5

mantel (*m.*) tablecloth, 9

mantener (*irreg.*) to keep, maintain

mantequilla butter, 9

manzana apple, 9

maquillaje (*m.*) makeup, 5

maquillarse to put on makeup, 5

máquina de afeitar electric razor, 5

maravilla wonder

marcar (qu) to mark; to point out

marisco shellfish, 9

marrón brown, 4

martes (*m.*) Tuesday, 3

marzo March, 1

más more; **~ que** more than, 8

masculino(a) masculine

matemáticas (*f. pl.*) mathematics, 3

mayo May, 1

mayonesa mayonnaise, 9

mayor older, greater, 8

mayoría majority

mayúsculo(a) capital (letter)

me to / for me, 8

mecánico(a) mechanic, 5

medio(a) hermano(a) half-brother (half-sister), 5

medianoche (*f.*) midnight, 3

medicina medicine, 3

médico(a) doctor, 5

medida measurement, 9

medio ambiente (*m.*) environment

mediodía (*m.*) noon, 3

medios de transporte means of transportation, 6

medir (i, i) to measure

meditación (*f.*) meditation

mejilla cheek

mejor better, 8

melón (*m.*) melon, 9

memoria flash flash drive, 4

menor younger; less, 8

menos: ~ que less than, 8; **por lo ~** at least, 10

mensajero(a) messenger

mentiroso(a) dishonest, lying, 2

menú (*m.*) menu, 9

mercadeo marketing, 3

mercado market, 6; **~ al aire libre** open-air market, farmer's market, 6

merecer (zc) to deserve

merienda snack

mes (*m.*) month, 3; **~ pasado** last month, 7

mesa table, P; **poner la ~** to set the table, 9; **quitar la ~** to clear the table, 10

mesita de noche night table, 10

meta goal

metro: en ~ on the subway, 6

mexicano(a) Mexican, 2

mezcla mix

mezclar to mix, 9

mezclilla denim, 8

mi (*adj.*) my, 3

mí (*pron.*) me, 8

micro bus (*Chile*)

micrófono microphone, 4

microondas (*m. s.*) microwave, 10

miedo: tener (*irreg.*) **~ (a, de)** to be afraid (of), 7

mientras while, during

miércoles (*m.*) Wednesday, 3

mil (*m.*) one thousand, 8

miles (*pl.*) thousands

millón (*m.*)**: un ~** one million, 8; **dos millones** two million, 8

mío(a) (*adj.*) my, 10; (*pron.*) mine, 10

mirar televisión to watch television, 2

misionero(a) missionary

mismo(a) same; **lo mismo** the same (thing)

mitad (*f.*) half

mixto(a) mixed

mochila backpack, P; knapsack

moda fashion, 8; **(no) estar de ~** (not) to be fashionable, 8; **pasado(a) de ~** out of style, 8

modales (*m. pl.*) manners

modas: de ~ (*adj.*) fashion

módem (*m.*) **externo / interno** external / internal modem, 4

molestar to bother, 4

molido(a) crushed, ground, 9
monitor (*m.*) monitor, 4
mono monkey
montañoso(a) mountainous
montar to ride; **~ a caballo** to ride horseback, 7; **~ en bicicleta** to ride a bike, 7
monte (*m.*) mountain
morado(a) purple, 4
morirse (ue, u) to die, 8
mortalidad (*f.*) mortality
mostaza mustard, 9
mostrar (ue) to show
MP3 portátil portable MP3 player, P
muchacho(a) boy (girl), P
muchedumbre (*f.*) crowd
mucho a lot, 4; **~ que hacer** a lot to do; **No ~.** Not much. 1
mudarse to move (*change residence*)
muebles (*m. pl.*) furniture, 10
mujer (*f.*) woman, P; **~ de negocios** businesswoman, 5
mundo world
muñeca doll
museo museum, 6
música music, 3
muy very, 2

N

nacer (zc) to be born
nacionalidad (*f.*) nationality, 2
nada nothing, 1; **De ~.** You're welcome. 1
nadar to swim, 7
nadie no one, nobody, 6
naranja orange (*fruit*), 9
narrador(a) narrator
natación (*f.*) swimming, 7
naturaleza nature; **~ muerta** still life
navegación (*f.*) navigation; **~ en rápidos** whitewater rafting, 7
navegar (gu): ~ en rápidos to go whitewater rafting, 7; **~ por Internet** to browse the Internet, 2
necesitar to need, 2
negocio business, 3; (*pl.*) business
negro(a) black, 4
nervioso(a) nervous, 4
nevar to snow, 7; **Está nevando. (Nieva.)** It's snowing. 7

ni... ni neither . . . nor, 6
nicaragüense (*m., f.*) Nicaraguan, 2
nieto(a) grandson (granddaughter), 5
niñero(a) baby-sitter
ningún, ninguno(a) none, no, not any, 6
niño(a) boy (girl), P
nivel (*m.*) level
noche (*f.*) night, 3; **de la ~** in the evening (*with precise time*), 3; **por la ~** during the evening, 3
nombre (*m.*) name; **Mi ~ es...** My name is . . . , 1; **~ completo** full name
normal normal, 4
Norteamérica North America
norteamericano(a) North American
nos to / for us, 8; **¿~ vemos donde siempre?** See you at the usual place? 1
nosotros(as) we, 1; us, 8
nota grade, P
novato(a) newbie, novice
novecientos(as) nine hundred, 8
novedoso(a) novel, new
novelista (*m., f.*) novelist
noveno(a) ninth, 10
noventa ninety, P
noviembre November, 1
novio(a) boyfriend (girlfriend)
nublado: Está ~. It's cloudy. 7
nuera daughter-in-law, 5
nuestro(a) (*adj.*) our, 3; (*pron.*) ours, 10
nueve nine, P
número number, 8; **~ ordinal** ordinal number, 10
nunca never, 5

O

o... o either . . . or, 6
ochenta eighty, P
ocho eight, P
ochocientos(as) eight hundred, 8
octavo(a) eighth, 10
octubre October, 1
ocupado(a) busy, 4
ocupar to live in
odio hatred
oferta especial special offer, 8

oficina office, 6; **~ de correos** post office, 6
oír (*irreg.*) to hear, 5
ojear to scan
ola wave
ómnibus (*m.*) bus
once eleven, P
onda: en ~ in style
oprimir to push
opuesto(a) opposite
oración (*f.*) sentence
ordenar to order, 9
organización (*f.*) **benéfica** charity
orgulloso(a) proud
originar to originate
orilla shore
oro gold, 8
ortografía spelling
os to / for you (*fam. pl.*), 8
otoño fall, autumn, 7

P

paciente (*m., f.*) patient, 2
padrastro stepfather, 5
padre (*m.*) father, 5; **padres** (*m. pl.*) parents, 5
pagar (gu) to pay, 9
página page, P; **~ web** web page, 4
pago: método de ~ form of payment, 8**país** (*m.*) country
paisaje (*m.*) scenery
pájaro bird
pan (*m.*) bread, 6; **~ tostado** toast, 9
panameño(a) Panamanian, 2
pandilla gang
pantalla screen, 4
pantalones (*m. pl.*) pants, 8; **~ cortos** shorts, 8
pañuelo handkerchief
papá (*m.*) father, 5
papas fritas (*f. pl.*) French fries, 9
papel role; paper; **hoja de ~** sheet of paper, P
papelería stationery store, 6
papitas fritas (*f. pl.*) potato chips, 6
paquete (*m.*) package, 9
para for, toward, in the direction of, in order to (+ *inf.*), 10
paracaídas (*m.*) parachute
parada stop

paraguayo(a) Paraguayan, 2
parar to stop
parecer (zc) to seem
pared (*f.*) wall, P
pariente (*m., f.*) family member, relative, 5
parque (*m.*) park, 6
párrafo paragraph
parrilla: a la ~ grilled, 9
partido game, match, 7
pasar to pass (by), 2; **~ la aspiradora** to vacuum, 10
pasear: sacar a ~ al perro to take the dog for a walk, 10
pasillo hallway, 10
pasta de dientes toothpaste, 5
pastel (*m.*) cake, 9
patinar to skate, 2; **~ en línea** to inline skate (rollerblade), 7; **~ sobre hielo** to ice skate, 7
patio patio, 10
patrocinador(a) sponsor
pavo turkey, 6
paz (*f.*) peace
pedazo piece, slice, 9
pedir (i, i) to ask for (*something*), 1; to request, 10; **~ la hora** to ask for the time, 3
peinarse to brush / comb one's hair, 5
peine (*m.*) comb, 5
pelar to peel, 9
pelearse to have a fight, 5
peligro danger, 7
peligroso(a) dangerous, 7
pelirrojo(a) redheaded , 2
pelo hair; **~ castaño / rubio** brown / blond hair, 2
pelota ball, 7
peluquero(a) barber / hairdresser, 5
pendiente (*m.*) earring, 8
pendrive (*m.*) flash drive, 4
pensar (ie) to think, 4; **~ de** to have an opinion about, 4; **~ en (de)** to think about, to consider, 4
penúltimo(a) next-to-last
peor worse, 8
pequeño(a) small, 2
perder (ie) to lose, 4; **perderse (ie)** to lose oneself, to get lost
Perdón. Excuse me. 4
perejil (*m.*) parsley
perezoso(a) lazy, 2

periódico newspaper
periodismo journalism, 3
periodista (*m., f.*) journalist, 5
permiso: Con ~. Pardon me. 4
permitir to permit, to allow, 10
pero but, 2
perro(a) dog, 2; **perro caliente** hot dog, 9
persiana Venetian blind, 10
personalidad (*f.*) personality
peruano(a) Peruvian, 2
pesar: a ~ de in spite of
pesas: levantar ~ to lift weights, 2
pescado fish (*caught*), 9
pescar (qu) to fish, 7
pez (*m.*) fish (*alive*)
piano piano, 2
picante spicy, 9
picar (qu) to chop, to mince, 9
pie (*m.*): **a ~** on foot, walking, 6
piel (*f.*) leather, 8
pimienta pepper, 9
pingüino penguin
pintar to paint, 2
pintoresco(a) picturesque
pintura painting, 3
pirata (*m.*) pirate
pisar to step on
piscina swimming pool, 6
piso floor; **primer (segundo, etc.) ~** first (second, etc.) floor, 10
pista de atletismo athletics track, 6
pizarra interactiva interactive whiteboard, P
pizzería pizzeria, 6
placer: Un ~. My pleasure. 1
plancha iron, 10
planchar to iron, 10
plata silver, 8
plátano banana, 9
plato plate, 9; **~ hondo** bowl, 9; **~ principal** main dish, 9
plaza plaza, 6
plomero(a) plumber, 5
poblar (ue) to populate
pobre poor
poco little, small amount, 4; **muy ~** very little
poder (*m.*) power; (*irreg.*) to be able to, 4
poderoso(a) powerful
poesía poetry
poeta (poetisa) poet

policía (*m., f.*) policeman (policewoman), 5
político(a) political
pollo chicken, 6; **~ asado** roasted chicken, 9; **~ frito** fried chicken, 9
polvo dust
poner (*irreg.*) to put, 5; **~ en equilibro** to balance; **~ la mesa** to set the table, 9; **~ mis juguetes en su lugar** to put my toys where they belong, 10 to put on (clothing), 5
por for, during, in, through, along, on behalf of, by, 10; **~ avión** by plane, 6; **~ ejemplo** for example, 10; **~ eso** so, that's why, 10; **~ favor** please, 1; **~ fin** finally, 9; **~ lo menos** at least, 10; **~ supuesto** of course, 10
¿por qué? why? 3
porcentaje (*m.*) percentage
porque because, 3
portarse to behave
portátil: MP3 ~ portable MP3 player, P; **computadora ~** laptop computer, P
portugués (portuguesa) Portuguese, 2
postre (*m.*) dessert, 9
pozo well; hole
practicar (qu) to practice; **~ alpi-nismo** to hike, to (mountain) climb, 7; **~ deportes** to play sports, 2; **~ surfing** to surf, 7
precio: Está a muy buen ~. It's a very good price. 8
preferencia preference
preferir (ie, i) to prefer, 4
pregunta: hacer preguntas to ask questions, 3
premio prize
prenda de ropa article of clothing, 8
preocupado(a) worried, 4
preocuparse to worry, 5
preparación (*f.*) preparation, 9
preparar to prepare, 2; **~ la comida** to prepare the food, 10; **prepararse** to get ready, 5
preposición (*f.*) preposition, 6
presa dam
presentar a alguien to introduce someone, 1
préstamo loan, 8

prestar to loan, 8

primavera spring, 7

primer(o)(a) first, 10; **primer piso** first floor, 10

primo(a) cousin, 5

principiante(a) beginner

prisa haste, hurry; **tener** (*irreg.*) ~ to be in a hurry, 7

probarse (ue): Voy a probármelo / la(los / las). I'm going to try it (them) on. 8

procesador de comida food processor, 10

producto electrónico electronic product, 4

profesión (*f.*) profession, 5

profesor(a) professor, P

programa (*m.*) program; ~ **antivirus** anti-virus program, 4; ~ **de procesamiento de textos** word-processing program, 4

programador(a) programmer, 5

prohibir to forbid, 10

promover (ue) to promote

pronombre (*m.*) pronoun, 1

propina tip, 9

propósito purpose

proveedor (*m.*) **de acceso** Internet service provider, 4

provocador(a) provocative

próximo(a) next

proyector projector, P

psicología psychology, 3

publicidad (*f.*) public relations, 3

publicitario(a) (*adj.*) pertaining to advertising

pueblo town, 6

puerta door, P

puerto de USB USB port, 4

puertorriqueño(a) Puerto Rican, 2

pulgada inch

pulsera bracelet, 8

punto de vista viewpoint

punto period

Q

¿qué? what? which? 3; **¿~ hay de nuevo?** What's new? 1; **¿~ hora es?** What time is it? 3; **¿~ significa…?** What does . . . mean? P; **¿~ tal?** How are things going? 1; **¿~ te gusta**

hacer? What do you like to do? 2

quedar to fit; **Me queda bien / mal.** It fits nicely / badly. 8; **Me queda grande / apretado.** It's too big / too tight. 8; **quedar(se)** to remain; to be

quehacer (*m.*) **doméstico** housechore, 10

quejarse to complain, 5

querer (*irreg.*) to want, to love, 4; to wish, 10

queso cheese, 6

¿quién(es)? who? 3; **¿De ~ es?** Whose is this? 3; **¿De ~ son?** Whose are these? 3

química chemistry, 3

quince fifteen, P

quinientos(as) five hundred, 8

quinto(a) fifth, 10

quisiera (+ *inf.*) I'd like (+ *inf.*), 6

quitar to take off, to remove 5; ~ **la mesa** to clear the table, 10; **quitarse (la ropa)** to take off (one's clothing), 5

quizás perhaps

R

raíz (*f.*) root

rango rank

rápido(a) fast, 4

rasgado torn up

rasgar (gu) to tear up

rasuradora razor, 5

ratón (*m.*) mouse, 4

rayado(a) striped, 8

rayas: a ~ striped, 8

razón (*f.*) reason; **tener** (*irreg.*) ~ to be right, 7

realidad: en ~ actually

realizarse (c) to take place

rebajado(a): estar ~ to be reduced (in price) / on sale, 8

recámara bedroom, 10

recibir to receive, 3

reciclaje (*m.*) recycling, 10

recomendar (ie) to recommend, 10

reconocer (zc) to recognize

recordar (ue) to remember

recorte (*m.*) cutting

recuerdo souvenir

recurrir to fall back on, to resort to

red (*f.*) web, Internet; ~ **mundial** World Wide Web, 4; ~ **social** social networking site, 4

redactar to edit

reflejar to reflect

reflexión (*f.*) reflection

refresco soft drink, 6; beverage, 9; **tomar un ~** to have a soft drink, 2

refrigerador (*m.*) refrigerator, 10

regalar to give (as a gift), 8

regalo present, gift, 8

regar (ie) (gu) las plantas to water the plants, 10

regla rule

regresar to return, 2

regular so-so, 1

reina queen

reírse (*irreg.*) to laugh, 5

relajarse to relax, 5

reloj (*m.*) watch, 8

remar to row, 7

remero(a) rower

renombre (*m.*) renown

renovar (ue) to renovate

repente: de ~ suddenly, 9

repetir (i, i) to repeat, 4; **Repitan.** Repeat. P

reproductor (*m.*) **de discos compactos / DVD** CD / DVD recorder, 4

requerir (ie, i) to require, 10

residencia estudiantil dorm, 3

respirar to breathe

responder to respond, 1

responsable responsible, 2

restaurante (*m.*) restaurant, 6

resumen: en ~ in short, to sum up

reto challenge

reunión (*f.*) meeting

reunirse to meet, to get together, 5

revista magazine; ~ **de moda** fashion magazine

rey (*m.*) king

riesgo risk

rima rhyme

río river, 7

riqueza wealth

rodeado(a) surrounded

rojo(a) red, 4

ropa clothing, 5

rosa rose, 4

rosado(a) pink, 4

rubio(a) blond(e), 2
rueda wheel
ruta route

S

sábado Saturday, 2
saber (*irreg.*) to know (*a fact, information*), 5; ~ (+ *inf.*) to know how (*to do something*), 5
sabor (*m.*) flavor
sacar (**qu**) to take out; ~ **a pasear al perro** to take the dog for a walk, 10; ~ **fotos** to take photos, 2; ~ **la basura** to take out the garbage, 10
sacerdote (*m.*) priest
saco jacket, sports coat, 8
sacudir los muebles to dust the furniture, 10
sal (*f.*) salt, 9
sala living room, 10
salchicha sausage, 6
salir (*irreg.*) to leave, to go out, 5
salmón (*m.*) salmon, 9
salón (*m.*) **de clase** classroom, P
salud (*f.*) health, 3
saludable healthy
saludar to greet, 1
saludo greeting
salvadoreño(a) Salvadoran, 2
salvaje wild, untamed
salvavidas (*m. s.*) lifejacket
sandalia sandal, 8
sandwich (*m.*) sandwich, 9; ~ **de jamón y queso con aguacate** ham and cheese sandwich with avocado, 9
secadora dryer, 10
secar (**qu**) to dry (*something*), 5; **secarse** (**qu**) **el pelo** to dry one's hair, 5
secretario(a) secretary, 5
secreto secret
sed (*f.*) thirst; **tener** (*irreg.*) ~ to be thirsty, 7
seda silk, 8
seguido(a) continued
seguir (**i, i**) to continue, 6; ~ **derecho** to go straight ahead
según according to
segundo(a) second, 10
seguro(a) sure, 4; safe, 7
seis six, P
seiscientos(as) six hundred, 8

semana week, 3; ~ **pasada** last week, 7; **fin** (*m.*) **de ~** weekend, 2; **todas las semanas** every week, 5
semejanza similarity
sencillo(a) simple; single (*room*)
sentarse (**ie**) to sit down, 5
sentir (**ie, i**) to feel, 4; **Lo siento.** I'm sorry. 4
señalar to point out
señor (*abbrev.* **Sr.**) Mr., Sir, 1
señora (*abbrev.* **Sra.**) Mrs., Ms., Madam, 1
señorita (*abbrev.* **Srta.**) Miss, Ms., 1
separarse to get separated, 5
septiembre September, 1
séptimo(a) seventh, 10
ser (*irreg.*) to be, 1
serio(a) serious, 2
servicio service **servilleta** napkin, 9
servir (**i, i**) to serve, 4; **¿En qué puedo servirle?** How can I help you? 8
sesenta sixty, P
setecientos(as) seven hundred, 8
setenta seventy, P
sexto(a) sixth, 10
sí yes, 1
siempre always, 5
siete seven, P
siglo century
significar (**qu**): **Significa...** It means . . . , P
significado meaning
siguiente following, next
silla chair, P
sillón (*m.*) armchair, 10
símbolo symbol
simpático(a) nice, 2
sin without; ~ **control** uncontrolled
sincero(a) sincere, 2
sino but instead
sistemático(a) systematic
sitio place; ~ **web** website, 4
smartphone smartphone, 4
snowboarding snowboarding, 7
soberanía sovereignty
sobre on, above, 6
sobrepasar to surpass
sobresaliente outstanding
sobrino(a) nephew (niece), 5
sofá (*m.*) sofa, 10

software (*m.*) software, 4
sol (*m.*) sun; **Hace ~.** It's sunny. 7
soltero(a) single (unmarried)
sombrero hat, 8
sonar (**ue**) to ring, to go off (*phone, alarm clock, etc.*), 4
sonido sound
sonreír (*irreg.*) to smile, 8
sonrisa smile
soñar (**ue**) **con** to dream about, 4
sopa soup, 9; ~ **de fideos** noodle soup, 9
sorpresa surprise
sorteo raffle; evasion
sortija ring
sótano basement, cellar, 10
su (*adj.*) your (*s. form., pl.*), his, her, their, 3
suave soft
subir to go up, to get on, 6; to upload, 4
suburbio suburb, 10
sucio(a) dirty
sudadera sweatsuit, track suit, 8
Sudamérica South America
suegro(a) father-in-law (mother-in-law), 5
sueño dream; **tener** (*irreg.*) ~ to be sleepy, 7
suéter (*m.*) sweater, 8
sugerencia suggestion
sugerir (**ie, i**) to suggest, 8
superación (*f.*) overcoming
supermercado supermarket, 6
supuesto: por ~ of course, 10
surfing: hacer / practicar (**qu**) ~ to surf, 7
sustantivo noun
sustituir (**y**) to substitute
suyo(a) (*adj.*) your (*form. s., pl.*), his, her, its, their, 10; (*pron.*) yours (*form. s., pl.*), his, hers, its, theirs, 10

T

tabla de snowboard snowboard, 7
tableta tablet computer, 4
tal vez perhaps
talla size, 8
taller (*m.*) workshop
también also, 2
tampoco neither, not either, 2
tan... como as . . . as, 8
tanto(a)(s)... como as much (many) . . . as, 8

tarde (*f.*) afternoon, 3; **de la ~** in the afternoon (*with precise time*), 3; **por la ~** during the afternoon, 3; (*adv.*) late, 3

tarea homework, P

tarjeta ~ de crédito credit card, 8; **~ de débito** (bank) debit card, 8

te to / for you (*fam. s.*), 8

té hot tea, 9; **~ helado** iced tea, 9

teatro theater, 6

tecnología technology, 4

techo roof, 10

tecla key (*on a keyboard*), 4

teclado keyboard, 4

tejer to weave

tejido weaving

tela fabric, 8

teléfono inteligente smartphone, 4

televisor (*m.*) television set, 10

temperatura temperature, 7; **La ~ está a 20 grados Celsio(s) (Fahrenheit).** It's 20 degrees Celsius (Fahrenheit). 7

temporada: ~ de lluvias rainy season; **~ de secas** dry season

temprano early, 3

tender to tend (to)

tenedor (*m.*) fork, 9

tener (*irreg.*) to have, 1; **~ ... años** to be . . . years old, 1; **~ calor** to be hot, 7; **~ cuidado** to be careful, 7; **~ frío** to be cold, 7; **~ ganas de** to have the urge to, to feel like (doing), 7; **~ hambre** to be hungry, 7; **~ miedo (a, de)** to be afraid (of), 7; **~ prisa** to be in a hurry, 7; **~ que** (*+ inf.*) to have to (+ *verb*), 1; **~ razón** to be right, 7; **~ sed** to be thirsty, 7; **~ sueño** to be sleepy, 7; **~ vergüenza** to be embarrassed, ashamed, 7

tenis (*m.*) tennis, 7

teoría theory

tercer(o, a) third, 10

término term

terrible terrible, awful, 1

tesoro treasure

texto text

tez (*f.*) skin, complexion

ti you (*fam. s.*), 8

tiburón (*m.*) shark

tiempo weather, 7; **¿Qué ~ hace?** What's the weather like? 7

tienda store, 6; **~ de equipo deportivo** sporting goods store, 6; **~ de juegos electrónicos** electronic games store, 6; **~ de ropa** clothing store, 6

tierra earth, ground

tímido(a) shy, 2

tinto: vino ~ red wine, 9

tío(a) uncle (aunt), 5

típico(a) typical, 9

tira cómica comic strip

tiroteo shooting

titular to title

título title, 1

tiza chalk, P

toalla towel, 5; **~ de mano** handtowel, 5

tocador (*m.*) dresser, 10

tocar (qu) un instrumento musical to play a musical instrument, 2

todavía still

todo everything

todo(a) all, every; **todas las semanas** every week, 5; **todos los días (años)** every day (year), 9

tomar to take; **~ un refresco** to have a soft drink, 2; **~ el sol** to sunbathe, 2

tonto(a) silly, stupid, 2

tormenta thunderstorm

torpe awkward

tostadora toaster, 10

trabajador(a) (*adj.*) hard-working, 2; (*noun*) worker, 5

trabajar to work, 2

traducir (zc) to translate, 5

traer (*irreg.*) to bring, 5

traje (*m.*) suit, 8; **~ de baño** bathing suit, 8

trama plot

tramos sections

transmitir to broadcast, 3

trapear el piso to mop the floor, 10

tratar de to try

tratarse de to be a matter of; to be

través: a ~ de across, throughout

trece thirteen, P

trecho distance, period

treinta thirty, P

tren: en ~ by train, 6

tres three, P

trescientos(as) three hundred, 8

trigo wheat

tripulación (*f.*) crew

triste sad, 4

triunfar to triumph

trompeta trumpet, 2

trozo chunk, 9

trucha trout, 9

truco trick

tu your (*fam.*), 3

tú you (*fam.*), 1

tuyo(a) (*adj.*) your (*fam.*), 10; (*pron.*) yours (*fam.*), 10

U

ubicado(a) located

Ud. (*abbrev. of* **usted**) you (*form. s.*), 8

Uds. (*abbrev. of* **ustedes**) you (*fam. or form. pl.*), 8

último: lo ~ the latest (thing)

un(a) a, 1

único(a) only, unique

unido(a) united

unir to mix together, to incorporate, 9

universidad (*f.*) university, 6

uno one, P

unos(as) some, 1

uruguayo(a) Uruguayan, 2

usar to use, 2

usted you (*s. form.*), 1

ustedes you (*fam. or form. pl.*), 1

usuario(a) user, 4

útil useful

uva grape, 9

V

vacío(a) empty

valer (*irreg.*) **la pena** to be worthwhile

valioso(a) valuable

valle (*m.*) valley

valor (*m.*) value

vanidoso(a) vain

vapor: al ~ steamed, 9

vaquero cowboy

variedad (*f.*) variety

varios(as) various, several

varonil   manly

vaso   glass, 9

veces (*f. pl.*)   times; **a ~** sometimes, 5; **(dos) ~ al día / por semana**   (two) times a day / per week, 5

vecino(a)   neighbor, 6

vegano: algo ~ something vegan, 9

vegetal (*m.*)   vegetable, 6

vegetariano(a)   vegetarian; **~ estricto**   vegan, 9

vehículo   vehicle

veinte   twenty, P

veintiuno   twenty-one, P

vender   to sell, 3

venezolano(a)   Venezuelan, 2

venir (*irreg.*)   to come, 5

venta: estar en ~   to be on sale, 8

ventana   window, P

ver (*irreg.*)   to see, 5; **Nos vemos.**   See you later. 1

verano   summer, 7

veras: de ~   truly, really

verbo   verb, 3

verdad   true; **~** (*f.*)   truth

verde   green, 4

vergüenza shame;   **tener** (*irreg.*) **~** to be embarrassed, ashamed, 7

verso libre   blank verse

vestido   dress, 8

vestir (i, i)   to dress (*someone*), 5; **vestirse (i, i)**   to get dressed, 5

veterinario(a)   veterinarian, 5

vez (*f.*)   time; **de ~ en cuando**   sometimes; **en ~ de**   instead of; **rara ~**   hardly ever; **tal ~** perhaps; **una ~**   once, 9

viajar   to travel, 2

vida   life

videocámara   videocamera, 4

viejo(a)   old, 2

viento   wind; **Hace ~.**   It's windy. 7

viernes (*m.*)   Friday, 2

vinagre (*m.*)   vinegar, 9

vino: ~ blanco   white wine, 9; **~ tinto**   red wine, 9

violín (*m.*)   violin, 2

viraje (*m.*)   turn

visitante (*m., f.*)   visitor

visitar a amigos   to visit friends, 2

vivienda   housing

vivir   to live, 3

volibol (*m.*)   volleyball, 7

volver (ue)   to return, 4

vosotros(as)   you (*fam. pl.*), 1

voz (*f.*)   voice

vuestro(a) (*adj.*)   your (*fam. pl.*), 3; (*pron.*)   yours (*fam. pl.*), 3

W

wifi (*m.*)   wifi, wireless connection, 4

Y

yerno   son-in-law, 5

yo   I, 1

yogur (*m.*)   yogurt, 6

Z

zanahoria   carrot, 9

zapato   shoe, 8; **~ de tacón alto**   high-heeled shoe, 8; **~ de tenis**   tennis shoe, 8

English–Spanish Glossary

A

a un(a), 1
à la carte a la carta, 9
above sobre, 6
abundance abundancia
academic académico(a)
access acceder, 4
accessory accesorio, 8
according to según
accountant contador(a), 5
accounting contabilidad (f.), 3
achieve alcanzar (c), lograr
acquisition adquisición (f.)
across a través de
action acción (f.), 5
active activo(a), 2
activity actividad (f.), P
actor actor (m.), 5
actress actriz (f.), 5
actually en realidad
ad: personal ~ anuncio personal
add agregar, añadir, 9
address dirección (f.)
advertising (adj.) publicitario(a)
advise aconsejar, 10
affection cariño
afternoon tarde (f.), 3;
  during the ~ por la tarde, 3;
  Good ~. Buenas tardes. 1;
  in the ~ (with precise time)
  de la tarde, 3;
  late ~ atardecer (m.)
age edad (f.)
agreement concordancia
agricultural agrícola (m., f.)
ahead adelante
airport aeropuerto, 6
all todo(a)
alligator aligátor (m.), caimán
  (m.)
along por, 10
alphabet alfabeto
also también, 2
altitude altitud (f.)
always siempre, 5
ambassador embajador(a)
ambiguity ambigüedad (f.)
amusement diversión (f.)
ancestor antecesor(a),
  antepasado(a)
anger cólera

angry enojado(a), 4
anonymous anónimo(a)
answer contestar;
  Answer. Contesten. P
Antarctica Antártida
antiquated anticuado(a)
any algún, alguno(a) 6
apartment apartamento, 6
appear aparecer (zc)
apple manzana, 9
appliance electrodoméstico, 10
application aplicación (f.), 4
appreciate apreciar
appropriate apropiado(a)
April abril, 1
apt apto(a)
architect arquitecto(a), 5
architecture arquitectura, 3
Argentinian argentino(a), 2
armchair sillón (m.), 10
around alrededor de
arrive llegar, 2
arrogant altivo(a)
art arte (m.), 3
article artículo, 1
artist artista (m., f.), 5
as como; **~ . . . ~** tan... como, 8;
  ~ many . . . ~ tantos(as)...
  como, 8; **~ much . . . ~**
  tanto(a)(s)... como, 8
ask: ~ questions hacer
  (irreg.) preguntas, 3; **~ for**
  something pedir (i, i), 1; **~ for**
  the time pedir (i, i) la hora, 3
asparagus espárragos (m. pl.), 9
at en; **~ least** por lo menos, 10;
  ~ low heat a fuego suave /
  lento, 9
athletics track pista de
  atletismo, 6
atmosphere ambiente (m.)
attachment anexo
attack ataque (m.)
attempt intentar
attend acudir; asistir a, 3
attractive guapo(a), 2
audio audio, P
audiotape cinta, P
auditorium auditorio, 6
August agosto, 1
aunt tía, 5
Australian australiano(a), 2

automated bank teller
  (ATM) cajero automático, 6
autumn otoño, 7
availability disponibilidad (f.)
avenue avenida, 1
avoid evitar
awful fatal, terrible, 1
awkward torpe

B

baby-sitter niñero(a)
background fondo
backpack mochila, P
bad malo(a), 2
badly mal, 4
balance poner (irreg.) en
  equilibro
ball pelota, 7
ballpoint pen bolígrafo, P
banana plátano, 9
bank (commercial) banco, 6
barber peluquero(a), 5
barefooted descalzo(a)
baseball béisbol (m.), 7
basement sótano, 10
basket canasta
basketball básquetbol (m.), 7
bather bañador(a)
bathing suit traje (m.) de baño, 8
bathroom baño, 10
be estar (irreg.), ser (irreg.), 1;
  ~ . . . years old tener (irreg.)...
  años, 1; **~ a matter of** tratarse
  de; **~ able to** poder (irreg.),
  4; **~ afraid (of)** tener
  (irreg.) miedo (a, de), 7;
  ~ ashamed tener (irreg.)
  vergüenza, 7; **~ born** nacer
  (zc); **~ careful** tener (irreg.)
  cuidado, 7; **~ certain of** contar
  (ue) con; **~ cold** tener (irreg.)
  frío, 7; **~ embarrassed** tener
  (irreg.) vergüenza, 7; **~ familiar**
  with conocer (zc), 5; **~ going**
  to ir a, 3; **~ hot** tener (irreg.)
  calor, 7; **~ hungry** tener
  (irreg.) hambre, 7;
  ~ important importar, 4; **~ in**
  a hurry tener (irreg.) prisa,
  7; **~ interesting** interesar, 4;
  ~ jealous tener (irreg.) celos;

~ right tener (*irreg.*) razón, 7; **~ sleepy** tener (*irreg.*) sueño, 7; **~ thirsty** tener (*irreg.*) sed, 7; **~ worthwhile** valer (*irreg.*) la pena

bean haba (*f. but* el haba); **(green) ~** habichuela, 9; **refried beans** frijoles refritos, 9

beat batir

beautiful bello(a), hermoso(a)

beauty belleza

because porque, 3

bed cama, 10

bedroom cuarto, dormitorio, habitación (*f.*), recámara, 10

beef stew guisado, 9

beer cerveza, 9

before antes, 5

begin comenzar (ie) (c), empezar (ie) (c), 4

beginner principiante

behave portarse

behavior comportamiento

behind detrás de, 6

believe (in) creer (en), 3

below debajo de, 6

belt cinturón (*m.*), 8

besides además

better mejor, 8

between entre, 6

beverage bebida, refresco, 9

bicycle: on ~ en bicicleta, 6

big grande, 2

bilingual bilingüe

bill cuenta, 9

biology biología, 3

bird pájaro

birthplace lugar (*m.*) de nacimiento

black negro(a), 4

blank verse verso libre

blender licuadora, 10

blind ciego(a); **~ date** cita a ciegas

block cuadra, 6

blog blog, 4

blond(e) rubio(a), 2

blouse blusa, 8

blue azul, 4

boat barco, bote (*m.*)

boil hervir (ie, i), 9

boiled hervido(a), 9

Bolivian boliviano(a), 2

book libro, P

bookstore librería, 3

boot bota, 8

border frontera

boredom aburrimiento

bored aburrido(a), 4

boring aburrido(a), 2

both ambos(as)

bother molestar, 4

bowl plato hondo, 9

box: large ~ cajón (*m.*)

boxing boxeo, 7

boy chico, P; muchacho, P; niño, P

boyfriend novio

bracelet brazalete (*m.*), pulsera, 8

bread pan (*m.*), 6

break (a record) batir

breakfast desayuno, 9

breathe respirar

brick ladrillo

brief breve

bring traer (*irreg.*), 5

broadcast transmitir, 3

broccoli brócoli (*m.*), 9

brother (younger, older) hermano (menor, mayor), 5

brother-in-law cuñado, 5

brown castaño, 2; café, marrón, 4

browse: the Internet navegar por Internet, 2

brush cepillo, 5; **~ one's hair** cepillarse el pelo, peinarse, 5; **~ one's teeth** lavarse los dientes, 5

buddy cuate(a)

building edificio, 6

burn arder

burning encendida

bus ómnibus (*m.*), colectivo, guagua (*Cuba, Puerto Rico*), micro (*Chile*)

business negocio, 3; **~ administration** administración (*f.*) de empresas, 3; **~ district** centro comercial, 10

businessman hombre (*m.*) de negocios, 5

businesswoman mujer (*f.*) de negocios, 5

busy ocupado(a), 4

but pero, 2; **~ instead** sino

butcher shop carnicería, 6

butter mantequilla, 9

buy comprar, 2

by por, 10; **~ bus** en autobús, 6; **~ car** en carro / coche / automóvil, 6; **~ check** con cheque, 8; **~ plane** por avión, 6; **~ train** en tren, 6

Bye. Chau. 1

C

cable cable (*m.*), 4

cafeteria cafetería, 3

cake pastel (*m.*), 9

calculator calculadora, P

calculus cálculo, 3

call llamar, 2

can opener (electric) abrelatas (*m.*) (eléctrico), 10

Canadian canadiense (*m., f.*), 2

cap gorra, 8

capital (letter) mayúsculo(a)

card tarjeta; **credit ~** tarjeta de crédito, 8; **debit ~** tarjeta de débito, 8

cardboard cartón (*m.*)

career carrera, 5

Careful! ¡Cuidado!

Caribbean (Sea) Caribe (*m., f.*)

carpenter carpintero(a), 5

carpet alfombra, 10

carrot zanahoria, 9

carry llevar

cash: in ~ en efectivo, al contado, 8

cashmere cachemira

cat gato(a), 2

cattle ganado, ganadería

cattle-raising industry industria ganadera

cautious cuidadoso(a), 2

CD: CD / DVD recorder grabador (*m.*) de discos compactos / DVD, reproductor (*m.*) de discos compactos / DVD, 4

celebration celebración (*f.*)

cellar sótano, 10

Celsius degree grado Celsio(s), 7

census censo

cent centavo

center centro

Central America Centroamérica

century siglo

cereal cereal (*m.*), 9

certain cierto(a)

chain cadena, 8

chair silla, P

chalk tiza, P

challenge reto

change cambio; convertir (ie, i);

chapter capítulo, P

charity organización (f.) benéfica

chat chatear (online), 4; **~ room** grupo de conversación, 4

check cheque (m.); (restaurant check) cuenta, 9

cheek mejilla

cheese queso, 6

cheeseburger hamburguesa con queso, 9

chef cocinero(a), 5

chemistry química, 3

chess ajedrez (m.)

chicken pollo, 6; **~ soup** caldo de pollo, 9; **~ with rice** arroz (m.) con pollo, 9; **fried ~** pollo frito, 9; **roasted ~** pollo asado, 9;

Chilean chileno(a), 2

Chinese chino(a), 2; **~ language** chino, 3

chocolate cacao

choose escoger (j)

chronology cronología

chunk trozo, 9

church iglesia, 6

cinema cine (m.), 6

cinnamon canela

city ciudad (f.), 6

clam almeja, 9

clarity claridad (f.)

class clase (f.), P; **lower ~** clase baja

classroom salón (m.) de clase, P

clean the bathroom limpiar el baño, 10

clear the table quitar la mesa, 10

click hacer (irreg.) clic, 4; **double ~** hacer (irreg.) doble clic, 4

close cerrar (ie), 4; **~ your books.** Cierren los libros. P

close to cerca de, 6

closet clóset (m.), 10

clothing ropa, 5; **article of ~** prenda de ropa, 8; **~ store** tienda de ropa, 6

cloudburst chaparrón (m.)

cloudy: It's ~. Está nublado. 7

coat abrigo, 8

code código

codfish bacalao, 9

coffee café (m.), 9

cold (adj.) frío(a); **It's ~.** Hace frío. 7

Colombian colombiano(a), 2

color color (m.), 4; **solid ~** de un solo color, 8

comb peine (m.), 5; **~ one's hair** peinarse, 5

come venir (irreg.), 5

comic strip tira cómica

comma coma

command mandato

compact disc CD, disco compacto (m.)

comparison comparación (f.), 8

compete competir (i, i)

competition competencia, 7

complain quejarse, 5

complexion tez (f.)

complicity complicidad (f.)

computer computadora, P; **~ center** centro de computación, 3; **~ functions** funciones (f. pl.) de la computadora, 4; **~ science** computación (f.), informática, 3

conduct conducir (zc), 5

confection confección (f.)

connect conectar, 4

connection conexión (f.), 4

consider pensar (ie) en (de), 4

contest concurso

continue seguir (i, i), 6

continued seguido(a)

contraction contracción (f.), 3

contrary: on the ~ al contrario

conversation conversación (f.)

cook cocinar, 2; cocer (-z) (ue), 9; cocinero(a), 5

cookie galleta, 9

cool, chévere; It's cool. Hace fresco. 7

copper cobre (m.)

corn maíz (m.)

corner esquina, 6

correct corregir (i, i) (j)

Costa Rican costarricense (m., f.), 2

cotton algodón (m.), 8

country país (m.)

courage coraje (m.)

course: basic ~ curso básico, 3

courtesy cortesía, 4

cousin primo(a), 5

cowboy vaquero

cradle cuna

create crear

creative creativo(a)

crew tripulación (f.)

crowd muchedumbre (f.)

cruise ship crucero

crushed molido(a), 9

Cuban cubano(a), 2

culinary culinario(a)

culture cultura

cumin comino, 9

cup taza, 9

curtain cortina, 10

custard flan (m.), 9

customer cliente (m., f.), 8

cutting recorte (m.)

cyberspace ciberespacio, 4

cycling ciclismo, 7

D

daily cotidiano(a)

dam presa

dance bailar, 2; baile (m.), 3

danger peligro, 7

dangerous peligroso(a), 7

date fecha, 3; **blind ~** cita a ciegas

daughter hija, 5

daughter-in-law nuera, 5

dawn amanecer (zc)

day día (m.), 3; **~ before yesterday** anteayer, 7; **~ of the week** día de la semana, 3; **every ~** todos los días, 3

December diciembre, 1

decoration decoración (f.), 10

definite definido(a), 1

degree grado

Delighted to meet you. Encantado(a). 1

demand exigir (j)

demonstrate demostrar (ue)

demonstrative demostrativo(a), 6

denim mezclilla, 8

dentist dentista (m., f.), 5

deodorant desodorante (m.), 5

describe describir, 2

deserve merecer (zc)

design diseño; **graphic ~** diseño gráfico, 3

designer: graphic ~ diseñador(a) gráfico(a), 5

desire afán (m.); anhelo

desk escritorio, P

dessert postre (*m.*), 9

detail detalle (*m.*)

determined resuelto (*p.p. of* resolver)

develop desarrollar

dialect dialecto

dictionary diccionario, P

die morirse (ue, u), 8

difference diferencia

difficult difícil, 4

digital camera cámara digital, 4

dining room comedor (*m.*), 10

dinner cena

dirty sucio(a)

disappointment desilusión (*f.*)

disaster desastre (*m.*)

discount descuento, 8

discover descubrir, 3

disgusting asco

dish: main ~ plato principal, 9

dishonest mentiroso(a), 2

dishwasher lavaplatos (*m. s.*), 10

disillusionment desengaño

dispatch despachar

disqualify descalificar (qu)

distance trecho

diversity diversidad (*f.*)

divide dividir

do hacer (*irreg.*), 5; **a lot to ~** mucho que hacer; **~ the homework for tomorrow.** Hagan la tarea para mañana. P; **~ the recycling** hacer el reciclaje, 10

doctor doctor(a); médico(a), 5

dog perro(a), 2

doll muñeca

dollar dólar (*m.*)

Dominican dominicano(a), 2

door puerta, P

dorm residencia estudiantil, 3; dormitorio estudiantil, 6

download descargar, bajar, 4

downpour chaparrón (*m.*)

downtown centro de la ciudad, 10

dozen docena, 9

drawing dibujo, P

dream sueño; **~ (about)** soñar (ue) con, 4

drenched empapado(a)

dress vestido, 8; **~ (someone)** vestir (i, i), 5; **get dressed** vestirse (i, i), 5

dresser cómoda, tocador (*m.*), 10

drink beber, 3

drive manejar, conducir (zc), 5

driver's license licencia de manejar

dry (something) secar (qu), 5; **~ one's hair** secarse (qu) el pelo, 5

dryer secadora, 10

during mientras, por, 10

dust polvo; **~ the furniture** sacudir los muebles, 10

DVD / CD-ROM drive lector (*m.*) de CD-ROM / DVD, 4

E

early temprano, 3

earphones audífonos (*m. pl.*), 4

earring arete (*m.*), pendiente (*m.*), 8

earth tierra

easy fácil, 4

eat comer, 3; **~ dinner** cenar, 2

e-book libro electrónico, P

economics economía, 3

Ecuadoran ecuatoriano(a), 2

edit redactar

education educación (*f.*), 3

egg huevo, 6; **~ sunny-side up** huevo estrellado, 9; **scrambled ~** huevo revuelto, 9

egotistic egoísta, 2

eight ocho, P; **~ hundred** ochocientos(as), 8

eighteen dieciocho, P

eighth octavo(a), 10

eighty ochenta, P

either . . . or o... o, 6

electricity electricidad (*f.*)

electronic electrónico(a); **~ games store** tienda de juegos electrónicos, 6; **~ mailbox** buzón (*m.*) electrónico, 4; **~ notebook** asistente (*m.*) electrónico, 4; **electronics** aparatos electrónicos, 4

elephant elefante (*m.*)

eleven once, P

e-mail correo electrónico, e-mail (*m.*), P

embarrass avergonzar (ue) (c)

embarrassed avergonzado(a)

embroidered bordado(a), 8

emotion emoción (*f.*), 4

emphasize destacar (qu), enfatizar (c)

empty vacío(a)

encounter encuentro

end cabo; fin (*m.*)

engineer ingeniero(a), 5

engineering ingeniería, 3

English inglés (inglesa), 2; **~ language** inglés (*m.*), 3

enjoy gozar (c); **~ (life)** disfrutar (la vida)

enough: it is ~ basta

enroll alistar

entertain entretener (*like* tener)

entertaining divertido(a), 2

environment medio ambiente (*m.*)

equator ecuador (*m.*)

era etapa

essay ensayo

Europe Europa

evaluation calificación (*f.*)

evasion sorteo

even aun

evening noche (*f.*); **during the ~** por la noche, 3; **Good ~.** Buenas noches. 1; **in the ~** (*with precise time*) de la noche, 3

everything todo

everywhere por dondequiera

example ejemplo, 10

exchange intercambiar; **in ~ for** a cambio de; **~ rate** cambio

Excuse me. Disculpe. Perdón. 4

exercise hacer (*irreg.*) ejercicio, 7

exhibit exhibir

exotic exótico(a)

expensive: It's (too) ~. Es (demasiado) caro(a). 8

express preferences expresar preferencias, 2

expression expresión (*f.*), 1

extroverted extrovertido(a), 2

eyeglasses lentes (*m. pl.*), anteojos (*m. pl.*)

F

fabric tela, 8

fact dato, hecho

Fahrenheit degree grado Fahrenheit, 7

fairy tale cuento de hadas

fall caer (*irreg.*);
(*autumn*) otoño, 7;
~ **asleep** dormirse (ue, u), 5;
~ **back on** recurrir; ~ **in**
love enamorarse, 5
false falso(a)
family familia;
~ **member** pariente (*m., f.*), 5;
nuclear ~ familia nuclear, 5;
~ **tree** árbol (*m.*) genealógico
fantasy fantasía
far from lejos de, 6
fascinate fascinar, 4
fashion (*adj.*) de modas
fashion moda, 8;
~ **magazine** revista de moda
fashionable: (not) to be ~ (no)
estar de moda, 8
fast rápido(a), 4
fat gordo(a), 2
father padre (*m.*), papá (*m.*), 5
father-in-law suegro, 5
fax: external / internal ~ fax
(*m.*) externo / interno, 4
February febrero, 1
feed the dog darle de comer al
perro, 10
feel sentir (ie, i), 4; ~ **like**
(**doing**) tener (*irreg.*) ganas
de, 7
feminine femenino(a)
field of study campo de estudio, 3
fifteen quince, P
fifth quinto(a), 10
fifty cincuenta, P
file archivar, 4; archivo, 4
fill llenar
final final
finally por fin, 9
financial financiero(a)
find encontrar (ue), 4
find out averiguar (gü)
Fine, thank you. Bien, gracias. 1
fire fuego; ~ **fighter**
bombero(a), 5
fired despedido(a)
fireplace chimenea, 10
first primer(o)(a), 10;
~ **floor** primer piso, 10
fish pescar (qu), 7; pez (*m.*)
(*alive*); pescado (*caught*), 9
fit apto(a); **It fits nicely /**
badly. Me queda bien / mal. 8
five cinco, P;
~ **hundred** quinientos(as), 8;
~ **thousand** cinco mil, 8

flash drive la memoria flash, el
pendrive, 4
flat llano(a)
flavor sabor (*m.*)
floating flotador(a)
floor piso; **first** ~
primer piso, 10
flour harina, 9
flourish florecer (zc)
flower florecer (zc); flor (*f.*)
fold doblar, 6

following siguiente
fondness cariño
food comida, 6
food processor procesador
(*m.*) de comida, 10
fool engañar
foot: on ~ a pie, 6
football fútbol americano, 7
footprint huella
for para, por, 10; ~ **example** por
ejemplo, 10
forbid prohibir, 10

fork tenedor (*m.*), 9
fortress fortaleza
forty cuarenta, P
forum foro, 4
founder fundador(a)
four cuatro, P; ~ **hundred**
cuatrocientos(as), 8
fourteen catorce, P
fourth cuarto(a), 10
free libre
freezer congelador (*m.*), 10
French francés (francesa), 2;
~ **fries** papas fritas, 9;
~ **language** francés (*m.*), 3
frequently frecuentemente, 4
fresh fresco(a), 9
Friday viernes (*m.*), 2
fried frito(a), 9
friend amigo(a), P; cuate(a)
from the del (de + el), 3
front: in ~ **of** delante de, frente a,
enfrente de, 6
frozen congelado(a), 9
fruit fruta, 6; ~ **juice** jugo de
fruta, 9; ~ **salad** ensalada
de fruta, 9; ~ **shake** licuado
de fruta
fry freír (i, i), 9
fun divertido(a), 2
function funcionar, 4
funny cómico(a), 2

furious furioso(a), 4
furniture muebles (*m. pl.*), 10

G

gallon galón (*m.*), 9
game partido, 7; **interactive** ~
juego interactivo, 4
gang pandilla
garage garaje (*m.*), 10
garbage basura, 10
garden jardín (*m.*), 10
garlic ajo, 9
generally por lo general, 9
generous generoso(a), 2
genre género
gentle apacible
geography geografía, 3
German alemán (alemana), 2;
~ **language** alemán (*m.*), 3
get conseguir (i, i), 8;
~ **ahead** adelantar;
~ **cold** enfriarse, 9;
~ **divorced** divorciarse, 5;
~ **down from** bajar, 6;
~ **dressed** vestirse (i, i), 5;
~ **engaged** comprometerse, 5;
~ **married** casarse, 5;
~ **off of** (*a bus, etc.*) bajar, 6;
~ **on** subir, 6;
~ **ready** prepararse, 5;
~ **separated** separarse, 5;
~ **sick** enfermarse, 5;
~ **together** reunirse, 5;
~ **up** levantarse, 5
gift regalo
girl chica, P; muchacha, P; niña, P
girlfriend novia
give dar (*irreg.*), 5;
~ **as a gift** regalar, 8;
~ **directions** decir (*irreg.*)
cómo llegar, 6; ~ **personal**
information dar (*irreg.*)
información personal, 1;
~ **preference** anteponer;
~ **someone a bath** bañar, 5;
~ **the time** dar (*irreg.*) la
hora, 3
glass vaso, 9
glove guante (*m.*), 8
go acudir; ir (*irreg.*), 3;
~ **away** irse (*irreg.*), 5;
~ **off** (*alarm clock, etc.*) sonar
(ue), 4; ~ **offline** cortar la
conexión, 4; ~ **online** hacer
(*irreg.*) una conexión, 4;

~ out salir (*irreg.*), 5;
~ shopping hacer (*irreg.*)
las compras, 6; ir de compras,
8; **~ straight** seguir (i, i) (g)
derecho; **~ to bed** acostarse
(ue), 5; **~ up** subir, 6
goal meta
gold oro, 8
golden dorado(a), 9
golf golf (*m.*), 7
good bueno(a), 2; bondadoso(a)
goodbye adiós, 1
gossip chisme (*m.*)
gossiping chismoso(a)
governor gobernador(a)
grade nota, P
granddaughter nieta, 5
grandfather abuelo, 5
grandmother abuela, 5
grandson nieto, 5
grape uva, 9
graph gráfica
gray gris, 4
great chévere (*Cuba, Puerto
Rico*); grande, 2
greater mayor, 8
green verde, 4
greet saludar, 1
greeting saludo
grilled asado(a); a la parrilla, 9
ground molido(a), 9; tierra
group (*m.*) conjunto; **group**
(*v.*) juntar
growth crecimiento
Guatemalan guatemalteco(a), 2
guess adivinar;
Guess. Adivina. P
guinea pig cuy (*m.*)
guitar guitarra, 2
gymnasium gimnasio, 3

H

hair: blond ~ pelo rubio, 2;
brown ~ pelo castaño, 2
hairdresser peluquero(a), 5
half mitad (*f.*)
half-brother medio hermano, 5
half-sister media hermana, 5
hallway pasillo, 10
ham jamón (*m.*), 6
hamburger hamburguesa, 9
handicrafts artesanía
handkerchief pañuelo
handsome hermoso(a);
guapo(a), 2

handtowel toalla de mano, 5
happiness dicha; felicidad (*f.*)
happy contento(a), 4
hard duro(a); **~ drive** disco
duro, 4
hardly ever rara vez
hardware hardware (*m.*), 4
hard-working trabajador(a), 2
haste prisa
hat sombrero, 8
hatred odio
have tener (*irreg.*), 1; **~ a
fight** pelearse, 5; **~ a soft
drink** tomar un refresco, 2;
~ fun divertirse (ie, i), 5;
~ the urge to tener (*irreg.*)
ganas de, 7; **~ to** (+ *inf.*) tener
(*irreg.*) que (+ *inf.*), 1
he él, 1
health salud (*f.*), 3
healthy saludable
hear oír (*irreg.*), 5
heat calentar (ie), 9
heavy fuerte, 9
height altitud (*f.*), altura; (*of a
person*) estatura
hello hola, ¿Aló? (*on the
phone*), 1
helmet casco
help ayudar; ayuda
her (*pron.*) ella, 8; (*adj.*) su, 3;
suyo(a), 10; **to / for ~** le, 8
here aquí, 6
heritage herencia
hers (*pron.*) suyo(a), 10
hide esconder
hike hacer (*irreg.*) alpinismo,
practicar (qu) alpinismo, 7
him (*pron.*) él, 8; **to / for ~** le, 8
his (*adj.*) su, 3; (*adj., pron.*)
suyo(a), 10
Hispanic hispano(a)
history historia, 3
hoax engaño
hockey: field ~ hockey (*m.*)
sobre hierba, 7; **ice ~**
hockey (*m.*) sobre hielo, 7
hole pozo
home hogar (*m.*)
homeless sin hogar
homemade casero(a)
homework tarea, P
Honduran hondureño(a), 2
honest honesto(a)
hope esperanza; esperar, 10
hospital hospital (*m.*), 6

hot: be ~ tener (*irreg.*) calor, 7;
~ dog perro caliente, 9;
It's ~. Hace calor. 7
hour hora
house casa, 6; **the ~ special** la
especialidad de la casa, 9
housechore quehacer (*m.*)
doméstico, 10
housing vivienda
how? ¿cómo? 3; **~ are things
going?** ¿Qué tal? 1; **~ are
you?** (*form. s.*) ¿Cómo
está (usted)? / (*form. pl.*)
¿Cómo están (ustedes)? /
(*s. fam.*) ¿Cómo estás (tú)? 1;
~ can I help you? ¿En
qué puedo servirle? 8; **~ do
you say . . . ?** ¿Cómo se
dice…? P; **~ do you wish to
pay?** ¿Cómo desea pagar?, 8;
~ many? ¿cuántos(as)? 3;
~ much? ¿cuánto(a)? 3;
~ much does it cost? ¿Cuánto
cuesta? 8; **How's it going with
you?** ¿Cómo te / le(s) va? 1
humanities humanidades
(*f. pl.*), 3
humble humilde
humid húmedo(a)
hunger hambre (*f. but* el hambre)
hurry prisa; **be in a ~** tener
(*irreg.*) prisa, 7
husband esposo, 5
hymn himno

I

I yo, 1
**ice: (vanilla / chocolate)
~ cream** helado (de vainilla /
de chocolate), 9;
~ hockey hockey (*m.*) sobre
hielo, 7; **~ skate** patinar sobre
hielo, 7
identity identidad (*f.*)
immigration inmigración (*f.*)
impatient impaciente, 2
impressive impresionante
impulsive impulsivo(a), 2
in en; por, 10; **~ charge
of** encargardo de; **~ order to**
(+ *inf.*) para, 10; **~ relation
to** en cuanto a; **~ short** en
resumen; **~ spite of** a pesar
de; **~ the direction of** para,
10; **the "in" place** "antro"

inch pulgada
increase acrecentar (ie), aumentar
incredible increíble
indefinite indefinido(a), 1
index índice (*m.*)
Indian indio(a), 2
indigenous indígena
influence influir (y); influencia
ingredient ingrediente (*m.*), 9
inhabitant habitante (*m., f.*)
in-laws familia política, 5
inline skate (rollerblade) patinar en línea, 7
inside of dentro de, 6; **~ the house** dentro de la casa, 10
insist insistir, 10
install instalar, 4
instead of en vez de
instructor instructor(a), P
intelligent inteligente, 2
intention fin (*m.*)
interactive whiteboard pizarra interactiva, P
interest interesar, 4
interesting interesante, 2
Internet Internet (*m.* or *f.*), red (*f.*); **~ provider** proveedor (*m.*) de acceso, 4
interpreter intérprete (*m., f.*)
intimate íntimo(a)
introduce someone presentar a alguien, 1
introverted introvertido(a), 2
invest invertir
iron planchar, 10; (*metal*) hierro; (*appliance*) plancha, 10
irresponsible irresponsable, 2
Italian italiano(a), 2; **~ language** italiano, 3
its (*adj.*) su, 3; (*pron.*) suyo(a), 10

J

jacket (*suit jacket, blazer*) saco; (*outdoor, non-suit coat*) chaqueta 8
January enero, 1
Japanese japonés (japonesa), 2; **~ language** japonés (*m.*), 3
jealous celoso(a); **be ~** tener (*irreg.*) celos
jealously celosamente
jeans jeans (*m. pl.*), 8
jewelry store joyería, 6
jewelry joyas (*f. pl.*), 8

---

join juntarse
joke broma
journalism periodismo, 3
journalist periodista (*m., f.*), 5
July julio, 1
June junio, 1

K

keep: (oneself) separate mantenerse apartado
key (*on a keyboard*) tecla, 4
keyboard teclado, 4
kilo kilo, 9; **half a ~** medio kilo, 9
kind bondadoso(a)
king rey (*m.*)
kiss besar
kitchen cocina, 10
knapsack mochila, P
knife cuchillo, 9
know: ~ a person conocer (zc), 5; **~ a fact, ~ how to** saber (*irreg.*), 5
Korean coreano(a), 2

L

lake lago, 7
lamp lámpara, 10
language idioma (*m.*), lengua, 3
laptop computer computadora portátil, P
late tarde, 3
later luego, 5
latest: the ~ lo último
laugh reírse (*irreg.*), 5
laundry room lavandería, 10
lawn césped (*m.*), 10; **mow the ~** cortar el césped, 10
lawyer abogado(a), 5
lazy perezoso(a), 2
learn aprender, 3
learning aprendizaje (*m.*)
leather piel (*f.*), cuero, 8
leave dejar, 2; salir (*irreg.*), irse (*irreg.*), 5
left: to the ~ a la izquierda, 6
lemonade limonada, 9
less menor, 8; **~ than** menos que, 8
lesson lección (*f.*), P
level nivel (*m.*)
life vida
lifejacket salvavidas (*m. s.*)

---

lift levantar, 5; **~ weights** levantar pesas, 2
light luz (*f.*); (*adj.*) ligero(a), 9
like gustar; **~ a lot** encantar, 4; **(They / You** [*pl.*]**) ~ . . .** A... les gusta... 2; **He / She likes . . .** A... le gusta... 2; **I / You ~ . . .** A mí / ti me / te gusta... 2; **I'd ~** (+ *inf.*) quisiera (+ *inf.*), 6; Me gustaría (+ *inf.*)... 6
Likewise. Igualmente. 1
linen lino, 8
linguistic lingüístico(a)
link enlace (*m.*), 4
lip labio
listen escuchar; **~ to music** escuchar música, 2; **~ to the audio** Escuchen el audio. P
liter litro, 9
literature literatura, 3
little poco, 4
live vivir, 3, ocupar
livestock ganadería
living room sala, 10
loan préstamo, 8; (*v.*) prestar, 8
lobster langosta, 9
located ubicado(a); **is ~** queda
long for apetecer (zc)
look: ~ for buscar (qu), 2
lose perder (ie), 4; **~ oneself** perderse (ie)
love querer (*irreg.*), 4; amar; amor (*m.*), cariño
lover amante (*m., f.*)
lunch almuerzo, 9
luxurious lujoso(a)
lying mentiroso(a), 2

M

made: It's ~ out of . . . Está hecho(a) de... 8; **They're ~ out of . . .** Están hechos(as) de... 8
magazine revista
mailbox buzón (*m.*)
majority mayoría
make hacer (*irreg.*), 5; **~ sure** asegurarse; **~ the bed** hacer la cama, 10
makeup maquillaje (*m.*), 5
mall centro comercial, 6
man hombre (*m.*), P
manager gerente (*m., f.*), 5
manly varonil

manners modales (*m. pl.*)
March marzo, 1
marital status estado civil
mark marcar (qu)
market mercado, 6; **open-air ~ ,
  farmer's ~** mercado al aire
  libre, 6
marketing mercadeo, 3
masculine masculino(a)
match emparejar; (*sports*)
  partido, 7
mathematics matemáticas
  (*f. pl.*), 3
matter (to someone) importar, 4
May mayo, 1
mayonnaise mayonesa, 9
mayor alcalde (alcaldesa)
me mí, 8; **to / for ~** me, 8;
  with ~ conmigo, 8
mean: It means . . . Significa… P
meaning significado
means of transportation medios
  de transporte, 6
measure medir (i, i)
measurement medida, 9
meat carne (*f.*), 9
meatball albóndiga
mechanic mecánico(a), 5
media center centro de
  comunicaciones, 3
medicine medicina, 3
meditation meditación (*f.*)
meet conocer (zc), reunirse, 5
meeting encuentro, reunión (*f.*)
melon melón (*m.*), 9
menu menú (*m.*), 9
messenger mensajero(a)
Mexican mexicano(a), 2
microphone micrófono, 4
microwave microondas (*m. s.*), 10
midnight medianoche (*f.*), 3
mild apacible
milk leche (*f.*), 6
mine (*pron.*) mío, 10
mirror espejo, 10
Miss señorita (*abbrev.* Srta.), 1
missionary misionero(a)
mix mezclar, 9; mezcla
mixed mixto(a)
modem: external / internal ~
  módem (*m.*) externo /
  interno, 4
Monday lunes (*m.*), 3
money dinero
monitor monitor (*m.*), 4
monkey mono

month mes (*m.*), 3; **last ~** mes
  pasado, 7
mop the floor trapear el piso, 10
more más; **~ than** más que, 8
morning mañana, 3; **during the ~**
  por la mañana, 3; **Good ~.**
  Buenos días. 1; **in the ~**
  (*with precise time*) de la
  mañana, 3
mortality mortalidad (*f.*)
mother madre (*f.*), mamá, 5;
  Mother's Day día (*m.*) de las
  Madres, 3
mother-in-law suegra, 5
mountain monte (*m.*);
  ~ range cordillera
mountainous montañoso(a)
mouse ratón (*m.*), 4
move (*change residence*)
  mudarse
mow the lawn cortar el
  césped, 10
Mr. señor (*abbrev.* Sr.), 1
Mrs. señora (*abbrev.* Sra.), 1
Ms. señorita (*abbrev.* Srta.), 1
much mucho, 4
mud lodo
museum museo, 6
music música, 3
mustard mostaza, 9
my (*adj.*) mi, 3; (*pron.*) mío(a), 10;
  ~ pleasure. Mucho gusto. Un
  placer. 1

N

name llamar, 2; nombre (*m.*);
  full ~ nombre (*m.*) completo;
  My ~ is . . . Me llamo…, Mi
  nombre es…, 1
napkin servilleta, 9
narrator narrador(a)
nationality nacionalidad (*f.*), 2
nature naturaleza
navigation navegación (*f.*)
necklace collar (*m.*), 8
need necesitar, 2
neighbor vecino(a), 6
neighborhood barrio, colonia, 1
neither tampoco, 2; **~ . . .
  nor** ni… ni, 6
nephew sobrino, 5
nervous nervioso(a), 4
never nunca, 5; jamás, 6
nevertheless sin embargo
new novedoso(a)

news: ~ group grupo de
  noticias, 4
newspaper periódico
next próximo(a); **~ to** al lado
  de, 6; **~ to last** penúltimo(a)
Nicaraguan nicaragüense
  (*m., f.*), 2
nice simpático(a), 2
nickname apodo
niece sobrina, 5
night noche (*f.*), 3; **Good ~.**
  Buenas noches. 1; **last ~**
  anoche, 7
nine hundred novecientos(as), 8
nine nueve, P
nineteen diecinueve, P
ninety noventa, P
ninth noveno(a), 10
no one nadie, 6
nobody nadie, 6
none ningún, ninguno(a), 6
noodle soup sopa de fideos, 9
noon mediodía (*m.*), 3
normal normal, 4
North America Norteamérica
not: ~ any ningún, ninguno(a),
  6; **~ either** tampoco, 2;
  ~ much no mucho, 1
notebook cuaderno, P
notes apuntes (*m. pl.*), P
nothing nada, 1
noun sustantivo
novel novedoso(a)
novelist novelista (*m., f.*)
November noviembre, 1
novice novato(a)
number número, 8
nurse enfermero(a), 5

O

obey hacer (*irreg.*) caso
obtain conseguir (i, i), 8
October octubre, 1
of: ~ course cómo no, 6; por
  supuesto, 10; **~ the** del
  (de + el), 3
offer: special ~ oferta
  especial, 8
office oficina, 6
old viejo(a), 2
old-fashioned anticuado(a)
olive oil aceite (*m.*) de oliva, 9
on en, sobre, encima de, 6;
  ~ behalf of por, 10
once una vez, 9

one uno, P; **~ hundred** cien, P; **~ hundred and ~** ciento uno, 8; **~ hundred thousand** cien mil, 8; **~ million** millón (*m.*), un millón, 8; **~ thousand** mil (*m.*), 8

onion cebolla, 9

online en línea, 4

only único(a)

open abrir, 3; **~ your books.** Abran los libros. P

opposite enfrente de, frente a, 6; opuesto(a)

orange (*color*) anaranjado(a), 4; (*fruit*) naranja, 9

order ordenar, 9; mandar, 10

ordinal number número ordinal, 10

originate originar

ought deber (+ *inf.*), 3

our (*adj.*) nuestro(a)(s), 3

ours (*pron.*) nuestro(a)(s), 10

outline bosquejo

outside of fuera de, 6; **~ the house** fuera de la casa, 10

outskirts afueras (*f. pl.*), 10

outstanding sobresaliente

oven horno

overcoming superación (*f.*)

owner dueño(a), 5

P

package paquete (*m.*), 9

page página, P

paint pintar, 2

painting pintura, 3; cuadro, 10

Panamanian panameño(a), 2

pants pantalones (*m. pl.*), 8

paper papel (*m.*), P

parachute paracaídas (*m. s.*)

paragraph párrafo

Paraguayan paraguayo(a), 2

Pardon me. Con permiso. 4

parents padres (*m. pl.*), 5

park parque (*m.*), 6

parking lot estacionamiento, 6

parsley perejil (*m.*)

pass (by) pasar, 2

password contraseña, 4

patient paciente (*m., f.*), 2

patio patio, 10

paving stone baldosa

pay pagar (gu), 9; **~ attention** hacer (*irreg.*) caso

payment: form of ~ método de pago, 8

PDF file archivo PDF, 4

pea guisante (*m.*), 9

peace paz (*f.*)

peel pelar, 9

pencil lápiz (*m.*), P

penguin pingüino

people gente (*f.*)

pepper pimienta, 9

percentage porcentaje (*m.*)

perhaps quizás, tal vez

period (*punctuation*) punto; trecho

permit permitir, 10

personality personalidad (*f.*); **~ trait** característica de la personalidad, 2

Peruvian peruano(a), 2

pharmacy farmacia, 6

philanthropic filantrópico(a)

philosophy filosofía, 3

photo foto (*f.*), P

physical físico(a), 5; **~ appearance** apariencia física; **~ trait** característica física, 2

physics física, 3

piano piano, 2

picturesque pintoresco(a)

piece pedazo, 9

pillow almohada

pink rosado(a), 4

pirate pirata (*m.*)

pizzeria pizzería, 6

place lugar (*m.*), sitio

plaid a cuadros, 8

plain llanura

plate plato, 9

play jugar (ue) (gu), 4; **~ a musical instrument** tocar (qu) un instrumento musical, 2; **~ sports** practicar (qu) deportes, 2; **~ tennis (baseball, etc.)** jugar tenis (béisbol, etc), 7

playful juguetón (juguetona)

plaza plaza, 6

please por favor, 1

pleasure: A ~ to meet you. Mucho gusto en conocerte. 1

plot trama

plumber plomero(a), 5

poet poeta (poetisa)

poetry poesía

point: ~ out marcar (qu), señalar; **to the ~** al grano

policeman (policewoman) policía (*m., f.*), 5

political político(a); **~ science** ciencias políticas (*f. pl.*), 3

polka-dotted de lunares, 8

poor pobre

populate poblar (ue)

pork chop chuleta de puerco, 6

portable CD / MP3 player CD portátil / MP3, P

Portuguese portugués (portuguesa), 2

post office oficina de correos, 6

potato: ~ chips papitas fritas, 6; **~ salad** ensalada de papa

pound libra, 9

power poder (*m.*)

powerful poderoso(a)

practice practicar (qu)

prefer preferir (ie, i), 4

preference preferencia

prenuptual agreement contrato prenupcial

preparation preparación (*f.*), 9

prepare preparar, 2; **~ the food** preparar la comida, 10

preposition preposición (*f.*), 6

present (*gift*) regalo; **at the ~ time** en la actualidad

pretty bonito(a); lindo(a), 2

price: It's a very good ~. Está a muy buen precio. 8

priest sacerdote (*m.*)

prime rib lomo de res, 9

print imprimir, 3; (*patterned fabric*) estampado(a), 8; (*art*) cuadro, 10

printer impresora, 4

prize premio

profession profesión (*f.*), 5

professor profesor(a), P

program programa (*m.*); **antivirus ~** programa antivirus, 4; **~ icon** ícono del programa, 4

programmer programador(a), 5

projector proyector, P

promote adelantar, promover (ue)

pronoun pronombre (*m.*), 1

proud orgulloso(a)

provocative provocador(a)

psychology psicología, 3

public: ~ communications comunicación (*f.*) pública, 3; **~ relations** publicidad (*f.*), 3

Puerto Rican puertorriqueño(a), 2

purple morado(a), 4

purpose propósito
purse bolsa, 8
push oprimir
put poner (*irreg.*), 5; **~ away the clothes** guardar la ropa, 10; **~ my toys where they belong** poner mis juguetes en su lugar, 10; **~ on (clothing)** ponerse (la ropa), 5; **~ on makeup** maquillarse, 5

Q

quality calidad (*f.*); **of good (high) ~** de buena (alta) calidad, 8
queen reina
questionnaire cuestionario
quotation cita

R

raffle sorteo
railroad ferrocarril (*m.*)
rain llover (ue); **~ forest** bosque (*m.*) tropical, bosque (*m.*) pluvial; **It's raining.** Está lloviendo. (Llueve.), 7
raincoat impermeable (*m.*), 8
raise levantar, 5
ranch estancia
rank rango
rather bastante, 4
raw crudo(a), 9
razor rasuradora, 5; **electric ~** máquina de afeitar, 5
read leer (y), 3; **~ Chapter 1.** Lean el Capítulo 1. P
really de veras
reason razón (*f.*)
receive recibir, 3
recipe receta, 9
recognize reconocer (zc)
recommend recomendar (ie), 10
record grabar, 4
recruit alistar
recycling reciclaje (*m.*), 10
red rojo(a), 4
redheaded pelirrojo(a), 2
reduced: It's ~. Está rebajado(a). 8
reflect reflejar
reflection reflexión (*f.*)
refrigerator refrigerador (*m.*), 10
relate contar (ue), 4
relative pariente (*m., f.*), 5

relax relajarse, 5
remain quedar(se)
remember recordar (ue)
renovate renovar (ue)
renown renombre (*m.*)
rent alquiler (*m.*); **~ videos** alquilar videos, 2; **~ movies** alquilar películas, 2
repeat repetir (i, i), 4; **~.** Repitan. P
report informe (*m.*)
request pedir (i, i), 10
require requerir (ie, i), 10
residential neighborhood barrio residencial, 10
resort to recurrir
respond responder, 1
responsible responsable, 2
rest descansar, 2
restaurant restaurante (*m.*), 6
return regresar, 2; volver (ue), 4
revenue ingreso
rhyme rima
rich adinerado(a)
ride montar; **~ a bike** montar en bicicleta, 7; **~ horseback** montar a caballo, 7
right: to the ~ a la derecha, 6
ring sonar (ue), 4; anillo, 8; sortija
ripped rasgado
risk riesgo
river río, 7
roasted (in the oven) al horno, 9
role papel (*m.*)
roof techo, 10
room cuarto, **Proommate** compañero(a) de cuarto, P
root raíz (*f.*)
rose rosa, 4
rough draft borrador (*m.*)
route ruta
row remar, 7
rower remero(a)
rude descortés
rug alfombra, 10
rule regla
run correr, 3
rural campestre

S

sad triste, 4
safe seguro(a), 7

said: It's said . . . Se dice..., P
salad ensalada, 9; **lettuce and tomato ~** ensalada de lechuga y tomate, 9; **tossed ~** ensalada mixta, 9
sale: It's on ~. Está en venta. 8
salesclerk dependiente (*m., f.*), 5
salmon salmón (*m.*), 9
salt sal (*f.*), 9
Salvadoran salvadoreño(a), 2
same mismo(a); **~ (thing)** lo mismo
sandal sandalia, 8
sandwich bocadillo, sandwich (*m.*), 9; **ham and cheese ~ with avocado** sandwich de jamón y queso con aguacate, 9
Saturday sábado, 2
sausage salchicha, 6
save guardar, 4
say decir (*irreg.*), 5; **~ good-bye** despedirse (i, i), 1
saying dicho
scan ojear
scarcely apenas
scarf bufanda, 8
scenery paisaje (*m.*)
schedule horario
school escuela, 3
science ciencia, 3
scientific científico(a)
scream gritar; grito
screen pantalla, 4
script guión (*m.*); **~ writer** guionista (*m., f.*)
search engine buscador (*m.*), 4
season estación (*f.*), 7; **dry ~** temporada de secas; **rainy ~** temporada de lluvias
second segundo(a), 10
secret secreto
secretary secretario(a), 5
sections tramos
see ver (*irreg.*), 5; **~ you at the usual place?** ¿Nos vemos donde siempre? 1; **~ you later.** Hasta luego. Nos vemos. 1; **~ you soon.** Hasta pronto. 1; **~ you tomorrow.** Hasta mañana. 1
seem parecer (zc)
selfish egoísta, 2
sell vender, 3
send enviar, 4; mandar, 8
sentence oración (*f.*)
separate apartado

September septiembre, 1
serious serio(a), 2
serve servir (i, i), 4
set the table poner (*irreg.*) la mesa, 9
seven siete, P; **~ hundred** setecientos(as), 8
seventeen diecisiete, P
seventh séptimo(a), 10
seventy setenta, P
several varios(as)
shame vergüenza
shampoo champú (*m.*), 5
share compartir, 3
shark tiburón (*m.*)
shave oneself afeitarse, 5
she ella, 1
sheet of paper hoja de papel, P
shellfish marisco, 9
shelter albergar (gu)
shirt camisa, 8
shoe zapato, 8; **high-heeled ~** zapato de tacón alto, 8; **tennis ~** zapato de tenis, 8
shooting tiroteo
shore orilla
short (*in length*) corto(a); (*in height*) bajo(a), 2
shorts pantalones (*m. pl.*) cortos, 8
should deber (+ *inf.*), 3
shout gritar
show demostrar (ue), mostrar (ue)
shred picar (qu), 9
shrimp camarón (*m.*), 9
shy tímido(a), 2
sick enfermo(a), 4
side lado; **on the ~ of** al lado de, 6
sign letrero
silk seda, 8
silly tonto(a), 2
silver plata, 8
similarity semejanza
simple sencillo(a)
sincere sincero(a), 2
sing cantar, 2
singer cantante (*m., f.*)
single soltero(a)
sister (younger, older) hermana (menor, mayor), 5
sister-in-law cuñada, 5
sit down sentarse (ie), 5
six seis, P; **~ hundred** seiscientos(as), 8

sixteen dieciséis, P
sixth sexto(a), 10
sixty sesenta, P
size talla, 8
skate patinar, 2
ski esquiar, 7; esquí (*m.*)
skiing esquí (*m.*); **downhill ~** esquí alpino, 7; **water ~** esquí acuático, 7
skin tez (*f.*)
skirt falda, 8
slave esclavo(a)
sleep dormir (ue, u), 4
slice pedazo, 9
slogan lema (*m.*)
slow lento(a), 4
slowly despacio
small pequeño(a), 2; **a ~ amount** un poco, 4
smartphone teléfono inteligente, smartphone, 4
smile sonreír (*irreg.*), 8; sonrisa
snack merienda
snow nevar (ie); **It's snowing.** Está nevando. (Nieva.), 7
snowboard tabla de snowboard, 7
snowboarding snowboarding, 7
so por eso, 10
soap jabón (*m.*), 5
soccer fútbol (*m.*), 7; **~ field** cancha, campo de fútbol, 6
social: media director director(a) de social media, 5; **~ networking site** red social, 4
sock calcetín (*m.*), 8
sofa sofá (*m.*), 10
soft suave; **~ drink** refresco, 6
software software (*m.*), 4
solved resuelto
some unos(as), 1; algún, alguno(a), 6
someone alguien, 6
something algo, 6; **~ vegan** algo vegano, 9
sometimes de vez en cuando; a veces, 5
somewhat bastante, 4
son hijo, 5
son-in-law yerno, 5
sorry: I'm sorry. Lo siento. 4
So-so. Regular. 1
soul alma (*f.*) (*but* el alma)
sound sonido
soup sopa, 9; **cold ~** gazpacho (*Spain*), 9

source fuente (*f.*)
South America Sudamérica
souvenir recuerdo
sovereignty soberanía
spa balneario
Spain España
Spanish español (a), 2; **~ language** español (*m.*), 3
Spanish-speaking hispanohablante
speaker conferencista (*m., f.*); altoparlante (*m., f.*), 4
species especie (*f.*)
spelling ortografía
spicy picante, 9
sponsor patrocinador(a)
spoon cuchara, 9
sport deporte (*m.*), 7; **~ activity** actividad (*f.*) deportiva, 7
sporting goods store tienda de equipo deportivo, 6
sports coat saco, 8
spring primavera, 7
stadium estadio, 6
stairs escaleras (*f. pl.*), 10
state estado, 5
station estación (*f.*); **train / bus ~** estación de trenes / autobuses, 6
stationery store papelería, 6
statistics estadística, 3
steak bistec (*m.*), 6
steamed al vapor, 9
steel acero
step on pisar
stepbrother hermanastro, 5
stepfather padrastro, 5
stepmother madrastra, 5
stepsister hermanastra, 5
still todavía; **~ life** naturaleza muerta
stop (*e.g., bus stop*) parada; **~ (doing something)** dejar de (+ *inf.*), 2; parar (de), 3
store guardar; almacén (*m.*), tienda, 6; **music (clothing, video) ~** tienda de música (ropa, videos), 6
stove estufa, 10
straight ahead todo derecho, 6
straighten out the bedroom arreglar el dormitorio, 10
strategy estrategia
strawberry fresa, 9

street calle (*f.*), 1
strengthen acrecentar (ie)
stringed al hilo, 9
striped rayado(a), a rayas, 8
strong fuerte
student estudiante (*m., f.*), P;
~ **center** centro estudiantil, 6
studio estudio, 3
study estudiar; ~ **at the library**
(**at home**) estudiar en la
biblioteca (en casa), 2;
~ **pages ... to ...**
Estudien las páginas ...
a ..., P
stupid tonto(a), 2
style estilo; **in** ~ en onda; **out**
of ~ pasado(a) de moda, 8
substitute sustituir (y)
suburb barrio residencial,
suburbio, 10
subway: on the ~ en metro, 6
success éxito
suddenly de repente, 9
sugar azúcar (*m., f.*), 9;
~ **cane** caña de azúcar
suggest sugerir (ie, i), 8
suggestion sugerencia
suit traje (*m.*), 8; **bathing** ~
traje (*m.*) de baño, 8
summer verano, 7
sun sol (*m.*)
sunbathe tomar el sol, 2
Sunday domingo, 2
sunglasses gafas (*f. pl.*)
de sol, 8
sunlight luz (*f.*) solar
sunny: It's ~. Hace sol. 7
supermarket supermercado, 6
support apoyar
sure seguro(a), 4
surf hacer (*irreg.*) surfing,
practicar (qu) surfing, 7
surpass sobrepasar
surprise sorpresa
surrounded rodeado(a)
survey encuesta
sweater suéter (*m.*), 8;
chompa
sweatsuit sudadera, 8
sweep the floor barrer el suelo /
el piso, 10
sweet dulce (*m.*); (*adj.*)
dulce
swim bañar, 5; nadar, 7
swimming natación (*f.*), 7;
~ **pool** piscina, 6

symbol símbolo
systematic sistemático(a)

T

table mesa, P; **night** ~ mesita
de noche, 10; **set the** ~ poner
(*irreg.*) la mesa, 9
tablecloth mantel (*m.*), 9
tablespoon cucharada, 9
tablet: ~ **computer** tableta, 4
take tomar, llevar; ~ **a**
bath bañarse, 5; ~ **a**
shower ducharse, 5; ~ **off**
clothing quitarse la ropa, 5;
~ **out the garbage** sacar (qu)
la basura, 10; ~ **photos** sacar
(qu) fotos, 2; ~ **place** realizarse
(c); ~ **the dog for a walk**
sacar (qu) a pasear al
perro, 10
talk hablar; ~ **on the telephone**
hablar por teléfono, 2
tall alto(a), 2
tamed domesticado(a)
taste gusto; **to individual** ~ al
gusto, 9
tavern bodegón (*m.*)
tea: hot ~ té (*m.*), 9; **iced** ~ té
(*m.*) helado, 9
teach enseñar
teacher maestro(a), 5
team equipo, 7
tear up rasgar (gu)
teaspoon cucharadita, 9
technology tecnología, 4
television: ~ **set** televisor
(*m.*), 10;
tell contar (ue), 4; decir (*irreg.*),
5; ~ **the time** decir la hora, 3
temperature temperatura, 7
ten diez, P; ~ **thousand** diez
mil, 8
tend tender
tennis tenis (*m.*), 7;
~ **court** cancha de tenis, 6;
~ **shoes** zapatos (*m. pl.*) de
tenis, 8
tenth décimo(a), 10
term término
terrible fatal, terrible, 1
terrific chévere (*Cuba, Puerto*
Rico)
text texto
Thank you very much. Muchas
gracias. 1

that (*adj.*) ese(a), 6; (*pron.*)
ése(a), 6; ~ **over there** (*adj.*)
aquel (aquella), 6; (*pron.*) aquél
(aquélla), 6
that's why por eso, 10
the el, la, los, las, 1
theater teatro, 6
their su, 3; suyo(a), 10
theirs (*pron.*) suyo(a), 10
them ellos(as), 8; **to / for** ~ les, 8
then entonces
theory teoría
there allí, 6; **over** ~ allá, 6; ~ **is /**
~ **are** hay, 1
these (*adj.*) estos(as), 6; (*pron.*)
éstos(as), 6
they ellos(as), 1
thin delgado(a), 2
think (about) pensar (ie)
(en, de), 4
third tercer(o, a), 10
thirst sed (*f.*)
thirsty: be ~ tener (*irreg.*) sed, 7
thirteen trece, P
thirty treinta, P
this (*adj.*) este(a), 6; (*pron.*)
éste(a), 6
those (*adj.*) esos, 6; (*pron.*)
ésos(as), 6; ~ (**over there**)
(adj.) aquellos(as), 6; (*pron.*)
aquéllos(as), 6
thousands miles
threat amenaza
three tres, P; ~ **hundred**
trescientos(as), 8
through por, 10
throughout a través de
throw: ~ **oneself** lanzarse (c);
~ **out** botar
thunderstorm tormenta
Thursday jueves (*m.*), 3
time hora; vez (*f.*)
times veces (*f. pl.*); (**two, three,**
etc.) ~ **a day / per week** (dos,
tres, etc.) veces al día / por
semana, 5
tip propina, 9
tired cansado(a), 4
title titular; título, 1
to a; **to the** al (a + el), 3
toast pan (*m.*) tostado, 9
toaster tostadora, 10
today hoy, 3; ~ **is Tuesday the**
30th. Hoy es martes treinta. 3
tomorrow mañana, 3
too much demasiado, 4

toothbrush cepillo de dientes, 5
toothpaste pasta de dientes, 5
top: on ~ of encima de, 6
toward para, 10
towel toalla, 5
town pueblo, 6
toy juguete (*m.*), 10
track suit sudadera, 8
train (*for sports*) entrenarse, 7; tren, 6
trainer entrenador(a) (*m.*)
trait característica
translate traducir (zc), 5
traveler's check cheque (*m.*) de viajero, 8
treasure tesoro
tree árbol (*m.*)
trick truco
triumph triunfar
trout trucha, 9
true verdad
truly de veras
trumpet trompeta, 2
try intentar, tratar de; **I'm going to ~ it on.** Voy a probármelo(la). 8
t-shirt camiseta, 8
Tuesday martes (*m.*), 3
tuna atún (*m.*), 9
turkey pavo, 6
turn cruzar (c), doblar, 6; viraje (*m.*); **~ in** entregar; **~ in your homework.** Entreguen la tarea. P; **~ off** apagar (gu), 2
twelve doce, P
twenty veinte, P
twenty-one veintiuno, P
twice dos veces, 9
two dos, P; **~ hundred** doscientos(as), 8; **~ million** dos millones, 8; **~ thousand** dos mil, 8
typical típico(a), 9

U

U.S. citizen estadounidense (*m., f.*), 2
ugly feo(a), 2
uncle tío, 5
underneath debajo de, 6
understand comprender, 3; entender (ie), 4
understanding comprensión (*f.*)
unique único(a)

unite unir, 9
united unido(a); **~ States** Estados Unidos
university universidad (*f.*), 6
unpleasant antipático(a), 2
untamed salvaje
upload subir, cargar, 4
Uruguayan uruguayo(a), 2
us nosotros(as), 8; **to / for ~** nos, 8
use usar, 2
useful útil
user usuario(a), 4

V

vacuum (*verb*) pasar la aspiradora, 10; **~ cleaner** aspiradora, 10
vain vanidoso(a)
valley valle (*m.*)
valuable valioso(a)
value valor (*m.*)
variety variedad (*f.*)
various varios(as)
vegan vegetariano(a) estricto(a), 9
vegetable vegetal (*m.*), 6
vegetarian vegetariano(a)
vehicle vehículo
Venetian blind persiana, 10
Venezuelan venezolano(a), 2
verb verbo, 3
very muy, 2; **~ little** muy poco
vest chaleco, 8
veterinarian veterinario(a), 5
videocamera videocámara, 4
videotape (*noun*) video
viewpoint punto de vista
vinegar vinagre (*m.*), 9
violin violín (*m.*), 2
visit friends visitar a amigos, 2
visitor visitante (*m., f.*)
voice voz (*f.*)
volcanic eruption erupción (*f.*) volcánica
volleyball volibol (*m.*), 7

W

waiter camarero, 5
waitress camarera, 5
wake up despertarse (ie), 5; **wake someone up** despertar (ie), 5
walk caminar, 2; andar (*irreg.*), 8

walking a pie, 6
wall pared (*f.*), P
wallet cartera, 8
want desear, querer (*irreg.*), 10
warm caluroso(a)
warning aviso
wash lavar, 5; **~ one's hair** lavarse el pelo, 5; **~ oneself** lavarse, 5; **~ the dishes (the clothes)** lavar los platos (la ropa), 10
washer lavadora, 10
wastebasket basurero
watch reloj (*m.*), 8; **~ television** mirar televisión, 2
water agua (*f.*) (*but:* el agua); **fresh ~** agua dulce; **sparkling ~** agua mineral, 9; **~ skiing** esquí acuático, 7; **~ the plants** regar (ie) las plantas, 10
watercress berro
waterfall catarata
wave ola
we nosotros(as), 1
wealth riqueza
wealthy adinerado(a)
weather tiempo, 7; **It's nice / bad ~.** Hace buen / mal tiempo. 7
weave tejer
weaving tejido
web red (*f.*); **~ page** página web, 4
webcam cámara web, 4
website sitio web, 4
wedding boda
Wednesday miércoles (*m.*), 3
week semana, 3; **during the ~** entresemana, 3; **every ~** todas las semanas, 5; **last ~** semana pasada, 7
weekend fin (*m.*) de semana, 2
welcome bienvenido(a); **You're ~.** De nada. 1
well bien, 4; **(Not) Very ~.** (No) Muy bien. 1; **Quite ~.** Bastante bien. 1; (*for drawing water*) pozo
well-being bienestar (*m.*)
what? ¿cuál(es)? ¿qué? 3; **~ day is today?** ¿Qué día es hoy? 3; **~ do you like to do?** ¿Qué te gusta hacer? 2; **~ does . . . mean?** ¿Qué significa…? P; **~ is today's date?** ¿A qué

fecha estamos? 3; **~ is your phone number?** ¿Cuál es tu / su número de teléfono? (*s. fam. / form.*), 1; **~ time is it?** ¿Qué hora es? 3; **~'s he / she / it like?** ¿Cómo es? 2; **~'s the weather like?** ¿Qué tiempo hace? 7; **~'s your (e-mail) address?** ¿Cuál es tu / su dirección (electrónica)? (*s. fam. / form.*), 1; **~'s your name?** ¿Cómo se llama (*s. form.*) / te llamas (*s. fam.*)? 1; **~ 's new?** ¿Qué hay de nuevo? 1

whatever cualquier

which? ¿qué? 3; **~ one(s)?** ¿cuál(es)? 3

wheat trigo

wheel rueda

when? ¿cuándo? 3; **~ is your birthday?** ¿Cuándo es tu cumpleaños? 1

where? ¿dónde? 3; **~ (to)?** ¿adónde?; **~ do you live?** ¿Dónde vives / vive? (*s. fam. / form.*), 1; **~ does your . . . class meet?** ¿Dónde tienes la clase de… ? 3

while mientras

white blanco(a), 4

whitewater rafting: go ~ navegar en rápidos, 7

who? ¿quién(es)? 3

whose cuyo(a)(s); **~ are these?** ¿De quiénes son? 3; **~ is this?** ¿De quién es? 3

why? ¿por qué? 3

wife esposa, 5

wifi wifi, 4

wild salvaje

willing dispuesto(a)

win ganar, 7

wind viento

window ventana, P

windy: It's ~. Hace viento. 7

wine: red ~ vino tinto, 9; **white ~** vino blanco, 9

wineglass copa, 9

winter invierno, 7

wireless connection wifi, 4

wish desear, querer (*irreg.*), 10; esperanza

with con

wolf lobo

woman mujer (*f.*), P

wonder maravilla

wood madera

wooden cart carreta

wool lana, 8

word-processing program programa (*m.*) de procesamiento de textos, 4

work trabajar, 2

workday jornada laboral

worker trabajador(a), 5

workshop taller (*m.*)

world mundo; **~ Wide Web** red (*f.*) mundial, 4; **~wide** a nivel mundial

worried preocupado(a), 4

worry preocuparse, 5

worse peor, 8

wrinkled arrugado(a)

write escribir, 3; **~ in your notebooks.** Escriban en sus cuadernos. P

Y

year año, 3; **every ~** todos los años, 9; **last ~** año pasado, 7

yellow amarillo(a), 4

yes sí, 1

yesterday ayer, 3

yogurt yogur (*m.*), 6

you vosotros(as) (*fam. pl.*), tú (*fam. s.*), usted (Ud.) (*form. s.*), ustedes (Uds.) (*fam. or form. pl.*), 1; ti (*fam. s.*), Ud(s). (*form.*), 8; **to / for ~** os (*fam. pl.*), te (*fam. s.*), le (*form. s.*), les (*form, pl.*), 8; **with ~** contigo (*fam.*), 8

young joven, 2

younger menor, 8

your (*adj.*) tu (*fam.*), su (*s. form. pl.*), vuestro(a) (*fam.*), 3; suyo(a) (*form. s., pl.*), tuyo(a) (*fam.*), 10

yours (*pron.*) vuestro(a) (*fam. pl.*), suyo(a) (*form. s., pl.*), tuyo(a) (*fam. s.*), 10

youth juventud (*f.*)

Z

zero cero, P

Index